WOMEN IN
CHINESE SOCIETY

Contributors

Emily M. Ahern	Mary Backus Rankin
Delia Davin	Marjorie Topley
Yi-tsi Feuerwerker	Roxane Witke
Joanna F. Handlin	Arthur P. Wolf
Elizabeth Johnson	Margery Wolf

WOMEN IN CHINESE SOCIETY

Edited by MARGERY WOLF *and* ROXANE WITKE

Stanford University Press, Stanford, California 1975

Stanford University Press, Stanford, California
© 1975 by the Board of Trustees of the Leland Stanford Junior University
Printed in the United States of America
ISBN 0-8047-0874-6   LC 74-82782

Preface

In June 1973 a conference on women in Chinese society was held in San Francisco under the sponsorship of the Joint Committee on Contemporary China of the Social Science Research Council and the American Council of Learned Societies. The papers in this book were presented in preliminary form at that conference, and have benefited in their current form from the criticism of other conferees. We are very grateful for this contribution from Marilyn Young, who served as a general discussant, and from Charlotte Beahan, Fu-mei Chang Chen, Norma Diamond, Leo Lee, Victor Li, G. William Skinner, and Sophie Sa Winckler. Since the thoughts expressed in the Introduction grew out of these five days of meetings and cannot be properly attributed to any single individual, we have chosen to leave it unsigned, accepting responsibility for any misinterpretation of ideas, but giving credit where it is due: to the intellectual effort of the entire group.

We would like to express our appreciation to John Creighton Campbell, then Staff for the Joint Committee, for his administrative assistance in organizing our meetings and for his thoughtful participation in our discussions. We are, of course, extremely grateful to the Joint Committee for sponsoring our meetings.

This book now becomes part of the series originally sponsored by that Committee's Subcommittee on Research on Chinese Society and published by Stanford University Press. Other books in the series are listed on the back of the title page. We are grateful to our editor, Muriel Bell, for improving our prose and for graciously tearing her hair rather than ours over errors in our references and vagaries in our notes. We also thank Margaret Sung, whose calligraphy graces the Character List.

M.W.
R.W.

December 1974

Contents

Contributors

EMILY M. AHERN received her Ph.D. from Cornell University in 1971. She has taught at the University of California, Irvine, and Yale University, and is currently at the Johns Hopkins University. She is the author of *The Cult of the Dead in a Chinese Village*.

DELIA DAVIN is a lecturer in Social and Economic History at York University (England). She is the author of *Women and the Party in Revolutionary China* (forthcoming, 1975) and of several articles on modern Chinese society. She is currently on leave from York University, working at the Foreign Languages Press in Peking.

YI-TSI FEUERWERKER (MEI I-TZ'U) began her studies at National Chekiang University, Hangchow, China, and continued her education in this country, at Mount Holyoke College and Harvard University. She is now teaching at the Residential College, University of Michigan, and doing research in the field of modern Chinese literature.

JOANNA F. HANDLIN is Assistant Professor of History at the University of Rochester. She is currently working on two projects: a study of how Lü K'un and his contemporaries accommodated themselves to popular values, and a study of late Ming sources for the Ch'ing interest in statecraft.

ELIZABETH JOHNSON is a doctoral candidate at Cornell University, and is currently serving as Coordinator of the China Resources Project at the University of British Columbia. She has done field work in Hong Kong, where she spent the years 1968–70 studying family organization, and in the People's Republic, where she did research on commune organization in Kwangtung province.

MARY BACKUS RANKIN received her Ph.D. from Harvard University in 1966. She does independent research on modern Chinese history and is the author of *Early Chinese Revolutionaries: Radical Intellectuals in Shanghai and Chekiang, 1902–1911.*

MARJORIE TOPLEY is an Associate in Research at the Centre of Asian Studies, University of Hong Kong, and a member of the Centre's Committee of Management. She is currently working on a study of the Hong Kong medical system and the interaction of Chinese and Western medicine.

ROXANE WITKE is a Research Associate at the East Asian Research Center at Harvard University. She is currently readying two books for publication, one on Chiang Ch'ing's life in revolution and another on revolutionary women leaders of twentieth-century China.

ARTHUR P. WOLF is Associate Professor of Anthropology at Stanford University. He has done extensive field research in Taiwan, and edited one of the volumes in this series, *Religion and Ritual in Chinese Society.* He is at present a Visiting Fellow at All Souls, Oxford, where he is finishing a book on marriage and adoption in Taiwan.

MARGERY WOLF has drawn on her field experience in Taiwan to write two books: *The House of Lim: A Study of a Chinese Farm Family* and *Women and the Family in Rural Taiwan.*

WOMEN IN
CHINESE SOCIETY

Introduction

Until recently, the role of women has been largely ignored or, worse, considered irrelevant to an understanding of Chinese institutions. These essays prove the error of such a narrow perspective and serve as well to dispel some old myths about Chinese women by examining their lives with scholarly objectivity in the context of the society in which they live. Geographically that context ranges from Taiwan to Yenan, socially from the wealthy urban families of the intelligentsia to rural workers in silk factories, temporally from the late Ming to the first decade of the People's Republic. For those of us who come to this task as historians, the canvas is large and some areas must be left in deep shadow. By contrast, those of us who are anthropologists tend to avoid the large canvas and to strive for photographic accuracy in the subtle details of one small corner. In our opinion the two approaches complement each other, and their combination is particularly appropriate in a volume addressing itself to a topic as elusive as the reality of women's lives in Chinese society.

In the conference for which these essays were written, a number of recurrent themes emerged. We have selected three for discussion here because of their importance and the interest they hold for scholars in all disciplines.

Conflicting Images of Women

Stereotypes—ideological, ethnic, and sexual—seem to exist in all societies. We may condemn them as sources of baseless prejudice, but as social scientists we must also class them as data, facts of culture, like kin terms and funeral rites. The presence in a culture of conflicting stereotypes does not affect their validity as cultural data and may be even more revealing because of the inconsistency. In several of the essays in this volume we find evidence for a Chinese conception of women as weak, timid, and sexually exploitable *as well as* dangerous, powerful, and sexually insatiable. What do these divergent images tell us?

Lü K'un, a Ming official who wrote a handbook of moral guidance for women, is used by Joanna Handlin as a source for Ming assumptions about women. In her thoughtful essay on Lü's writings, Handlin provides us with a fair sampling of the then current female stereotypes. She describes Lü's attitudes toward women as sympathetic for his time, but there runs through his work a presumption of women's timidity, irresponsibility, and limited moral capacity. When one of the Model Women he is writing about behaves with "manly courage," he expresses astonishment. Lü concluded that women were in fact beings that could be compared with men (a progressive statement in his intellectual era), citing as evidence their increasing literacy and the good use they made of it.

Handlin suggests that the apparent decline in the status of women in the Ch'ing and the new emphasis in men's writings on chastity, foot-binding, and such notions as "only the untalented woman is virtuous" were reactions to a changing social scene. They were attempts to realign a faltering reality with the ideal. Thus we have the female on the one hand portrayed as timid and subordinate, but on the other forced to bear responsibility for the moral decay and disruption of society. Another attitude expressed in Lü's work sheds more light on the discrepancy between these two images. Members of the elite who had some knowledge of life in the lower classes, as Lü apparently did, were conscious of the energy and determination of women when aroused. The fact that women had participated in White Lotus groups and that "demonic women" had led a rebellion earlier in the Ming seemed to give rise to an uneasiness in men, a recognition of the havoc that might result if upper-class women rejected the rules of propriety governing their position in society. Men's image of women as socially and politically incompetent was violated by these visions. The result was quiet anxiety and increased repression.

Emily Ahern's essay, based primarily on field interviews from rural Taiwan, addresses a problem in anthropology that is currently attracting much interest: the relationship between ritual pollution, the bodies of women, and social beliefs about women. Here we have another perspective, from a different time period and class, on the disquietude the Ming elite felt toward women's potential for power. Ahern contrasts the *power* in women's contribution to the formation of the fetus, and the physical and social *danger* of contact with birth and menstrual fluids, with the *power* women's fertility has over the future of the patrilineal descent group and the *danger* their influence over descendants of the family can have for its survival as a unit. She rejects a causal interpretation, but an intriguing paradox remains: gestation and childbirth, a source of great good as well as immense unacknowledged female power, have acquired over the centuries an enormous ritual burden of negative sentiment. Women are labeled unclean and polluting in life, and are promised horrible punishment in the Buddhist hell after death. Marjorie Topley in her essay provides more evidence of this paradox when she reports (1) that silkworms were believed to die as a result of being handled by pregnant women, and (2) that religious sects in Kwangtung handed out tracts describing in strong language the dire underworld punishment awaiting women who bore children.

Sexual intercourse, according to Ahern, is less polluting ritually (although it holds some dangers for men in certain circumstances) than are the events and effluvia associated with women's fertility. Nonetheless, the attitudes of Chinese men toward women's sexuality are charged with the same feeling of threat. As Yi-tsi Feuerwerker tells us in her essay on women writers, "A man done in by lust, for which the woman is to blame, was a common theme in popular fiction." She mentions in particular the heroine of the novel *Golden Lotus*, who "combines in her person both the fascination and the horror felt toward female sexuality." In Elizabeth Johnson's essay we read of a Hakka woman who was required to abstain from sex with her husband for several years after their marriage because he was still a student and sex was believed to have an adverse effect on studying. Johnson reports another case in which a woman was warned to avoid sexual relations with her husband for several years lest the brain disease that afflicted him prove fatal.

Besides these threatening aspects of women's sexuality, there is also a presumption that women's sexual appetites keep them ever on the alert for sexual adventures. Feuerwerker notes this as a frequent theme in literature. In the early years of the People's Republic, Delia Davin tells us in her essay, men suspected "that women who left home to work were just looking for love affairs." And Handlin reports that Lü found the "leisure available to young girls was also disturbing; would they not be susceptible to illicit amorous affairs?" One begins to suspect that the elaborate techniques to protect elite women's reputations were motivated more by men's suspicions about the improper inclinations of their ostensibly chaste daughters and virtuous wives than by the concern they expressed for women's inability to fend off aggressive males.

The irony of this suspicion is that insofar as Chinese women have revealed their attitude toward sex, it tends to be both negative and heavily influenced by a fear of the exploitation of their sexuality. Some of the women from Kwan Mun Hau village in Hong Kong implied in conversations with Johnson that the poor quality of sexual relationships accounted for the low birth rate in "the old days." And the impression women in all age groups in rural Taiwan left with Margery Wolf in the late 1950's and 1960's was not one of salacious enterprise but of resigned submission to an inevitable but not particularly satisfying act. Of course such attitudes may have been merely a protective façade, and that in itself would be an interesting counterpoint to the male assumption.

This brief survey of some of the divergent images Chinese have of women tells us very little about the "nature" of women in Chinese society, but it tells us a good deal about the confusing social context that encouraged women's conservatism, and points directly at some of the strains in the fabric of Chinese society. Since our purpose in studying women in China, as elsewhere, is to increase our understanding of the total society, this result is neither disappointing nor unexpected. With this context for women's lives sketched in, let us now move on to look at some of the ways women exerted influence to improve their condition.

Feminism and Revolution

If, as Handlin explains, the comparability of women with men was considered a radical concept during the Ming, feminism as a doctrine advocating the social and political equality of men and women was unthinkable. Feminism as a social movement, of course, came late in the Ch'ing, among the foreign ideas introduced into China around the turn of the century. By then a number of talented women had demonstrated their "comparability" by pursuing a modern education and publicly participating in nationalist and feminist causes. However, as we learn from Mary Rankin's essay on Ch'iu Chin, feminism as a social movement was quickly set aside in favor of the more urgent needs of nationalism. As Rankin observes, "She [Ch'iu] implicitly recognized that sexual equality was not likely to be achieved without some major structural changes, and saw the liberation of women as one result of the revolution to which she chose to devote her greatest energy." Ch'iu's execution in 1907 enshrined her as a revolutionary martyr for Communists and Nationalists alike. The circumstances of her death suggest that Ch'iu chose martyrdom, in an act that could be interpreted as suicide, for her ultimate statement about the heroic role women could assume in political action.

Ch'iu's legacy of poems and essays reveals the great personal cost of her liberation. Although she had the talent and the financial means to maintain herself independently, she did not turn away from the traditional roles of daughter, wife, and mother without moments of real anguish. This anguish echoes again and again in the works of the women writers described by Feuerwerker. They struggled to gain an education, struggled to gain their physical freedom, and then found they must struggle yet again to escape the emotional bonds their mothers and families used to draw them back. Feuerwerker tells us, "They wrote at the time in their personal lives when, having made the brave effort to break away from traditional molds, they were rebellious and defiant, but also lonely and anxious, and they wrote to clarify and interpret to themselves the rush of impetuous, unsettling experiences they were living through. In these works of their youth they wrote to keep up with their own lives; they wrote, over and over again, the story of their own lives."

So also Chiang Ch'ing's recollection of her early life, which appears in Roxane Witke's biographical essay, conveys the pain of breaking away from social conventions and seeking identity in new worlds. Born to such social ignominy as not to have been exposed to the moral decorum of the Confucian elite, Chiang Ch'ing had to fight her way out of the poverty cycle that absorbed the vast majority of women (and men) until a systematized revolutionary movement made women's liberation a fundamental obligation. Like other nonconformist women of her generation, from childhood she was defiant of authority, eager to break the family bond, athirst for education, and fiercely nationalistic and radical in her politics. But unlike many other young women who tested themselves in modern careers and revolutionary political movements, Chiang Ch'ing did not allow herself to wallow in sentimentalism, nor did she pursue the peculiar justice and solace of a suicidal course. From the beginning she was bent upon survival—on her own terms.

Feuerwerker tells us that many of the young writers of the 1920's did not survive as writers much beyond their adolescence; instead they slipped into other activities, from wife and mother to teacher or editor. It is as if they burned themselves out in their ardent struggle for personal liberty, leaving too little to sustain them through the emotional ordeal of a lifetime of literary creativity. Perhaps in the same way that their writing echoes Ch'iu Chin's despair, their lives exemplify her fears. Conscious of the severe drain her career had already made on her spiritual resources, she may have chosen to use her remaining strength to provide a heroic model for others because she feared she would not have the endurance necessary for the long, tedious job of making revolution.

To the women discussed by Rankin and Feuerwerker, feminism was a concept that had meaning, that they could apply to their own future. To women of the less privileged classes, by contrast, feminism was as alien as the automobile. Feuerwerker's liberated women writers were appalled to discover "that whereas women had been repressed and confined under the traditional system, they now were in a precarious and exposed situation, and no less vulnerable." This aspect of liberation would come as no surprise to women of the lower classes, for whom alternatives to the family system were grim. The Hakka women Johnson describes knew they could support themselves as laborers; and elsewhere women who left their husbands earned a living of sorts as servants and prostitutes. But most peasant women understandably preferred to cope, to make their way within the system.

Peasant women did not simply submit to the oppressions of the traditional family. They searched out and made use of every source of power they could to gain some influence over their fate. The women Topley discusses from the silk-producing regions of Kwangtung were certainly the most successful. Some of these women rejected marriage in favor of the rare economic independence available to them; others agreed to marry but to delay consummation (sometimes forever), to limit the number of children they would bear, and to demand other unheard-of concessions from their husbands' families. But women under more routine conditions found other ways of manipulating their circumstances. Margery Wolf argues, for instance, that women are careful to retain the first loyalty of their young sons for themselves, and later try to prevent their daughters-in-law from interfering with this loyalty. If their control over these male sources of power fails them, some women resort to threats of suicide, or, if all else fails, to suicide itself. The pecuniary and social cost of a suicide to a family is sufficient to make the senior members of a family cautious even when threatened by the most lowly daughter-in-law.

Peasant women also use less drastic means of acquiring some control over their lives. As Ahern tells us, Chinese beliefs about conception allot women their full share in the creation and development of the unborn child, and peasant women seem to have some awareness of the power this fertility gives them. In Shun-te, Topley reports that marriage contracts may specify a limit on the number of children the bride will bear. From Arthur Wolf's analysis of household registers from Taiwan we learn that many widows in the first half of this century neither remarried nor remained celibate. Drawing from his field experience with modern farm families, Wolf suggests two possible explanations for this finding.

One is conventional: that parents-in-law who insisted on making an uxorilocal marriage for their son's widow, in order to have an extra hand on the farm and a father of sorts for their grandchildren, failed by reason of the deep-seated prejudice against such marriages on the part of prospective husbands. The other is less conventional: that young widows simply were not interested in remarriage. If a woman has borne sons by her deceased husband, her progeny give her a claim on his estate and authority in his family superior to any she might have with a living husband, first or second. Should the family need more descendants or temporary income, these needs could be met (and according to the household records often were) by "informal marriages." Thus with typical peasant pragmatism the ideal of the chaste widow was honored by ignoring its substance but calling on its forms to ratify a woman's independence.

Since educated elite women and lower-class peasant women came from such very different environments, it seems in retrospect not surprising that early Communists in China found difficulty incorporating them into a single women's movement. Elite women, who had little contact with the men of their families and even less opportunity to influence their behavior, saw a solution to many of their problems in the independence equal opportunity would give them. Peasant women, sharing closely in the lives of men whose limited opportunities were all too obvious, questioned the utility of attaining sexual equality if no one ate. And yet the burden of the Chinese family system, in both the huge families of the elite and the sometimes painfully fragmented families of the poor, fell on women, rich or poor, far more heavily than on men. The struggle to maintain a place in the system, to stay afloat in a sea of male and generational prerogatives, was familiar to every woman regardless of her class. On this issue women could and eventually did unite.

Today in the People's Republic of China the rights of women to social, political, and economic equality with men have been formally proclaimed. The implementation of these rights may seem at times cynically superficial to the Western observer, but it is clear that Mao Tse-tung's confidence in future improvement is shared by the people. National strength and the basic human needs have highest priority. To meet them progress toward less basic social needs such as equality of the sexes must frequently be slowed, but women as well as men accept the delays without losing faith. As outsiders, we can only watch with interest, for the complicated interaction between the needs of women and the needs of revolution is a chapter in China's history still only half written.

Women and Productive Labor

The relationship between the status of women and their role in the economy, currently a fundamental research problem in social science, comes up in several of the essays in this book. The hypothesis central to Marxian thinking about the "woman problem"—i.e., that women are oppressed primarily because they are cut off from socially productive labor—is considered in Davin's essay. In the People's Republic the presumed relationship has been incorporated into policy: if women's status is to improve, they must be a part of the labor force. The difficulty of testing such a hypothesis conclusively becomes apparent when one attempts to define "improvement in women's status" or "amount of oppression," and to observe the effects of such contributing variables as general economic conditions and concurrent social reforms. Nonetheless, evidence for and against the hypothesis is now accumulating from a variety of cultures, and it is perhaps time that the Chinese case be considered.

Davin looks at the degree to which rural women in China participated in agriculture before 1949 and in the first decade after liberation. She also describes the many improvements in women's lives under the People's Republic. The 1929–30 Buck survey of twenty-two provinces used by Davin for a prerevolutionary baseline found that of the men, women, and children involved in farm labor, 24 percent were women, and that 13 percent of all farm work was done by women. In 1956, according to a paper presented at the Third National Representative Congress of Chinese Women, 25 percent of the workpoints allocated by the agricultural cooperatives were earned by women. Although Davin interprets this 25 percent as a decided increase in women's involvement in productive labor, she is careful to point out that these data are difficult to evaluate and dangerous to compare. She knows, for example, that the Buck estimate appears to be significantly lower than that made by Fei and Chang in a study in the Yunnan area only seven years later; and two studies by Sidney Gamble in North China also indicate somewhat higher agricultural participation than Buck reports. Any satisfactory estimate of women's involvement in agriculture in Republican China (if one is even possible) would require sorting out the Chinese, Japanese, and European surveys and village studies by crop and by area. According to some reports, women played a crucial role in the rural economy of some areas long before the campaigns of the People's Republic. In others their role may have been less important or less obvious. Should matching data from the People's Republic someday be made available, there is the possibility of a controlled study of social change.

The Hakka village Johnson studied in the New Territories of Hong Kong brings another kind of data to bear on the productive labor hypothesis. Until after the Second World War most of the women of the village were primarily or solely responsible for farming the family's land, which provided the basic subsistence for their households. In the years following the war much of the farmland was sold for factory sites. In 1964 the entire village, by then surrounded by an industrial city, was moved to the suburbs, where its members now live off rental income or, for those who sold their land before its value skyrocketed, off factory earnings. Johnson, who shared the life of these "urban villagers" for two years, tells us the women's response to the dramatic changes. "I detected no feeling of anomie among the women. From their point of view, the loss of apparently meaningful and productive work in agriculture has been more than compensated for by the relative ease of their lives, particularly the absence of hard physical labor. The men seem to feel this change less keenly, and some felt a nostalgia for the past that was not expressed by the women." This group of women, at least, felt that oppression was lifted by the *end* of their involvement in productive labor.

Topley's paper on the marriage resistance movement in the area in and around Shun-te hsien in Kwangtung provides a third temporal and social setting in which to examine the Marxian hypothesis. Unmarried women were essential sources of labor in sericulture; married women, because they were considered a source of pollution and hence a danger to the silkworms, were excluded from certain processes in the silkworm's life cycle. In the middle of the nineteenth century, mechanization and the introduction of large factories severely curtailed the domestic production of silk, cutting off married women and many men from sources of income. However, young unmarried women, many of them living in the "girls' houses" common to the area, were employed in even larger numbers in the factories. For some families the earnings of daughters and "independent" daughters-in-law became the major source of income. Of all the factors that led these young women to resist marriage or the consummation of marriage, Topley found the most important to be their ability to support themselves in a socially respectable manner.

What then have these Chinese examples told us about the productive labor hypothesis? Davin, working with inadequate survey data from prerevolutionary China and incomplete data from the first decade of the People's Republic, asserts that there is a correlation between the improvement of women's condition in China and their apparent increased participation in agriculture. Johnson finds that women released from the major burden of family support neither regret its passing nor ac-knowledge any loss of status as a result. Topley demonstrates the ex-traordinary social independence that accompanied women's economic independence, even in the conservative society of the last century. These seemingly contradictory findings suggest the need for some revision in the classical hypothesis. Contributing to socially productive labor is not enough, as Johnson's paper indicates, nor is simply controlling the rewards for that labor. For a woman's lot to improve appreciably in Chinese society, her labor must be able to provide her with a life style that is a respected alternative to marriage and family. Only then can she set a value on her fertility and her domestic services, rather than allow them to be taken for granted as natural to her female existence irrespective of her economic contribution.

So far, except in nineteenth-century Shun-te, no effective test of this hypothesis seems to be in the offing in China. Women in the People's Republic are still struggling to get equal workpoints for equal labor, and after the day's labor is done they return home to the domestic duties "natural" to their sex. Even the campaigns to get them into productive labor vary with the economic needs of the country. Delayed marriage is urged, and dormitory living is common for the unmarried urban young, but these are temporary adjustments, not alternatives to marriage and motherhood. On the other end of the hypothesis, however, it is obvious to even the most critical observer that the status of Chinese women, by any definition, has improved dramatically in the last twenty-five years. Oddly enough, then, it appears that the original Marxian hypothesis, though fundamental to revolutionary development in social-ist countries in general and China in particular, works out variously in practice. The uncertainty of that hypothesis offers numerous possi-bilities for research on the changing role of women in China and else-where.

Prospects

It would be gratifying to be able to provide the reader with a list of solid conclusions about the roles, status, and condition of women in Chinese society, past and present. The closest we can come to that goal is to list some key questions and to indicate research begun or antici-pated. We have much to learn. Our understanding of the shifts in the status of women in China is shaky; the information we have about his-torical attitudes toward women is much too limited. We need to know more about women's legal status under the Ch'ing, the Republic, and the People's Republic, and we need a comparison of the legal codes with customary law. We must give more analytic attention to autobiographies and biographies, and to the more subjective data provided by women in literature. We need to know more about women's relations with women. We know that within the family, at least the family resulting from what Arthur Wolf calls a major marriage, women quarreled and competed, and dissatisfaction on this score must have had considerable effect on family reform in the post-1949 period. But we know very little about the informal groups women formed in the villages or the strength of the relationships they formed in factory dormitories, and these are factors that must have contributed to the success or failure of social reforms. There was and still is tremendous variation in custom from province to province, but few researchers have focused on that variation as a research problem. Such a study might well clear up many apparent discrepancies in interpretation.

Our gravest handicap in the study of women in Chinese society is the inadequacy of data on the attitudes and opinions of ordinary women. We can go to a village in Taiwan and interview a hundred women, but we cannot go back to the late Ch'ing or the early Republic for a matching sample. Nor, unfortunately, can we interview rural women in the People's Republic in ways of our own choosing, though this may change. But difficulties with sources are not new to students of China, and the quality of the essays in this book attests to how well such handicaps can be overcome.

Lü K'un's New Audience: The Influence of Women's Literacy on Sixteenth-Century Thought

JOANNA F. HANDLIN

An understanding of women in premodern China has been made diffi-cult both by contemporary concerns and by traditional Chinese ideals. The cry of twentieth-century Chinese women for social and economic equality has led to an overemphasis on the subordination of women at the expense of other important features of traditional Chinese life.

In accordance with the widely accepted formula of "thrice obeying" (*san-tsung*) women were expected to comply with their fathers or elder brothers in youth, their husbands in marriage, and their sons after their husbands' death. But the force of such precepts was undercut by a hier-archical concept of society that extended to men as well as women. Just as women were expected to serve their husbands, so were officials ex-pected to serve their rulers. Similarly, didactic works for women such as Pan Chao's *Nü chieh* (Admonitions for women) and Liu Hsiang's *Lieh nü chuan* (Biographies of model women), at first glance oppres-sive, should be understood in the broader context of *li*, norms of proper behavior, to which boys no less than girls were expected to conform.

The principles of female subordination and li, designed to order soci-ety, tell us more about how the upper class thought women should be-have than how they actually did. The patrilineal descent of property and surname that demonstrates women's social and legal inferiority to men was an institutional form that, like li, persisted unchanged over centuries, even as actual behavior and the values it expressed changed

Many have helped me through various stages in the writing of this paper, but I would like to thank above all Professors Frederic Wakeman, Jr., and Wei-ming Tu for their generous encouragement and guidance and Professor Eugene D. Genovese for his painstaking care in editing the penultimate draft. I would also like to thank the American Association of University Women for its support.

markedly. It is the numerous practical changes that did in fact take place which should have first claim on our attention.[1]

The writings of the scholar-official class, committed to the ideals of hierarchy and li, obscured the real world behind the visions. Changes in the ideals or shifts in emphasis did, to some degree, reflect real social changes: we know, for example, that there was a turning point in the middle of the Sung dynasty, when a period of diverging opinions gave way to a period in which attitudes toward women were consolidated. Thus Chu Hsi (1130–1200), promoting the severe opinion that widows should not remarry, followed upon the heels of the innovative eleventh-century reformers Fan Chung-yen, who had advocated giving widows money to remarry, and Wang An-shih, who proposed allowing a girl whose husband had killed her child to remarry.[2] The increasing importance attached to the fidelity of widows can be tenuously related to the rise of an urban culture in which women ceased to work and became status symbols for men. However, the precise links between social realities and changes in values remain unclear. The writings about women do not reveal the world that prompted the emergence of new attitudes; rather, they reveal idealistic reactions to a changing society. We see only a series of reaffirmations of the traditional view, and consequently, surveys of the position of women in China typically conclude that the status of women either remained unchanged or deteriorated.[3] Foot-binding, the cults of chastity and virginity, and stricter rules against the remarriage of widows are cited as evidence of the growing oppression of women. They should, however, be interpreted as reactions to the aggressive behavior of women, as described in the vernacular fiction, and to the expansion of opportunities for women living in cities.

Sixteenth-century materials reveal the social realities as well as the ideals, and make it feasible to study elite attitudes toward women as a dialectic between the actual and the ideal. A notable example of the shift from idealism to realism is Lü K'un's manual *Kuei fan* (Regulations for the women's quarters). Whereas sixteenth-century fiction writers portrayed the illicit affairs of their heroines with a certain amount of relish and sympathy, Lü K'un tried to draw the attention of female readers to more didactic works. Yet he did not merely reassert old values in reaction to departures from the approved path; indeed, his very act of addressing a female audience was accompanied by curious and significant shifts in his philosophical views. In particular, the distinctions between right and wrong, so clear in earlier didactic works, give way in *Kuei fan* to more ambiguous attitudes toward women.

Lü's *Kuei fan* and such other works of his as those on local government and self-discipline, which also comment frequently on women, were so widely read both during his own time and during the Ch'ing dynasty that they can justly be interpreted as reflections or expressions of prevailing sentiments. But more important, his works constitute especially rich sources for the sixteenth century. Lü proved receptive to the kaleidoscopic social and intellectual currents of his era; at the same time, he strove to incorporate the numerous conflicting attitudes into one consistent view.

Superficially, little distinguishes Lü K'un from numerous other sixteenth-century scholar-officials. He had a conventionally successful career, rising from magistrate to governor to vice-minister of justice. While his more colorful contemporaries, rebelling against a brutal and despotic government, gained notoriety for iconoclastic eccentricities, Lü K'un appeared to be such a conformist that after his death he quietly joined the ranks of the most upright scholars in the Confucian Temple. Others became famous through their affiliations with the philosophical schools then thriving throughout China, but Lü eschewed the empty philosophizing of the academies and remained socially isolated. He wrote prolifically, but was by no means a seminal thinker. Later scholars quoted him from time to time, but they borrowed his ideas piecemeal, without taking the whole Lü K'un as their model.[4]

Yet Lü K'un, although in so many ways conventional, reflects the extremes of his time. The failings of the court had caused widespread disaffection from the ideals associated with the imperial government at a time when flourishing urban centers were exerting an unprecedented centrifugal pull on the educated. Consequently, many avoided political involvement altogether, and instead derived a sense of purpose by associating with the artisans and shopkeepers who flocked to join the circles of teachers like Wang Ken. Lü K'un, however, remained in a pivotal position, serving the government for most of his life while directing much of his energy to educating the commoners. Those no longer committed to the imperial government easily abandoned orthodox ideals for individualistic philosophies. Lü, in contrast, sought to compromise between those ideals and the everyday demands of the uneducated. Hence, his writings incorporate both idealistic and pragmatic features.

According to Confucian theory Lü's dual orientation, serving simultaneously the people and the state, entailed no conflict. But the social and political conditions of the Ming created tension in those occupying such pivotal positions. Uncertain about the validity of orthodox ideals, Lü was receptive, even vulnerable, to the impact of realities, in particular the many social changes wrought by the expansion of the market economy. Thus Lü perceived and attempted to deal with such activities as women's working outside the home and participating in the heterodox White Lotus sects, activities ignored by the more resolutely idealistic.

In previous centuries scholar-officials who were alienated from the imperial government had turned their attention to the people, but the spread of literacy during the Ming created an unprecedented bond between the elite and the commoners. The large receptive audience not only bolstered the courage of scholars inclined to quit the civil service, but also moved Lü and his contemporaries to express their views not in idealized abstractions, but in concrete terms that related to everyday life. As scholar-officials shifted to values that they could share with their new audience, the distinctions between them and the commoners became blurred. Most important, as the new audience attracted the attention of the educated, it came also to command their respect, for men like Lü K'un identified themselves closely with the views and interests of their readers.

Accordingly, the presence of a female audience influenced Lü's consciousness. The idealized view of the position of women had gone unaltered for centuries, but in the sixteenth century widespread female literacy provoked men for the first time to perceive not the equality of women but their comparability, and to ask just how, given their obvious talents, they differed from men. These questions, once articulated during the late Ming, continued to worry writers during the Ch'ing. Thus a study of the sixteenth-century attitudes toward women will suggest that long before the intrusion of the West, the serious literature of the scholar-official class had laid the foundation for the presumably revolutionary twentieth-century belief in the equality of the sexes.

Lü K'un's "Kuei fan"

For his Kuei fan (preface, 1590), Lü drew on the Lieh nü chuan, a work that enjoyed great popularity during the early Ming.[5] Whether or not it was indeed authored by the Han dynasty scholar Liu Hsiang, and whether or not his son, Liu Hsin, was responsible for the prefaces and encomiums, the extant Lieh nü chuan took its present form—various categories of biographies of women, each followed by a brief encomium—by the beginning of the thirteenth century.[6] Lü K'un rearranged the categories, eliminated the section on evil women, added a few biographies of his own choosing, and, most important, replaced the laconic encomiums of the Lieh nü chuan with his own. Unlike those of the Lieh nü chuan, which merely reiterate that the heroine was virtuous indeed, Lü K'un's bear the stamp of an opinionated and powerful editor. Often departing from the obvious biographical content, Lü specifies the precise purpose for which he thinks a story important. He explains, for example, that the trials of the woman of Ch'i-shih are significant "*not* to show that she was extraordinary, but to shame those officials who plot for the state";[7] that Huai Ying falls short of being a noteworthy example of fidelity, but has been selected as an example of someone who "manages matters well";[8] and that he normally does not record wives who follow their husbands to death.[9] In addition Lü indulges in lengthy comments and, departing freely from the original accounts, raises questions and explores problems that preoccupy him. In this manner he brings arcane anecdotes to life for his sixteenth-century readers, who responded with enthusiasm: the *Kuei fan* went through many editions even before the end of Lü's life.[10]

In his preface to the *Kuei fan*, Lü K'un explains his interest in the instruction of women. The behavior of women is degenerating. Those born in villages hear vulgar expressions. Those living in wealthy homes are slipping into extravagance and think only of gold and pearls; although clever, they neither speak good words nor perform good deeds.[11] Such criticisms of degenerating morals are so commonplace among Chinese authors that Lü might be thought to be merely echoing earlier didactic works. However, the urban culture of the sixteenth century, with its pornographic novels, sexual handbooks, and information on the depraved customs of various regions,[12] provided understandable cause for special concern. Lü worried about the leisure now enjoyed by women of all classes, even in Shansi and Honan, the backward northern provinces of his acquaintance. Accordingly, in his *Shih cheng lu* (Records on practical government) Lü complains: one need not discuss the laziness of wealthy women (which, though regrettable, can be taken for granted); but now even poor village women shirk their many tasks and sit around discussing clothes and ornaments. They exchange their garments for fruits and cake, enriching their stomachs while impoverishing themselves. Should a bad harvest befall them, will they not starve to death?[13] The leisure available to young girls was also disturbing; would they not be susceptible to illicit amorous affairs?[14]

Earlier didactic literature such as Pan Chao's *Nü chieh* of the Han dynasty, *Nü lun-yü* (The girls' analects) of the T'ang, and *Nei hsün* (Instructions for the inner quarters) of the early Ming[15] exhorted women to avoid laziness and arise early to attend to household duties. But these works had been written for upper-class women, whereas the prosperity of the late Ming made leisure available to the poor as well as the rich. This had a profound influence on Lü's consciousness, for he tailored many of his writings for those "women and girls among the people (*min-chien fu-nü*) who suddenly have three or five volumes in their chests."[16]

Although it is difficult to determine quantitatively how far literacy had spread during the Ming, contemporary reports offer some clues. According to a visiting Korean monk, Ch'oe Pu (1454–1504), for instance, literacy as early as the 1480's had penetrated the lower classes in the area south of the Yangtze:

> People south of the river, moreover, read books. Even village children, ferrymen, and sailors can read. When I came to their region and wrote questions to ask them, they understood everything about the mountains, rivers, old ruins, places, and dynastic changes, and told me about it minutely.
>
> North of the river, the unschooled are many. That is why when I wanted to ask them something they would all say, "We do not understand the characters." They were illiterate.[17]

The proliferation of academies and popular educational works in the sixteenth century suggests that literacy had become even more widespread by Lü's time.[18] Although Lü came from a backward region, he clearly had in mind female readers "from among the people." Furthermore, he had been so influenced in his youth by the educational activities of a magistrate from the prosperous Kiangnan region[19] that he tried to create an even wider audience by accommodating semiliterate and even illiterate women. For the illiterate he composed songs that could be transmitted orally.[20] For the semiliterate, Lü made the biographies in the *Kuei fan* more attractive in a number of ways. He provided brief glosses and indicated the proper pronunciation by inserting two characters to represent the initial and final sounds, thus explicating any obscure characters that might confuse his readers. He condensed the original biographies, almost always deleting allusions to difficult classical texts. He played to his readers' emotions. And he had the *Kuei fan* richly illustrated;[21] for example, a wood-block print accompanied each brief anecdote in an edition from the Wan-li period.

The expansion of the market economy brought with it a dangerous superabundance not only of leisure, but also of money. Money contributed to the "vanity and extravagance of today's girls"[22] and to the spoiling of children[23] that Lü so deplored. Even worse, according to Lü, was the divisive effect money was having on the family. In songs composed for the illiterate members of his clan, Lü admonishes his audience: "If brothers disagree, it is because of money. . . . If [only] you would yield more of the household things and listen less to [your wife's] pillow talk."[24] Poignantly, he blames the financial demands of wives and children for the neglect of ancestral worship:

Ask where your body comes from. Think of those ancestors and parents who raised you children. Alas, in vain does a home have several children. In the winter, who offers a glass of wine at the tomb? (You will certainly say you do not have the money.) Did you spend money entertaining guests? And you did not begrudge money for your wife and children. Ah! You see that lonely ghost returning for the three sacrifices at the northern tomb? If it comes to this, it is better not to have children.[25]

So far from ideals has the world fallen, Lü wails, that "recently marriages, if not for wealth, have been for sexual attraction."[26]

Given the many potential objects of criticism that abounded in Lü's day, the tone of his commentary to the *Kuei fan* is surprisingly moderate. Unlike the authors of earlier didactic works, he eschews moral censure and idealized prescriptions in favor of a more sympathetic and tolerant attitude toward women.

From External Norms to Self-Determination

At first glance it might appear that Lü upholds the subordination of women. Agreeing with the *Li chi* (Book of rites), Lü writes: "Women are those who submit to others. Compliant and humble . . . , their nature and feelings serve others."[27] But on careful reading, Lü's commentary to the *Kuei fan* reveals that for him li represents only a set of ideals in sharp conflict with his perception of reality. Lü praises his heroines not for their submissiveness, but for independent thinking,[28] for thwarting the demands of their parents that they remarry when widowed,[29] and for their ingenious use of persuasion.[30] When philosophizing in abstract terms, Lü values highly the role of li in ordering society: "If one eliminates the word li from the women's quarters, then the world will turn upside down. A hundred calamities and a thousand disasters, loss of life and destruction of family, will all result from this."[31]

But when Lü inspects real situations closely, a more ambivalent attitude emerges. Lü explicitly criticizes exaggerated li (*kuo li*). Thus in his encomium of Miao-yüan, whom he admires for continuing to live out her life after her fiancé's death, Lü writes: "As for those who have been promised in marriage, and who, . . . weeping, follow [their fiancés] to death, their falling in love is carrying li too far and cannot be considered instructive."[32] Also illuminating is Lü's comment on a woman who, when a dangerous fire broke out, refused to leave her rooms unless properly accompanied by her tutor and governess. Lü considered her refusal especially senseless because she had other companions to testify that her departure had no illicit motives, and because, even when the governess came to escort her, she still refused to leave without the tutor:

Po-chi thought it more important to preserve li than to preserve her own body. Now li are used to preserve one's body. If one transgresses li, then what can one do with one's body? . . . When it came to the night when the house caught fire, having other girls accompany her would have been enough to make her true intentions clear. Li in coping with emergencies [*ch'u pien chih li*] are naturally like this. That [Po-chi] would go only after waiting for her governess was in itself excessive caution. Then, when the governess came but the tutor did not, she finally died in the fire [because] she would not go. In a thousand years there is only one person who adheres so strictly to li. Gentlemen will grieve over her determination; but they will also regret that she was blind to the expediency [necessary] in emergencies.[33]

In another *Lieh nü chuan* anecdote, the heroine, Meng Chi, tries to commit suicide when faced with the prospect of riding in an open carriage that would improperly expose her. While the *Lieh nü chuan* encomium simply praises Meng Chi for steadfast adherence to the rules of right conduct, Lü uses this story to explore the two extremes of rigid compliance with li and utter permissiveness:

When the ancient kings set up restrictions in the world, only li were most serious, and li in regard to [the relations between] men and women were even more serious [because the ancients] feared that that is whence disasters came. . . . Today when women go out, they walk and do not even cover their faces. And when they ride in carriages, they themselves also pull aside the curtains, [their faces] abundantly adorned to please the eyes of crafty youths. The gentry, moreover, are unaware that it is wrong. How can we expect others [to know]?[34]

As in the story of the fire, Lü seems torn between the two extremes— excessive and mindless compliance with li and total moral laxity. There even creeps into the end of the passage a hint of resignation to the decadent but prevailing customs of his time.

Unable to choose between rigid compliance with li and disconcerting contemporary decadence, Lü becomes obsessed with the means of managing affairs expediently (*ch'u shih chih ch'üan*). In the cases of Po-chi and Meng Chi, expediency is important because a life is at stake. Cherishing life, Lü writes of the heroine of the Han family who risked her reputation by going disguised as a man among Ming soldiers for seven years: "One need not give up one's life to stick to righteousness. How could the sages value death?! The daughter of the Han family acted expediently without losing her integrity."[35]

Lü also admires those heroines who found a way to cope with emergencies (*ch'u pien chih ts'ai*) that posed a moral dilemma. Huai Ying, for example, was torn between her duty toward her father, Duke Mu of Ch'in, and her loyalty to her husband, who was the duke's hostage but wished to flee to his own home. To avoid overt disloyalty to either man, Huai Ying decides to remain behind but to feign ignorance of her husband's escape. Lü cites Huai Ying not as a worthy example of fidelity, but for her "expediency in managing matters."[36]

Lü advocates expediency not only to avoid making an extreme choice between li and death, but to make the most of a situation even when the moral choice is ultimately clear. He agrees with the Sung scholar who said, "To die for something in the world is easy; to accomplish something in the world is difficult." "Accordingly," Lü explains, "the sages value virtue, but more than that, they value virtue accompanied by talent."[37]

Thus at every turn Lü distinguishes between mere virtuousness and the ability to salvage or accomplish as much as possible before meeting death. Of Chao Huai—who requested permission to bury her slaughtered husband before serving the victorious general and who, after burying the dead man, committed suicide to preserve her fidelity to him— Lü, moved to tears, observes, "Is this not how one should deal with the unexpected?!"[38] And he admires Yen, who stalled bandits with promises of submission so her brother and father could escape. Had she cursed the bandits without submitting to them, Lü explains, the whole family would have suffered. "Would that not be virtuous!" he exclaims sarcastically, and then concludes, "But no one would have benefited from it. Those who are wise will pity her. An illustrious girl such as Yen can be regarded as [knowing how to] manage emergencies."[39]

Again, Lü commends a heroine of the Cheng family for confronting her captor (who was fond of eating female flesh) so boldly that he lost the heart to kill her. In addition, she successfully shamed another general for wanting to make her his mistress. For edifying the villains, Lü praises her at length:

Whether you explain the great principles to shame them or use agreeable words and sad feelings to move them, all bandits have the mind for righteousness [i] and principles [li]. Would you consider it preferable that not one of them be enlightened? If one's body falls into the hands of bandits, one method of preserving one's chastity would be [to assume that] nothing but death would suffice to keep one's reputation and nothing but cursing would suffice to accomplish death. [The bandits] would get very angry and their desires would wane. But I must express a reservation about this [method]. One girl cannot face down two bullies. If she arouses their anger they will necessarily want to disgrace her, and even death will not be enough to wipe clean the wrong done her. Therefore, one can be assured that it is better to shame and move them to get [death].[40]

The above passage, like many others,[41] illustrates how Lü's preoccupation with the means of coping with emergencies overshadows orthodox moral precepts. Even where the heroine's action is beyond question correct, Lü keeps alternative courses before our eyes. Thus he has mixed feelings about Wang Kuang's daughter, a widow who committed suicide after a vain attempt to kill the barbarian who murdered her father. While acknowledging her sterling virtue and her fidelity to her deceased husband, Lü nevertheless regretfully observes that she might have succeeded if, instead of acting so precipitously, she had allowed the barbarian one night of pleasure and waited for him to fall asleep.[42]

The extent to which Lü's interest in dictating rules of behavior (along the lines of earlier didactic works) had yielded to an interest in helping women solve problems on their own appears most clearly in his comments on the story of a "wife who took her husband's place": An enemy who wanted to kill the woman's husband forced her father to use her as an inside contact. The father told his daughter, who thought the matter over. If she did not comply, the thief would kill her father; if she did, he would kill her husband. She finally decided to save both men by letting herself be murdered in her husband's stead, occupying his place in bed at night when the thief could not detect the substitution. Although this heroine wins unqualified praise in the *Lieh nü chuan*, Lü critically and somewhat incredulously comments:

Someone who dares coerce a father to force the daughter [to be an inside contact] is a powerful bravo! Why did he not openly kill the husband on bumping into him during the day? . . . Why not have the father and husband together flee to a place where they could not be traced? Alas—virtuous women! How regrettable![43]

Lü not only scoffs at the protagonist's lack of ingenuity, but suggests a realistic solution.

Throughout his *Kuei fan*, Lü replaces advocacy of abstract ideals with explorations of means of achieving those ideals and of the conflicts involved. He thus departs from Pan Chao's prescriptive *Nü chieh* and the models given in Liu Hsiang's *Lieh nü chuan*. In fact, Lü almost impatiently declares that "the numbers of virtuous women are too great to record."[44] Isolated models of virtue interest him little. He has made his selection carefully, embroidering upon the anecdotes in a way that encourages his readers to cultivate themselves by pondering such problems as how to strike a balance between achievement and the preservation of life on the one hand and the maintenance of moral integrity on the other.

His belief that women should be taught to think for themselves rather than merely to accept external norms reflects a new attitude. In fact, Lü even upholds the moral autonomy of his heroines at the expense of the traditional deference to parents and husbands. Accordingly, Lü applauds two young women who uphold li by refusing their parents' orders to remarry.[45] In another case, Lü explicitly reproaches a father for forcing his daughter into a second marriage.[46] With a similar disregard for the formal structure of hierarchical relationships, Lü writes of a mother who beat her irresponsible son: "If the son is upright, the mother will follow; if the mother is upright, the son will follow."[47]

The extent to which Lü believed that one's moral integrity, not one's sex, should determine who is worthy of leading is clear in the following passage on Mu-lan, who for 12 years disguised herself as a boy to take her father's place in the army:

Those who do not have confidence in themselves are unable to trust others. For someone like Mu-lan, how could others gossip about her losing her purity? The multitude of three armies over a period of 12 years did not know that she was a girl. How could they gossip about her? A gentleman in managing the world has a mind of which he alone is aware and which can be tested before the sun in heaven; and his sympathy with others [reaches the standard of] being able to mix [without blighting] his splendor with dust. Indeed, Mu-lan is my teacher.[48]

Mu-lan's individual conscience—the mind of which she alone was aware —not only was sufficient to sanction her behavior, but moved Lü to take her, although a woman, as his model.

The Comparability of Men and Women

In addition to raising questions about the conflicting demands of ideal li and real emergencies, Lü enriches the biographies by contrasting and comparing, as the original *Lieh nü chuan* does not, men with women and the rich with the poor. His inability simply to accept—indeed, his need to explore—the differences between these groups suggests how faded the distinctions had in fact become.

Frequently Lü enhances a heroine's virtue by declaring that even men would have found her dilemma difficult. Thus throughout his commentary run such declarations as: "The two words loyalty and purity are difficult for a gentleman; how much more so for a servant woman!"[49] "How are there in the world people who do not fear tigers? How much more so of a timid girl!"[50] Hsiao-o's "wisdom and bravery are such that there are some brave fellows who cannot match her,"[51] and "This is a matter for a great fellow. Now, that a woman can do it, alas! How heroic!"[52]

Indeed Lü K'un often unwittingly refers to his heroines as "fellows" (*chang-fu*), counting them among the ranks of men. I have already mentioned Mu-lan, whom Lü not only deems a worthy example of self-confidence to "gentlemen of the world" but himself takes as teacher.[53] Similarly advising gentlemen to follow Yen Kung's example of protecting a city against bandits, Lü declares, "How can we say Yen Kung is not an eminent fellow!"[54] Again, in his prefatory remarks, Lü asserts that women can serve as examples of virtuous men. "There are many virtuous . . . men, so why have I written about women?" Lü asks. And answers: "To manifest the teaching of women [yin-chiao]. These are all women who are [examples of] benevolent people, filial sons, upright scholars, and loyal officials."[55]

These passages, which might be dismissed as one man's eccentric view, take on more general significance in the light of other sixteenth-century writings. The story of Mu-lan, for instance, although originating much earlier, seized the imaginations of many of Lü's contemporaries. T'ien I-heng, a poet and bon vivant of the latter part of the sixteenth century, reports as "seeing twice again Mu-lan" two other instances of girls who disguised themselves as men—one to avoid being captured by rebels, the other to pursue a livelihood as a merchant after her parents died.[56] Similarly, the playwright Hsü Wei (1521–93), who was obsessed with clothing and forms of disguise,[57] wrote one of his four plays on Mu-lan. Other writings by these two authors confirm that their interest in Mu-lan's disguise was not superficial. For a second play Hsü Wei takes as his theme a girl who, contrary to custom, took the civil service examinations.[58] And T'ien I-heng was disconcerted by the report of a boy who suddenly changed into a woman and married one of his companions.[59]

Although Lü does not indulge in such frivolous literature as notes on strange events or plays, his comment in the Kuei fan that "this is the deed of a fellow but the body of a woman"[60] reveals that he, too, entertained, however unwittingly, ideas about the interchangeability of sex roles.

Lü also exploits every opportunity that the original biographies provide to contrast and compare the rich and the poor. One biography, for example, tells of a great general who asked a talented singer to become his mistress. When she refused, he found a pretext to have her husband killed and then tried to win her with pearls and silks. Unmoved, she first tried to kill him, and, failing that, killed herself. In his encomium Lü finds her story all the more moving because she, of poor background, withstood the temptations of the great general's wealth.[61] Of another heroine Lü similarly exclaims, "Who would have said there would be a person like this among poor women!"[62]

In accord with the sixteenth-century view that commoners can share the Way with the sages Yao and Shun,[63] Lü K'un asserts that moral values transcend social status: "Wealth is not enough for glory; nor does it mean disgrace. Poverty cannot excuse tempestuous behavior, and it should not merit shame."[64] Lü elaborates on this belief in defending his inclusion of biographies of lowly women: "Servants are lowly; why record them? [Because I am] recording worthies. If one is speaking of allotted influence and status, then the wives of members of the gentry and of commoners should not be put together. If one speaks of the Way and righteousness, then [people] in ditches and starving to death can share the same hall with Yao and Shun. Why speak of high and low?"[65] In this manner, Lü addressed the rich and the poor in common terms, simultaneously, as one audience.

Lü's consciousness of the lower classes, for whom social and economic distinctions between the sexes were minimal, contributed to his awareness that women had capacities equal to men's. A sympathetic account of a female beggar, drawn from Lü's personal experience, illustrates Lü's acceptance of women's working outside the home. Ts'un-erh, "the little survivor," born blind and with no means of support, begged alone in the capital. A band of beggars tried to violate her, whereupon she screamed, knocked her head against the ground, and wept aloud: "My poor fate! Even if I have no matchmaker, must I become a wanton woman making a damnable reputation for myself?!" A sympathetic official arranged for her to marry a blind street singer; after a year, the husband died. The official buried him and wished to arrange another marriage for Ts'un-erh, but she refused, insisting that she should remain faithful to her husband until death. "Moreover," she added, "I have learned my husband's songs to beg for food; and [now] I eat more than when I was a maiden. How could I bear using these songs to feed another?"[66]

Lü's account does much more than commemorate Ts'un-erh's fidelity to her husband or prove that the poor, too, are capable of virtue. It not only accepts her working in public, it emphasizes that she improved her material well-being by acquiring skills. Finally, the story shows Lü's awareness that a woman could easily assume a man's occupation.

Numerous tantalizing hints suggest that in the sixteenth century women were finding more opportunities for outside work, and that scholars began to focus more on working women. Certainly the prosperous cotton industry of the period opened up new opportunities for women, who were seen, for example, daily taking thread to market to exchange for more raw cotton to spin.[67] Indeed, contemporary accounts of artisans often lump together "ignorant men and women,"[68] without any differentiation whatsoever. Such statements as "men and women of the entire hsien all make stomachers for their living"[69] and "both men and women braid sandals, knot hemp, and weave cloth"[70] further demonstrate how blurred some of the occupational distinctions between the sexes had become.*

One of Lü's contemporaries, Hai Jui (1514–87) was so disturbed by the disappearance of such distinctions that he tried to teach townspeople to differentiate their occupations according to sex. Forbidding women to go onto the streets, Hai Jui insisted that only men be allowed to go to and fro among the houses or undertake capitalistic (tzu-sheng) enterprises: women, he instructed, should limit themselves to work within the home.[71]

Lü, by contrast, recognizing that women have the capacity to serve the society at large as well as the home, outlines an elaborate plan for mobilizing female labor:

In Yü-tz'u and T'ai-yüan hsien, weaving is very widespread among the people. The Keeper-of-the-Seal of the Prefecture should select about ten carpenters to train the carpenters of the province to make spinning wheels and looms to sell in the markets. Then they should see that the village headmen and directors of the garrisons and yamen make a list of all the people within the covenant [yüeh], excluding those of wealthy families and those men and women who have occupations such as selling wine and food and such skills; the rest, whether of commoner or military status, should, if they are women without work, be reported to the officials. First the officials should be touched for silver to buy a thousand catties of clean cotton, one catty for each family; and the Keeper-of-the-Seal should make a record of it and distribute it to be reeled into thread. . . . As soon as the cotton has been spun, the garrison should dispatch it to the world at large. Twenty or thirty weavers sent from such hsien as Yü-tz'u [should] teach the people to weave cloth. The men and women who reeled thread should on successive appointed days learn weaving from the weavers. Within a year a thousand people will be able to spin and weave. . . . Within two years there will be many weavers within the province. When this has been accomplished, not only will women have jobs, but will the province not enjoy the profit as well?[72]

In contrast to Hai Jui, Lü makes no objection to women's selling wine or mingling with male weavers. He wishes only that women become productive members of the province.

In one more way Lü's exposure to the lower classes made him aware of the energy of women. Earlier in the dynasty "demonic women" had

---

* Marjorie Topley's findings, reported later in this volume, on how the demand for female labor bolstered the independence of women in the nineteenth century suggests that a similar correlation might have existed for the sixteenth century.

led a rebellion,[73] and it was widely known that women were as numerous as men in the rebels' ranks.[74] In his writings on local government, Lü condemned the numerous secret societies that deceived people in general and even seduced women.[75] Likewise Ho Shih-chin, also of the late sixteenth century, worried that "the understanding of women and girls is so simple and humble that they like even more [than men] to coax spirits and seek wealth and are deluded by heterodox sorcerers."[76]

The participation of women in rebellions, already known to students of the Ch'ing dynasty, is discussed further by Mary Rankin in the following paper in this volume. Suffice it to note here that Lü K'un and Ho Shih-chin, unlike earlier scholar-officials who had limited their vision to an ideal world, were impressed and troubled by the potential power of women. A third writer, Shen Te-fu, less serious than Lü and Ho, even wrote an essay, "Fear of the Inner Quarters," on henpecked husbands.[77]

Social and economic changes contributed to but do not suffice to explain the enlarged view of Lü and Ho. The earning power of women undoubtedly increased during the sixteenth century with the expansion of the textile industry, the spread of a money economy and contractual labor, and the burgeoning of intermediate market towns. But a female role in the economy had developed prior to the sixteenth century without precipitating a change in the elite's attitude toward women. Peddling women appear, for example, in the early *ch'uan-ch'i* stories,[78] but, significantly, those accounts did not alter the consciousness of the literate world. Therefore, we must look further for an explanation of Lü's broadened vision.

Disillusionment with fellow officials detached Lü and other sixteenth-century writers from the ideal hierarchical conception of society, making them receptive to new impressions. But even this does not fully account for their novel opinions. In addition to the disaffection of the scholar-official class and the altered economic position of women, another change—increased literacy among women—made men aware of the comparability of the two sexes.

Thus, T'ang Shun-chih (1507–60)—whose role in replacing the stilted "palace" (*t'ai-ko*) style with the informal "ancient" (*ku-wen*) style in itself suggests a novel outlook[79]—observes that his younger sister was so bright and so easy to teach, "it is a pity that girls are not fellows."[80] Moreover, T'ang maintains that girls can be transformed, or edified, by reading a wide range of books. Accordingly, he has the highest praise for his sister-in-law, who not only liked to read conventional didactic works such as the *Hsiao ching* (Classic of filial piety) and the *Lieh nü chuan*, but had mastered manuals of medicine, divination, and tree-planting. "Although she certainly was not as good as a specialist," observes T'ang, "she never failed to understand the main points; and often she put them into practice with successful results. If she were not a girl," T'ang concludes, "would she not be able to discuss the philosophical precept of 'Nature and feelings' with Confucian scholars? If not [that], there is no doubt that she would certainly be a capable person, widely read and having many skills."[81]

For T'ang Shun-chih, who thought it "a pity that girls are not fellows," literacy had virtually obliterated the distinctions between the sexes. But, in the wake of such unselfconscious enthusiasm for the literate woman, there set in a reaction, epitomized by a saying that gained wide currency in the late Ming: "Only the virtuous man is talented; only the untalented woman is virtuous." Ho Shih-chin, for example, was distressed that groups of twenty or thirty women and girls were forming associations (*she*) to study the classics.[82] Other scholars must have feared the pernicious influence on female readers of vernacular fiction. Even more insidious than pornographic fiction were those stories which pretended to be sternly didactic, but which stimulated romantic titillation. These warned of impending disasters while indulging at great length the reader's taste for spicy love affairs. Still worse were stories that condoned and even romanticized illicit affairs between handsome, talented youths and beautiful, equally talented maidens who finally win the approval of their parents. Such stories, in short, taught that independence could bring happiness. At least one tale suggested an alternative to marriage and thereby strengthened the independent aspirations of female readers in a manner especially threatening to the social order: one night a girl escapes from her chaperon to have a talk with a Buddhist elder; later, on her wedding day, she is transformed into a Bodhisattva when she is supposed to descend from her betrothal carriage.[83]

Lü senses how disruptive such literature might be, for he cautiously distinguishes virtue from literacy. Explaining his selection of biographies of literary women, he writes:

Literary women—those recorded in histories and biographies—are known to all. Although they are not perfect, their many good points cannot be overlooked. . . . [Yet] even those whose palindromes show extraordinary skill and talent erred and came to know regret. Their virtue still reaches others, so I do not take note of them. . . . But there are also chaste girls and faithful wives whose poetry and prose are not recorded; they certainly did not gain respect through literature.[84]

Lü similarly says of young women poets, "Women are not known for their outstanding behavior, nor do they become famous through learning—and still less through poetry!" Lü then explains that while there have been numerous women poets, he is including only those two whose understanding of the Way is admirable.[85]

These limits to Lü's appreciation of women reflect the same standards he applied to men. Lü, who wrote few, mostly didactic, poems, has no patience for flowery compositions and approves of fiction only so long as it serves a useful purpose.

Some of Lü's contemporaries, in contrast, allow men but not women frivolous displays of their literary talents. For example, the famous Feng Meng-lung (1574–1646), who was responsible for editing and publishing much of the vernacular fiction, heartily concurs that "only the virtuous man is talented; only the untalented woman is virtuous."[86] Feng explains that men and women resemble the sun and the moon; since the (female) moon reflects the light of the (male) sun, there is no need for both to sparkle.[87] Since Feng's livelihood depended on his success as a publisher, he had a vested interest in leaving some room for trivial literature. But like Lü he wished to communicate with women, and shifted from a hierarchical to a reciprocal relationship with them. Thus Feng, like Lü, so respects his heroines that he notes of one: "There are fellows whose wisdom cannot match hers."[88] At the same time, both tried to compromise between their desire to relate to their female readers and the conventional hierarchical concept of society. So, while female literacy commanded their respect, in deference to traditional values they limited their acknowledgment of women's comparability to the areas of moral and practical capacities. Nonetheless the question raised by T'ang Shun-chih—how are women, if literate, different from men?—disturbed Lü and Feng, and by the late Ming, women's literacy had become an open issue. Chao Ju-yüan, in contrast to Lü and Feng, argued: "'To be virtuous is to be untalented' are overly strict words. 'If one is virtuous, there is no need to constrain one's talent' is a more equitable view."[89] The opposing sides in a debate that stirred up much controversy in the eighteenth century emerged clearly during the late Ming.

Emotion, the Great Equalizer

Lü's disillusionment with officials partially accounts for his openness to the strengths of women. Thus, he lauds one heroine's concern for the welfare of the state "not to say that she is extraordinary, but to shame those officials who make plans for the state."[90] Moreover, he could easily

identify his own dangerous position—serving a ruthless dynasty while
treading cautiously among self-seeking officials—with that of a maid-
servant he describes who survived a treacherous predicament while remaining loyal to her master. According to Lü's version of the biography,
the wife of a minister has a love affair with her neighbor and instructs
her personal maid to poison the husband upon his return. The maid
finds herself in a dilemma: she wishes neither to murder her master nor
to disgrace her mistress. Therefore she contrives to trip and spill the
poison. Writes Lü:

In this example of a loyal servant, she was completely in accord with good-
ness. That she did not reveal the evil of her mistress was generosity; that she
could not bear seeing her master poisoned was loyalty; that she slipped
intentionally, spilling the wine, was wisdom. . . . This can be called the
method [fa] of a gentleman; how much more so of a woman.[91]

Lü can conceive no higher praise for the servant than describing her
actions as worthy of a true gentleman.

The notion that Lü identifies with women because of a similar pre-
cariousness of social position throws light on his preoccupation with his
heroines' expedient management of emergencies. More important, precisely because of comparable pressures in his own life, Lü perceives
in a remarkably detached manner that the moral demands on women
reflect their peculiar social position, rather than transcendent values:

A girl protects her body as [securely as] she holds a jade goblet or [something]
overflowing with water. Her mind does not want to be perturbed by [what
the] eyes and ears [perceive]; and her inner feelings do not want to be thrown
into doubt by [the discrepancy between] inner and outer. Only then can she
perfect a steadfast and pure behavior and keep her body chaste. Why? The
husband undertakes work in the world at large; if he is reckless and defiles
the proper relationships, his restraint in small matters still suffices to redeem
him. [But] the girl's reputation rests in her one body; and if there is the
slightest fault, ten thousand good [deeds] cannot cover it. Thus nine out of
ten girls remain constant.[92]

The moral confusion of the Wan-li period (1572–1620) further contributed to Lü's sympathetic attitude toward women. No longer convinced of the validity of rational social rules and hierarchical distinctions,
men became increasingly emotional. Lü's comment on the biography of
Wang Chang's wife illustrates his occasional inability to make a clear-
cut moral choice. When Wang Chang was poor, his wife wisely advised
him not to feel sorry for himself; when he prospered, she urged him not

to call for the dismissal of the powerful and corrupt minister Wang Feng. Wang Chang ignored his wife's counsel and ultimately suffered death for his courage. Writes Lü most ambivalently:

Wang Chang and his wife exemplify the different roads to accomplishment. The [wish to] stop the letter [denouncing] Feng was a normal feeling on the part of Chang's wife; but Chang in the end would not follow [her advice] and persisted in his intention to speak out. If one considers it from the viewpoint of success and failure, then the wife was not unwise; if one considers it from the viewpoint of right and wrong, then Chang was not disloyal.[93]

Instead of singling out either party as ultimately right, Lü retreats into comments about the good companionship spouses should share. And instead of reinforcing the husband's authority, Lü stresses the equality of the relationship by asserting that spouses should not conceal even a single word or deed from each other. Sympathetic to both the wife's counsel and the husband's act, Lü submerges his ambivalence in the emotional conclusion, "I am moved by this account."[94]

One reason for Lü's moral uncertainty—his inability to judge solely "from the viewpoint of right and wrong"—emerges from his sympathetic comment on Chih's wife:

When a husband dies and the wife kills herself in order to accompany him, I do not record it. . . . But I have taken note of Chih's wife. Why? . . . When the customs of the state are changing, it is most agonizing to preserve one's integrity [*ch'eng*]. Lamenting that she had no one to rely on, she drowned herself in the waters of the Tzu. These are not the feelings customary between boys and girls. I sympathize with her worthiness and frequently marvel at her, but not because of her fidelity.[95]

The departing words of Chih's wife—"Above I have no parents; below I have no children; in the middle I have no brothers. Can human suffering reach this point? Where can I go?"—meant to Lü that she drowned herself primarily because she had no one to rely on. He was touched not by her desire to follow her husband—he explicitly denied sympathy for women who needlessly give up their lives—but because he shared her sense of dislocation and anguish at a time when "the customs of the state are changing."[96]

In earlier centuries scholar-officials, anxious about their precarious careers, or confused by the conflicting values of their times, had also identified with women, but with specific categories of concubines and courtesans. Lü sympathized with a generalized womankind. Moreover, he did not merely slip into occasional emotionalism, but articulated and celebrated the role of emotions in communicating with others. His efforts to reach a stratified audience of both rich and poor women led him to emotions—that common ground which everyone could share.

In his preface to the *Kuei fan*, Lü explains that earlier didactic works for women are inadequate because "they are dull, without any flavor, so they cannot make men feel awe."[97] Just as Lü enlivens the stale *Lieh nü chuan* accounts by bringing out the tensions between li and the preservation of life, so too he sprinkles his encomiums with explicit declarations of emotion. The account of a mother willing to sacrifice her own son to save a stepson "makes men wipe tears away";[98] moved by a mother who sacrifices much to entertain a guest, Lü "wants to cry";[99] and a filial girl who tries to save her stepmother from the death penalty "makes ghosts and spirits weep."[100] He also liberally scatters such terms as "aroused" and "moved" throughout his commentary.

Lü's desire to move his readers can be better understood in the light of his concept of "feelings" (*ch'ing*) as a basis for human communication. Like earlier philosophers, Lü believed the feelings should be restrained by li and laws.[101] Nonetheless, Lü's concept of feelings departs radically from that of Chu Hsi and Wang Yang-ming.

Both Wang and Chu accept the importance of feelings. In reaction to the Buddhist scorn for emotions (which signify an attachment to this world), Chu Hsi strove to define a place in his philosophical system for "feelings." For this reason he finds congenial Chang Ts'ai's view that "the mind unified Nature and feelings."[102] And Wang Yang-ming, going further than Chu, boldly asserts that "there is no event outside of human feelings and human affairs."[103] Thus whereas Chu maintained that principle (*li*) existed outside the mind and Wang that it existed within it, they agreed on the importance of feelings in perceiving such virtues as humanity, righteousness, propriety, and wisdom (*jen, i, li, chih*).[104]

Lü gives feelings a much more prominent place than does Chu Hsi, who subordinates feelings to nature and nature to the mind,[105] or Wang, for whom feelings are incidental to the main tasks of "cultivation of the personal life" and "rectification of the mind."[106] According to Wang, "the feelings of the sage are in accord with all things and yet of himself he has no feelings."[107] But Lü cannot attain such equilibrium, for feelings have an irresistible hold on him: "they cannot be disposed of . . . cannot be stopped."[108] Consequently, going far beyond Chu and Wang, Lü proudly asserts, "I am not afraid of [having] many emotions [*kan*]; I am afraid of being too attached to emotions."[109]

Lü finds feelings so compelling that he repeatedly defines li, those rites which order society, in terms of feelings: "the mourning regulations follow human feelings";[110] "favor [en] and li come from the naturalness of human feelings and cannot be reached by force";[111] and "the sages originally regulated li by embodying human feelings, not by brushing them away."[112]

For earlier Neo-Confucian writers, feelings played an important role in the relationship between the individual man and his world. For Lü, feelings are crucial as a medium for communication among people. Thus, Lü talks of "those who are good at putting themselves in the place of others";[113] or "how the sage can feel the hearts of others";[114] and declares that "the more one personally becomes familiar with human feelings, the more interesting they will be."[115]

Communication and empathy require the rooting out of all *ch'ing ko*, which literally means "separation of feelings" but which can loosely be translated as "lack of communication" or "emotional detachment." "The single word 'separation,'" writes Lü, "is the great disaster for human feelings."[116] Such separation should be eliminated from all relationships, without regard to status:

The ancients said, "When the gate of the emperor is ten thousand li away, it is called 'separation of feelings.'" How is it [that this refers to] the gate of the emperor alone? When father and son are of different minds, they are, [although] in one room, over ten thousand *li* apart; when older and younger brothers are divided in feelings [*li-ch'ing*], they are, [although] within the same gate, over ten thousand li apart; when husband and wife quarrel, they are, [although] in one bed, ten thousand li apart. If feelings are joined and intentions communicated, then, [despite] a distance of ten thousand li, it is like sharing the same hall, the same gate, and rubbing shoulders together in one bed. Using this example, [one could also say that] one's spirits can communicate up and down hundreds and thousands of generations while remaining unfamiliar with those of the same period. This implies that separation and meeting refer to the meeting of minds and do not rely on personal encounters. [Of course, the simultaneous] meeting of persons and minds is the greatest encounter in the world. Examples are: the ruler and the official, Yao and Shun; the father and the son, King Wen and the Duke of Chou; and the master and the disciple, Confucius and Yen Yüan.[117]

In this respect Lü resembles the eccentric and passionate Li Chih (1527–1602), who, according to W. T. De Bary, also abstracted from the complementary husband-wife (rather than from the hierarchical parent-child or ruler-subject) relationship the basis for all human relationships.[118] Although Li's *Ch'u t'an chi*, on which De Bary's observations are based, is undated, the essay that serves as its preface also appears in his *Fen shu* of 1590, the year in which Lü first published his *Kuei fan*.

Thus when Li Chih declared "husband and wife are the beginning of men,"[119] Lü K'un observed: "The way of the gentleman originates in man and wife. . . . The man and wife are a small-scale heaven and earth. . . . Therefore the myriad deeds and transformations begin in the bedroom quarters; and the five relationships and five li begin with the boy-girl [relationship]."[120]

Just as Lü K'un was impressed by female readers but wary of them, so he valued feelings but fearfully clung to the forms of discipline and structure necessary to rational order. He recognized the tension between the need to preserve sexual distinctions and the primacy of emotions between men and women:

Among the sources of affection in the world, men and women are among the most important. The sage kings did not wish to tear them apart; nor could they tear them apart. Therefore they united them with feelings that cannot be stopped, restrained them with rites [li] that cannot be transgressed, and bound them with immutable laws. If one indulges [the feelings, male and female] will be mutually content and long-lived. . . . Therefore, of the five human relationships, [the sages] again and again attached great importance to [feelings] and again and again were tolerant of [feelings] in regard to [the four relationships between] father and son, ruler and servant, older brother and younger brother, and friend and friend. I fear the significance of feelings were slighted only in regard to the one relationship between man and woman, which has given the minds of sages difficulty. Consequently, differentiation first began with [the relationship] between husband and wife. Originally there was no distinction between them, but then they were instructed with [the concept of] differentiation. How much more [important] when there are [true] distinctions [e.g., between men and women who are not husband and wife]; should one yet wish to confound them? The sage uses meaning deeply. It is the crossroads of life and death and [potentially] the beginning of great disorder. One cannot but beware.[121]

Summary of Lü's Novel Attitudes Toward Women

First, Lü calls for according women due respect. In reference to the virtuous Su Liu, who "had deep understanding and far sight," Lü asks, "How is it that women are good only for sex and beauty [se]?"[122] On this question Lü resembles such sixteenth-century writers as T'ang Shun-chih, who wrote so many epitaphs on women,[123] and Wen Huang, who recorded the instructions of his mother.[124]

Second, Lü stresses the value of a woman's life. Like many of his contemporaries, such as Kuei Yu-kuang (1506–71),[125] Lü deplored the popular view that a woman should commit suicide if her husband died.[126] More important, he denounced men in the Kiangnan area who, having no consciences (*liang-hsin*), committed female infanticide to avoid providing lavish dowries.[127] Citing the example of T'i Ying, who offered to become a servant in exchange for her father's release from prison, he argued that "giving birth to boys is not necessarily advantageous."[128]

Third, Lü holds the husband as responsible as the wife for a harmonious marriage. Departing from earlier views, he maintains that a husband's unsympathetic treatment or a son's unfilial behavior can make being a good wife or stepmother difficult:

The harshness of a stepmother, the jealousy of a first wife—ancients and contemporaries have considered [these] detestable. But the unfilial behavior of the sons by the first wife and the licentiousness of the husband, these, clearly, no one asks about. For a long time the feelings of the world [*shih-ch'ing*] have been biased. . . . Only if the son is filial and the husband is upright will the stepmother and the first wife have no apologies to make to the relatives.[129]

Lü criticizes avaricious grooms who contend for wives with large dowries:

After [the bride] has entered his door, if the earlier engagement and festival gifts and furnishings, and even the dowry that he has just asked the new bride to bring in are not lavish and numerous, he then treats his new wife like a servant. Once she has entered his door, if the offerings for the periodic festivals are in the least bit unsatisfactory, he will forbid her to come and go, or sometimes beat and curse her to the point where she contracts a fatal illness or commits suicide. He does not think of the thousands of miseries that people raising daughters go through that we might give birth to sons to make a livelihood; and more than that, he causes others to put out money and to suffer indignities.[130]

Finally and most important, Lü acknowledges and seeks to promote the capabilities of women. Rather than merely admonishing men to treat widows kindly, Lü instructs widows directly on how they might fend for themselves:

Everything is hard for widows and orphans. To remain faithful [to one's deceased husband] when childless is even more pitiable. If wealthy, one [will be treated] generously; but if poor, who will look after you? You are cheated and harmed in a hundred different ways and with no place to go. They persistently make false accusations before heaven. If the wife is determined to inherit her husband's share—she should look carefully into the legal codes.[131]

Confident that women could master useful knowledge, Lü planned to teach women to circulate information among themselves. To curb the practices of female quacks, most frequently consulted by women and children, Lü compiled songs with simple prescriptions, in the hope they would be circulated by women to teach the practitioners (*shih-p'o*).[132] In sum, Lü's desire to teach women weaving and medicine and to instruct widows in their legal rights illustrate how his respect for women was translated into practical innovations.

Continuity into the Ch'ing

Some writers during the Ch'ing dynasty reacted against the openly sympathetic attitude toward women of the late Ming. Lu Ch'i, who was born in 1614 when Lü K'un was an old man, wrote:

Now, all those youths who like to study have unusual feelings and a spirit of adventure, which is not something girls can understand; whether composing poems on climbing mountains, approaching waters, and looking down from a height; or writing essays on pawning clothes, buying wine, and snuffing out candles; or freely chatting with friends; or embracing prostitutes—all are necessary to [the development of] talent and feelings [*ts'ai-ch'ing*]. The wife must consistently go along [with these activities] without opposition. Only if she thinks that they might damage his health may she agreeably [try to] restrict him; and then she must not nag or talk too much.[133]

Thus Lu Ch'i, in sharp contrast to Feng Meng-lung, who admired a woman for her ingenious method of winning back her husband from the tempting brothel quarters,[134] or Lü K'un, who sympathized with the wives of licentious husbands, calls for the wife's unmitigated submission to her husband.

Lu Ch'i's work bears the peculiar stamp of a self-centered profligate husband, but nevertheless remains significant both because it was widely read during the Ch'ing[135] and because it grew out of the same social milieu that drove Shen Te-fu (1578–1642) to write a short essay on the "Fear of the Inner Quarters."[136] In short, writers had become conscious of the growing power of women and were reacting to it.

Though popular, Lu Ch'i's piece was not included in *Chiao-nü i-kuei*, a collection of works for the education of women compiled by the Ch'ing scholar Ch'en Hung-mou (1696–1771).[137] Probably Ch'en deliberately excluded it, for unlike Lu Ch'i, he shared Lü's sympathetic attitude toward women. As the younger scholar declares in his preface to the *Kuei fan*, Lü's work was moving even in Ch'en's day:

Not less than several tens of thousands of copies were published [during the Ming]—to the extent that it reached the inner quarters of the palace.[138] Among those within [the palace] it gave rise to [a sense of] shame through emotions; and through [a sense of] shame, determination. Among womenfolk, [it has been used] to encourage one another to do good and to deter evil, by how many I do not know. . . . The virtuous deeds it records can move heaven and earth and cause the spirits to weep. To this day, when reading it, [the characters] seem so real, as though still alive.[139]

Lü's commentary on the *Lieh nü chuan* biographies continued to elicit an emotional and intellectual response in the eighteenth century. Ch'en perpetuates the view that women should be educated:

There is no one in the world who is not educable; and there is no one whom we can afford not to educate; why be neglectful only in regard to girls? Just after leaving infancy, they are raised and protected deep in the women's quarters. They are not like the boys who go out to follow an outside teacher; who benefit from the encouragement of teachers and friends; and who are steeped in literature. Although parents love [girls] very much, they do not give them attention and sympathy [in matters] beyond daily eating and dressing. And when [girls] grow older, they are taught to embroider to prepare their dowries and that is all. It reaches the point that [parents] go to extremes in lavishing affection and doting on [girls]; rarely do they ask whether correct words [are used to] move them or whether they are complying with the ancient [sense of] righteousness or not. This is to regard girls as not requiring education, as though this is how it should be.[140]

Like Lü, who recognized that "the success of a family rests half upon the wife,"[141] Ch'en believes the education of women important because "the kingly transformation [*wang-hua*] begins in the women's quarters."[142] And hoping, like Lü, to reach a large audience, Ch'en "has selected those events which, being plain and simple [*p'ing-yi*], are close to the people; and [he has selected] those principles, which being lucid and shallow, are easy to understand."[143]

Like Lü, Ch'en had to mediate between the views of his peers and his own sense of mission vis-à-vis the uneducated women. Although preparing a collection of readings for women and buoyed by the vision that everyone can be reached through education, he defensively addresses the preface to those of his peers who question the need for female education:

Some will suspect that because girls who can read books are few, they cannot be educated through writings; those who wield brushes and compose poetry at times care about female virtue; [but even] they do not know that all girls are clever and that if they cannot all learn the classics and histories thoroughly, there are also [some] among them who know the rough meaning of the texts. Even when it comes to village women who have not mastered the characters, within the home their fathers and sons, children and brothers, will explain and narrate stories for them and discourse on the writings that have been handed down; and there will be areas where [the women] will comprehend and where their emotions will be aroused according to the deeds [described]. If one family is like this, one can infer that a whole village and a whole city [can understand]—who cannot be reached through teaching? If [even] those who devote themselves to essays and ink cannot understand the main meaning, then it is the fault of the instructors and not entirely the fault of the girls.

I have also seen women and girls today, holding onto something they [only] half understand or onto a formula they are used to hearing; and everywhere [they go] they believe it firmly, to the end of their lives. Moreover, circulating and spreading [instruction] orally, and encouraging and warning one another—how are these as good as reading literature aloud, from which their actions and knowledge would benefit doubly? For those who think about it, it is the nature of girls [to be] single-minded and very reverent; and would they not be even easier to reach through teaching? Those who are responsible for families of leisure should give first consideration to this.[144]

The debate continued fifty years later, in the 1790's, when Yüan Mei (1716–98) opened his doors to female students,[145] while his arch-rival Chang Hsüeh-ch'eng (1738–1801) proclaimed in his famous "Studies for Women" that women of his day were undermining li in their pursuit of poetry.[146] The eighteenth-century debate on the education of women, discussed in Rankin's essay, did not grow out of the accidental appearance of an independent and allegedly libertine Yüan Mei, but from tensions that, following the spread of literacy among women, found expression as early as the sixteenth century.

The Emergence of Women at the End of the Ch'ing: The Case of Ch'iu Chin

MARY BACKUS RANKIN

During the last years of the Ch'ing dynasty, modern feminism found its first Chinese exponents among those members of the urban elite who were influenced by Western attitudes and the 1898 Reform Movement. Women formed anti-foot-binding associations, girls' schools, and newspapers. In a period of uncertainty and change, educated women benefited from the growth of new professions and political groups, in which roles were not yet rigidly defined as they were in the exclusively male bureaucracy. New attitudes toward women and new opportunities for them were among the clearest indications that real, if limited, change was occurring within the elite strata of Chinese society. Although the entire women's movement before the 1911 Revolution was elitist, it was also potentially radical because it seriously challenged the dominant system of Confucian social relations. Women's activities at the end of the Ch'ing thus paved the way for the feminism that was to blossom a few years after the Revolution as part of the May Fourth Movement.

Many women stayed within reformist bounds. A smaller number pursued feminist goals more intensely and iconoclastically. They joined radical male students in the treaty ports and Tokyo, and formed small women's adjuncts to male student circles. Within these groups some women linked feminism to the revolutionaries' goal of overthrowing the Ch'ing dynasty. Ch'iu Chin, beheaded in 1907 after leading an abortive anti-dynastic rising in Chekiang province, was the most famous of the "new women" of this period.[1] A dramatic and appealing personality, she joined in many women's activities typical of her time: study, teaching, journalism, political involvement. In particular, she illustrates the wedding of feminist and revolutionary commitments. In some respects she displayed the traditional skills typical of earlier outstanding women; in

others she foreshadowed the individualistic liberated women of the
May Fourth Movement, and in still others she anticipated later leftist
women who, as Roxane Witke has shown, subordinated feminist goals
to the broader one of social revolution.[2] Certain dominant themes in her
life were to pervade women's history during the Republican period:
rebellion against the family system, involvement in problems of students
and youth, rejection of feminine for martially heroic masculine roles,
the association of women's liberation with larger political causes, and
severe emotional strain.

Since her death Ch'iu Chin has become an exemplary heroine, and
as such has inspired many Chinese women and exerted a romantic appeal on Chinese of all political persuasions. Yet the mythology that soon
embellished the real facts of her life has tended to set her apart, ob-
scuring similarities between her story and those of other educated
women who first demanded independence. Although her aspirations and
achievements were extraordinary, her career illustrates the problems
faced by her contemporaries and the motives that inspired them.

Changes in Elite Attitudes

Women under the Ch'ing. Although the history of women during the
Ch'ing has been little studied,[3] there is evidence that the usually accepted dark picture needs modification. Such evils as bound feet, seclusion, curtailed education, and a rigid one-sided morality epitomized
in the cults of chastity and virginity were real enough. However, the
actual lives of gentry women often deviated markedly from the restrictive Confucian ideal. The sympathetic male attitudes that Joanna
Handlin describes for the end of the Ming persisted and broadened.
There were general trends toward liberation that prepared the way for
more far-reaching, Western-inspired change.

The fragmenting of government power and diminution of faith in
orthodox Neo-Confucianism during the late Ming and early Ch'ing gave
women unusual opportunities to participate in public life. Ch'in Liang-
yü (d. 1668) was the most striking of several women famed for their
political and military exploits. A Ming loyalist, she sent troops under
the command of her son and daughter-in-law to aid the dynasty. When
the Ming government collapsed, she managed to keep her base in
Szechwan intact, and her family's position there was eventually recognized by the Ch'ing.* As late as the 1670's, a woman named K'ung

---

* Besides Ch'in Liang-yü, her daughter-in-law, Ma Feng-i, and Shen Yün-ying
(1624-61), who commanded her dead father's troops in a successful defense of a
city against bandits, attained military fame. Arthur W. Hummel, ed., *Eminent Chi-*

Ssu-chen was active in high-level political maneuvering during the rebellion of Wu San-kuei.[4]

After government power was securely reestablished in the late seventeenth century, there was some tightening of orthodox standards. Nonetheless, educational opportunities for women were not cut back. Beginning with Lan Ting-yüan in the early part of the eighteenth century, a series of writers took the view that, although girls could study only for a limited time before taking up household duties, both their domestic skills and their comprehension of the ideals of female virtue would benefit if they learned to read.[5] It was widely accepted that women could learn. Even so conservative a moralist as the Chekiang historian Chang Hsüeh-ch'eng argued that the oft-quoted maxim proclaiming the absence of talent to be a virtue in women did not preclude female capability. It meant, he explained, simply that women with literary pretensions who had not first absorbed the traditional female virtues would be prone to ridiculous improprieties.[6] The instant popularity of *Dream of the Red Chamber*, with its very sympathetic characterizations of women, indicates that by the time the book was published in the 1790's, many men were much less grudging than Chang in acknowledging female ability. By the end of the century many educated women were achieving reputations as poets, painters, and calligraphers. Volumes by women had appeared in the Ming and early Ch'ing, but more were published during the late eighteenth and early nineteenth centuries. Women poets were particularly abundant in Kiangsu and Chekiang, and many also came from Anhwei and Kiangsi.* These provinces were noted for a high level of literacy and scholarship. Women's achievements in this region may also be related to its being an early center of Ch'ing reaction against the "Sung Learning" that had dominated intellectual life during the Ming.[7]

---

nese of the Ch'ing Period (2 vols.; Washington, D.C., 1943–44), pp. 168–69; Tung Te-han, *Ai-kuo nü-ch'ing-nien shih-hua* (Words about the history of patriotic young women; Taipei, 1954), pp. 27–44.

* For a survey of names of women poets and collections of their poetry, see Ch'en Tung-yüan, *Chung-kuo fu-nü sheng-huo shih* (A history of Chinese women; Shanghai, 1928), pp. 257–74. Evidence for geographic concentration of learned women is based on two narrow samples, which give strongly similar results. Of 85 women poets included in Ts'ai Tien-ch'i, *Kuo-chao kuei-ko shih-ch'ao* (Poems from the women's quarters of the Ch'ing dynasty, n.p., 1844) whose native district is unambiguously listed, 33 percent came from Kiangsu, 25 percent from Chekiang and 11 percent each from Anhwei and Kiangsi. Of 61 women mentioned for their own accomplishments in Hummel, *Eminent Chinese of the Ch'ing Period*, 41 percent came from Chekiang or married Chekiang men, and 33 percent from Kiangsu. Twelve of these women were mainly active before the end of Wu San-kuei's rebellion about 1680, 19 from 1680 to 1796, and 30 from 1796 to 1890.

By the end of the eighteenth century, accomplished women were presenting conservatives with a heightened moral dilemma. Many such
women enjoyed rich social and intellectual lives, gained public recognition, and associated frequently with men. Husbands with poetic and
artistic interests found companionship with wives of similar abilities.
In some respects, women's education, with its emphasis on art and
poetry, must have seemed enviable to young men from good families
with plenty of money and no taste for studying the eight-legged essays
required for the official examinations.*

The issue of moral decline was dramatized at the end of the eighteenth
century by the controversy between Chang Hsüeh-ch'eng and the poet
Yüan Mei. The iconoclastic Yüan Mei ostentatiously enjoyed female
company and beauty, but also seriously encouraged the women poets
he befriended to publish their works. Moreover, he spoke out against
foot-binding and an exaggerated emphasis on female chastity. Although
Yüan accepted concubinage and did not really regard women as equals,
he advocated opening up relations between the sexes in ways that con-
flicted with many of the Confucian restrictions.[8]

Chang Hsüeh-ch'eng attacked this attitude in his essay "Women's
Education" ("Fu-hsüeh") in which he said girls should not study
poetry, and insisted that their education should concentrate on virtuous
behavior and decorous speech. Although Chang is considered an opponent of female education, he actually was attacking the contemporary
moral laxity of both sexes, not learned women per se. He could admire
ancient women scholars who studied poetry to heighten their understanding of propriety (li). Now, however, Chang saw poetry subverting
propriety by drawing women away from the study of traditional virtues,
increasing their contact with men, and encouraging conceited notions
with public recognition. Girls of good family should remain quietly
within the women's quarters and not advance to further study until they
had thoroughly learned to practice modesty and other traditional virtues.[9] Many conservatives may have agreed with Chang's mixture of
restriction and respect, but it does not follow that he effectively stemmed
the reformist tide.

* The novel *The Scholars* (*Ju-lin wai-shih*), written in the 1740's, satirizes the
absurdities of divergent male and female education in the story of the disappoint-
ments that arose on both sides in the marriage of a beautiful, talented woman, who
had been lovingly trained to write polished eight-legged essays by her devoted
father and scorned more frivolous literary forms, and an accomplished young man,
who turned out to write poetry and have no interest in studying for the examinations.
The novel also depicts companionable relations between husbands and wives, and
tells of a gentry girl who for a time supported herself in Nanking by selling her
poetry and calligraphy. Wu Ching-tzu, *The Scholars*, tr. Yang Hsien-yi and Gladys
Yang (Peking, 1957), pp. 171, 449, 661–64.

In the 1830's, a number of scholars denounced the traditional treatment of women. The famous scholar-reformer Kung Tzu-chen (1792–1841) opposed foot-binding.[10] Yü Cheng-hsieh (1775–1840) used careful historical, classical, and humane arguments to attack foot-binding, the preoccupation with female chastity, and concubinage, and to insist that men should be held to the same standards of virtue as women.[11] Li Ju-chen (1763–c.1830) made the broadest attack in *Flowers in the Mirror* (*Ching-hua yüan*), in which he satirized almost all oppressive aspects of the treatment of women, whom, moreover, he presented as equal to men in activity and intelligence, skilled in war and scholarship and capable of holding office.[12]

The cumulative effect of increasing contacts between men and women may help account for the flowering of pro-feminine literature at this time. Intellectual reaction to the narrow, pedantic scholarship of the School of Empirical Research may also have been an influence. Most important was the revived interest in the New Text School of Han dynasty scholarship that began during the eighteenth century and became an influential current of thought during the nineteenth.[13] This school's freer ideological interpretations of Confucianism, openness to institutional reform, and less rigid attitudes toward women encouraged new ideas. Kung Tzu-chen was a leading advocate of this view in the early nineteenth century. Later the values of New Text School influenced the attitudes of leading 1898 Reformers, who advocated changes in the treatment of women among other Western-inspired reforms.

After the 1830's, the evolution of attitudes toward women within the Confucian tradition became increasingly intertwined with other factors generated by outside Western influence and internal political decline. The early reformers Wang T'ao and Cheng Kuan-ying were impressed by Western women, and broadened existing demands for reform for women during the 1860's. Dynastic weakness again gave women wider opportunities. For most of the last forty years of the Ch'ing, the most important political figure in China was the Empress Dowager Tzuhsi. Women were also important among rebel groups. A woman saltsmuggler and gambler led a troublesome Triad rising in Kwangtung during the 1850's.[14] The Taiping rebels did not live up to their theoretical sexual egalitarianism. Even so, the spectacle of Hakka women soldiers and the (largely unpopular) policy of unbinding women's feet in areas under their control may have had more impact than is generally recognized on the same gentry who despised Taiping ideology. Arthur Wolf demonstrates in his paper for this volume that supposedly deviant patterns of behavior could greatly influence elite practices. The disruptions of the mid and late nineteenth century perhaps encouraged such influence. Certainly there emerged from the disorders examples of females who might be assimilated to the tradition of martial heroines that for centuries had been a minor thread in popular fiction.

By the 1890's orthodox views of women had been compromised in many ways. Nonetheless, it was still accepted that women functioned mainly within the household and men without. Education and literary skills, which for men were stepping-stones to power and prestige, remained largely an adornment even for the most admired and able women. They might bring individual satisfaction, but were not important to society.[15] At best, women outside the family were integrated into the high culture that was an inseparable part of the Confucian tradition, but art and poetry, when cut off from the serious pursuits of statesmanship or classical scholarship, potentially were associated with heterodox bohemianism.

Whether changes within the Confucian tradition might eventually have become more substantial is conjectural. As it turned out, the immediate influences that broke the barriers keeping women out of public life came from the West. The main significance of previous developments was to predispose a portion of the elite to accept Western ideas that would bring far greater independence and equality.

The Western impact. Although some Chinese had been exposed to Western ideas and examples of Western women for several decades, such influences were minor until the 1898 Reform Movement, when the traditional position of women was reexamined along with numerous other institutions. The decisive step came when several intellectual leaders linked the woman question to nationalism, which provided a functional justification for the employment of women outside the home and gave women themselves new goals and values.[16] Both sexes were thereby encouraged to look once more at inequities.

Many of the new themes were introduced by Liang Ch'i-ch'ao in his 1897 essay "On Women's Education" ("Lun nü-hsüeh"). First, he linked women's education to the requirements for national strength and survival in a Darwinian struggle for existence. The goals of national wealth and power required that everyone be producers. Thus it was folly to write off one-half the populace as incompetent when women could contribute in many fields, and, at the very least, were crucial to the rearing of productive, patriotic citizens. Second, Liang appealed to universalist principles of fairness and equality, which he related to economic independence and experience outside the home. Women were not naturally ignorant, and should be allowed to broaden their minds and prepare to earn a living through travel and study. Husbands and wives might then be equally intelligent, occupied, and independent. Each sex would be able to develop its different strong points and accomplish noteworthy things. Third, Liang condemned the old system in strong, emotional terms that more radical writers would soon echo. Women were treated as birds and beasts, humiliated and oppressed by stronger men, who turned them into slaves and concubines, stopped up their eyes and ears, and bound their feet, all the while conditioning them to view this treatment as natural.[17] Within a few years Liang's ideas had gained considerable currency, and in 1903 the anarchist Chin I took the further step of linking such reformist arguments to revolution in *Women's Bell* (*Nü-chieh chih chung*).[18]

Even though attitudes among the elite as a whole lagged well behind the vanguard thinkers, and some writers opposed any changes in women's status, some women became active outside their home, and a small-scale feminist movement developed in the treaty ports and Tokyo. Missionary girls' schools increased in number after 1890, and they began to attract girls from respectable gentry families. More important was the growth of girls' schools established by Chinese reformers after 1900. The founders of these schools and of the anti-foot-binding societies did not necessarily contemplate far-reaching changes in the position of women. However, these institutions were important in drawing girls out of the home and providing institutional bases from which some women moved into broader participation in public life.

The association of women's education with the reform movement was significant. To the extent that girls' education was conceived as a modern education, girls were introduced to new ideas and gained parity with boys in a still uncharted field. The women who taught in schools or managed associations achieved a new status from their public activities, a status that had eluded the talented women poets who stayed at home. The term "woman scholar" (*nü-shih*), used almost as a title, appeared in newspapers. It was in this environment—of expanding opportunities for women, female reform activity shading off into radical politics, and strong concern over China's future—that Ch'iu Chin pursued her brief, but extraordinary, career.

The Life of Ch'iu Chin

Childhood. Ch'iu Chin was born in Amoy in 1875 into a respectable but slightly declining gentry family, whose home was just outside the prefectural city of Shao-hsing, in Chekiang province.[19] Her great-grandfather served as hsien magistrate in various places and finally rose to the rank of prefect. Her grandfather was the prefect in charge of Amoy's coastal defense. Ch'iu Chin's father was probably a *chü-jen*, but spent much of his career as a secretary and never rose very high in the official hierarchy. Ch'iu's elder brother passed the *sheng-yüan* examinations and had a post in Peking, but when her father died in 1901 the financially straitened family turned to trade for support, opening a *ch'ien-chuang* ("native") bank.[20]

The family was exposed to Western ways during their years in Amoy, and her grandfather had sometimes unpleasant experiences with foreigners as part of his official duties. In the mid-1880's, Ch'iu's father served as a secretary in the governor's yamen in Taiwan, under the energetic, reformist administration of Liu Ming-ch'uan. Ch'iu's family was part of the elite segment that in the late nineteenth and early twentieth centuries was changing somewhat—finding new economic bases, becoming oriented toward the large cities, and entertaining some Western-inspired reformist ideas. By 1904, when Ch'iu Chin deserted her husband to study in Japan, her family's attitudes had evolved sufficiently that her mother and brothers gave her considerable support.

Chekiang was a center of female education, and Ch'iu's mother was a well-educated woman who was strongly devoted to her daughter's interests. Her father also favored her, and saw that she received a good education, along with her elder brother and younger sister and brother, in the family school. It is difficult to disentangle facts about her childhood from later mythology, but clearly she was indulged by her parents to an unusual extent. Her feet were almost certainly bound, but perhaps not very tightly.[21] She studied and wrote poetry, as was normal for talented girls of her class, but is also said to have engaged in romantic dreams of knight-errantry, fed by swashbuckling novels, and to have learned to ride horseback, use a sword, and drink considerable quantities of wine. Her brother recollected that she did not even begin to learn what was normally considered women's work until about age fifteen. Although she developed some skill at embroidery, she did not enjoy doing it and gradually gave it up.[22] All accounts indicate that, even for the favorite daughter of an elite family, her upbringing was extremely advantaged, a background that paved the way for her subsequent career, as was also true thirty years later of Ting Ling. Ch'iu matured into a talented, unconventional, and strong-willed young woman, accustomed to having her own way.

She also did not marry until the unusually late age of twenty-one. Both she and her parents must have wished to forestall their separation, but it also seems quite possible that she had developed a reputation in the places where she spent her girlhood that discouraged prospective mothers-in-law. In the early 1890's, however, the family moved to Hunan, where her father held office first in Changteh and then in the hsien capital and trading port of Hsiang-t'an. There he became a friend of the wealthy merchant and philanthropist Wang Fu-chen, who had the additional distinction of being related by marriage to the family of Tseng Kuo-fan. In 1896 the two men arranged for Ch'iu Chin to marry Wang Fu-chen's youngest son, Wang T'ing-chün.[23]

Marriage. The frustrations and sorrows of eight years of marriage had a decisive influence on Ch'iu's life. The Wang family is invariably described as conservative and her husband as a wastrel, yet Ch'iu appears to have been fortunate in her marriage. There is no indication that she was mistreated by her mother-in-law, her position in the family was soon strengthened by the birth of a son and a daughter, and within a few years she accompanied her husband to Peking, where she enjoyed far more freedom than most Chinese wives.[*] Nonetheless, her loneliness for her own family[24] was not assuaged by any particular affection for her probably rather spoiled husband. She found her new household duties boring and, while she was still living in Hunan, was much more restricted in her pastimes than before.

Immediately after marriage Ch'iu's life probably approximated that of the traditional woman of talent more closely than at any other time. Her chief occupation was writing poetry in traditional style (mostly *tz'u*), mainly on conventional subjects. Autumn, sorrow, loneliness, wind, and rain were recurrent, melancholy themes,[25] which had a special personal note because the Chinese character for Ch'iu's surname also means autumn and is an element in the character meaning sorrow. Later she would write on revolutionary and feminist topics, but she would continue to use the same poetical forms and in many cases to employ traditional references and imagery.[26]

When Ch'iu's husband purchased a post in Peking, probably early in 1900, she entered a much more congenial social milieu of reform-minded lower-grade metropolitan officials and their wives. The men were interested not only in the traditional pastimes of the privileged—lavish entertainment, art collecting, and gambling—but also in Western

---

[*] Ch'iu's son, Wang Yüan-te (1897–1955), was graduated from Cheng-feng University and worked as a journalist and a middle school teacher. He remained in China after 1949 and became Secretary of the Hunan Office for Research on Written History. Her daughter Wang (Ch'iu) Ts'an-chih (b. 1901) studied abroad, wrote, and sought to imitate her mother's physical daring. She went to Taiwan in 1949 and has been Ch'iu's persistent biographer. Wang Shih-tse, "Hui-i Ch'iu Chin" (Recollections of Ch'iu Chin), in *Hsin-hai ko-ming hui-i lu*, 4: 232; Florence Ayscough, *Chinese Women Yesterday and Today* (Boston, 1937), pp. 135–36.

ideas and customs. Their wives followed suit. Some had foreign acquaintances, and at one point both Ch'iu and her husband began to
study English. In this environment Ch'iu began to read "new books"
and take an increased interest in national affairs. According to one
source, she helped form a natural-foot society after the Boxer Rebellion
and also spoke on behalf of women's education.[27]

She also enjoyed a free social life with a group of women friends, the
chief of whom were the calligrapher, poet, and reformer Wu Chih-ying,
the wife of one of Wang T'ing-chün's colleagues, and the Japanese second wife of one of Ch'iu's own relatives, who was employed in the T'ung-
li yamen. These women visited one another, drank together, and exchanged poetry and modern ideas.[28] While these activities in part may
have reflected the freedom enjoyed by talented women poets in the past,
they also showed the influence of the independence exhibited by Western women. Similarly, although the group was patterned on traditional
coteries of male scholar friends, it foreshadowed social relations among
women radicals a few years later. From the experience of Ch'iu and her
companions, it appears that educated women in the large cities could
enjoy considerable social freedom by about 1900 without much resistance from their husbands. For Ch'iu personally her group of friends
not only made life more enjoyable, but proved an important outside
source of support when she left her family.

Most important, Ch'iu's experiences in Peking led her to develop a
strong nationalist concern with China's future. Some writers have suggested that as a child she had learned from her grandfather's experiences
in Amoy to resent Western encroachment. We know that she was distressed by the Sino-Japanese War.[29] It was the occupation of Peking by
Western troops, however, which convinced her that China was on the
brink of disaster, and that all Chinese should work for the country's
salvation.[30] Nationalism then called Ch'iu forth from her home and inspired many of her future actions.

Her nationalist ideas, as formulated in Peking and further developed
in Tokyo, resemble those generally pervading radical student circles
in her day. She had already obliquely criticized the Manchus as alien
before leaving for Japan, a sentiment that may have had traditional
xenophobic roots.[31] Soon thereafter she accepted the quasi–Social Dar-
winist analysis that China was on the verge of extinction in a struggle
for survival against the more vigorous imperialist West, though she still
often expressed her ideas through more traditional imagery.[32] Nationalism permeated her feminist views. She argued that equal education and
rights would kindle women's patriotic desire to contribute to national

strength, and would elicit contributions toward the new civilization that might be less tainted with traditional aspirations than men's.[33] Nationalism also demanded revolution, for only if China's rottenness, epitomized in the Ch'ing dynasty, was swept away and its uncomprehending populace awakened would the country gain the strength to survive.

Ch'iu and her husband paid a visit to the Wang home after the Boxer Rebellion. When they returned to Peking, her discontent became acute. Aware that attitudes toward women were changing, Ch'iu no longer found poetry and friendships a satisfactory outlet for her energies. Distressed by the contrast between her seemingly meaningless life and her aspirations to save the country,[34] she decided by the end of 1903 to leave her husband to study in Japan.

She was aided in this decision by her friends and her mother. The Wang family from whom she was escaping also helped unintentionally, for the family system functioned so that her mother-in-law naturally assumed responsibility for Ch'iu's children. Ch'iu had earlier persuaded her husband to divide their property but was unable to recover her share, which had been invested in a relative's unsuccessful business. She therefore sold her jewelry. Her women friends supported her decision and helped her leave Peking. Before sailing for Japan she visited her parents' home and, because she had quixotically spent most of her money to aid the imprisoned reformer Wang Chao,[35] was compelled to ask her mother for more funds.

Japan: the liberated woman. When Ch'iu arrived in Tokyo during the spring or summer of 1904, she was determined to make the most of her new freedom. If she had not previously done so, she now unbound her feet and threw herself into a plethora of activities. From then on her life revolved about the three interlocking themes of education, feminism, and, above all, revolution.

She saw her arrival in Japan as a blow both for women's rights in general and for her individual freedom of conscience. The courage to make such a decisive break with family life revealed the strength of the individualistic and independent character fostered by her upbringing. Unlike feminists of the May Fourth period, Ch'iu had not been exposed to the ideas of Ibsen and the example of Nora. She knew little about Western individualism, and attempted no sophisticated definition of a spiritual core on which individual integrity was based.[36]

Ch'iu did demand that women enjoy the same freedom as men, a goal inextricably bound up with ending domestic seclusion. The unhappiness felt by many recently married young women was intensified by Ch'iu's strong, unusual personality. Moreover, new ideas and goals trans-

formed traditionally futile dreams of escape, for Ch'iu firmly believed
that the social environment was changing in ways that offered genuine
hope of wider opportunities.[37] Education, outside friendships, useful and
gainful employment not only promised to enrich women's lives, but also
to elicit the respect necessary for them to be accepted as equal partners
by their husbands.[38] Outside family confines, a woman might act as a
recognizable person and demonstrate abilities that would justify equality. Ch'iu blamed women themselves, as well as male-dominated society,
for their traditionally subservient position. Women had failed to study
and leave inner compartments. Thus they had abdicated their naturally
equal rights and abilities by acquiescing in training that destroyed any
thought of independence.[39] Now, in the new circumstances, they could
leave and accomplish worthwhile things.

This solution, which tied individual female liberation to respect won
by performing traditionally male tasks valued by society, was really
open only to the most able and resolute. Ch'iu Chin did not seriously
expect most women to follow her path to freedom, but she never developed programs either for gradually reforming the family system
or for destroying it by concerted social action. Instead, barriers were to
be transcended by the exercise of individual wills, and women to become independent by the cumulative effect of personal rebellions.

By the time Ch'iu Chin arrived in Tokyo, there were over 1,500 Chinese students there and more arriving almost daily. A few of these were
women who were either students themselves or were accompanying
husbands or relatives. Special schools for Chinese girls had been founded
by Christian missionaries and Japanese and Chinese educators to meet
the demand.[40] Women were only a very small fraction of the Chinese
student population in Japan, but they were highly motivated and often
radical. They had also begun to organize. In 1903 a group of women
students had founded the Humanitarian Society (Kung-ai Hui) to promote women's rights and education. Members volunteered to be nurses
in the spring of 1903, when radical, nationalistic male students established the Volunteer Corps to Resist Russia (Chü-O I-yung Tui) with
the aim of expelling Russian troops still holding points in Manchuria
occupied during the Boxer Rebellion.[41] Ch'iu was preceded to Japan by
a number of women radicals important in the revolutionary movement,
including Ch'en Hsieh-fen, daughter of *Su-pao* editor Ch'en Fan, who
had fled from Shanghai with her father to escape arrest in 1903, Feng
Tzu-yu's wife, and Li Tzu-p'ing, the radical wife of Cantonese secret
society member Li Chih-sheng. Ho Chen, the anarchist, bohemian wife
of the revolutionary Liu Shih-p'ei, who joined her husband in journalism

and other radical activities, also was in Tokyo while Ch'iu was there, but it is uncertain whether the two met.[42]

On arriving in Japan, Ch'iu enrolled in the Japanese language school operated by the Chinese Students' Union. Subsequently she entered the normal school connected with the Aoyama Vocational Girls' School for Chinese women, and attended classes sporadically until the end of 1905. The student body included twenty Hunanese with government scholarships, about ten non-scholarship students, and three women in their forties. Ch'iu encouraged less dynamic women at the school to pursue their studies and urged those still in China to make the trip abroad. She also wrote articles on women's rights and soon befriended other Chinese women radicals then in Japan, reviving the Humanitarian Society with Ch'en Hsieh-fen. She is credited with encouraging Ch'en to resist her father's arrangement to give her as a concubine to one of his friends, and also with urging Ch'en Fan's own two concubines to assert their independence by becoming students.[43]

Nonetheless, most of her time must have been devoted to radical politics. Soon after her arrival she joined both the Hunanese and Chekiangese student clubs and associated with their more militant members. She helped found a radical Society for the Study of Oratory (Yen-shuo Lien-hsi Hui) and contributed articles to its *Vernacular Journal* (*Pai-hua pao*), six issues of which appeared during 1904–5.[44] Together with the Hunanese revolutionary Liu Tao-i and eight other radicals she formed a Ten Person Corps (Shih-jen T'uan),[45] and during the fall of 1904 was introduced into the Yokohama branch of the Triad Society along with several other radical women.[46]

Among her most significant Tokyo acquaintances was the Chekiangese revolutionary T'ao Ch'eng-chang, a leading member of the Restoration Society (Kuang-fu Hui) established in Shanghai in late 1904. T'ao was introduced to Ch'iu by the son of a relative whom she saw frequently in Peking. Although initially doubtful that a woman should engage in revolutionary work, he furnished her with introductions to other party leaders in Shanghai and Shao-hsing, including Ts'ai Yüan-p'ei and Hsü Hsi-lin. She met these men in the spring of 1905 on a trip home to ask her mother for more money to continue her studies. On the same trip she met some of the Chekiangese secret society leaders with whom she was to work at a later date. She probably joined the Restoration Society at this time. When she returned to Tokyo she had considerable entrée into the revolutionary movement. In August she joined the new Revolutionary Alliance (T'ung-meng Hui) and became party recruiter for Chekiang.[47] Possibly she also helped Wu Yüeh plan his attempt to assassinate five ministers sent abroad in September 1905 to study Western constitutions.[48]

During her stay in Japan, Ch'iu emerged as a compelling, attractive, somewhat flamboyant figure. She dressed in men's clothing, carried a short sword, practiced bomb-making and marksmanship. Her enthusiastic radicalism propelled her to discuss politics tirelessly, and prompted angry despair over what she considered the apathy of many students.[49] This behavior was closely tied to the image of the hero, which had already crept into her early poetry and now became the model about which she sought to organize her life.* The inspiration was mainly traditional, drawing upon heroic figures from Chinese history, fiction, and Taoist mythology, and to some extent the Buddhist bodhisattvas. There were also modern overtones. Ch'iu was impressed by such famous Western terrorist and nationalist figures as Napoleon, George Washington, Sophia Perovskaya (who helped assassinate Alexander II), and the nineteenth-century Polish patriots. She read Byron's poetry.[50] Most important, she saw the hero championing the new causes of republican revolution and feminine liberation.

The martial, self-sacrificing, sometimes superhuman, and often tragic hero was a well-defined figure in Chinese romance.[51] It was also mainly a masculine one, which raises the question—how did Ch'iu relate to this role? Although normally filled by the active and dominant male, the heroic role was neuter insofar as it could be assumed by a woman who displayed the proper characteristics. Popular literature was dotted with stories of female knights-errant and women warriors.[52] Ch'iu was thoroughly familiar with the notable women of Chinese history, and was particularly drawn to those such as Ch'in Liang-yü and her late Ming contemporaries or the brave and resolute Chin dynasty scholar Hsieh Tao-wei. She also referred to such mythical or semi-mythical figures as the Western Queen Mother (Hsi-wang Mu) and Hua Mu-lan, who, disguised as a man, served for years in the army in her father's stead. Sophia Perovskaya and Madame Roland were added to the list from Western history.[53] In dressing as a man, Ch'iu was in part imitating Hua Mu-lan and other popular heroines who wore male dress, but in the new atmosphere of her own day she was also demanding the right as a woman to play male roles and, relishing the impropriety of her behavior and dress, dramatizing her protest against restrictions.

---

* In Tokyo Ch'iu took two additional names: the *hao* Ch'ien-hu nü-hsia (the heroine of Ch'ien Lake, after the lake by her family home), and the *tzu* Ching-hsiung. The latter has been translated "challenger of men," but might also be interpreted to mean "emulate male bravery."

Ch'iu used the heroic idea to open up new possibilities for herself as a woman. In part the hero was an exalted, romantically compelling figure, but the image was also appealing as the antithesis of the ideal Confucian woman. Physically, it traded the effete beauty of lily-footed ladies for an alternative model in which glamour was closely linked to power and physical prowess. As a substitute for "moth eyebrows" she presented the spectacle of graceful and elegant women commanders, "Hair bound back, in battle dress, marvelous in appearance,/Each, like jade, astride a gilt camel."[54] Moreover, the heroic idea offered Ch'iu a way to participate in political affairs. Heroines of old had demonstrated their loyalty and filial piety as generals and saviors of the state;[55] Ch'iu would follow in their footsteps. Traditional heroine and revolutionary foreknower, she was to be one of the leaders shepherding the Chinese into the future. For all her concern with women's rights and sympathy toward other women, Ch'iu's main ambitions lay in the realm of political power.

Finally, the heroic role offered Ch'iu a new morality and a chance for self-redemption and integration into the new society. Heroism demanded fearless devotion to duty, absolute responsibility for one's acts, and, if necessary, severe sacrifice. Through heroic deeds women might wash away the shame of their former subservience and demonstrate their abilities and exalted moral capacities.[56] Rejection of her past life had been painful and difficult,[57] but Ch'iu found compensation in proving her determination by surmounting great barriers. Her own acts could thus demonstrate how an ardent spirit might qualify a woman for heroic action despite her relative frailty.[58]

The idea of the dedicated heroine appealed to male imaginations as well. All we know of Ch'iu in Japan indicates that her male colleagues were struck by her beauty, intelligence, and fervor. Nor was she unique. Lin Tsung-su, sister of the Fukienese revolutionary Lin Hsieh, who became a leader of the women's suffrage movement in 1912, impressed many in Tokyo and Shanghai before the Revolution with her intense dedication.[59] Equally dynamic was the Cantonese doctor and revolutionary Chang Chu-chün.[60] Like Ch'iu Chin, these women influenced others by their ability and extraordinary moral commitment.

Shanghai and indecision. In December 1905, Ch'iu Chin was among those radical students who most strongly protested the Japanese Ministry of Education's stricter regulation of Chinese studying in Japan. Early in 1906 she sailed for Shanghai with a group who believed the only possible course was to return home and work for revolution. Shanghai was then the main, though not the sole, center of the women's movement in China. As early as 1897 an anti-foot-binding society and a girls' school under the direction of Li Kuei, wife of T'an Ssu-t'ung, had been established by the group of reformers publishing *Shih-wu pai* (The Chinese progress).[61] By 1911 at least 21 Chinese and nine missionary schools for girls had been established in Shanghai, not counting those in the International Settlement.[62] As a result there were a sizable number of girl students and women teachers who took part in demonstrations and other political activities and founded their own associations and their own press.*

Women were part of Shanghai radical circles from the beginning. In late 1902 and early 1903 the Patriotic Girls' School (Ai-kuo Nü-hsüeh-hsiao) and the feminist *Women's Journal* (*Nü-pao*), under the editorship of the able essayist Ch'en Hsieh-fen, joined their male counterparts in radical activities that culminated in the open denunciation of the Manchu government by the newspaper *Su-pao* that June.[63] The following year Ts'ai Yüan-p'ei turned the Patriotic Girls' School into his revolutionary headquarters, and some of its students eventually joined the Revolutionary Alliance.

In late 1903 to 1904, a particularly striking group of radical feminists, including Lin Tsung-su, Ho Chen, and Chang Chu-chün, was associated with the school and the series of radical newspapers that succeeded *Su-pao*. These women contributed to the radical journals, but also founded their own associations and had their own social life, drinking together and exchanging poetry. Thus, all their activities acquired a distinct feminist cast.[64]

Such relatively visible groups, revolving about one or several extraordinary women, emerged periodically in the major cities. They had varying degrees of coherence and formal organization. In many cases they functioned only briefly, as leading women moved from place to place, but nonetheless provided focal points and set standards for continuing

---

* Women took part in the 1903 anti-Russian demonstrations (*Su-pao*, May 1, 1903 [The Kiangsu Journal; photolithograph, Taipei, 1965]: 368–69, the Tatsu Maru case, and local nationalistic agitation in Shanghai in 1910 (Mary C. Wright, ed., *China in Revolution: The First Phase, 1900–1913*, [New Haven, Conn., 1968], pp. 33–34). The role of women in the series of demonstrations over the Kiangsu and Chekiang Railways in 1907 indicates that their participation could be substantial and organized. Such figures as the educator, reformer, and philanthropist Wang Hsieh Chang-ta had influence well beyond their immediate circle of local women's groups. The history of early professional women and women reformers deserves study. Further research may also reveal female contributions to the constitutionalist movement. On women in the railway movement, see Kuomintang, Committee for the Compilation of Materials on the Party History of the Central Executive Committee, ed., *Chiang-Che t'ieh-lu feng-ch'ao* (The agitation over the Kiangsu and Chekiang Railways; reprint, Taipei, 1968), pp. 119, 132, 374–415 *passim*.

female activities. When Ch'iu returned to Shanghai, therefore, she entered a milieu in which strong, radical women had already made an impact. By this time she was fully committed to overthrowing the government, but for a year seemed uncertain how best to pursue her goals. She alternated between reformist feminist and revolutionary activities, grieved over the death of her mother, and felt frustrated by the lack of progress in revolution. Much of the time she was in Chekiang, but she kept returning to Shanghai, with its congenial intellectual environment and radical student circles.

Not long after her arrival in Shanghai she left to teach Japanese, science, and hygiene at the Hsün-ch'i Girls' School, recently established in the wealthy market town of Nan-hsün in the silk-producing area of northern Chekiang. By 1906 the government was giving moderate encouragement to girls' schools, which were no longer a rarity even in small cities. The educational fare varied greatly, but in some of the schools girls were exposed to radical teachers and revolutionary propaganda.[65]

Ch'iu Chin was probably introduced to the Hsün-ch'i Girls' School by the elite reformer Ch'u Fu-ch'eng, who had connections with the revolutionary parties. Her decision to go there may have reflected the Restoration Society strategy of tapping local wealth and revolutionary potential. From this point of view Ch'iu had little success. She acquired a devoted friend in the headmistress, Hsü Tzu-hua, and recruited a few students to the revolutionary movement. She was too radical for most members of the school, however, and so left for Shanghai when summer vacation began.[66]

There Ch'iu led the life of the radical students. She almost blew up her room experimenting with explosives, and helped raise funds (by blackmail, among other means) for the Chinese Public Institute (Chung-kuo Kung-hsüeh), which had been founded by radical students returning from Japan earlier that year. She visited home briefly when her mother died in the fall. Then, after temporarily flirting with the idea of teaching at a school founded by a Chekiangese radical in Java, she threw herself into preparations for a rising in Chekiang at the end of the year. This attempt was to coincide with the rising then being organized by Revolutionary Alliance members and secret societies in Liu-yang and Li-ling, in Hunan province, and P'ing-hsiang, in Kiangsi.[67]

In this way she became involved in the Ta-t'ung School at Shao-hsing. This revolutionary front, which had been founded by Hsü Hsi-lin in 1905, was then the center of Restoration Society efforts to infiltrate the local social structure and organize secret societies. Ch'iu had no formal position at the school during the fall, but contacted low-grade army officers and military students in Hangchow, joined in discussions with secret society leaders at the school, and met a broad spectrum of members in travels about Shao-hsing and Kinhwa prefectures.[68] By the end of the year she must have had a thorough knowledge of the revolutionary movement in Chekiang, and was angry and disappointed when the plans for a rising had to be canceled because the attempts in Hunan and Kiangsi had failed.

Back once again in Shanghai, Ch'iu Chin returned to her feminist interests, founding the *Chinese Women's Journal* (*Chung-kuo nü-pao*) in January 1907, with the aid and financial backing of Hsü Tzu-hua, Hsü's younger sister, and a handful of other associates. This group was close to Ch'en Chih-ch'ün, Lo Yen-pin, and others who published the rather erudite *Women's World* (*Nü-tzu shih-chieh*) and its successor, *New Women's World*. Despite political views ranging from moderately reformist to actively revolutionary, these women admired one another and contributed to one another's publications. What was left of the two groups merged at the end of 1907 to establish the *Shen-chou Women's Journal* to commemorate Ch'iu Chin and carry on her work.* Ch'iu Chin originally conceived of the *Chinese Women's Journal* as the nucleus of a women's association that would publish books and aid girl students. It was written in a fairly simple style, but for an educated audience. Although it did not call for revolution, it urged women to leave home, if necessary, to gain their rights. Examples of revolutionary heroines were provided. Although theoretically recognizing that most women had neither the desire nor the training to break totally with their past lives, it was not really designed for the casual reader. Only two issues were published. Funds were short, but, more importantly, Ch'iu left Shanghai for the last time to assume leadership of the Ta-t'ung School in Shao-hsing.[69]

In Japan Ch'iu had written about women's rights, but the publication of the *Chinese Women's Journal* was the high point of her feminist

---

* This journal's offices shifted to Tokyo. Thereafter a largely new group of women became active in and about the fringes of the Shanghai revolutionary parties until 1911, and a much larger number took part in the 1911 Revolution in that city. On the journals, see Roswell S. Britton, *The Chinese Periodical Press, 1800–1912* (reprint; Taipei, 1966), pp. 115–16; *Ch'iu Chin chi* (Collected works of Ch'iu Chin; Shanghai, 1960), pp. 10–16, 94, 113; P'eng Tzu-i, *Ch'iu Chin* (Shanghai, 1941), p. 11; Hsü Shuang-yün, "Chi Ch'iu Chin" (Recollections of Ch'iu Chin), in *Hsin-hai ko-ming hui* (Recorded recollections of the 1911 Revolution; 6 vols.; Peking, 1961–65), pp. 212–13; Liang Chan-mei, *Chung-kuo fu-nü fen-tou shih hua* (Words about the history of the struggles of Chinese women; Shanghai, 1928), p. 65; and *Chung-kuo T'ung-meng hui*, 2: 553–54.

activities, and it expressed best her views on the liberation of women. As one would expect, Ch'iu fiercely joined the contemporary feminist attack on such obvious targets as foot-binding, arranged marriages, enforced chastity, confinement, ignorance, and the alleged male disposition to view women as "horses and cattle" or adorn them as playthings. To break away from this legacy of oppression, Ch'iu stressed that girls should seek an education and women learn professions or handicrafts so that they might earn a living—thereby winning the respect of their families, ensuring their independence and social importance, and enjoying broadening friendships away from home.[70] Like most of her feminist contemporaries, Ch'iu attached particular importance to modern education for women.[71] This emphasis was in part an extension of elite traditions that led members of both sexes to consider modern education a key to national strength. Education also clearly related to strictly feminist goals because women needed additional training if they were to support themselves and enter modern professions. More immediately, attending school was the easiest way for girls to escape family life, and was the route that Ch'iu had used herself.

Despite some attention to specific grievances and their remedies, the main theme of Ch'iu Chin's writings was intense, total rejection of the traditional woman's role. Specific problems combined to create in her eyes an evil atmosphere of oppression, blackness, numbing confinement, degrading ignorance. In the "black prison" created by "darkness and ignorance," most women did not even realize the danger inherent in being divorced from the reality of the world, and even those who did wish to save themselves and others were robbed of the will and capacity to act.[72] The darkness pervading the world of women appeared to Ch'iu to be a particularly painful manifestation of that greater blackness which enveloped the whole Chinese nation. This perception did not lead her to a comprehensive theory of social revolution, but rather to a tremendous emphasis on breaking out of and eradicating the stifling prisons of traditional Confucian society—an analagous, but less specific and more romantic, approach. Buddhist-inspired visions of heaven and hell and the Bodhisattva's redemptive role suggested the way.[73] Ch'iu clearly differed from those reformers who believed women's problems could be solved by correcting the specific abuses that they (and she) condemned. Feminism was not an isolated matter for Ch'iu, but an integral part of the political problems to which she sought solutions.

The extent to which Ch'iu related feminism, nationalism, and revolution is indicated by the early chapters of her unfinished novel. *Stones of the Ching-wei Bird* (*Ching-wei shih*), which she evidently intended to

serialize in the *Chinese Women's Journal*. In this story five talented
girls from gentry families rebel against forced marriage, foot-binding,
and seclusion. A crisis is precipitated when one of them refuses to
acquiesce in plans for her marriage. Inspired by the most modern member of the group and supported by a sympathetic older woman, they
flee their homes together and go to Japan.

The action, which has some vague autobiographical overtones, is
interrupted by passionate harangues on the evils of women's life, which
are in turn set against alarmed descriptions of foreign encroachment
and government corruption. In Japan the girls earnestly study together
as a self-contained, sisterly group for several months. Then they join a
revolutionary party, attracted by the sincere resolve, nationalistic loyalty, and lofty aims of its members—whose qualities are approximately
those of traditional heroes.[74] Whatever the shortcomings of the *Stones
of the Ching-wei Bird* as literature, it probably describes Ch'iu Chin's
path to revolution quite closely.

Chekiang: revolutionary sacrifice. When Ch'iu again left Shanghai
for Shao-hsing about the end of February 1907, she was finally in a
position to realize her heroic aspirations. There were a number of
women in the revolutionary parties by 1907, but most were to perform
such secondary, though useful, tasks as managing party fronts, establishing temporary cells, or distributing radical literature. Ch'iu was the
only one to lead a major attempt to overthrow the government.

She arrived at a volatile time. Although Shao-hsing was considered a
conservative city, modern ideas had been introduced there through
trade and banking contacts with Shanghai and the influence of scholar-
reformers and returned students. At the same time that new ideas were
infiltrating the elite strata, peasant unrest was mounting. New secret
societies, loosely identified with the Triads, appeared during and after
the Taiping Rebellion. After 1900 there were one or two transitional
groups whose leaders had been influenced by modern ideas. Unrest was
exacerbated by "new government" reforms, which, as Ichiko and others
have shown, were financed mainly by increased taxation of the lower
classes. Finally, the spring of 1907 saw famine and riots in the wake of
heavy flooding throughout much of the Lower Yangtze area.[75]

In Shao-hsing, Ch'iu inherited the fruits of a two-year effort by the
Restoration Society to lay the basis for revolution in Chekiang by developing illegal contacts with secret societies and establishing apparently
legal reformist organizations such as schools. She energetically set about
planning a rising with Hsü Hsi-lin, who by then had become head of
the police school in Anking and a confidant of the Anhwei governor.

From her position at the Ta-t'ung School and as principal of the nearby Ming-tao Girls' School, Ch'iu reorganized the Restoration Society in Chekiang and established a Restoration Army of secret society members.[76] These were mainly paper schemes, but at the same time she received commitments from secret society leaders to participate in a rising, and organized a gymnasium at the Ta-t'ung School to provide military training with the help of New Army radicals from Hangchow.*

Ch'iu's accomplishments were not achieved quietly. She already had a local reputation as a scholar and educator, and a woman in her position was the likely object of curiosity. Ch'iu compounded the problem by behaving with the same deliberate iconoclasm as in Japan. A one-time student at the school remembers that she often wore a man's long gown and black leather shoes and combed her hair back into a queue. Even more scandalous, she rode horseback astride, and ordered girls to practice military drill. This kind of behavior was less appealing to respectable provincial merchants and gentry than to students in Japan, and by the end of the spring Ch'iu was the object of suspicion and resentment.[77]

This combination of relatively efficient organization with almost self-defeating flamboyance was pursued on behalf of a revolution whose aims Ch'iu never clearly defined. Her revolutionary views were mainly identical to the ideas then prevalent in radical student circles: modern anti-imperialism mixed with traditional anti-Manchuism; revulsion at government corruption, incompetence, and alleged oppression; anger at the Confucian family system; and a vague commitment to republicanism and individual liberty.[78] Ch'iu was most strongly drawn to the idea of revolution as a decisive, dramatic event that would dispel at a stroke the decadence and injustice of existing society.[79] She shared with many other radical intellectuals of her day a naive faith that overthrowing the dynasty would purge the country of corrupt and weakening influences and inaugurate a new era of national strength and individual freedom— a vision that placed a premium on the purity of motive of those who were to usher in the future.

Ch'iu clearly placed revolution ahead of feminist goals. In this she anticipated both post–May Fourth leftist women and the substantial sexual equality achieved in Communist China. Unlike the Communists

---

* It is not clear why the societies accepted Ch'iu Chin's leadership. They have been called Triad by T'ao Ch'eng-chang, who worked with them extensively. There is no record of women being important in them. Ch'iu was aided by having joined the San-ho Hui in Japan, and some of the educated leaders with whom she dealt had absorbed new ideas. Quite possibly, however, her main appeal may have derived from her successful emulation of the heroic model.

and other socialists she did not advocate union with the masses, though her writings sometimes suggest real sympathy for the common people.* On the other hand, she believed that women would benefit by revolution. Sexual restrictions would be swept away along with other old evils. In a new China influenced by Western civilization, men and women would strive together to reach shared goals.[80] In the short run, the revolutionary movement offered women the opportunity to join in the great work of saving the nation, and to prove themselves through heroic action, thus earning the right to future equality. All womenkind would be shamed if this opportunity were ignored.[81]

Ch'iu's concepts of the relations between women's freedom, heroic action, and revolution reflected an intensely personal commitment that brought her to her death. Despite reasonably thorough groundwork, the plans for a rising went awry. The school was under suspicion, secret societies were indiscreet, and Hsü Hsi-lin prematurely launched an insurrection in Anking by assassinating the Anhwei governor. Ch'iu knew the situation was hopeless and was forewarned that government troops were coming to close the school, but she was too emotionally committed to flee and try again at a later date. Deserted by all but a few gymnasium students, she resisted the soldiers in a brief battle and was easily captured. Literature found at the school clearly indicated her revolutionary aims.[82] Although she refused to confess under torture, angry and alarmed officials ordered her execution on July 15, 1907.

Because Ch'iu could easily have avoided arrest, her death has overtones of suicide. Her motives, insofar as they can be discerned, were complex. They included a desire to escape personal tensions and responsiveness to the tradition of female suicides; most important was the desire to climax a heroic life with a heroic death. Was Ch'iu mildly manic-depressive? We cannot gather the evidence now. Nonetheless, her poems reveal varying moods of intense exhilaration and great despair juxtaposed on a persistent melancholy strain. The gloom in her early poems, prompted by marriage and enforced idleness, was dispelled by her escape to Japan. Elated by this successful exercise of will, for the next three years Ch'iu was sometimes confident of success and fame.[83] Sadness persisted, however, fed now by the loneliness of her chosen

---

* Ch'iu occasionally used the phrase ho-ch'ün ("To Hsü Chi-ch'en," Ch'iu Chin chi; Collected works; Shanghai, 1960, p. 89; "Letter to first girls' school in Hunan, ibid., p. 32), but her dominant view was that revolution was the business of a heroic elite who would awaken and mold the sleeping populace into a militant citizenry, an attitude with definite authoritarian overtones (e.g., "To Chiang Lushan . . . ," ibid., pp. 77–78). The "Introduction" to the Collected Works presents a similar analysis.

course[84] and the frustrations of not being able to realize her ambitions quickly.[85] These problems she shared with other independent women and with many male radicals as well. Her emotional reactions, however, were more acute, resulting in increasing despair over the apathy of the country as it seemed to plunge toward destruction.[86]

Problems of identity and conflicting loyalties were compounded by Ch'iu's sex. Her break with her past was more shocking than it would have been for a man, and her position always required justification even within radical circles. She rejected a high degree of security and potential influence, which the traditional family offered a woman successful on its terms, without finding a wholly adequate substitute. The early radical schools and revolutionary parties were not well organized or backed by any comprehensive ideology. The close friendships with other women that Ch'iu developed at most stages of her career and the theoretical concept of sisterhood expressed in her writings[87] were also rather fragile substitutes. To maintain her resolve, Ch'iu dedicated herself to the interlocking causes of national salvation, revolution, and women's independence with a completeness approaching religious vocation.[88] The only serious reason to continue her life was to work for revolution.[89]

Elements in the Chinese tradition suggested that death might be as effective in realizing her aims as a lifetime devoted to party work. Suicides or quasi-suicidal acts were not uncommon in the radical movement. Two aspects of the suicide issue seem particularly relevant to Ch'iu Chin's case. As Margery Wolf discusses later in this volume, suicide has been a traditional response of Chinese women to intolerable but inescapable family situations, a way to bring blame and public censure upon those cited as responsible, or a way to achieve fame through a demonstration of virtue. Since Ch'iu had escaped family bonds, her death cannot be described as a surrender to the old, oppressive morality as were the suicides of some twentieth-century girls who tried but failed to win independence.[90] Nonetheless, certain old influences may have remained. Her concern with retaining the purity of her dedication amidst the complex opportunities for compromise that surrounded her[91] reminds us that the traditional cults of chastity and virginity placed a premium on female virtue of a different sort.

The model of the self-sacrificing hero, however, was the main inspiration behind Ch'iu's death. In one poem she mentions Ching K'o (d. 227 B.C.), who died trying to assassinate Ch'in Shih-huang-ti on behalf of a small state threatened with annihilation. Although unsuccessful, he had achieved fame as a model of nobleminded and selfless assault on a tyrant.[92] There were also female models: Ch'iu Chin retold the story of an anonymous woman in the palace of the Ming emperor who, after Peking had fallen to the bandit-rebel Li Tzu-ch'eng in 1644, stabbed one of Li's generals to avenge the dead emperor. When the general's cries brought help, she killed herself.[93] Neither this woman nor Ching K'o expected to survive their acts, but they were convinced their causes demanded the sacrifice. Ch'iu Chin, in another day, felt similar loyalty to nationalist and republican causes. By her death she focused the attention of radical students, whom she hoped to inspire to greater determination to overthrow the government. She hoped that women would take her as a model of female accomplishment, that the country as a whole (or at least the educated classes) would be angered by the spectacle of government oppression, and that future generations of Chinese would fulfill her aim of revolution and honor her sacrifice as they had honored previous martyrs.

With poetic justice, Ch'iu Chin attained most of what she sought through martyrdom. Word of her steadfast end spread quickly. Press coverage was in general highly sympathetic. Many members of the elite believed her innocent of illegal actions. Even more believed that the government had acted hastily and tyrannically, and in Chekiang, Anhwei, and Kiangsu some people felt threatened by arrests or other efforts to repress modern ideas. Her case was debated by Grand Councillors and other high officials in Peking. The careers of officials responsible for her execution were ended by the public reaction, and a magistrate unfairly blamed for the decision committed suicide.*

The myth of Ch'iu Chin began to develop right after her death. Newspapers reported the story (which may or may not be factual) that shortly before her execution she asked for pen and paper and wrote, "Autumn rain and autumn wind, I die of sorrow" (*Ch'iu-yü ch'iu-feng, ch'ou-sha jen*). Radicals in Shanghai and Tokyo formed societies and

---

* News of Ch'iu's death was spread within a few weeks by the Shanghai press, which circulated beyond the Lower Yangtze area, and by papers in other major cities. Students and others traveling to and from their home towns brought the news with them. Even conservative papers criticized the government for unnecessarily arousing public hostility through hasty and illegal procedures. Some believed that no woman should have been treated so harshly. Although not everyone believed that Ch'iu was innocent, her case occurred at a time when much of the reform-minded elite in Chekiang and Kiangsu was suspicious of government actions because of disagreement over railway policy. A sizable collection of newspaper clippings and other writings about Ch'iu's death appears in Ch'iu Tsan-chih, appendix. Also see *Hsin-hai ko-ming hui-i lu*, 1: 629, 4: 81; *North China Herald*, 84: 205 (July 26, 1907); and Denby to Jordan, July 26, 1907, British Foreign Office Archives, F.O. 228/1668.

held meetings in her honor. Her friends Wu Chih-ying and Hsü Tzu-hua wrote about her and risked arrest to bury her, emerging as heroines by association. Two editions of her poetry were published before 1911. Through a mixture of fact and fiction she was endowed with all the traditional heroic qualities: generosity, loyalty, bravery, martial skill, uncompromising morality, and devotion to duty.[94] Women's armies invoked her spirit during the 1911 Revolution,[95] and Sun Yat-sen attended a memorial service at a temple dedicated to her in 1912. Under the Republic she was admired by advocates of female independence—Kuo Mo-jo praised her as the incarnation of Ibsen's Nora[96]—and her determination, valor, and self-sacrifice inspired subsequent women revolutionaries. Now the subject of numerous biographies and works of fiction, she comes close to being a folk heroine to all Chinese, irrespective of political ideology.

Conclusion

Ch'iu Chin's life dramatized the rapid changes that were occurring in the expectations and opportunities of educated women at the end of the Ch'ing. New Western ideas and nationalist fears raised by imperialist encroachment, coming on top of a slow evolution in traditional attitudes, were all breaking down the Confucian framework in which men viewed women. Women with the requisite knowledge and determination were quick to take advantage of the new situation, and their achievements pointed toward the substantial degree of equality and sexual integration attained in the People's Republic.

The rapidity with which this change occurred suggests that underlying factors in Chinese society encouraged Chinese men to accept major changes in the status of women. Francis L. K. Hsü has argued that in traditional Chinese society—dominated ultimately by an authoritarian, family-directed, father-son relationship—concepts of sexual relationship tended to be specific and limited, that is, to be associated with either marriage to continue the family line or with pornography and prostitution, rather than generalized through all aspects of life as in the United States. This traditional view, he suggests, made it easier for Chinese men to treat women in the professions or in politics solely in terms of their competence once they had overcome the (often considerable) barriers to their assumption of these roles.[97] To this approach it can be added that the Chinese have a very strongly developed idea of role behavior, buttressed by the notion of sincerity and quintessentially expressed in the concept of the rectification of names. Thus a woman within the household was a daughter, wife, or mother, and had traditionally been supposed to conform to the accepted ways in which such people behaved. Moreover, those who did so admirably were respected and honored. A woman who succeeded in breaking away from family bonds and becoming a teacher, doctor, revolutionary, etc., was likewise expected to act in accord with well-defined concepts of behavior, and others often gave her the recognition accorded a person in that role.* Feminists assumed that women who developed their skills and earned their own living would be respected by men not only because they would be independent, but also because they would occupy positions that evoked respect from society. Most of the serious roles outside the household were reserved for men. Thus when a woman did enter one of these roles, she also assumed their normally male characteristics, a factor that may in part account for the sexual neutrality that Witke has noted in twentieth-century Chinese women.[98] In addition to the advantages accruing from submersion of sexual identity in male roles, women may also have benefited from transfer of some of the respect accorded the able woman within the family, where she had obviously important functions in a vital social unit, to the able woman outside the home.

There was a strong functional aspect to the history of liberation of women in China. Individualism, with its concomitant ideas of equality, natural rights, and personal development, was a dominant theme during the May Fourth Movement. At other times feminist arguments tended to be closely linked to or justified by the performance of a socially useful task or pursuit of a broad political cause, often with the ultimate goal of contributing to national strength. This functional linkage can be seen in the history of leftist women in the 1930's and 1940's, and in efforts to give substance to theoretical equality since 1949. In Ch'iu Chin's case, she desired independence so she could contribute to making a revolution that would save China.

When Ch'iu Chin turned to revolution she anticipated ways in which women were eventually liberated in China. She implicitly recognized that sexual equality was not likely to be achieved without some major structural changes, and saw the liberation of women as one result of the revolution to which she chose to devote her greatest energy. How-

* Chie Nakane makes a similar point about Japanese society when she says that Japanese women are nearly always ranked as inferiors not directly because their sex is considered inferior, but because they do not usually hold positions conferring high social status. Chie Nakane, *Japanese Society* (Berkeley, Calif., 1972), p. 32.

ever, she came from the elite layer of society, in which women were most likely to absorb Western ideas and have the education to take advantage of new opportunities. Insofar as she was concerned with social, as opposed to national, revolution, the objects of her attack were the authoritarian, hierarchical, Confucian relationships that shaped family life and many other social relations. If these bonds were dissolved—in itself a most radical step—freedom and equality would follow. Problems of liberating educated urban women were different from (and probably simpler than) those of freeing poor and uneducated peasant women from villages only lightly touched by the new influences. Ch'iu Chin did not take the step of seeking to make the freedom available to the most able women meaningful to all through the stronger prescription of class revolution, even though her revolutionary activities inspired those who did so after the May Fourth Movement.

Unlike some strikingly able contemporary women, Ch'iu did not subordinate political action to professional, educational, or feminist activities. Moreover, she saw herself as a leader, shaping the fundamental nature of the state. Thus she entered the sphere of high politics, from which women were theoretically most firmly excluded. Though some did exercise political power in practice, they were always vulnerable to criticism for doing so.

The heroine provided a model, diametrically opposed to those of unscrupulous empress or seductive concubine, which in effect cleansed a woman's connection with power and politics by demonstrating that she was governed by pure moral purpose, not personal ambition. This kind of imagery has been applied to the seventeenth-century Ch'in Liang-yü and to modern women of Chinese Communist fact and fiction who bravely endured hardships and sacrificed for the Revolution. Uneasiness over women who exercise political power, now focused on the figure of Chiang Ch'ing, has not disappeared from China. In Ch'iu Chin's time traditional feelings about women and politics had barely been challenged. Heroism then became a way for Ch'iu to justify her actions to herself and induce others to follow her lead.

Heroism traditionally meant great sacrifice, and for women, heavy emotional costs. Decades later, it still often required considerable toughness for women to break away from family bonds and defy authoritarian traditions. When Ch'iu left her husband such an act was almost unprecedented, and there were few substitutes for family ties. A heroic death to shame present oppressors and inspire future admirers was not only a readily available model of behavior, but also a personal escape from the feelings of frustration, despair, and impotence that were unbearably magnified by the revolutionaries' failure in Shao-hsing. The intensity with which Ch'iu pursued her goals made her an outstanding example of the new possibilities for feminine achievement that so quickly developed at the end of the Ch'ing. Ironically, it also made her an illustration of the difficulties faced by those caught in transition, difficulties that she herself finally transcended in death.

Marriage Resistance in Rural Kwangtung

MARJORIE TOPLEY

For approximately one hundred years, from the early nineteenth to the early twentieth century, numbers of women in a rural area of the Canton delta either refused to marry or, having married, refused to live with their husbands. Their resistance to marriage took regular forms. Typically they organized themselves into sisterhoods. The women remaining spinsters took vows before a deity, in front of witnesses, never to wed. Their vows were preceded by a hairdressing ritual resembling the one traditionally performed before marriage to signal a girl's arrival at social maturity. This earned them the title "women who dress their own hair," *tzu-shu nii*. The others, who were formally married but did not live with their husbands, were known as *pu lo-chia*, "women who do not go down to the family," i.e., women who refuse to join their husband's family. Such women took herbal medicines to suppress micturition and set off for their wedding ceremonies with strips of cloth wrapped, mummy fashion, under their bridal gown to prevent consummation. Three days after the wedding ceremonies they returned to their natal villages for the traditional home visit, which they prolonged for several years. Some women subsequently returned to their husbands, presumably to consummate their marriage and bear children. Others took the further decision to stay away until they were past childbearing age, and never consummated their marriage.

Most Cantonese grew up knowing something of this resistance, but were it not for a few brief, mostly anecdotal references, chiefly by Westerners, it might have passed unnoted by the outside world. The reasons for this are not difficult to guess. These were not the sort of customs traditional Confucians would be inclined to write about. The customs arose at a time when marriage and childbearing constituted the only socially valued way of life for a woman; they thus incurred the displeasure, sometimes active displeasure, of the State. Nor were they the sort of customs that would commend themselves to modern reformists. The women who eschewed marriage or cohabitation were not interested in marriage reform or in converting women elsewhere to their cause. Throughout the hundred years of the resistance, these practices never spread beyond a relatively small area. They were confined to those parts of the Canton delta engaged in sericulture: Shun-te hsien, particularly the eastern part; a small part of Nan-hai hsien, adjoining northern Shun-te and including the Hsi-ch'iao foothills; and a small part of P'an-yü, to the east of Shun-te.

Under what conditions did this unorthodox but nonreformist resistance emerge? How did it manage to persist for a century? And why did it eventually decline? Most sources stress fear of marriage as the women's principal impetus. A few refer to their unusual economic status: women in the area had worked outside the house in the domestic sericulture for centuries, and by the first third of the nineteenth century they were earning cash in filatures and other industrial establishments connected with silk production. These factors must have been very important, but we must bear in mind that women all over Kwangtung traditionally worked outside their home, and by this century women in other provinces were also working in cash-earning occupations. Yet marriage resistance remained unique to one small area. Was there, then, something special about the area itself, something that might have made the status of unattached women relatively more attractive than it was elsewhere, or the status of married women relatively less attractive? Was there anything particularly favoring female solidarity, or the obvious local acceptance of such heterodox behavior? Why was it that some members of the resistance married while some did not, and what implications did the two forms of resistance have for the women, their natal families, and their in-laws?

Unfortunately, though the few published accounts we have provide us with some insights into the area that occasionally can be followed up in the wider literature, questions of the kind I have raised are neither asked nor answered by these accounts. And none of them seem to be based on firsthand evidence from the women involved. In the last twenty years, however, a few social scientists have interviewed women from the resistance area who had emigrated to Hong Kong and Singapore. The interviews conducted by Ho It Chong, a former social work student at the University of Singapore, have been of particular value in this study. These firsthand data do not permit firm answers to the questions raised earlier, or allow us to make wide generalizations. First, like the earlier material, it comes almost exclusively from Shun-te and Hsi-ch'iao. Second, it comes from only a small fraction of the women involved and is derived in most cases from interviews that were not specifically oriented around the marriage resistance.* Third, the immense task of researching the Canton delta has just begun,† and many as yet undiscovered facts about the area will affect our ultimate assessment of the evidence gathered so far. Nevertheless, significant variables may emerge if all material now available is assembled and analyzed.

Was there anything unique about the area? I will begin by describing the physical environment and its effect on the local economy and culture. I will then try to isolate local factors that helped generate the resistance, encouraged the particular forms it took, and perpetuated its existence. Finally, I will look at changes in the area and elsewhere that may have contributed to the movement's decline, and see briefly if the local ecology and the resistance itself have left any visible mark on the status of women living in the area today.

Environment, Society, and Culture

P'an-yü is the largest of the three hsien involved, occupying about 1,800 square kilometers; Nan-hai and Shun-te are some 1,360 and 750 square kilometers. Nan-hai has the largest population (about 680,000 in 1947), and Shun-te the smallest (417,000 in 1947). But population densities have been highest in Shun-te; indeed, they are the highest in all Kwangtung province.

Much of the land is flat and criss-crossed by rivers. Shun-te, in the heart of the Pearl River delta, is mostly floodplain. The numerous waterways intersect in a spiderweb pattern, making communications relatively easy, but numerous hills rise up from the plain throughout much of the area. On the hills' outer rims—the highest are in Hsi-ch'iao—lie the large villages and market towns. Outside the hilly area, settlement was relatively dispersed.[1]

The wet, sandy soil, often affected by tides, is not everywhere suitable for rice. But it is suitable for both fish breeding and mulberry raising. These activities, together with other phases of sericulture, were the

---

* My own interviews were conducted in the early 1950's in connection with a study of women and religious institutions in Singapore, and in Hong Kong in 1973 for this essay. Ho It Chong's interviews were part of a study of domestic servants' organizations undertaken in Singapore in the late 1950's.

† The multidisciplinary Canton Delta Project is headed by Winston Hsieh, of the University of Missouri at St. Louis.

economic mainstays of the area. Fishponds and mulberry groves went together. Fish were fed on nightsoil and cocoon waste, and mulberry groves were fertilized with silt from the fishponds. When pits were dug to form ponds, the excavated earth was heaped over the rest of the farmer's land to raise it sufficiently above water level for the mulberry groves. A farmer wishing to increase his output would install additional ponds and groves; the characteristic scene was one of densely planted fields of mulberry shrubs, intersected by narrow canals and dotted with ponds scattered irregularly over the fields.[2]

In 1939 approximately 70 percent of Shun-te's land area was devoted to this economy, and about 90 percent of the population was engaged in one or another aspect of sericulture. Nan-hai had close to one-half the mulberry acreage of Shun-te; a little less than half its population was engaged in sericulture.[3] I have no figures for P'an-yü. I was told that much of the land in Shun-te had been reclaimed by wealthy lineage groups, who in many cases lived elsewhere and rented their land to tenant farmers. Some relatively large lineage villages flourished in the area, alongside many smaller multisurname villages, which were inhabited by tenant farmers. Some of these farmers were described as newcomers by informants, although by the nineteenth century they had been living in the area some time.

Because of the area's subtropical climate, everything grows rapidly. Silkworms produce six or seven broods a year, in contrast to the usual two broods of the Yangtze Valley—another area dissected by waterways. Indeed, throughout Central China, mulberry trees yield at most two pickings a year, which will support only one large brood of worms in spring and another in summer. In this delta area, six to eight leaves could be picked from a plant each month, thus feeding more abundant broods.[4]

Much labor was needed in every phase of sericulture, and a considerable proportion of it was performed by women. Women in Kwangtung did not have bound feet, and female infanticide in the silk area reportedly was relatively rare. B. C. Henry, a nineteenth-century traveler in Hsi-ch'iao, described the scene when the first crop of leaves was ready: "thousands of boys, women, and girls are employed to strip them and pack them in baskets. Hundreds of men in little boats propelled by paddles dart back and forth along the canals carrying these baskets ... to the market-places, where they are ... purchased by the owners of silk worms."[5]

There appears to have been a distinct division of labor between men and women. Men and boys were the exclusive rearers of fish: boys helped with the breeding and feeding, men took charge of the fully grown specimens. Catching the fish meant standing in waist-deep water and manipulating heavy nets. This, I was told, was too heavy a task for boys or women. Women cultivated the mulberry groves and together with young boys and girls picked the leaves. Adult men took charge of what was described to me by informants as the first "inside" phases of silk-worm raising: the hatching and early care. Later the worms were transferred to matsheds, and this "outside" aspect of rearing was entrusted exclusively to women. Finally the worms were brought inside again, when they formed cocoons and needed extra warmth; women took charge of this phase. When the cocoons were ready, women plunged them into hot water to loosen their silk threads. Reeling and spinning were exclusively women's work, although in some places men wove all the cloth.

Married women were less likely to be involved in sericulture than unmarried women. This was due in part to the time they expended on other household tasks, and in part to notions of pollution and female physiology. Women were considered unclean at certain times, notably during pregnancy and childbirth, when, it was believed, they could harm immature living things, such as young children and silkworms. (According to Winston Hsieh, a similar notion prevailed among silk-growers near Shanghai.) In Shun-te, married women were usually excluded from worm rearing and the care of cocoons. They were also excluded from the thread-loosening process because, my informants explained, this was "wet work": constant association with water was believed to interfere with menstruation and hence fertility.

There seems also to have been a spatial division of labor. Farmhouses were built not near the villages, but near groves and ponds. Glenn Trewartha, writing in 1939, observed that "nowhere else in Kwangtung . . . do most of the farm houses stand alone and isolated outside the villages." He describes the farmhouses as being made of mud plaster mixed with straw, contrasting these obviously more impermanent dwellings with the tile-roofed brick houses in the village.[6] According to informants, men spent much of their time at the farms, looking after the fish and the worms in their initial inside phases, but women usually lived in the villages. The married men visited their wives in their village, where they usually had a more permanent abode, and the women went out to the farms to pick mulberries and care for the worms in the matsheds. Reeling and spinning were done in the village; Henry observed hundreds of Hsi-ch'iao women sitting by their doors winding the gossamer threads from the cocoons.[7]

By the second third of the nineteenth century, however, the picture was beginning to change. Industrialization had gained a foothold, largely in response to outside competition. Large cocoonaries, some of them owned by lineages, were built in the bigger mulberry plantations. Filatures were set up, the first ones using foot-driven machinery. These industrial concerns employed women because women traditionally had worked with cocoons and at reeling and spinning. They used mainly unmarried women because unattached women had fewer family commitments and were believed to be more reliable in their attendance. By 1904, eleven market towns in the Hsi-ch'iao–Shun-te part of the area had filatures, some employing 500–1,000 women.[8] Weaving factories were also established, and at first they employed both men and women (men, we saw, had traditionally done the domestic weaving in some localities).

Steam-driven machinery was first introduced in the mid-nineteenth century. It was bitterly resented by the local population because it supplanted human labor. Henry reports that when machinery was introduced into one of the silk factories near Hsi-ch'iao, the place was twice mobbed and the owners were compelled to remove the machines. Steam machinery was associated with foreign influence, and as Henry remarks, "turbulent and bitterly anti-foreign" feelings were prevalent in the silk areas.[9] Nevertheless, there was no turning back.

One of the first effects of steam-driven machinery was to eliminate male labor in the silkworks. Some of the men may have joined the local militia, which the gentry was then organizing to fight British troops. Others may have returned to their farms. But the domestic economy had been seriously affected by the mechanization of industry. The labor supply necessary to some phases of sericulture was depleted by the exodus of unattached women to the towns. Both the scale and the range of occupations decreased, and in the rural areas both married women living at home with their husbands and married and unmarried men had a harder time finding gainful employment. Agnes Smedley, writing in the 1930's, contrasts the local weaving factories, which employed only women, with silk-weaving factories in other parts of China. She speculates that men were scarce because of heavy farming duties or because of emigration. As the domestic economy declined, men had begun to emigrate in large numbers to Singapore, Malaya, and Hong Kong. Smedley observed that "thousands of peasant homes depended for a large part of their livelihood upon the modest earnings of a wife or daughter."[10]

As a result of industrialization, village populations began to consist largely of women and children. But nubile girls formed a separate group, for another distinctive feature of the area was the "girls' house" or "girls' room," *nü-wu* or *nü-chien*. From my own evidence, and that of Mr. Ho in Singapore, it appears that many parts of Kwangtung had such houses and rooms, as well as similar houses for unmarried boys. There is only one publication on these houses—on boys' houses in a village in Chung-shan hsien, Kwangtung.[11] Clearly, such establishments differed from one another in important ways, but several features of the boys' houses, as described in the article on Chung-shan and by the informants of Mr. Ho and myself, seem to me directly relevant to our subject.

The bachelor houses of the Chung-shan village were owned by the ancestors, i.e., were part of the ancestral trust. Each lineage in the village had such a house, adjacent to its ancestral hall or shrine. Their functions were to provide (a) a sleeping place and recreational center for unmarried men, (b) temporary quarters for married men, (c) a guest house for visiting men, and (d) relief of household congestion. Residence was not compulsory, although it proved on careful investigation that if a household included daughters or other nubile young women, adolescent boys invariably slept in the bachelor house. Married men stayed there from the fifth month of their wives' pregnancies until 100 days after their child's birth[12]—the traditional Chinese period of childbearing pollution. In the Chung-shan village there were no girls' houses. But their function in villages where they were found in conjunction with boys' houses has been described by informants as follows: to provide (a) a sleeping place and recreational center for unmarried women, (b) a guest house for visiting women, (c) relief from household congestion, and (d) "modesty." Nightsoil buckets were kept in the sleeping quarters, where they could be used at night and also secured against theft (a valuable fertilizer, nightsoil was used in Shun-te to feed fish). I was told that it would be "inconvenient" for boys and girls to use the same bucket, in full view of members of the opposite sex.

It is not easy to see why, in that case, *both* boys' and girls' houses were necessary. However, a further explanation I was given for Tung-kuan hsien was that girls' houses were needed because girls could not be married straight from home: a girl who married from home made the house inauspicious; it became "empty," which affected the luck of her brothers who would later bring wives into the household, making it "full." According to informants, the girls' house in Shun-te served the same purpose. Separate houses for boys were not needed, my informants said, because they already lived apart—with the men on the farm. The girls' houses were found in the village, where again they were sometimes part of an ancestral trust. They were organized entirely by women, and in contrast to such houses elsewhere, were separated by some distance from the sleeping abode of the men.

Girls lived in these houses in Shun-te until they married or took their vows of spinsterhood. The older girls there, my informants said, were fond of visiting temples and other religious establishments and attending theatrical performances. Henry also observes that the women of Hsi-ch'iao "show their independence" by going "in large numbers" to theatrical performances associated with large religious festivals, with a separate gallery reserved for their use.[13] The hills of Hsi-ch'iao, which, as he noted, had been "peopled ... with spirits and deities of various kinds" by the inhabitants, provided an ideal environment for temples and monastic institutions, as did the other hills that dotted the area. The hilly area around Ta-liang, the hsien capital of Shun-te and a filature center, was noted for both its Buddhist nunneries and its other celibate institutions, which allowed members not to shave their heads and to live in their own homes.[14] The latter type of institution was a vegetarian hall, or chai-t'ang.

Vegetarian halls were residential establishments for lay members of the Buddhist faith, and for both lay and clerical members of several semisecret sects fragmenting from a syncretic religion called Hsien-t'ien Ta-tao: The Great Way of Former Heaven. These sects appear to have had connections with the famous White Lotus rebels.[15] According to leaders of these sects living in Singapore and Hong Kong, the sects entered Kwangtung from the north in the mid-nineteenth century, as a result of their suppression by the government in more populous areas and the exiling of their leaders.[16] Tucked away in the hills girding the delta, the sectarian halls escaped hostile attention by disguising themselves as Buddhist establishments.[17]

The syncretic Hsien-t'ien religion is messianic and millennial. Its sects stress the Chinese notion that natural and social disorders arise when earth is out of phase with Heaven; this happens when the country's leaders lack virtue. The sects thus appealed to people who felt threatened either by the social disorder resulting from the introduction of steam machinery, by foreign influences, or by the constant possibility of flooding in high-water-level areas. Several informants said their fathers and mothers had belonged to a Hsien-t'ien sect. The sects held a particular appeal for women. The highest deity is a "mother goddess" to whom many local children who had "bad fates" reportedly were bonded. Moreover, the religion stressed sexual equality, and men and women sat together in prayer (a practice earning it official displeasure). One local sect was run entirely by women.[18]

Both temples and monastic establishments printed and sold religious literature, including "good books" (*shan-shu*) written to convert people to the religious life. Aimed expressly at women was the "precious volume" (*pao-chüan*), which contained biographies of model women, usually recounted in ballad form. One such story, about Kuan Yin, the Goddess of Mercy, who is popularly believed to have been a princess who became a nun over her parents' objections, points out that she had no husband to claim her devotion, no mother-in-law to control her, and no children to hamper her movements.[19] Many of my informants had "precious volumes" they acquired in their homeland which further emphasize that refusing to marry is not morally wrong and even that religion can help those brave enough to resist; that men cannot be trusted; and that suicide is a virtue when committed to preserve one's purity.

The need for purity and chastity is explained in terms of pollution. Childbirth is a sin, for which women are punished after death by being sent to a "bloody pond," filled with birth fluids, from which they can be rescued only by ritual.[20] One pao-chüan says that women "taint Heaven and Earth when [they] give birth to children. . . . When you are a man's wife . . . you cannot avoid the blood-stained water . . . and the sin of offending the Sun, Moon, and Stars (*san-kuang*).[21] The only way a woman can improve her fate in life—after death she can go to the Happy Land (the Buddhist paradise) or be reborn as a man in another existence—is to remain celibate. Some of Ho's informants suggested that a person marries the same partner over and over again in many incarnations.[22] Occasionally, my own informants explained, a woman is born with a "blind" or "nonmarrying" fate: her predestined partner is not alive at the same time, not of suitable marriage age, or not of the appropriate sex. In these circumstances, a woman should remain unwed.

Many women in the Shun-te area were able to read this kind of literature. Dyer Ball observes that Shun-te women were considered "more intelligent than others," and "notwithstanding the want of schools for their instruction, those of the middle classes are generally able to read ballads."[23] My informants said numerous local women from farming families received instruction in reading from a tutor who called at the girls' house; also that they read pao-chüan stories in groups in the girls' houses. Ho talks of such women reading the classics.[24]

Tracts were distributed that pointed to more immediate incentives for a celibate woman who joined a Hsien-t'ien sect: an administrative appointment in a vegetarian hall, possibly even complete authority over a hall; permanent residence if desired (some halls were residential), but more freedom to come and go than Buddhist nunneries allowed; no requirement that members shave their heads or, except for ceremonies, wear religious garments; and the opportunity to be worshiped as an "ancestor" by religious "families" (a "master" and her or his disciples), a privilege not granted unmarried or childless women in secular society.[25]

Women visited religious establishments in groups. Members were often sworn sisters (*shuang chieh-pai*, "mutually tied by oath"). Several features of the local ecology encouraged the formation of such sisterhoods: teamwork in various phases of silk production; residence in girls' houses; membership in the same sectarian "family"; and the ties between girls who were bonded to the same deity because of their "bad" (often nonmarrying) fates and who worshiped the deity together on ceremonial occasions.

The term used by both my own and Mr. Ho's informants for sworn friendship between pairs of individuals or groups was *chin-lan hui*, Golden Orchid Association. An 1853 edition of the Shun-te gazetteer notes in its volume on customs that women's Golden Orchid Associations had long been a feature of the district.[26] Informants were not certain why this term was used, and the gazetteer does not enlighten us. James Liu of Stanford University has suggested to me that it may be derived from the following passage in the *I-ching*: "When two persons have the same heart its sharpness can cut gold; words from the same heart have a fragrance like the orchid." Winston Hsieh has suggested that the term may be a metaphor referring to structure—i.e., that such associations may "bud" or divide into subgroups as they enlarge, just as orchids bud into several flowers on one stem. Certainly Cantonese sometimes refer to societies as budding (rather than branching), although my informants said this happened to their sisterhoods only when members went elsewhere to work. Golden Orchid implies a semisecret association; it is used by the Triads for the name of a branch.[27] The women's sisterhoods were indeed semisecret; Dyer Ball talks of groups of girls in the area who used "an emblematical, or enigmatical, method of communication with each other."[28]

Several sources refer to lesbian practices in connection with sisterhoods in Shun-te and P'an-yü.[29] My own informants agreed that they sometimes occurred. One woman gave me a religious explanation. As we saw, a woman may be predestined to marry a certain man over and over again in different incarnations; even if her predestined husband should in one incarnation be born a female, she is nonetheless attracted to her predestined partner. Informants called lesbian practices "grinding bean curd" (*mo tou-fu*);[30] they also referred to the use of a dildo made of fine silk threads and filled with bean curd. A Hong Kong doctor of forensic medicine told me in the late 1950's of a similar type of dildo, filled with expandable raw silk.

Ho, writing about domestic servants in Singapore, says that some of his informants from the Shun-te area discussed sisterhoods that originated with married women who banded together to stop their husbands from taking concubines, promising to tell one another anything "not in order" they heard about the other women's husbands.[31] Concubinage was part of the system of marriage in many parts of China, and marriage for a woman in the Shun-te area had much in common with marriage for a Chinese woman elsewhere. Yet some features of the Chinese marriage system received particular emphasis in the resistance area; some found elsewhere were missing; and some local practices were peculiar to the area. Concubinage appears to have been widespread among tenant farmers as well as wealthier landowners. Children were wanted in large numbers because of the labor requirements of the domestic economy, and even when a wife had borne both sons and daughters (here daughters, too, were wanted for their labor), a concubine might nonetheless be taken to produce still more. In contrast to other parts of China, it was not the practice locally to adopt "little daughters-in-law," i.e., very young girls adopted into other families to be brought up as future brides for their foster-brothers. But girls might be adopted before a married couple had any children of their own, to "lead in" or encourage the birth of sons.*

In some parts of the area, as in many other parts of China, it was the custom for the eldest son to be married first. In some villages, I am told, the girls then had to marry before the rest of their brothers. By the beginning of this century it had become customary to marry girls to younger bridegrooms: the girl was typically about sixteen years old, the boy thirteen or fourteen. Concubines were usually recruited from the contingent of "bonded servants" (*mei-tsai*) who were daughters of poor, usually landless peasants, sold to families needing extra labor. Poor peasants took such girls as wives, but matchmakers specializing in concubines would inquire of families with mature bonded servants about the girls' availability for secondary unions (families taking mei-tsai were obliged to see them married at maturity).

It was not uncommon in the resistance area for girls to be married off to grooms who were on the point of death, or even already dead. The original object of these kinds of marriages was to ensure the continuance of the groom's family line; a son would be adopted for the post-

---

* On this practice see the following paper in this volume, "The Women of Hai-shan," by Arthur P. Wolf.

humous husband, and his living spouse would rear the child.* Girls were also married to men who were working overseas. In a proxy ceremony, the absent husband was represented by a white cock.[32]

Local Culture and the Resistance

Arthur Smith believed that the marriage resistance movement demonstrated "the reality of the evils of the Chinese system of marriage."[33] From both his own vivid nineteenth-century descriptions and Margery Wolf's descriptions of rural Taiwan in recent times, we can see that many women indeed bitterly resented the system.[34] But in many parts of traditional China, the life of a married woman was not so very much grimmer than the life of an unmarried daughter. As Smith and others observe, a Chinese girl was likely to be unwelcome from the moment of her first appearance in the world. She was "goods on which one loses" (she-pen huo), of little value to her natal family except perhaps as a partner to a marriage contract aimed at binding two kinship groups. The inferiority of women was supported by an ideological superstructure that equated them with the yin cosmic element: dark, empty, negative, and, in Confucian interpretations, inauspicious.[35] This idea seems to underly the notion already observed that girls cannot be married from home because that makes it empty and inauspicious. In the silk area, however, a girl was relatively more welcome: because of her labor potential, she was not "goods on which one loses." Girls did not have their feet bound, and infanticide was rare.

In many other parts of China, as Smith remarks, girls "never go anywhere to speak of, and live . . . the existence of a frog in a well."[36] Again there was an ideological justification: it was appropriate for girls, as "inner" beings, to stay inside. But in the silk area girls traveled freely around the countryside; they visited temples, vegetarian halls, and theaters. And, as we have seen, they even did "outside" work. Like other girls in Kwangtung, they had the companionship of other residents in the girls' houses. In addition, however, they had the companionship of other girls in their economic tasks, and they had sisterhoods. Unlike other peasant girls, they were taught to read. Together they read ballads that stressed the unpleasant aspects of marriage and even the equality of the sexes. By contrast, the local married woman who lived with her husband was of less economic value—after the establishment of filatures her value as a home spinner declined—she went out much

---

* Such practices were harshly condemned in the marriage-reform propaganda for South China put out by the People's Republic. Hsin-chiu hun-yin tui-pi t'u (Chart comparing old and new marriage; Canton, 1952).

less, had fewer opportunities for female companionship, and, doing only "inside" work, was kept busy producing and rearing children. In many cases she had also to accept a concubine into her home.

In discussing marriage in general, informants of mine who participated in both the marrying and the nonmarrying forms of resistance contrasted the status of married women unfavorably with that of single women. Many of them stressed the independence of an unmarried woman—her freedom from control by parents-in-law and her ability to move about and do what she liked. Ho's informants stressed their fear of becoming a "slave of man," of being a "human machine of propagation," and of marrying the "wrong type" of man.[37] Several of my own informants were daughters of concubines; they stressed the domestic disharmony arising out of quarrels between different consorts and their children. Many of them also stressed the loneliness of marriage and the lack of economic independence.

Several informants expressed a distaste for heterosexual relations and childbirth. Smith observed that women in the resistance believed "that their married lives would be miserable and unholy."[38] Informants talked of the pollution of childbirth, the punishment in purgatory awaiting women who had children, and the limitations that pregnancy and childbirth, because of their polluting effects, imposed on women in the domestic economy. Some of my informants belonged to Hsien-t'ien sects; a few of them managed vegetarian halls in Hong Kong. These women emphasized the religious advantages of celibacy: a celibate woman could assume a high rank in a sect and have many disciples; she could learn esoteric practices to protect her in her journeys about the countryside (e.g. against rape); and she could assure herself of a better fate in the next life. In other areas Buddhist nunneries provided one socially acceptable alternative to marriage, but our informants contrasted the restricted movements of a nun with the freedom of a vegetarian who was not obliged to reside in a religious institution.

Some women said their fears of sexual relations with men were exacerbated by tales visiting married women told in the girls' houses. One woman Ho interviewed said she had heard "weird stories about childbirth." She married at seventeen and became a pu lo-chia.[39] Some spoke of the frigidity that sometimes marred the wedding night and might last for several months, the consequent anger of the mother-in-law, and the bitter medicines a "stone girl" or frigid woman was forced to swallow. Other women said they had formed close friendships with girls in the girls' house or their work group and did not want any man's "affections." Some pointed to the very real possibility of dying in childbirth, which, they believed, brought even greater punishment after death. Several women said they had nonmarrying fates. They had learned this either from fortunetellers or from their own parents. This brings us to the question of local acceptance of the resistance, including the role of parents.

The local economic system was clearly a major factor in the development of the resistance. We saw how it led to striking contrasts in status between married and unmarried women. The local economy also provided an unmarried woman with a means of supporting herself—a rare option in traditional society. Elsewhere the only alternatives to marriage were religious orders or occupations connected with sex and procreation: prostitution, matchmaking, midwifery.[40] A married woman could sometimes supplement the family income and improve her status by engaging in cottage industry,[41] but it was unlikely that a separated wife could earn enough to support herself by such means. An unhappily married woman who returned to her natal home was not entitled to her parents' support.[42] Finally, an unmarried daughter could not live at home and take in work because of the Chinese conviction that "mature girls cannot be kept in the midst" of the family: nü-ta pu chung-liu.

As the silk economy industrialized, there were further inducements for women in the resistance area to remain single. As we have seen, unattached women were preferred by employers of female labor because of their freedom from family ties. And since an unmarried girl working in a silk factory could support not only herself but also her younger siblings and parents, the latter also had an incentive to keep her unwed. Of the women Ho interviewed in Singapore, not all, he notes, remained unmarried "because of a wish to abstain. Some felt they had a duty to provide extra income for their natal families."[43] What if they did not wish to abstain?

One Chinese description of unmarried girls in P'an-yü mentions their "sexual freedom" and "debauchery among the mulberry trees," adding that "they will neither marry the man chosen [by their parents] nor practice proper celibacy; they merely use the concept of celibacy as a pretext for promiscuity." The source goes on to moralize about the dangers of free love, saying that if an unmarried girl becomes pregnant, she has no recourse but the "inhuman device of abortion." It then describes the case of a girl who had been having an affair in the fields for whom a marriage was arranged by her parents; as it turned out, they had arranged for the girl to marry her lover.[44]

One cannot of course rule out the possibility that a girl who formally renounced heterosexual relationships might have done so not out of a positive commitment to celibacy, but out of economic necessity or out of resentment of the traditional marriage arrangements rather than of men as such. But my informants considered it most unlikely that a girl who had taken tzu-shu vows would enter into a forbidden relationship with a man. These vows were said to be absolutely binding—they were made before gods—and in violating them both the girl and her lover would risk terrible punishment from Heaven. I was also told that a girl who had gone through the hairdressing ritual could not be married off by her parents. The ritual meant that her parents had no further rights over her person, i.e., that she was socially mature. Indeed, it was added, it was precisely to avoid the risk that a daughter who did not want an arranged marriage might form a liaison with a man that parents made her take tzu-shu vows. If she did form such a liaison, particularly while away working in a town, her parents might lose an important source of income. The hairdressing ritual gave them further security: once the ritual had been performed, the girl had no further claim to parental support. Whether, as the Chinese source suggests, many tzu-shu nü risked Heaven's "terrible punishment" is difficult to say; no other available source mentions "free love." Moreover, Ho comments that a girl who becomes a tzu-shu nü in Shun-te "is respected . . . ; her parents may gain prestige through having [such a] daughter."[45] This seems unlikely to have been the case if illicit relations were common.

The Decision to Marry or Not

Some parents did not want their daughters to take vows of celibacy. Often betrothals were kept secret from the daughter to forestall objections and even suicide. We have seen that religious literature emphasized the merit of suicide committed to preserve chastity. Several sources mention mass suicides in which sisters of a betrothed girl who did not wish to wed joined her in death.[46] Some girls are said to have obtained magical charms from religious groups that they used to dissuade the other party to a marriage contract. According to Dyer Ball, "they were taught by the nuns" and vegetarian women "to kill their husbands by saying certain charms or incantations."[47] My informants said that a woman who intended to leave her husband without consummating the marriage tucked charms in her underwrappings to ward off his advances. Why were some girls encouraged by their parents to remain single and others married off against their will?

According to my informants, by the beginning of the century most families in the area tried to keep one daughter as a tzu-shu nü. Early signs of an aversion to marriage or of marked intelligence might be interpreted as indications of a "nonmarrying fate." If a horoscope-reader confirmed this view, the daughter's future was set. Daughters adopted to "lead in" sons might also be selected; they would be older than their oldest brother when his time came to marry, and possibly too old to make a good match when their turn came.[48] A girl might even be adopted with this purpose in mind. So-called daughters who were really mei-tsai might also be selected.

Some girls had to marry against their will, I am told, because it was believed that a family who sent out no daughters in marriage would get no wives in return. Once a girl had been betrothed, she could usually not withdraw, betrothal being actually the first step of the marriage ritual. The only course open to her was to refuse to cohabit. Just as not all girls became tzu-shu nü out of a positive desire for celibacy, not all pu lo-chia opposed eventual cohabitation. A girl might object to marrying a stranger or a very young boy, or to having many children. Some girls followed the custom of staying away three years, which gave them time to get to know their husbands (they returned for ceremonial visits) and very young husbands time to mature. In-laws often accepted this arrangement and in some cases even encouraged it, because during her time away the girl worked to support her husband and his family. Indeed, I was told, families began to find brides for younger and younger sons so they could be supported by their daughters-in-law.[49] A girl might, however, strike a bargain with her in-laws: when she returned, she would bear no more than two or three children, afterward being free to abstain from sexual relations.

During their time away, such women did not usually live in their natal homes, but in the cockloft of the girls' house (girls also slept in the cockloft for four days before they married). Usually they worked locally as hired labor. If after a few years they further decided not to return until past childbearing age—perhaps they found their husband or in-laws uncongenial or had resolved to remain celibate—they had to leave the village and buy a mei-tsai to act as their husband's concubine. They then had additionally to support the concubine and her children. According to Ho, "to maintain chastity and support a husband and his children . . . were acts admired and respected."[50]

Both the tzu-shu nü and the pu lo-chia who did not intend returning until old age usually had long-term economic obligations to their natal or conjugal families. Moreover, unattached women of either category could not stay in their natal homes, but had to find somewhere else to live. Let us now see what arrangements they made.

The tzu-shu nü. The nonmarrying woman's hairdressing ceremony, like the bride's, was a prerequisite to leaving home. As for the marriage ceremonies, an auspicious day was chosen for the ritual.[51] Whereas the bride was assisted at the hairdressing ceremony by an elderly woman with many sons, the nonmarrying woman was assisted by an elderly celibate female. Like wedding ceremonies, the tzu-shu ceremonies were followed by a banquet, and like the bride, the nonmarrying woman received red packets of money from her relatives, as well as from her "sisters" and friends. If she was lucky she also received money saved for her dowry, or against her departure if her parents had decided earlier that she would not wed. The peasant woman would eventually use the money she was given on this occasion to pay for residence in a special house for tzu-shu nü, known as a "spinsters' house" (*ku-p'o wu*) or "sisters' house" (*tzu-mei wu*), when she grew too old to work.

Spinsters' houses were found throughout the Shun-te area, usually adjoining a plot of farmland with which the elderly inmates helped support themselves.[52] Like some of the girls' houses, some of the spinsters' houses appear to have been built by lineages as retirement homes for their unmarried women, and perhaps also as residences for unattached women working in an economic operation of the lineage. Some gentry families allowed a daughter to remain unwed without requiring her to work, which enhanced the family's prestige, and in many instances built a house for the girl to live in.

Many women, however, had to finance their own house, or alternatively pay into a vegetarian hall when they retired. Spinsters' houses were in many cases practically indistinguishable from vegetarian halls. They had an altar for a patron deity, usually Kuan Yin, and on festival days they invited priests to officiate at religious ceremonies. But vegetarian food was not required at the spinsters' houses, and there was far less focus on religious activities in general.

During her active years the tzu-shu nü usually shared a rented room with her "sisters" in a town near the filature that employed them. Such residential groups often had elaborate arrangements for saving money. They ran death-benefit clubs, to which members made monthly payments against funeral expenses of one of their number or a parent's postmortuary ceremonies; in some groups women put a fixed percentage of their monthly earnings into a fund for festival celebrations; they contributed to funds for emergency assistance to the families of the "sisters"; and they saved for the retirement home they eventually would build. If they could save enough, they retired early—around forty—and adopted a mei-tsai, whom they brought up in their "faith."

The pu lo-chia. The pu lo-chia who did not return to her husband until old age usually had greater economic burdens than a tzu-shu nü. The nonmarrying woman supported her siblings and parents, but the separated wife had to support not only her in-laws and husband, but also her husband's concubine (for whom she paid) and their children. Expected to return eventually, she did not save for a retirement home. While she was working, however, her life followed much the same pattern as that of the nonmarrying woman. She, too, rented a room with other separated wives—her "sisters"—and with young widows and grass widows whose husbands were overseas, for they, too, in many cases left home to work for their in-laws. Whether the separated wife ever returned depended on many circumstances: whether she had made sufficient financial contributions to win acceptance by her husband's concubine and her children (who were technically the wife's); whether an overseas husband returned; or whether she was called back to care for an adopted child.

Many separated wives and young widows never returned. In the 1920's the silk industry began to decline, at first because of outside competition and later because of the worldwide depression. Earnings decreased, and many a woman's hard-pressed conjugal family refused to take her back. Olga Lang describes her visit to women's residences in and around Canton in the late 1930's, which the Kwangtung authorities had had to erect for women who "had no real contact with their husbands, thus becoming helpless in old age."[53] She also reports that some occupants were women who had lost all contact with their father's families—presumably tzu-shu nü who could not save enough money to build themselves a house or buy into a vegetarian hall.

Decline of the Resistance

By 1935 the slump hit bottom. Writing during the period, Smedley reports that the collapse of industrial life had forced all the filatures in some areas to close down.[54] I am told that some tzu-shu nü and separated wives retired early to spinsters' houses and vegetarian halls; those still young enough to seek employment elsewhere found work as domestic servants in Canton and other cities.

Malaya and Singapore, similarly affected by the depression, began to restrict male immigration. The cost of a man's passage increased as a result of competition for the limited number of quota tickets available. At first there was no immigration quota for women, and their tickets were therefore cheaper. To fill their ships, ticket brokers would sell lodging houses and local ticket agents a quota ticket only if they bought three or four nonquota tickets at the same time. Parents, brothers, and in-laws therefore encouraged their daughters, sisters, and young daughters-in-law to emigrate. I am told that more girls were urged to become tzu-shu nü so they would not marry overseas, and it was impressed upon newly married women that noncohabitation was an honorable practice. From 1933 to 1938, when a quota of 500 females a month was introduced, shiploads of Cantonese women entered Malaya and Singapore. A large contingent came from Shun-te.[55]

Some women left the area in anticipation of the Japanese occupation of Canton and the consequent social and economic dislocations. When the Japanese took Canton in 1938, many young unattached women escaped sexual exploitation by taking up residence in vegetarian halls. After the Japanese left, life scarcely had time to settle down again before the Communists came to power. The People's Republic was sympathetic to the plight of these women who were described as suffering "terrible hardships . . . and [leading] sad and lonely lives."[56] But it considered their resistance essentially negative, and disapproved, I am told, of the "exploitative" custom of purchasing mei-tsai as concubines. The spinsters' houses were gradually phased out. Many women were forcibly removed to the homes of kinsmen. Only those with nobody to take them in were allowed to remain.[57]

Most of the unattached women who migrated to Singapore and Hong Kong from the Shun-te area worked as domestic servants. Many never returned to their homeland. While working they made arrangements similar to those of the silkworkers: they rented workers' rooms, or *kongsi* as they are called in Singapore, and ran several kinds of loan clubs.[58] Some are said eventually to have married and had children,[59] but it is noticeable that with the influx of unattached women in the 1930's, vegetarian halls, particularly sectarian ones, sprang up in large numbers. My own investigations in the 1950's showed that much of their membership was drawn from the nonmarrying and noncohabiting women of the resistance area.[60] Some of these women adopted daughters with the intention of having them follow in their footsteps, but such plans usually went awry. A film made for the female Cantonese audience in the early 1950's in Hong Kong, entitled *Tzu-shu nü*, tells the story of one such adopted daughter and her foster-mother. The girl refuses to take tzu-shu vows, telling her foster-mother that it is old-fashioned and superstitious to reject marriage, that nowadays marriage is much better for women than it was in the past, and that women should work to further improve their marital status.

In Hong Kong today, unmarried women are in demand in factories, offices, and commercial establishments. Demographic data show that many girls are postponing marriage, and one demographer, Janet Salaff, argues that this may reflect the significant contributions they make to their parents' and siblings' support and the higher status they enjoy as a result.[61] But most women in Hong Kong marry eventually. The resistance has not attracted women brought up in a society, economy, and culture that differ so markedly from those of prewar Shun-te.

The Legacy of the Resistance

I have argued that a particular local economy and settlement pattern, tied to a particular physical environment, raised the status of the unmarried or unattached woman considerably above that of the conventionally married woman; and further, that with the industrialization of the economy, women wishing to remain unwed were financially able to act on their preferences. Although unmarried women apparently had already participated to a greater extent than their married sisters in the domestic economy, once industrialization took hold, unattached women were almost the only class of labor in demand. The emigration of thousands of men who could not find work at home made parents more dependent than ever on the earnings of their unattached daughters and their daughters-in-law, which gave them a strong incentive to encourage marriage resistance.

In other parts of China where unattached women were in demand as factory labor, the traditional marriage arrangements were undercut. Fei Hsiao-t'ung, for example, cites the case of an illicit union between a married but detached factory worker and a man in Wusih. The woman's parents-in-law eventually decided to treat her as before because of her earning capacity.[62] One source on P'an-yü also talks of disruptive effects—"debauchery," free love, and abortion—but the overwhelming evidence is that in the resistance area, traditional values relating to premarital chastity and marital fidelity were preserved, and that the system of marriage, though modified, remained more or less intact. Many women remained celibate, but concubines, of whom there was a plentiful local supply, assumed the responsibility of bearing children. The women who chose celibacy were influenced by the high local valuation of chastity, which stemmed in large part from dissident religious groups with whom local inhabitants sympathized. These groups, driven from other parts of China but safely entrenched in the relatively isolated hilly regions around Shun-te, reached the relatively large numbers of literate or semiliterate women in the area with anti-marriage propaganda. In most of industrializing China, families had to balance the financial gain from an unmarried daughter or noncohabiting daughter-in-law who worked away from home against the risk of losing her, and hence her earnings, to another man. In the resistance area, however, the system of sanctions and beliefs surrounding institutionalized celibacy made such defections unlikely. It is not surprising, then, that many parents supported the commitment to celibacy once it was made or even encouraged their daughters and daughters-in-law to make such a commitment.

None of the features I have discussed appears unique to the resistance area, but their combination does. The Yangtze Valley, for example, had a similar terrain, practiced sericulture, and apparently had similar notions of female pollution and silkworm production; but because the climate supported only two broods of silkworms a year, less domestic labor was needed and women played a less important role in the village economy than they did in the resistance area. In the Yangtze Valley, moreover, there were no girls' houses and no sisterhoods, and by the mid-nineteenth century the Hsien-t'ien sects had been driven out or effectively hamstrung. Elsewhere in Kwangtung province there were girls' houses and girls working in the domestic economy; furthermore there was a significant male out-migration, as there was not in the Yangtze Valley. Outside the resistance area, however, women were seldom able to work for cash, at least cash enough to support themselves and their kinsmen, and nowhere else does sectarianism appear to have been so strong. Sectarianism also flourished in parts of Fukien province,[63] but a higher proportion of girls there had bound feet, and they did not work outside. There were no girls' houses in Fukien, so far as I know, and educational opportunities for women were rarer.

Clearly we do not yet know enough either about village-to-village variation in the resistance area or about other superficially similar areas with no history of marriage resistance to assess the relative importance of the variables discussed in this paper.

What about the resistance area today? Has the resistance, or the ecology that produced it, left a legacy discernible even under the People's Republic? Graham Johnson, a sociologist who visited the delta region in 1973, writes that on the average women there participate in collective work only slightly less than men, and that they constitute slightly over 50 percent of the labor force. He contrasts this pattern with that of a village in Honan, described by a recent observer, where there is a low level of female involvement in many aspects of collective production and where few women are rated as fully able-bodied members of the workforce.[64] In Shun-te the silk-and-fish economy persists, although other crops have been introduced or brought under more intensive cultivation. As a result of collectivization, fishponds and mulberry groves have been enlarged, and isolated farms are less in evidence. According to my own informants, there are no active celibate establishments in Shun-te today, although recent interviews recorded by China specialists working in Hong Kong suggest that girls' houses may still exist in some villages, and that there may still be women who do not join their husbands immediately after their wedding ceremonies. Women, moreover, are still the main workers in silk production. Unmarried girls are in exclusive charge of the outside phase of silkworm breeding and predominate in filatures. In a private report, Johnson says that one filature he visited employed nearly 1,300 workers, of whom 1,100 were women.

Johnson also contrasts Shun-te with Tung-kuan, another hsien in the Canton delta but outside the resistance area. In Shun-te there were, in 1973, 2,600 nurseries for workers' children, an average of one per work team. In Tung-kuan there were very few nurseries; instead, women work in the fields with young children on their backs. Family-planning propaganda appears to have been far more successful in Shun-te. Between 1965 and 1972 the birthrate in Shun-te is said to have fallen from 3.4 percent to 1.8 percent (0.9 percent in Ta-liang, the hsien capital), whereas in Tung-kuan the birthrate for the hsien as a whole remained at 2.2 percent, with higher rates in the rural areas. In Tung-kuan, though, abortion is widely practiced, whereas in Shun-te it is rare. As Johnson remarks, traditional notions concerning family and household are "presumably critical."[65] In a private report he writes that with respect to family planning, "it is openly admitted that the major problems stem not so much from parents as grandparents." In Shun-te many former members of the marriage resistance must now be members of the grandparent generation. One imagines that the high value they have always placed on freedom of movement for women—on their being unencumbered by children—and the low value they place on procreation might today find their expression in the distinctive work patterns and extraordinary population statistics of the former resistance area.

The Women of Hai-shan: A Demographic Portrait

ARTHUR P. WOLF

Though very little research has focused on the lives and concerns of Chinese peasant women, most analyses of Chinese institutions assume that the great majority of women's lives followed a common pattern. In hard times peasant families were forced to sell their daughters as slave girls (*ya-t'ou*) or give them out in adoption as little daughters-in-law (*t'ung-yang-hsi*). Otherwise, girls were raised by their natal families until shortly after puberty, when they were removed by marriage to their husband's home. Because women married early and were constrained by prudishness and bound feet, virtually all brides were virgins whose primary assignment in life was to bear male children to perpetuate their husband's line of descent. And once a woman was married, she was committed to her husband's family for life. Despite conditions that encouraged an exceptionally high suicide rate among young married women,[*] divorce was rare and granted only on the initiative of the husband's family. A widow's parents-in-law might arrange a second marriage for her with a man who agreed to join their family as a substitute for their son, but except among the poorest and least representative segments of society, women never broke their ties with their first husband's family. A woman came to her husband's family as a virgin and after his death remained there as a celibate widow.

We all recognize that this biography does not apply to every Chinese woman. In addition to those women who were removed from their natal families as ya-t'ou or t'ung-yang-hsi, some women became Buddhist or Taoist nuns, others were forced into prostitution, and a few

---

[*] For evidence on this point and a discussion of the causes of suicide among young women, see the following paper in this volume, by Margery Wolf.

changed the course of their lives by joining a marriage resistance sisterhood.* But while exceptions are granted, most discussions of traditional
China assume that they were so few in number and so obviously the
result of special circumstances that there is no need to inquire further.
The prevailing attitude appears to be that once you have allowed for
certain obvious differences between social classes, you can proceed as
though throughout Chinese history, in every area of the country, wom-
en's lives ran a common course set by the principles that governed
family life. My primary purpose in this paper is to demonstrate that in
at least one area of the country, exceptions were the rule. My hope is
that this demonstration will encourage others to reexamine the evidence
from other areas of China. I suspect that the uniformity of women's
lives is an illusion fostered by such elite documents as the Ch'ing code.
The reality appears to be both more complex and a great deal more
interesting.

The area of China to which my data refer is northern Taiwan, specifically Shu-lin *chen* (township), San-hsia chen, and a part of Pan-
ch'iao chen, an area known in the late Ch'ing and during the Japanese
period as Hai-shan. This region of Taiwan was settled in the eighteenth
and early nineteenth centuries by immigrants from An-ch'i hsien in
Ch'üan-chou, and until recently formed an ethnic enclave identified by
allegiance to the great Ch'ang Fu Yen temple in San-hsia. During the
fifty-year period with which I am concerned, 1895 to 1945, most of the
inhabitants were tenant farmers and farm laborers. Until the Land Reform Program initiated in 1952 broke up the landlords' estates, more than
a third of all farm land in Hai-shan was owned by the famous Lin
family, whose once elegant home in Pan-ch'iao remains one of the most
impressive architectural sights in Taiwan.

My data are drawn from two sources: interviews and observations
made during five years of fieldwork, and the household registers maintained by the Japanese colonial government. The Japanese household
registers are best introduced by asking the reader to visualize a wide
sheet of paper divided into six vertical columns. The first column notes
the address of the family in question and tells us that the former head
of this household died or retired on a certain date. The second column
is always labeled "Head of household"; the remaining columns vary,
each presenting one member of the household identified by his relationship to the head, for example, "Mother," "Wife," "Eldest Son," etc. At
the bottom of the column, in appropriately labeled boxes, we find the

---

* A fascinating account of marriage resistance is presented in the preceding paper in this volume, by Marjorie Topley.

person's name and birthdate, his father's name and birthdate, his mother's name and birthdate, and his own same-sex sibling order; a second row of notations immediately above these tells us that the person is Hokkien rather than Hakka, that he has been vaccinated for smallpox, that he is or is not an opium addict, and, in the case of a woman, whether or not she has bound feet.

The remainder of each column is taken up with handwritten notations made over a number of years. They tell us when the person became a member of the household, by what means, and, if not by birth, his former address, the name of the head of his former household, and his relationship to the head of that household. If the person has lived away from home for any period of time, as he will have if he has worked in the city or another part of the island, the dates of his departure and return are also noted, along with his temporary address. Looking through a record selected at random, we discover that the head of household was adopted in 1908, and that his wife also entered the household by adoption, in 1910. They were married in 1925, produced their first child, a son, in 1928, and then only a few months later adopted a girl to raise as the boy's wife. The addresses given tell us that the adopted girl came from the same village as her foster-mother, and the fact that they also bear the same surname suggests they are related. The girl is probably her foster-mother's brother's daughter.

When a child is born or the family acquires a new member by way of marriage or adoption, the appropriate information is entered in the next blank column, new sheets being appended to the original record as necessary. When a family member dies or otherwise leaves the household, or when a segment of the family hives off to form an independent household, the departure is noted in the appropriate column in red, after which the column is crossed out. This process continues until the head of household dies or retires. All information concerning the surviving members of the household is then copied onto new forms, and the old record is crossed with a diagonal red line and set aside. Fortunately for the researcher interested in the history of the Chinese family in Taiwan, these dead registers have been carefully preserved in all but a few offices. By putting together the registers current at the end of the Japanese period with the accumulated dead registers, one can reconstruct the precise composition of every family at every point in time between the initiation of the system in December 1905 through the departure of the Japanese at the end of World War II.

To interpret the information in the household registers, one must know something of the various forms of marriage and adoption practiced in northern Taiwan.* Marriages can be divided into three types—major marriage, minor marriage, and uxorilocal marriage. The major marriage removes the bride from her natal home as a young adult, makes her a member of her husband's father's household, and accords her husband's line the right to decide the descent of the children she bears. From the native point of view, the major marriage is the proper way to marry, the form of marriage that everyone would choose in an ideal world. Minor and uxorilocal marriages are best viewed as negotiated exceptions to the legal model provided by the major form of marriage; they are the product of compromises with social and economic reality.

The primary difference between major and minor marriages is that whereas the bride taken in a major marriage joins her husband's family as a young adult, the bride acquired in a minor marriage enters the family as a very young child, usually before 18 months of age and often as early as three or four months. Her change of residence makes the girl a *sim-pua*, a "little daughter-in-law," but not a wife.† She does not enter into a conjugal relationship until ten or fifteen years later, when she and one of her foster-family's sons together worship his ancestors and thereby complete the marriage.

The legal consequences of a minor marriage are essentially the same as those of a major marriage, the only difference being that a sim-pua is expected to love her husband's parents as though she were their daughter. Uxorilocal marriages involve a more radical departure from the model. All marriages of this type reverse the usual rule of residence and give the husband definite economic obligations to his wife's parents; many of them involve an agreement that qualifies the right of the husband's line to decide the descent of his children. In the most extreme case, the husband changes his surname and takes on the duties of a son with respect to his wife's parents. Under these conditions all children of the union take their descent from their mother's father. More commonly, a man who agrees to reside uxorilocally insists on retaining his name and the right to name some of his children to his line. One arrangement is to name the first-born son to the mother's father's line and all other children to their father's line; another is to alternate the descent of

---

* What follows is a much simplified account of complex institutions. For further details see my "Marriage and Adoption in Northern Taiwan," to appear in *Social Organization and the Applications of Anthropology: Essays in Honor of Lauriston Sharp*, ed. Robert J. Smith.

† My romanization of Hokkien terms follows the orthography outlined in Nicholas C. Bodman's *Spoken Amoy Hokkien*. I use Hokkien terms in referring to local institutions to remind the reader that Chinese institutions do vary. A sim-pua is like a t'ung-yang-hsi, but is not the precise equivalent.

the children irrespective of their sex. In either case the result is a sibling set split between two lines of descent. Those children who take their descent from their father inherit from him and are obliged to take his forebears as ancestors; those who take their descent from their maternal grandfather inherit his estate and are obliged to him and his forebears.

If by "adoption" one means simply the transfer of rights over a child, without stipulating the rights transferred, it can be said that customary law in northern Taiwan recognizes four distinct forms of adoption, two for females and two for males. By far the most common form of female adoption is the one that makes the girl a sim-pua with respect to her foster-parents, an adoption that is in fact the first step of marriage. The other is the purchase of female children as *ca-bo-kan*, servant-slaves whose status is best indicated by the fact that they are divided among a family's heirs on a per stirpes basis, like landed property. Until recently there was no institutional means of adopting a girl as a daughter, but there were two distinct ways of taking boys as sons. A family could either adopt a boy as a *ke-pang-kia:* from an agnate or purchase a boy as a *pieng-lieng-kia:* from a stranger. The essential difference between the two is that whereas the ke-pang-kia: retains strong ties with his natural parents, including the right to inherit a share of his father's estate, the pieng-lieng-kia: must break all ties with his natural parents and with respect to his foster-parents assume the full, exclusive duties of a son.

All the data presented in the tables that are the basis of this paper are drawn from the household registers of six districts (*li*), four in San-hsia chen and two in Pan-ch'iao chen. Work in progress on five other districts indicates that these six can be taken as representative of Hai-shan, which is to be expected of a community in which every village has kinship ties with every other village. The only striking variations one sees in the data are changes that occur as social and economic programs initiated by the Japanese take effect. The direction and magnitude of these changes is apparent in many of the tables, but I will not attempt to interpret them here. It will be enough if I can outline the general nature of women's lives and indicate some of the causal relationships that were important in the first forty years of our period. The reader should note, however, that as traditional institutions decay, the pattern of women's lives comes closer and closer to the one recommended by elite ideals. This is important because it suggests that field studies conducted on the mainland in the 1930's may have been too late for those of us interested in the women of traditional China.

In December 1951 an article appearing in the *Nanfang Jihpao* re-

ARTHUR P. WOLF

TABLE 1. PROBABILITY OF ADOPTION AMONG FEMALE CHILDREN
(All girls born 1906–35)

Year of birth	Number of girls born	Probability of adoption
1906–10	492	.712
1911–15	517	.678
1916–20	503	.636
1921–25	634	.595
1926–30	656	.586
1931–35	774	.454

ported that in certain villages near Canton, t'ung-yang-hsi constituted "80 to 90 percent of the total female population," and in February 1953 an article in the *Hopei Jihpao* claimed that "of all the women in Pingho hsien in Fukien, 70 percent are or have been t'ung-yang-hsi." Are these reports anything more than propaganda manufactured to support the marriage-reform campaigns of the 1950's? After a careful study of family composition in Ting hsien, near Peking, Sidney D. Gamble reports finding only two "future daughters-in-law" in a total of 5,255 farm families.[1] Is it possible that the incidence of female adoption could have varied so widely from one area of the country to another? It seems unlikely that we will ever be able to verify reports in the mainland press, but I can show that their estimates of female adoption are not wholly implausible. And I can prove that the incidence of female adoption did vary from the very low figure reported for Ting hsien to more than 70 percent of all female children.

Table 1 takes as its universe all female children born into our six districts during the years 1906–35. Because many female children died as infants and did not experience the full risk of adoption, the percent of adoptions among all girls born underestimates the true likelihood of adoption. I therefore report as an adoption rate the probability that a girl will be given out in adoption if she survives to age fifteen, a figure obtained by adding the probabilities for 0–30 days, 31–91 days, 92–182 days, 183–365 days, 1–4 years, and 5–14 years.* For girls born in the years 1906–10, the probability of adoption was a remarkable .712. This figure says that if all the girls born during the period had lived, 71.2 percent would have been given out in adoption.

---

* The probability for each of these periods was obtained by dividing the number of girls given out in adoption by the number of girls who reached the lower age limit, minus one-half the number of girls who died or migrated during the period. Because the likelihood of a child's dying declines during the early years of life, my assumption that all deaths occurred at the midpoint results in a slight underestimation of the true probability of adoption.

TABLE 2. CHILDHOOD MORTALITY
(All children born 1906–35)

Days from birth	Female deaths per 100 male deaths		Days from birth	Female deaths per 100 male deaths	
	Daughters	Adopted daughters		Daughters	Adopted daughters
1–99	83	—	600–99	125	217
100–99	109	—	700–99	57	129
200–99	93	148	800–99	140	160
300–99	78	104	900–99	89	156
400–99	89	168	1,000–99	63	213
500–99	100	163			

NOTE: I have omitted the number of deaths recorded for girls adopted within 200 days of birth because the figures are obviously unreliable: they say that girls adopted at this age almost never died within the first 100 days after adoption. Probably the adoption was simply not reported if the girl died shortly after adoption. The girl's natal family reported the death as the death of a daughter and saved themselves and the other family the trouble of registering an adoption.

I cannot explain why adoption rates were so high in some areas of the country and so low in others, but I can show that these differences were important. Whether or not a girl was given out in adoption was, literally, a matter of life and death. Probably because people wanted to bind their son's wife to them by ties of sentiment as well as by formal obligations, they preferred to adopt sim-pua at the earliest possible age. During the period 1906–35 more than 50 percent of all adopted daughters were given away before they were six months old, which means that most girls were adopted before the normal age for weaning.* In many cases the child's future mother-in-law gave away her own daughter and nursed her son's wife in the daughter's stead. Unfortunately this was not always possible, and as a result adopted daughters were far less likely to survive than girls lucky enough to be raised by their own parents. George W. Barclay is mistaken in attributing the relatively high mortality rates among female children to differential treatment of sons and daughters.[2] The evidence presented in Table 2 indicates that daughters enjoyed better survival chances than sons. Mortality among female children exceeded that of male children solely because of the very high mortality rates among adopted daughters.

Whether or not any particular female child was given out in adoption depended primarily on the composition of the family into which she was born. Because of the strong belief that adopting a female child enhances a woman's chances of bearing a son, many mothers in Hai-shan gave

* Data Margery Wolf and I collected in 1957–60 indicate that the mean age of weaning in Hai-shan was then 15.9 months for female children and 17.5 months for male children.

TABLE 3a. NUMBER OF GIRLS BORN, BY COMPOSITION OF SIBLING SET
(All girls born 1906–35)

Year of birth	Number of siblings present at birth					
	0	1	2	3	4	5+
1906–10	104	123	103	75	49	38
1911–15	126	113	93	62	72	51
1916–20	130	116	106	61	45	45
1921–25	151	157	135	82	56	53
1926–30	132	143	142	105	72	62
1931–35	163	174	135	127	92	83

TABLE 3b. PROBABILITY OF ADOPTION, BY COMPOSITION OF SIBLING SET
(All girls born 1906–35)

Year of birth	Number of siblings present at birth					
	0	1	2	3	4	5+
1906–10	.459	.710	.774	.829	.814	.793
1911–15	.385	.669	.809	.792	.757	.890
1916–20	.344	.687	.787	.796	.734	.688
1921–25	.208	.608	.774	.684	.862	.786
1926–30	.268	.503	.738	.716	.728	.688
1931–35	.131	.358	.540	.603	.598	.699

away the daughter who was an only child and adopted another girl in her stead, hoping that the adopted daughter would "lead in" a son. But with the exception of those who were replaced by a girl adopted for such therapeutic purposes, most girls born into childless families were raised by their own parents. Though their mothers were probably happy to keep their only child, these were not sentimental decisions. A primary goal of every married couple was to obtain male descendants to support them in their old age and to provide for their souls after death. Since most people could not afford to buy a boy as a pieng-lieng-kia: and could not count on finding a ke-pang-kia:, those who had no male children raised a daughter as insurance against the possibility they would fail to produce a son. One consequence of the high female mortality rate promoted by early adoption was that even poor families could usually find a man willing to perform the services of a son in return for a wife. A large proportion of the male population had to marry uxorilocally or not marry at all.

Girls born into families who already had one child or more were not so fortunate. People who already had children to support them in this life and the next saw no point in raising a "useless" daughter who would "only grow up and marry out of the family anyway." Consequently, the great majority of these girls were given out in adoption at an early age. Table 3 says that throughout the period 1906–35, the probability of adoption among girls born into families with one or more children was more than double that of girls born into childless families. That these differences became increasingly pronounced during the course of the Japanese occupation is probably a reflection of the selective impact of social change. Women with one or two children would be younger than women with four or five children, and for this reason would be the first to respond to changing conditions by choosing to raise their female offspring as well as their sons.

A female child's chances of being given out in adoption were also affected by the sex of the other children present when she was born, her mother's marital status, the form of her mother's marriage if she was married, her father's position among his brothers, and her mother's age at the time of the child's birth. I cannot demonstrate the effect of each of these variables here, but it is important to show that when certain combinations occurred, adoption was almost inevitable. An example is given in Table 4, which takes as its universe all legitimate children born into families with three or more children of whom at least two were males. When these girls are arranged by birth cohorts and subdivided by their mothers' age at the time they were born, we find that adoption was all but certain among those born in the years 1906–15 to mothers under thirty. In fact, of the 47 girls born under these conditions, only

TABLE 4a. NUMBER OF GIRLS BORN, BY AGE OF
MOTHER AT BIRTH

*(Only girls born into families with 3 or more
children, including at least 2 boys)*

Year of birth	Age of mother		
	29 and under	30–34	35 and over
1906–15	47	86	109
1916–25	38	77	116
1926–35	95	124	152

TABLE 4b. PROBABILITY OF ADOPTION BY AGE
OF MOTHER

Year of birth	Age of mother		
	29 and under	30–34	35 and over
1906–15	.967	.805	.777
1916–25	.840	.759	.730
1926–35	.708	.692	.688

one was raised by her natal family. The other 46 either died before age fifteen or were given out in adoption. The marked impact her mother's age had on a girl's chances of being given away can be explained in two ways. One possibility is that whereas the fate of a young mother's child was decided by her mother-in-law, that of an older woman's child was decided by the mother herself. The other is that young mothers with three or more children were more likely to have borne another child in the recent past and were therefore more likely to relieve the burden of caring for two infants by giving away their next child.

Two important conclusions follow from the evidence summarized in Tables 3 and 4. First, within the range of socioeconomic statuses represented in Hai-shan, the relative wealth of a girl's family was not the primary determinant of whether or not she would be given out in adoption. A few very poor families may have given away a girl who was an only child because they could not afford the luxury of raising a daughter as insurance, but most families would raise a girl who was an only child. And though a few families may have retained later-born daughters because they could afford to do so and wanted to display their wealth, the very great majority gave these girls away. Most of the exceptions were girls whose mothers were more than thirty-five years old. Clearly, the primary determinant of decisions about female adoption was not wealth, but the composition of the girl's natal family.

The second and more important conclusion to be drawn from Table 4 follows from the evidence that parents who wanted to give away a female child could always find someone to adopt her. This suggests a very strong demand for adopted daughters, which may not have been satisfied by the supply of girls available for adoption. If all female children had been placed on the adoption market, the rate of adoption would probably have been even higher than reported in Table 1.

Why was the demand for adopted daughters so great? What role did these girls play in their foster-families? Of all the girls adopted in Hai-shan in the years 1906–20, only two were entered on the household registers as ca-bo-kan. But the actual frequency of this form of adoption may have been higher, if not during this period, then at least during the previous decade. Table 5 reports the incidence of bound feet among 132 girls adopted before the Japanese campaign to eradicate the custom got under way in the rural areas. We see that where the great majority of adopted daughters who married uxorilocally or in the minor fashion had bound feet, a comparatively large proportion of those who did not marry or married in the major fashion had natural feet. This argues that people bound the feet of girls adopted to serve as daughters and daughters-in-

TABLE 5. FOOT-BINDING AMONG WOMEN BORN 1891–1900

Type of marriage	Daughters		Adopted daughters	
	Number of women	Pct. with bound feet	Number of women	Pct. with bound feet
Major	99	95.0%	78	78.2%
Uxorilocal	23	100.0	45	97.8
Minor	—	—	162	92.0
No marriage	10	90.0	31	77.4

law and suggests that girls whose feet were not bound were adopted for some other purpose. I suspect that although they were registered as sim-pua, many of these girls were in fact ca-bo-kan.

By far the most common reason for adopting a female child was to raise her as a wife for one's son. Indeed, there is good reason to conclude that despite the socially superior status of a major marriage, most parents preferred to raise their sons' wives. Table 6 indicates that minor marriage was almost as common in Hai-shan as major marriage, accounting for 40 percent of all marriages made by women born prior to 1910. And it must be remembered that the incidence of minor marriage would have been much higher if all of the girls adopted as sim-pua had survived to marry their foster-brothers. In many cases a man married in the major fashion only because the girl adopted as his future wife died in childhood. Moreover, there is a good possibility that many parents who desired a minor marriage for their son were forced to arrange a major marriage because they could not find a girl to adopt. We have already seen evidence suggesting that the supply of girls available for adoption was inadequate to meet the demand. My guess is that if every family that wanted a sim-pua had been able to adopt one and if all these girls had survived to marry, minor marriages would have accounted for more than 70 percent of all marriages.

The preference for minor marriages in Hai-shan was in part a conse-

TABLE 6. TYPE OF FIRST MARRIAGE MADE BY WOMEN BORN 1891–1920

Year of birth	Number of women	Percent of women by type of marriage		
		Major marriage	Minor marriage	Uxorilocal marriage
1891–95	167	41.3%	37.1%	21.6%
1896–1900	241	45.2	41.5	13.3
1901–5	245	44.5	41.6	13.9
1906–10	250	45.2	42.0	12.8
1911–15	256	57.7	30.9	11.3
1916–20	253	65.6	25.3	9.1

quence of their being less expensive than major marriages. By giving away their daughters and raising in their stead wives for their sons, people saved the bride price required by a major marriage, the money lost on their daughters' dowries, and the very considerable expense of several weddings in the major fashion. But economy was not the only reason for raising a son's wife. As in many other societies that emphasize agnatic kinship, a woman's best chance for power was control of her sons. The danger was always that a son would prove unfilial, which, from a mother's point of view, often meant that he would listen to his wife. The solution was to adopt and raise your son's wife, an arrangement that allowed women to bind their daughters-in-law to them by the same web of sentiment they used to control their sons. As Fei Hsiao-t'ung observes in commenting on minor marriages in Kaihsienkung, "The girl brought up from an early age by her future mother-in-law becomes . . . very closely attached to the latter and feels towards her just like a daughter," the result being that "the conflict between the mother-in-law and the daughter-in-law is often not so acute, even if not entirely avoided."[3] Or, as one of my more articulate informants in Hai-shan put it, "It is always better to raise your son's wife. The girl you raise yourself will listen to what you tell her and won't always be saying things to your son behind your back."

One reason for the low incidence of minor marriage in a community that appears to have preferred this form was the desire of many families to keep one daughter as insurance. The other was the belief that by adopting a female child a woman could improve her chances of bearing a male child. Because of this belief, a large percentage of all the girls available for adoption were taken by families who did not have sons for them to marry. Though these girls were occasionally matched with a boy born after their adoption, such marriages were in many cases precluded by the belief that a wife should be no more than three or four years older than her husband. Consequently, the majority of the girls adopted to lead in sons married out of their foster-families in the major fashion. Most of the exceptions were girls whose foster-parents failed to bear a son and were therefore compelled to bring a man into the family by arranging an uxorilocal marriage for their adopted daughter.

The strength of people's belief in the therapeutic potential of female adoption is indicated by the evidence presented in Table 7. We see there that of all the girls adopted in Hai-shan in the years 1906–35, over 40 percent were taken by families who did not have a son at the time of the adoption. A few of these adoptions were made by older people who had given up all hope of bearing sons of their own, their motive being to

TABLE 7. ADOPTED DAUGHTERS TAKEN BY FAMILIES WITH NO SONS
(All girls adopted 1906–35)

Year of birth	Number of girls adopted	Number adopted by families with no male children	Percent adopted by families with no male children
1906–10	322	117	36.3%
1911–15	324	125	38.6
1916–20	348	158	45.4
1921–25	375	156	41.6
1926–30	418	177	42.3
1931–35	400	185	46.3

obtain the means of arranging an uxorilocal marriage. But these were the exceptions. The majority of the girls adopted by families without sons were taken by women who were less than twenty-five years of age, most of whom had not been married more than five years—i.e., by women who still had good reason to hope for a son. What in fact probably happened in the majority of these cases is that an impatient mother-in-law, anxious to see her grandchildren before she died, arranged the adoption as a means of changing her daughter-in-law's fortune. My field notes indicate that this was also one of the many ways older women expressed their dissatisfaction with a daughter-in-law who had failed to provide her husband's family with male descendants.

We have so far seen that by the time they were one or two years old, women were divided into two classes whose lives followed very different courses. A fortunate few were raised by their natal families, usually because their parents felt they might be needed to substitute for sons. The majority were given out in adoption to people who wanted to raise them as wives for their sons or who hoped that adopting a girl would improve their chances of bearing sons. The primary determinant of which of these two courses a woman's life would take was the composition of the family into which she was born. Whereas most girls born into childless families were raised by their own parents, the great majority of those born into families that already had one or more children were given out in adoption at an early age.

The fate of girls adopted as sim-pua by families who had a son for them to marry was decided by the time they were weaned. Assuming that both the girl and her intended husband survived childhood, they were "pushed together" shortly after puberty. Because the girl was already a member of her husband's family, there was no need for a wedding. The head of the family simply announced that the two young people were old enough to consummate the match and told them it was time for them to share a bed. Only girls raised by their natal family or adopted by a family with no son could hope to marry in the major fashion, and this was by no means assured. It depended on whether or not the girl's parents (or foster-parents) produced sons and how soon. Those who failed to obtain sons or did so only late in life had no choice but to use their daughter (or adopted daughter) as a substitute. At best, this meant that the girl would have to marry a man willing to reside uxorilocally, a prospect most women dreaded because it was assumed that no decent man would desert his own parents. At worst, the girl would be sent out to work as a prostitute, this being the only way she could contribute significantly to her parents' income. Many of these women did not marry at all.

The extent to which the course of women's lives was influenced by their parents' fortunes with respect to sons is displayed in Table 8. This evidence argues that the pattern of a young woman's life was a highly predictable consequence of the composition of her sibling set at age fifteen. The lives of women whose sibling sets included older brothers (or older foster-brothers) followed the course assumed to hold for most women in Chinese society. But the lives of the majority of all other women departed from this course in a radical fashion. A large percentage of these women did not marry, an even larger percentage married uxorilocally, and, what is perhaps most surprising of all, a still larger percentage bore children before marriage. Despite an early marrying age and a puritanical attitude toward premarital sexual relations in our six districts, 12.3 percent of all the women raised there bore at least one illegitimate child. But this does not mean that most young women experimented with sex before marriage. Since the majority of those who bore illegitimate children were the daughters (or adopted daughters) of people who were dependent on them because they had no sons, most of these children were probably the fruits of prostitution. The tolerant

TABLE 8. SOME CONSEQUENCES OF THE COMPOSITION OF WOMEN'S
SIBLING SETS AT AGE FIFTEEN
(All women born 1896–1915)

Composition of sibling sets	Number of women	Survived to age thirty but never married	Married uxorilocally	Bore children before marriage
No siblings	71	19.7%	36.6%	42.5%
Sisters but no brothers	91	20.9	36.3	40.7
Younger but no older brothers	314	9.9	15.6	21.3
At least one older brother	568	2.8	3.5	8.3

TABLE 9a. NUMBER OF MAJOR MARRIAGE BIRTHS PER 100
MINOR MARRIAGE BIRTHS

(1st marriages of all women born 1881–1915)

Date of wife's birth	Age of wife					
	15–19	20–24	25–29	30–34	35–39	40–44
1881–85	*126*	*152*	161	156	185	135
1886–90	*151*	127	121	109	127	173
1891–95	131	159	134	137	120	139
1896–1900	107	137	136	139	169	118
1901–5	139	126	122	119	104	*138*
1906–10	117	131	120	115	*108*	—
1911–15	117	143	141	*192*	—	—

TABLE 9b. NUMBER OF UXORILOCAL MARRIAGE BIRTHS PER 100
MINOR MARRIAGE BIRTHS

(1st marriages of all women born 1881–1915)

Date of wife's birth	Age of wife					
	15–19	20–24	25–29	30–34	35–39	40–44
1881–85	*162*	*115*	131	104	139	168
1886–90	*241*	139	135	154	150	272
1891–95	131	137	121	169	108	165
1896–1900	176	99	112	115	131	110
1901–5	142	119	121	129	107	*177*
1906–10	161	135	133	116	85	—
1911–15	183	116	144	*143*	—	—

TABLE 9c. SUMMARY: NUMBER OF BIRTHS PER 100 MINOR MARRIAGE BIRTHS

(1st marriages of all women born 1881–1915)

Form of marriage	Age of wife					
	15–19	20–24	25–29	30–34	35–39	40–44
Major	126	140	134	133	133	137
Uxorilocal	167	124	128	133	119	153

NOTE: Two points should be noted with regard to the data presented in this table. The first has to do with the time boundaries of the registration system, which was initiated in late 1905 and began to deteriorate in the mid-1940's as World War II moved closer to Taiwan. This makes it difficult to measure the early marital fertility of women born in the years 1881–90 and the later marital fertility of women born in the years 1895–1915. Many of the former were married before the registration system began and may have borne children who did not survive long enough to be included in the registers, while many of the latter may have borne children who were not registered as a result of wartime dislocations. Because I have no way of determining whether or not these problems affect the three forms of marriage equally, the italicized figures should be treated with caution.

The second point concerns the effect of bridal pregnancy and the accuracy of the registered marriage date. Although many more brides who married in the major fashion were pregnant at marriage than the stereotype suggests, the frequency was somewhat lower than among girls marrying in the minor fashion. I think the explanation is that the groom's parents often took advantage of the ease with which marriages between foster-siblings could be concealed, and registered the union only after a pregnancy indicated the young couple had accepted the match. If this is

TABLE 10. FERTILITY OF ADOPTED DAUGHTERS, BY TYPE OF MARRIAGE
(1st marriages of all women born 1881–1915)

| Age of woman | Births per 100 births by daughters in major marriages | | |
	Adopted daughters married in the major fashion	Adopted daughters married uxorilocally	Adopted daughters married in the minor fashion
15–19	87	123	77
20–24	100	88	71
25–29	97	90	74
30–34	104	98	77
35–39	114	100	76
40–44	118	104	73

treatment accorded former prostitutes reflects a feeling that as filial daughters they deserve sympathy. They may have engaged in an immoral profession, but only for the sake of their parents.

A woman could count herself lucky if she was adopted by a family who wanted to raise her as a wife for one of their sons, since in this case there was little chance of her being called upon to support her parents. But such a situation had disadvantages as well. Probably because they were raised together from early childhood as intimately as any brother and sister, foster-siblings seldom found each other sexually attractive. Indeed, older informants claim that many couples had to be forced to consummate their marriage. That this reluctance was something more than momentary embarrassment is indicated by the relatively low fertility rates of couples married in the minor fashion. Table 9 reports the age-specific marital fertility of seven cohorts of women born in the years 1881–1915. In every case the fertility of major and uxorilocal marriages exceeds that of minor marriages by a substantial margin. A population that married at age fifteen and survived through age forty-five would bear an average of 7.6 children if they all married in the major fashion, 7.8 if they all married uxorilocally, and only 5.7 children if they all married in the minor fashion.

I have argued elsewhere that the cause of the lower fertility of couples

---

right, Table 9 underestimates the difference between major and minor marriages. The ratios for the age category 15–19 should be adjusted upward to take account of the fact that many minor marriages were initiated earlier than the registered date of marriage indicates.

The ratios comparing minor and uxorilocal marriages also require adjustment, but in the opposite direction. The reason is simply that women who marry uxorilocally are even more likely to be pregnant at marriage than women who marry virilocally. Of the women born in the years 1881–1915, 34.0 percent of those who married uxorilocally were pregnant at marriage, compared with only 16.2 percent of those who married in the major fashion and 21.9 percent of those who married a foster-brother.

TABLE 11. INCIDENCE OF DIVORCE, BY TYPE OF FIRST MARRIAGE
(1st marriages of all women born 1881–1915)

Year of wife's birth	Major marriage		Uxorilocal marriage		Minor marriage	
	No. of marriages	Pct. ending in divorce	No. of marriages	Pct. ending in divorce	No. of marriages	Pct. ending in divorce
1881–1900	424	6.4%	131	18.3%	409	14.7%
1901–15	484	7.0	112	17.0	375	20.8
1881–1915	908	6.7	243	17.7	784	17.6

married in the minor fashion was a sexual aversion aroused by intimate and prolonged childhood association.[4] Needless to say, there are other ways of interpreting the evidence, but the only point relevant here is that whatever the cause of lower fertility among minor marriages, it was specific to the conjugal relationship and not a consequence of adoption. Table 10 shows that adopted daughters who married out of their foster-families bore just as many children as women raised by their natal families. Adopted daughters experienced lower fertility only when they were forced to marry their foster-brothers.

The remarkable similarity in fertility between major and uxorilocal marriages should not be taken to indicate that these two forms of marriage were similar in other respects. Table 11 says that the divorce rate among uxorilocal marriages was almost three times as high as among major marriages. With respect to divorce, it was major marriages that stood out against minor and uxorilocal marriages. Essentially, each of the three forms of marriage exhibited a distinctive pattern. Major marriages were characterized by high fertility and a low divorce rate; minor marriages, by low fertility and a high divorce rate; and uxorilocal marriages, by high fertility and a high divorce rate. This argues that each of the three forms of marriage practiced in Hai-shan created a distinctive type of conjugal relationship and suggests that women who married in different ways led very different lives.

The fact that uxorilocal marriages were almost three times as likely to end in divorce as major marriages appears to confirm Lloyd Fallers's suggestion that "common corporate group memberships tend to reinforce the marriage bond, different corporate group memberships to work against it."[5] Where major marriages cut a woman off from her natal family and made her a dependent member of her husband's descent group, most uxorilocal marriages allowed the husband to retain his position as a member of his father's line. He lived with his wife and her father, but remained a member of another group. As a result, the conjugal bonds established by uxorilocal marriages were more brittle than those created by major marriages. The man who married out of his natal family could always go home; the woman who married out could not. When she stepped over the threshold of her father's house on the day of her wedding, the door of the hall was closed behind her and with that "the rice was cooked."

The more surprising finding is the high divorce rate among minor marriages. Whereas women who married out of their families in the major fashion retained emotional if not jural ties with their parents and siblings, girls given out in adoption at an early age were totally absorbed into their husband's group. By their own report, many adopted daughters refused to visit their natal family, often because they hated their parents for having given them away. Nevertheless, minor marriages exhibit a divorce rate equal to that of uxorilocal marriages. I think the reason is that the sexual aversion aroused by the experience of childhood association was strong enough to overwhelm the structural barriers to divorce implicit in minor marriages. Many women preferred to leave their husband's family and risk having to support themselves as prostitutes rather than continue an emotionally intolerable relationship. Put in other words, my argument is that whereas uxorilocal marriages had a high divorce rate because they were structurally brittle, minor marriages had a high divorce rate despite their structural soundness, an anomaly explained by sexual aversion.

What happened to divorced women also depended, in large part, on the form of their first marriage. Whereas women married in the major fashion always left their husband's household at the time of the divorce, this was not invariably the case among women married in the minor fashion. One girl married her former husband's brother; two married uxorilocally; and three remained members of the family without remarrying. Because many of the women who left their husband's family after divorce moved to communities outside the area covered by the registers I have analyzed to date, their subsequent marital history is difficult to follow. So far I have managed to trace only 58 of 160 cases. This is a biased sample because the women I cannot trace include all those who moved to Taipei City, and this is where women probably would go if they could not remarry and were forced into prostitution or domestic service. Nonetheless, it is interesting that all the women I can trace did remarry within a short time. The mean interval between divorce and remarriage was only 12.9 months, suggesting that women did not precipitate a divorce unless they were reasonably certain of an opportunity to remarry.

The evidence for what happened to women who divorced an uxori-locally married husband is more complete. Not surprisingly, a large percentage of those who remarried (10 of 23, or 43.5 percent) married uxorilocally, probably for the same reason they had married this way the first time. The more interesting facts are that many of these women did not marry a second time, and that those who did remarry took their time. Out of 40 uxorilocally married women whose first marriages ended in divorce, 17 (42.5 percent) did not remarry, including 11 women who were less than twenty-five years old at the time of the divorce. And for those 23 women who did marry a second time, the mean interval between divorce and remarriage was 54 months. This could be because their parents insisted on an uxorilocal marriage and had difficulty finding a man willing to marry into the family of a divorced woman. But it could also reflect reluctance on the part of the woman. Whereas women who leave their husband's family lose their children and the right to claim support, women whose husbands leave retain their children and the right to claim property in their name. Perhaps they are less likely to remarry because they have less need to do so.

Aware of the many discrepancies between the elite model for female behavior and the lives actually led by women in Hai-shan, I expected to find that the great majority of women widowed before age thirty would remarry. In fact, the data presented in Table 12 say that many widows, including women widowed before twenty-five years of age, did not remarry. Moreover, a high percentage of those who did remarry married uxorilocally. Of 106 women widowed before thirty years of age, only 41 (38.7 percent) left their former husband's home.

Though the behavior of widows with regard to remarriage comes closer to the elite ideal than I had anticipated, their record should not be attributed to a desire to live up to that ideal. The elite ideal was that of a celibate widow, and widows in Hai-shan were definitely not celibate.

TABLE 12. Percent of Widows Who Remarried, by Age at
Husband's Death
(All women widowed 1906–40)

Age at husband's death	Number of women	Married uxorilocally	Married virilocally	Did not remarry
19 and under	16	12.5%	56.3%	31.3%
20–24	38	18.4	39.4	42.1
25–29	52	21.2	32.7	46.2
30–34	38	10.5	21.1	68.4
35–39	32	6.3	6.3	87.5
40–44	30	0.0	0.0	100.0

In fact, widows and divorcees who did not remarry bore almost as many children as those who did. My data include 76 widows who were less than thirty-five years old when their husbands died; 41 (53.9 percent) of these women bore at least one child after their husband's death, and 24 (31.6 percent) bore two or more children. The number of births to women who did not remarry per 100 births to women who did remarry are as follows:

Age of woman	Births	Age of woman	Births
15–19	—	30–34	60
20–24	79	35–39	43
25–29	68	40–41	38

There are at least two ways to explain the fact that many widows did not remarry but continued to bear children. The former husband's parents (or the woman's own parents in the case of an uxorilocal marriage) may have needed their daughter-in-law to raise their grandchildren and therefore insisted on an uxorilocal marriage or none at all. Since it was always difficult to find a man willing to marry into his wife's family, the more so when the wife was older and a widow, many widows could not remarry and instead entered into a series of casual sexual relationships. Alternatively, it could be argued that women who had borne children and established what Margery Wolf calls a "uterine family" were reluctant to remarry.[6] Their children gave them the right to a share of their husband's father's estate, and this in turn allowed them an independence normally denied to women. Had they married out of their husband's family, they would have lost both their children and their claim to family property. They therefore preferred informal to formal relationships and resisted marrying a second time.

Table 13 reports what I consider one of the most intriguing findings to emerge from the household registers. The table says that regardless of age, women in second marriages bore fewer children than women in first marriages. This could be because the less fertile women in the population were more likely to make second marriages. For example, women who had had a number of children may have been less interested in marrying a second time; or women with several children may have had greater difficulty finding a second husband; or infertile women may have been more likely to be divorced and available for second marriages. Another line of argument, relevant to the point raised in the last paragraph, is that women in second marriages were in a better position to limit their fertility than women in first marriages. Whereas a woman in her first marriage was dependent on her husband and his line of descent,

TABLE 13. COMPARATIVE FERTILITY OF FIRST AND SECOND MARRIAGES
(All women born 1881–1915)

Age of woman	2d marriage births per 100 1st marriage births			
	Major marriages	Minor marriages	Uxorilocal marriages	All 1st marriages
15–19	66	84	50	72
20–24	73	103	83	85
25–29	82	110	86	91
30–34	81	108	81	89
35–39	74	99	83	83
40–44	71	98	64	78

a woman marrying a second time often controlled property through her sons and could make her husband dependent on her. To explain the lower fertility of second marriages one need only assume that most women wanted fewer children than their husbands did, and there is evidence suggesting that this was the case. Asked why they generally weaned their daughters two months earlier than their sons, many of my informants told me that it was for the girl's own sake: "The earlier you wean a girl, the earlier she will pass through menopause and be done with the business of bearing children."

I began by promising to demonstrate that the lives of women in Hai-shan did not conform to the pattern recommended by elite ideals and assumed by most analyses of the Chinese family. That has now been accomplished. I will therefore conclude with what I see as the main implications of this finding. The first is simply that we must reassess the incidence of "deviant" biographies in other areas of China. Although Hai-shan is not representative of Taiwan let alone China, neither is it an island of exotic foliage in an otherwise homogeneous sea. The likelihood is that the pattern of women's lives varied widely from one area of the country to another and from one period of history to another within the same area. The phrase "women in China" should appear in quotation marks until we discover the core of experience that justifies the use of such a categorical term.

If this view of our subject is correct, or even nearly so, our primary task is to explain the variation we find, not because it is there, but because it offers us an opportunity to test our assumptions about the forces that shape women's lives. I have been able to show that the biographies of women in Hai-shan reflect the composition of the families in which they were raised, but I have had to take as givens the preference for the minor form of marriage and the belief that adoption encourages conception. What is needed is carefully controlled comparative studies that allow us to see the conditions that promoted female adoption and the widespread acceptance of beliefs that had a significant impact on the lives of women. I think we will find that one of these conditions is the extent to which decisions about marriage and adoption were left in the hands of women. My guess is that many institutions that were deviant from the elite point of view were female creations.

Women and Suicide in China

MARGERY WOLF

Chinese Attitudes Toward Suicide Among Women

The dramatic public suicides of young Chinese widows in the last century became almost as well known in the West as the Hindu custom of suttee. Although the Chinese custom was apparently neither as widespread nor as common as readers of newspaper fillers were led to believe, like suttee it made a strong statement about the status of women. In genteel Chinese society a young widow, particularly a childless young widow, could expect little from the future. After marriage, a woman was no longer the responsibility of her natal family, and the only improvement she could hope for in her lowly status within her husband's family was to become the mother of one of their descendants. With the death of her husband, that possibility ended. If she remarried, it could only be to a man of lower status (or, even worse, to one who already had a wife), and she might also have to contend with the ill will of either her natal or her marital family, depending on which had arranged the second marriage. Once she announced her intention to "follow" her late husband, she would in the short time left to her be honored by officials, admired, and pampered, and would die in the knowledge that her name would be commemorated as a chaste widow. For women raised in the tradition of the gentry, this alternative was probably more attractive than it might appear.

Suicide was also considered a proper response for gentry women whose honor had been tampered with, even accidentally. Ernest Alabaster relates two cases in which the women were posthumously awarded "tablets of honor."[1] In one, an elderly unmarried woman killed herself after discovering that a drunken man, mistaking her bed for that of a friend, had fallen asleep on it. In the other case, a woman took her own life because a thief had taken refuge under her sleeping couch. She was awarded a posthumous tablet for "the nobility of her mind."

For peasant women, these niceties of thinking and behavior were understandable, but not compelling. Suicide was for them, and still is for farm women, a socially acceptable solution to a variety of problems that offer no other solution. The knowledge that suicide was highly honored by the upper classes undoubtedly colors the attitude of modern farm women, but the frequency with which they encounter suicide in their own communities probably has more influence on their personal behavior. Suicide rates for adult women in some areas of Taiwan run as high as 25 deaths per year for every 100,000 people. Translated into rural terms this means that about every other year a community with a population of 2,500 women would expect a suicide or two. By the time a girl is old enough to marry, she probably has heard the details of a suicide in a friend's family or even been privy to the personal misery that led to a suicide. Among peasant women the act is not exotic. It is a part of their repertoire of threats, a conceivable course of action, and for some the pathetic finale of their existence.

A common outcome of "unsuccessful" suicide attempts in Western societies is a decided improvement in the life of the victim. Friends and relatives express concern, guilt, and anxious sympathy, and often with the help of a public agency attempt to help the victim reshape her life into a more tolerable pattern. But suicide has other meanings in China, meanings that may make life less rather than more tolerable for the survivor of a suicide attempt. Like so much Chinese behavior, suicide is not only an individual act, a gesture of personal despair, but also an act that implicates others. For a young person it is the ultimate rebellion in a society that requires respectful submission to the will of one's seniors, and for a woman it is the most damning public accusation she can make of her mother-in-law, her husband, or her son. In the West we ask of a suicide, "Why?" In China the question is more commonly "Who? Who drove her to this? Who is responsible?"* After the two suicides that occurred during our first trip to the northern Taiwanese site of our field research, village conversations centered on who caused the acts. One victim, a young woman who threw herself into the river, was driven to suicide by the unwanted attentions of a mainland soldier who threatened her family when she refused him. (Her young male relatives and their friends were plotting revenge even before her body was re-

---

* Under the Ch'ing this was a question of some legal significance: someone who caused another's suicide was subject to punishment, which varied with their relationship and the degree of culpability.

moved from the riverbank.) The other suicide was that of a middle-aged man who hanged himself. This man's first wife had also killed herself, thirteen years before (because, we were told, of her mother-in-law's cruelty), and the family had been in a decline ever since. Many people said it was the first wife's ghost who had caused the suicide, as well as the other misfortunes afflicting the family.

The severity of the problems a suicide can cause her family is suggested in the following quote from one of the life histories collected by Adele Fielde in southern China.

Two months later my sister-in-law hung herself, and in the disgrace and trouble that followed, I was left at my father's for some time. There was one woman in our village whose daughter-in-law hung herself, and when the mother-in-law came in and found her thus, she, fearing the demands that could be made upon her by the girl's parents, got another rope at once, and hanged herself beside her daughter-in-law. There could be then no exactions by the friends of either party, for each had harmed the other to the same degree.[2]

To bring such disgrace to one's husband's family and so much trouble to one's natal family would not be likely to alleviate a survivor's original wretchedness. Male representatives from her natal family must, for their own face, indignantly demand explanations and guarantees of better treatment from her parents-in-law, no matter how "inconvenient" bad relations with the in-laws might be. The girl must be taken home to recuperate (and probably to be berated for her hasty actions) and complicated negotiations must commence over her return, a journey her male relatives may be even more eager to arrange than her in-laws. By the time she returns, her husband's family has been humiliated by the negotiations, and by the gossip of curious neighbors; her mother-in-law has heard her treatment of her son's wife openly discussed by her women friends; and, worse yet, the older woman may discover her son (who considers her responsible for managing his wife) looking at her askance. The family, as individuals and as a group, will resent this adverse publicity and the continuing attention the slightest row in the family brings. They are unlikely to feel very charitable toward the young woman who has caused them so much trouble.

Fei Hsiao-t'ung, writing of customs in a village in the Yangtze Valley, says of suicide: "According to popular belief [a suicide] becomes a spirit and is able to revenge herself; furthermore her own parents and brothers will seek redress, sometimes even destroying part of her husband's house."[3] The motive of revenge often comes up in discussions of suicide, both in determining the responsibility for actual cases and in discussing the danger inherent in family disharmony. It is also not an uncommon threat by young women at their wits' end, a threat that gives pause to mothers-in-law. Revenge is not, however, confined to the structurally helpless young women. The physical and mental illness of a middle-aged woman who lived in a village near ours in Taiwan was attributed to the suicide of her brother-in-law, who vowed to return and avenge the ill treatment the woman had afforded his mother when they lived in a joint family. Elderly parents who kill themselves are not dependent on purely mystical means of revenge, for their act itself convicts their sons and daughters-in-law of the most immoral of crimes, unfilial behavior.

To the young woman who, in her misery, is brought to the contemplation of suicide as a means of escape, and who sees as the source of her misery oppression by familiar people whose authority over her is their only mark of superiority, revenge must be a strong motive for suicide. Death brings not only an end to suffering, but power, the means to punish her tormentors. M.F.C., an anonymous writer who displays in the following quote much understanding of Chinese women, enters for a moment into the mind of a young suicide:

She intends that her mother-in-law, or other offender, shall be brought to terms,—shall be made to repent keenly of her cruelty to her. She gloats upon thoughts of what a disturbance her death will create, pictures to herself the consternation that will fill all hearts, when they enter her room and find her dead,—the stern anger of her own father and brothers,—the settlement that will ensue,—the lawsuit her tormentor will be obliged to bear the heavy expenses of,—the grand funeral that will be exacted for the repose of her soul,— the probability that her mother-in-law or the whole family will be compelled to follow her coffin as mourners, and the opportunity her ghost will have of inflicting all imaginable evils! Yes, she who has always been despised will now be felt as a power for once,—and the deed is done,—she commits suicide.[4]

In this paper I do not test hypotheses or attempt to develop a theory of suicide, although I do succumb briefly to the temptation to generalize about international differences in the sex ratio of suicide and its relationship to domestic settings. I also make some fairly elementary assertions about the effect of the Chinese social system on men and women in the various roles and statuses it assigns them. Alex Inkeles cites Durkheim's classic study *Le Suicide* as an example of the difficulties sociologists can get into by ignoring (or disdaining) any theory of personality functioning.[5] Inkeles shows how a simple notion like psychic pain (a psychological parallel of physical pain) can be used to resolve discrepancies in Durkheim's theory without threatening its integrity as a sociological explanation. In some social systems the pressure on certain roles is sufficient to cause some incumbents of these roles to seek relief from that pain with suicide. For our purposes, I find this a satisfactory level of analysis. With only statistical data available to me (as opposed to individual case histories), I cannot analyze the reasons some women in stressful roles coped and others did not. Nor can I "prove" that the correlation I predict between high-stress roles and high suicide rates reflects a causal relationship. Moreover, although I have objective suicide statistics for one side of this prediction, my analysis of the other side is totally subjective, being based almost entirely on my own description of the life cycle of Chinese peasant women. And neither side allows for the manipulation that might point a causal arrow.

Since my interest in suicide is not theoretical (and, in fact, arose incidentally to my efforts to understand the dynamics of the Chinese family), I do not compare the material presented here with findings in other studies. The student of suicide will find in the Chinese material relationships that contradict Durkheim and more recent studies of suicide in Western societies; he will also find that with some reinterpretation of terms, Durkheim's theory of the relationship between social integration and suicide can be made to apply to at least some aspects of the Chinese case. The implications of the Chinese material for a general understanding of the motivation for suicide is better left to someone who walks less self-consciously in the garden of theory.

The best source of census material and suicide statistics for a Chinese population of any size is the compilations of the Japanese Colonial Administration in Taiwan. By 1905 the Japanese had established their authority over most areas of their newly acquired Chinese province. Along with their many economic and social research projects on the island, they set up the elaborate household registration system described elsewhere in this volume,* and began to collect and collate other statistics describing aspects of Chinese life and death. The published summaries of these statistics, plus the seven island-wide censuses taken by the Japanese between 1905 and 1940, provide us with more information about the Chinese of Taiwan than we have for any other Chinese province.[6] Although some cities and a few districts in other provinces occasionally kept records and might report the number of suicides that came to the authorities' attention in a particular year, that year is rarely also covered by census material. Without a reliable estimate of the population, no suicide rate can be calculated, and unless transformed

---

* See the preceding paper in this volume, by Arthur P. Wolf.

into a rate, the number of suicides in an area has little meaning. I report here only the data from Sidney Gamble's 1917 study in Peking and the 1928–30 statistics given by Lin-po for Shanghai, Hangchow, Peking, and Canton.[7] Since the most complete records are those for Taiwan, I have taken 1905 to 1945, the period covered by the Japanese registers, as the time base for this study. P. M. Yap's excellent study of suicide in Hong Kong falls outside this period, but since my choice of dates is fairly arbitrary anyway, I have cited it whenever it seemed particularly relevant.[8]

To put the Chinese material in some kind of international perspective, I have selected suicide statistics from those published by the World Health Organization (WHO) for the first half of this century.[9] I present them in the next section with some misgivings and blanket qualifications. The decision to classify a death as an accident, a suicide, a murder, or as due to "natural causes" may seem a relatively simple matter. It is not. In many cases the victim himself is unclear about what he hopes or expects will result from a potentially fatal act. In other cases the victim may have legal, economic, and emotional reasons for concealing the cause of his death. In still others the family may arrange to have the death certificate record an accidental death. Even if there has been no conscious manipulation of the facts by either the victim or the survivors, the user of the statistics still cannot be sure what he has (or has not). Very little attention, cross-culturally or even within a single country, has been given to standardizing the definition of suicide. An extreme example of the resulting confusion is mentioned by Jack Douglas in describing a major American city that had a very low yearly suicide rate: the coroner of the city classified as suicide only those cases in which a note was found with the body.[10]

I believe the suicide statistics for Taiwan to be unusually accurate for several reasons. In contrast to most countries, where the collection of statistics was begun at the whim of local officials, in Taiwan the Japanese Colonial Government devised and imposed a uniform system. Moreover, although all the works of man are subject to errors of carelessness, the suicide statistics for Taiwan were probably less subject to conscious manipulation by people who wished to conceal the cause of a relative's death; the pressures that well-placed citizens can bring to bear on their countrymen probably had little influence on the Japanese colonial administrators who categorized cause of death. And finally, internal evidence indicates the data are reliable. For example, changes over time in age-specific suicide rates for certain age groups are gradual and consistent with social changes; local differences in gross rates are

TABLE 1. INTERNATIONAL SUICIDE RATES BY SEX
(*Crude rates per 100,000*)

Date and category	Taiwan	U.S. (all races)	Germany	Japan	Spain	Ireland	Sweden	Italy
1905								
M	13.5	20.2	33.4	—	3.8	5.4	26.2	11.4
F	19.3	6.8	9.5	—	0.9	1.8	4.8	3.0
M/F ratio	0.7	3.0	3.5	—	4.2	3.0	5.5	3.8
1915								
M	19.1	24.3	22.7	24.2	9.5	4.9	24.8	12.8
F	19.1	7.6	10.7	13.9	3.2	1.3	6.4	4.4
M/F ratio	1.0	3.2	2.1	1.7	3.0	3.8	3.9	2.9
1925								
M	17.0	18.0	36.4	25.2	9.2	4.4	21.8	14.0
F	17.6	5.8	13.3	16.0	2.6	1.4	5.6	4.9
M/F ratio	1.0	3.1	2.7	1.6	3.5	3.1	3.9	2.9
1935								
M	20.5	21.7	39.7	25.1	7.4	5.1	24.9	11.5
F	16.4	6.8	16.2	15.8	2.0	1.0	6.4	4.1
M/F ratio	1.3	3.2	2.5	1.6	3.7	5.1	3.9	2.8

SOURCES: World Health Organization, *Rapport épidémiologique et démographique*, 9.4 (1956); Sotoku-fu, *Taiwan jinko dotai tokei*, 1906–42; Sotoku-fu, *Rinji Taiwan kokō chōsa*, 1905, 1915; Sotoku-fu, *Taiwan kokusei chōsa*, 1920, 1925, 1930, 1935.

associated with differences in ethnic origins. The extraordinary degree of consistency in the rates over nearly forty years, years in which the population nearly doubled, attests to the quality of the data.

International Comparisons

The most striking single fact about Chinese suicide that makes it so different from Western suicide is its relationship to gender. In contrast to every other country for which we have statistical data, Chinese women are as likely as men to kill themselves and in some time periods more likely. Table 1 shows crude suicide rates for eight countries as well as the male-female ratio of those rates.* Assuming whatever bias was built into a country's collection system affected both sexes equally, a comparison of ratios probably has more validity than a comparison of rates. But, without putting undue weight on numerical differences, it is noteworthy that whereas the rates for Taiwan males in all four time periods are neither particularly high nor particularly low, the rates for Taiwan females are always the highest. Clearly it is this fact, the extraor-

* Crude suicide rates are based on the total population which, of course, includes infants and children. I use them here because they are often all that is given for other countries. Obviously, rates based on age-specific populations are more informative, and I have used them whenever practicable.

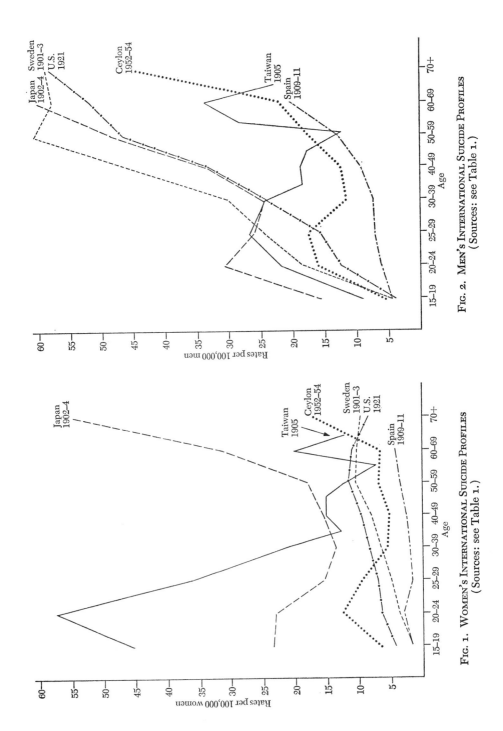

FIG. 1. WOMEN'S INTERNATIONAL SUICIDE PROFILES
(Sources: see Table 1.)

FIG. 2. MEN'S INTERNATIONAL SUICIDE PROFILES
(Sources: see Table 1.)

dinarily high rate at which Chinese women take their own lives, that controls the ratio. Only Japanese women (and in 1935, German women) rival the Chinese women's rate, but in Japan the higher male rates have more influence on the ratio.

There is another way of looking at the Chinese data in an international context without comparing possibly incomparable rates. Figures 1 and 2 show frequency distributions of age-specific suicide rates for five countries in the WHO sample and for Taiwan (based on the earliest years for which complete data were available for each country). Plotting the incidence of suicide in each age category gives us suicide profiles for each nation's men and women. It is the patterning of suicides by age—the profiles—rather than the rates to which I direct the reader's attention.

In the women's profiles there seems to be very little consistency. The three Asian countries—Japan, Ceylon, and Taiwan—show somewhat similar patterns among young women, but in the middle years the patterns diverge. The Swedish and American profiles are very different from the others but similar to each other until the final age group. (This apparent difference may reflect a methodological problem: the population in elderly categories is much reduced, and a chance error produces much greater discrepancies than it might in a younger, more populous age group.) The Spanish profile is nearly flat, indicating little variation with age.

The men's profiles show considerably less variation. Except for a sharp drop among sixty-year-old Swedish men, the three Western countries evince a steady increase in suicide with age. This male pattern appears in nearly all the European countries in the WHO sample, the major variation being in the steepness of the increase. Japan and Ceylon share the Western pattern except for a drop during the middle years. For this particular time period, the Taiwan sample is unique, resembling neither the other Asian nations nor the Western nations. Space limitations made it impossible to include changes over time in Figure 2, but a later table will demonstrate that by the end of the first half of this century Taiwan's male profile followed the Western pattern.

In summary, what Figures 1 and 2 seem to be telling us is that the patterns of suicide for women are complex and vary from one culture to the next, but the men's have greater and apparently increasing uniformity. On the face of it, these patterns seem irreconcilable with the usual stereotype of a monotonous similarity of women's lives in their domestic settings and the great opportunity for variation in the more public setting of men's lives. If, for the moment, we accept suicide as an index of psychic stress, it would seem that life starts out not badly for men, wherever they live, but its negative pressures increase with age. In some cultures the dissatisfactions of men's public lives in their middle years is countered by their increasing stature within their families. In others, the family is apparently no palliative for the strains of public life, and as age brings diminishing public rewards (or alternatives), the suicide rate increases. It may be that as technological changes weaken the economic and emotional power of the Asian family, this second pattern will exert a stronger influence on the suicide profiles of Asian males.

But what of the diverse and more complicated suicide profiles for women? Women have far fewer alternatives in life than men, and nearly all of them lead eventually to a domestic setting. Yet any anthropologist's library contains plentiful evidence of the variety of domestic arrangements found in the world. In some cultures the status "young married woman" is the happiest; in others it is the status of highest stress. In some cultures the age of childbearing is one of loneliness; in others this affliction most commonly strikes after the children are grown; in others, loneliness is a complaint of young and old alike. The reverse side of the coin that allows men in some cultures to turn to their families when public life proves disappointing also permits their total absorption in public life if their family life proves disagreeable. Women have *no* alternative to an unpleasant domestic situation. They must tolerate the people responsible for their distress, and they must endure their current status until the family cycle moves them into a more comfortable one. Those who cannot endure become cases in the national suicide profile.

The notion that international variation in domestic and individual life cycles accounts for the complexity of the women's suicide profiles is a testable hypothesis. Obviously the task is not appropriate to this paper, but the pages that follow might be viewed as a rather extravagant example of the kind of analysis necessary.

Chinese Comparisons

Unfortunately, Taiwan is the only province in China with reliable nonurban suicide statistics.* Some attempts were made to organize statistical bureaus on the mainland in the late 1920's and 1930's, but reports were so inconsistent that the material is unusable. Available records for urban areas are only slightly better, but I include them here in order to put the Taiwan findings in the context of the rest of China. In the

---

* Yap's study reports on suicide in the rural New Territories, but there are special problems there, which are more appropriately discussed under the section Rural-Urban Differences below.

TABLE 2. SUICIDE IN CHINESE CITIES
(*No. of female suicides per 100 male suicides*)

City	1917	1928	1929	1930	1954
Canton			121 (171)	105 (141)	
Hangchow		123 (185)	113 (175)		
Hong Kong					(74)
Kaohsiung				78 (87)	
Peking	35 (62)			95 (149)	
Shanghai			118 (159)	105 (141)	
Tainan				75 (82)	
Taipei				56 (60)	

SOURCES: Sidney D. Gamble, Peking: *A Social Survey* (Oxford, 1921); P. M. Yap. *Suicide in Hong Kong* (Hong Kong, 1958); Sotoku-fu, *Taiwan jinko dotai tokei* (Vital statistics of the population), 1926–32; Sotoku-fu, *Taiwan kokusei chōsa*, census of 1930; Lin-po, pseud., "Chung-kuo ssu ta tu shih tzu sha hsing pi wen t'i" (The sex ratio of suicides in four major Chinese cities), *Ch'ing hua chou k'an*, 38.1 (Oct. 1, 1932).
NOTE: Numbers in parentheses are ratios corrected for the unbalanced sex ratio indicated for each city.

essay from which the ratios in Table 2 for Canton, Hangchow, Shanghai, and Peking were taken, Lin-po comments on the inadequacy of his sources—government reports, police records, and newspaper accounts.[11] I stress this point because the ratios are quite extraordinary in a world that presumes male suicide to be at least twice as frequent as female suicide. Lin-po points out that if the imbalanced sex ratio of the urban populations is taken into consideration (there were, for example, 67 women for every 100 men in Hangchow in 1930), the ratio of female suicides would be even higher.[12] The figures in parentheses in Table 2 are estimates (based on ratios provided by the sources cited) of the appropriate correction. The most conservative statement to be made about the data in Table 2 is that they suggest that the Taiwan pattern by no means exaggerates the Chinese sex difference in proclivity for suicide.

Suicide and Age

Age-specific suicide rates for Chinese women in Taiwan are presented in Table 3 and in graph form in the next section (Fig. 3).* The very high rates with which young women took their own lives between 1905 and

* The rates were computed for an average of the suicides for the five years closest to each census date. Between 1905 and 1915 no census was taken so I took an average of the population in those two censuses as an estimate of the 1910 population. Unless otherwise indicated, all rates were developed in this way. In age-specific rates such as those in Table 3, the population figure is, of course, the number of people in the indicated age category. Japanese and other foreign residents are not included in any table.

TABLE 3. AGE-SPECIFIC SUICIDE RATES FOR WOMEN IN TAIWAN
(Rate per 100,000 women)

Age	1905	1910	1915	1920	1925	1930	1935	1940
15–19	45.4	42.6	40.7	39.2	35.1	30.5	32.0	21.1
20–24	57.4	57.8	50.8	47.8	39.5	38.8	36.4	28.7
25–29	36.1	39.2	38.5	36.4	28.6	26.3	26.4	21.4
30–34	21.4	27.9	25.8	30.4	23.0	20.5	19.2	14.1
35–39	12.9	17.3	20.5	20.6	21.8	15.2	17.7	11.7
40–44	15.0	17.8	20.5	17.8	19.0	16.2	20.0	17.5
45–49	15.1	13.1	18.7	25.5	17.6	20.0	22.2	18.1
50–54	12.3	14.9	15.7	15.2	23.0	21.8	23.3	19.6
55–59	6.4	15.2	20.3	18.0	24.0	26.3	22.1	23.6
60–64	20.0	19.2	20.4	23.6	30.9	29.4	32.9 ⎫	42.7
65+	12.1	14.4	25.4	33.4	33.3	42.7	49.5 ⎭	
Total (15 yrs. and over)	28.5	30.1	30.4	30.8	27.4	26.9	27.9	22.4

SOURCES: Sotoku-fu, *Taiwan jinko dotai tokei* (Vital statistics of the population), 1906–42; Sotoku-fu, *Rinji Taiwan kokō chōsa*, censuses of 1905, 1915; Sotoku-fu, *Taiwan kokusei chōsa*, censuses of 1920, 1925, 1930, 1935; Taiwan Provincial Government, Bureau of Accounting and Statistics, Results of the Seventh Population Census of Taiwan, 1940 (Taiwan, 1953).

1915 began to decline in the next two decades, and by 1940 had dropped to half the 1905 rate for ages 20–24, or 28.7 per 100,000 population. Even this rate would be considered shockingly high in many other countries. In the early decades of this century Chinese women between thirty-five and sixty were least likely to commit suicide, but by 1930 a new profile was established that retains high rates for young women, low rates between thirty and forty-five years, and a new rise in suicide for women over forty-five. Also in Table 3, notice that even though the total suicide rate for women is decreasing throughout our time period, the rate of suicide for older women steadily increases.

Before examining in the next section the domestic and economic changes that coincide with the shift in women's suicide profiles, I must make a brief but relevant digression. Since the Japanese statisticians did not report the marital status of suicide victims, and the largest single age category of suicides is between twenty and twenty-four years, we need some evidence on the probable marital status of women in this age group. The data in Table 4 do not tell us whether young suicides were married or single, but they do insist that most women in the highest sui-cide-risk category were married. The possibility remains that suicides were drawn entirely from the small percentage of unmarried women. If this were the case, it would mean a truly phenomenal rate of suicide among such women, a striking social fact that surely would have been remarked upon by both foreign and local observers. The model present-

TABLE 4. PROPORTIONS OF WOMEN EVER MARRIED, BY AGE, 1905–35

Age	1905	1915	1920	1925	1930	1935
15–19	47.3	34.7	32.8	29.4	32.6	28.1
20–24	91.6	87.4	86.6	84.4	86.3	83.0
25–29	98.2	96.6	96.9	96.2	96.1	95.9
30–34	99.2	98.5	98.5	98.3	98.0	97.7
35+	99.7	99.5	99.4	99.3	99.3	99.0

SOURCE: George W. Barclay, *Colonial Development and Population in Taiwan* (Princeton, N.J., 1954), Table 59. Reprinted by permission of Princeton University Press.

ed in the next section assumes the contrary, that most of the young women who killed themselves belonged to the population of the recently married.

The Setting for Suicide

Life is often particularly pleasant for a young woman in the year or two that precedes her marriage. Although peasant families cannot afford to pamper any of their female members, the mother of an about-to-be-married daughter usually tries to spare her the more arduous tasks, loading them instead onto her son's young wife, or even taking up the slack herself. This happy time, followed by the excitement of accumulating a dowry and a trousseau of new clothes and climaxed by the ritual of marriage, which focuses all eyes on "the new bride," must make the contrasting misery of her first years of married life all the harder to bear.

In the recent past, a bride entered the home that was to be hers for the rest of her days as a stranger. She may previously have met her mother-in-law, but rarely her husband, and probably none of the other family members. A farm family goes to considerable trouble and great expense to acquire a daughter-in-law, and the members of the household expect more from their bargain than any naive, ignorant young country girl can provide. The go-between exaggerates the girl's domestic competence (drudgery from which her mother spared her) in order to bring the future mother-in-law to a decision; her new sisters-in-law are resentful of her before she appears for the tightened budget her marriage has required of the family; her father-in-law is irritated at the stiff bargaining her family put him through; and her husband, who probably was in no hurry to marry anyway, solaced himself with fantasies of a delicately beautiful young woman, a type his mother who wanted a daughter-in-law capable of bearing numerous sons and of coping with heavy farmhouse work told the go-between not even to consider.

Within a few months the poor bride cannot help being painfully aware of the family's disappointment with her. Her mother-in-law has finally lost patience, no longer finding her desire to please sufficient compensation for culinary incompetence; her sisters-in-law resent her new clothes and mistake their mother-in-law's tolerance for favoritism, a mistake the bride may also make; and her husband, whom she sees alone only in the bedroom, where he forces unpleasant attentions on her after a trying day, is frequently well on the path to being her arch-enemy.

Perhaps most painful of all for the young woman is her sense of isolation, of emotional aloneness. It is considered bad form for her to visit her natal family often, and even her mother discourages frequent trips home. If she is seriously maltreated by her husband or his family, her father and brothers might intervene, but occasional slaps and frequent harsh words are too unexceptional to rate more than commiseration by her mother. Her closest and most important source of protection from her husband's family and solace in her most unbearable hours of loneliness is the group of women who live nearby but are not related to her husband's family. For her first few months in the village they treat her with the suspicion that is any stranger's portion, but in time, if she does not behave foolishly, she will find a friend or two among the older women who will listen to her problems and give her advice. The advice usually amounts to "Don't pay any attention to them," and "Hurry up and have a baby—then they can't treat you that way."

The marriage ritual, her mother-in-law, her mother, her women friends, and her own knowledge of her culture tell the young woman that until she has a child, preferably a male child, her life is not going to improve and may even get worse. If she never produces a son, it will get much worse. The pressures on a young woman to conceive are so intense it is amazing that sheer anxiety doesn't produce infertility.* Once she has produced a son, a woman has undeniable status in her husband's family as the mother of one of its descendants. Her mother-in-law is relieved to have the bride she chose for her son at last live up to her expectations, and her husband is pleased to have the status of father, a status that brings him full adulthood. Both are grateful to the young woman, although neither could or would say so openly. The new mother is relieved to have finally justified her existence, is more confident about her future (all Chinese women, even young women, seem to worry about who will support them in their old age), and most important of all, sees

---

* With immensely reduced infant mortality rates on Taiwan, the anxiety about producing children has lessened, but the first pregnancy is still a grave matter in the countryside.

her child as the beginning of a small personal circle of security in the midst of the alien world of her husband's family. I have elsewhere described in detail the ways in which a woman develops and ensures the loyalty of her uterine family, a task that occupies her totally for the next twenty years of her life.[18] The birth of her son signals, for the young mother, the end of a very unhappy period in her life, a period so painful that, as we saw in Table 3, many young women do not survive it.

What come next for a Chinese farm wife are satisfying if strenuous years. The insecure young bride gradually becomes the confident mother and competent housewife. Her mother-in-law turns over to her more

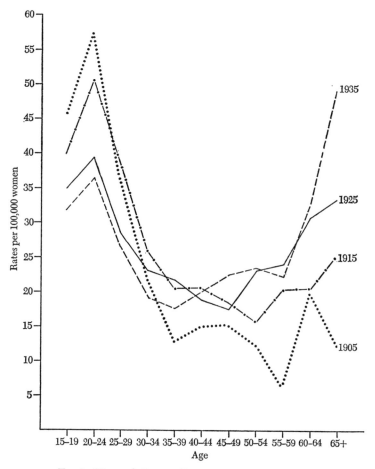

FIG. 3. WOMEN'S SUICIDE PROFILES, TAIWAN, 1905–35
(Sources: see Table 3.)

and more of the household responsibilities and, in time, authority. For many women these years are spent primarily in nuclear families, with their husbands' parents either living with other siblings or dead. The peacefulness of this phase of the life cycle is reflected in the suicide rates, which in 1905 and 1910 decline steadily until old age. The rise after sixty is probably more a function of the reduced population in that age category (see p. 122) and of the desire to escape from physical illnesses than it is of any social fact.

In 1915 and 1920, however, suicide in older women seems to increase and to include in the upsurge women in their late fifties (see Fig. 3). By 1925 a new suicide profile is obvious, and this profile holds till the end of our records. Suicide rates for young women remain high by any international standard, but are considerably lower than the first quarter of the century. Suicide rates for older women, women over forty-five, rise rather than decline as they did in the old profile. The increasing rate of suicide in older women is one of many social statistics reflecting critical changes in Taiwan in the 1920's and early 1930's. Improved transportation, new commercial enterprises, and generally expanding economic opportunities introduced by the Japanese Colonial Administration produced marked readjustments in the social system. The better education of the younger generations gave them real advantages over their illiterate seniors in finding jobs and exploiting economic opportunities. Young men were no longer dependent on land held by their fathers to feed their wives. They could rebel and some did, at least enough of them to make parents pay more attention to their sons' wishes.

Obviously, economic opportunities for women were still few, but the gust of fresh air in the family's authority structure had decided effects on the quality of young women's lives. As young men demanded and received more say in the selection of their wives, they also accepted more responsibility for their wives, to the point of defending them in conflicts with their parents. Faced with an obstinate son in possession of an income over which his father had no control, many parents found themselves sidestepping issues before they came to a head. For women this was a familiar technique in dealing with their sons, and since most mothers felt more strongly allied to their sons than to their husbands, older women did not feel particularly threatened by the young men's revolt against their father's authority. However, when a son's revolt grew out of a conflict between his mother and her daughter-in-law, when a mother saw the very center of her uterine family being drawn into her daughter-in-law's sphere of influence, tragedy threatened. A Chinese woman expects her middle years to be full of rewards for the long hard years that went before. She has a daughter-in-law to do the more onerous chores, and a son whose loyalty is assured by the years she spent cultivating it. If the son proves disloyal and in collusion with the daughter-in-law, the older woman finds herself not in the best years of her life but back in conflict, struggling this time not with her mother-in-law and her husband's family, but with a young woman whose potential for intimacy with her son was until now hers alone. In generations past an emotional tie between husband and wife came later in life, if at all, and was not expected in the young strangers who were married at their parents' convenience. A young wife who enters as her husband's choice has emotional and sexual advantages over her mother-in-law from the outset. When the apparently inevitable conflicts arise between mother-in-law and daughter-in-law and the son intervenes on his wife's behalf, the effect on the older woman is stunning. All the old anxieties about her physical welfare in her now near old age return. Even worse, all the years of struggle and sacrifice seem to be negated, lost to the wiles of an ignorant young woman. In despair over her powerlessness or in a fit of revengeful fury at her fickle son, the aging mother contemplates, threatens, and in some cases commits suicide.

To this point in my analysis I have ignored the alternative forms of marriage found on Taiwan, and the very different domestic climates they create. Arthur Wolf's paper in this volume shows that these "variants" accounted for more than half the marriages in northern Taiwan in the early part of this century, and at least a third as late as 1940. I will not develop here as detailed a picture of the settings these other marriage types create for women, both because I lack the space and because I think these settings contributed very little to the suicide statistics under discussion. Unfortunately, the Japanese did not categorize suicide victims by marital status, let alone form of marriage, so I cannot provide any satisfactory proof for my supposition. The most I can offer is a description of the different climates in families created by these other forms of marriage, climates which suggest that they do not create the same patterns of stress for women as the major form of marriage. If the psychic stress explanation of suicide has any validity, these alternative marriage forms are unlikely to be the source of significant numbers of suicides.

A young woman who makes a minor marriage enters her husband's family as a child, often as an infant. By the time she and her foster-brother marry, the young woman is at least as knowledgeable of the family's particular culture as her brother is. The traumatic severing of familiar, supportive relationships that marks the marriage of a woman who weds in the major form is absent in the minor marriage. Her mother becomes also her mother-in-law. The older woman has had a good many years to decide whether or not she wished to spend the rest of her days in the younger's company, and if there had been a major conflict of personality, the girl would have been married out. The primary adjustment for the bride lies in overcoming the incestuous feelings (or sexual revulsion) her new relationship with her foster-brother arouses. Serious as this problem may be, it is focused on that one relationship, and the other areas of the girl's life continue on much as they always have. The pervading stress of loneliness, of isolation, and of a generalized sense of threat from all sides that gives rise to suicide in the brides of major marriages is spared the girl who marries her foster-brother. Other miseries may have preceded her marriage (foster-daughters are frequently ill-treated as children), and she and her brother-husband may never achieve a sexual relationship sufficiently satisfactory to produce children, but the most dramatic result is likely to be divorce, not suicide.

What relation do minor marriages have to the second peak in the suicide profiles, that created by the suicides of mothers-in-law? My analysis of the domestic setting suggests that in minor marriages mothers-in-law are not likely candidates for suicide either. Whereas the mother-in-law in a major marriage watches with growing concern the increasing intimacy between her son and the stranger who is his wife, the mother-in-law in a minor marriage is more likely to have a closer relationship with her daughter-in-law and with her son than they have with each other. She enters her old age with her uterine family intact.

Young women who make uxorilocal marriages are also less likely to commit suicide than their sisters in major marriages. They may resent the inferior (by definition if not in fact) husbands chosen for them,* but their resentment is experienced while they still enjoy the security of their own families and the familiar setting of the villages in which they were raised. For their mothers, however, this form of marriage is a cause of anxiety. Having no sons (the usual reason for imposing an uxorilocal marriage on a daughter), they are dependent on their resentful daughters for the security of their old age. Coping with a son-in-law can be touchier than controlling a daughter-in-law. If the man is dealt with too harshly he may simply depart, leaving the family bereft. Even worse, he may seduce his wife into leaving with him. Older female suicides probably include a proportional share of women who arranged

---

* It is assumed that any man willing to "abandon his ancestors" and marry into his wife's family is morally flawed and probably inadequate in other ways as well.

uxorilocal marriages for their daughters that were either too successful or not successful at all.

Suicides can occur among women in all forms of marriage, as well as among that small group of women who never marry. An adopted daughter may prefer death to spending the rest of her life with a cruel foster-mother and a loutish brother-husband. A young woman in an uxorilocal marriage may find suicide the only solution when her loyalties are torn between a beloved husband who wants her to desert her parents and parents who wish to replace a disruptive son-in-law. Nonetheless, the category of women whose peaks of psychic stress coincide most closely with the suicide profile for Taiwanese women are those involved in the major form of marriage.

By Way of Contrast: Male Suicide

The quality of a woman's domestic relationships may determine whether or not she commits suicide, but though the domestic situation has some influence on a man's disposition toward suicide, it is less likely to be the single determining factor. A young man who finds his father's cool authority unpleasant and the emotional tug-of-war between his wife and his mother intolerable can respectably spend the majority of his time quite removed from the family, working diligently in the fields, spending his leisure hours with friends in such reputable occupations as practicing with the village band or attending agricultural association meetings. Men who work in factories or elsewhere for wages have a still wider range of activities open to them. And even the less respectable alternatives to home life—gambling and visits to tea houses and brothels —do not injure a man's reputation if they are not excessive.

Taiwanese villagers say that a young man becomes more responsible after the birth of his first child. As a father, he is fully adult, and as his own father ages and his family grows, his economic burdens become greater. The years pass, and the more expensive gratifications of flesh and spirit he found in the world outside are harder to come by, the other non-domestic activities less satisfying. If by his middle years a man has not found some pleasure in his family, particularly in a culture that places such high value on the family, life begins to seem bleak indeed. And for old men, whose alternatives to the domestic setting are almost as few as those of the young bride, family relationships become crucial to his well-being. Unlike their wives, old men have no residual tasks from their active years of value to an extended family. Again unlike their aged wives, they are dependent on sons who formally express respect for them and are obliged to treat them well but often have no real affection for them. The grimness of this supposedly golden age in the Chinese life cycle is reflected in the very high suicide rates of older men.

In Table 5 the differences in the suicide rates for adult men and adult women are not large, an unusual fact in itself, and reverse themselves over time. The suicide rate for adult women rose between 1905 and 1910, but stayed at about the same level for the next fifteen years, after which it began to decline. Adult male rates started uphill in 1905 and, except for 1925 and 1940, increased steadily. Female suicide rates were either higher than men's or about the same until 1930, after which the rise of men's rates and the decline of women's reversed their relationship. We have seen in the last section how the suicide profiles for women changed during the 35-year span of this study, and the data in Table 3 show us that the decrease in the total suicide rate of women is primarily the result of a pronounced decrease in the rate at which *young* women killed themselves. The age-specific suicide rates for men in Table 6 show a different pattern. Setting aside the 1905 data for a moment, the suicide rates of men under thirty-five fluctuate from year to year but

TABLE 5. ADULT MALE AND FEMALE SUICIDE RATES
(*Rates per 100,000 of each sex over 15 years of age*)

Sex	1905	1910	1915	1920	1925	1930	1935	1940
Male	20.9	25.8	29.9	31.0	26.6	30.8	35.6	33.5
Female	28.5	30.1	30.4	30.8	27.4	26.9	27.9	22.4

SOURCES: See Table 3.

TABLE 6. AGE-SPECIFIC SUICIDE RATES FOR MEN IN TAIWAN
(*Rates per 100,000 men*)

Age	1905	1910	1915	1920	1925	1930	1935	1940
15–19	9.3	11.7	13.3	12.3	11.0	11.1	16.3	10.8
20–24	21.6	27.0	28.1	26.7	23.9	31.5	31.9	26.8
25–29	27.0	27.3	35.6	33.4	23.8	27.5	33.1	27.4
30–34	24.3	27.7	30.2	37.5	30.3	29.5	32.5	33.8
35–39	18.8	26.0	33.3	34.8	33.5	30.2	36.6	31.4
40–44	18.9	30.9	28.7	32.5	27.6	35.3	33.2	37.4
45–49	17.8	25.7	36.1	35.1	34.9	35.4	42.7	41.6
50–54	12.4	28.0	33.2	47.0	30.1	44.5	44.8	50.7
55–59	28.5	38.6	34.6	36.5	33.5	47.0	57.6	58.0
60–64	34.0	41.1	46.0	44.5	50.8	51.8	61.2⎤	76.7
65+	23.0	33.7	52.7	48.2	53.7	78.0	85.7⎦	
Total (15 yrs. and over)	20.9	25.8	29.9	31.0	26.6	30.8	35.6	33.5

SOURCES: See Table 3.

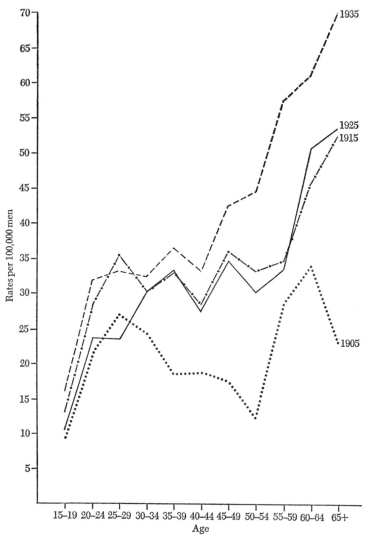

FIG. 4. MEN'S SUICIDE PROFILES, TAIWAN, 1905–35
(Sources: see Table 6.)

remain essentially on the same level over the period of the study. For older men, however, the rates increase more or less steadily with each time period. Thus it is the increase in suicide among older men, unaccompanied by a decrease in younger men's suicide rates, that accounts for the higher total rates over the years.

Since the focus of this essay is on women, I cannot examine here the non-domestic influences on men's lives that make them more or less prone to suicidal acts. It is intriguing, however, that young men, those most directly affected by the loosening of the authority structure in the family in the 1920's, show virtually no effect from this change in their suicide profiles. I would have expected a substantial drop, but apparently the non-domestic pressures on this age group were sufficient to maintain male suicide at a steady rate. The rates of older men both before and after this period of social change seem more sensitive to their relations within the family. The 1905 profile (see Fig. 4) shows a trough in the middle years, perhaps indicating the same satisfaction women have in their growing families and gradually increasing status at home. The profiles for later years reflect the increasing emptiness in the lives of the older men, who found their last solace, their position as master of the household, eroded by their own sons (and wives).

In interpreting men's suicide profiles it is also fruitful to consider men's relations not with the patrilineal family, but with the uterine families of their wives and mothers. Mothers forge uterine families for their own welfare, but their sons, the nuclei of these units, benefit greatly from their existence. When a son runs afoul of his father and the patrilineal family, he has the private family of his mother to turn to for succor and support. Even after a son marries, he can depend on his mother for encouragement, advice, and "loans" from her private savings. However, as men get older and the knocks from the world sharper, more and more of them find that the uterine families on which they depended evaporated with the deaths of their mothers (sisters come home to visit less frequently and the often frayed relations with brothers may finally be severed completely). If in search of human warmth a man then turns to the uterine family formed by his wife and their own children, he may be welcomed by the politeness reserved for high-status strangers. Finally, in old age, a man may find himself as isolated as any new bride, perhaps even more frustratingly because the isolation occurs in the midst of familiars and from the perspective of high (if token) status.

District Variation in Women's Suicide Rates

The data in Table 7 show a good deal of variation in suicide rates for different districts in Taiwan. All the districts follow to some extent the general decrease in suicides for the 35-year time span, but most also maintain a distinctive pattern. Tainan, for example, from 1905 to 1940 is nearly always higher than other districts and—putting aside for a

TABLE 7. WOMEN'S SUICIDE RATES BY DISTRICT
(*Crude rates per 100,000*)

District	1905	1915	1920	1925	1930	1935	1940
Populated areas							
Taipei	16.8	16.0	17.3	13.8	14.1	18.9	13.0
Hsinchu	12.3	15.2	12.1	14.5	15.4	14.1	10.2
Taichung	16.2	17.3	19.0	16.8	15.6	16.5	13.2
Tainan	28.3	25.8	27.8	24.0	21.2	18.4	15.7
Kaohsiung	14.3	20.0	20.8	17.3	13.3	13.4	10.5
Frontier areas							
Taitung	12.6	1.2	9.6	5.3	5.3	9.7	8.8
Hwalien	—	5.2	13.3	9.3	7.6	9.0	9.1
Penghu	44.5	16.5	—	—	19.3	16.6	8.4

SOURCES: See Table 3.

moment the special situations in Taitung, Hwalien, and Penghu—Hsinchu is usually, but not always, the lowest. Taitung, Hwalien, and Penghu are separated from the other districts because their sparse population makes a single suicide loom large statistically, and because Taitung and Hwalien were at least 50 percent aborigine. The aborigine population is categorically excluded from the suicide statistics, but the likelihood of sinicized aborigine wives of Chinese men appearing in census statistics seems high. More important, the frontier conditions in these two areas and the impossibility of accurate record-keeping under such conditions must have had considerable influence on the striking lowness of the reported suicide rates.

No single factor can account for the propensity of one district, such as Tainan, to produce high suicide rates while a neighboring district does not. I know that the rural people of the Taipei Basin consider Tainan an old, socially conservative, tradition-bound place, but how closely this picture resembles any reality, past or present, I cannot tell. If the stereotype has truth to it, conservatism might help explain Tainan's unusually high suicide rates. Young women would probably be more strictly controlled by their mothers-in-law, have fewer tolerable alternatives to the indignities of traditional marriage, and less opportunity to lighten the isolation of their early years of marriage with friendships outside the family. Moreover, women who deviated from the traditional ways would be more sharply condemned.

But what of the districts with consistently low female suicide rates? Hsinchu is the lowest or next to lowest in all but one time period in our sample, excluding the three isolated districts. It also has the highest

TABLE 8. COMPARISON OF WOMEN'S SUICIDE RATES AND
PROPORTION OF HAKKA IN POPULATION
(*Ranked; 5 is high*)

Date and category	Taipei	Hsinchu	Taichung	Tainan	Kaohsiung
1905					
Suicide rate	4	1	3	5	2
Proportion Hakka	1.5	5	3	1.5	4
1925					
Suicide rate	1	2	3	5	4
Proportion Hakka	1	5	3	2	4
1940					
Suicide rate	3	1	4	5	2
Proportion Hakka	2	5	3	1	4

SOURCES: See Table 3.

concentration of Hakka-speaking residents of any district on Taiwan. To illustrate the influence of Hakka population on suicide rates, Table 8 shows the rankings of the five major districts for suicide and for the percentage of Hakka in the population. In 1905 the rankings are in near perfect accordance, in 1925 they disagree considerably, and in 1940 they are very close to perfect agreement. The higher the proportion of Hakka, the lower the suicide rate. Between 1905 and 1930, the Japanese statisticians provided an ethnic breakdown of suicides, and Table 9 shows us the reason for the influence of the Hakka population on the rates: for some time periods Hakka, men and women, commit suicide at about half the rate of their Hokkien-speaking neighbors.

Unfortunately, not enough material is available on the Hakka family in Taiwan to compare the women's life cycles with those of the Hokkien-speaking women I am familiar with. Turning again to stereotypes, Hokkien speakers and their ethnographers characterize Hakka women as strong, domineering, and of independent mind.* Although the stereotype may derive from the particular personalities Hokkien speakers have happened to encounter, any reality in the stereotype may be based on the different status Hakka women occupy in their husbands' families from the outset. The Hokkien bride comes to marriage with a dowry as large and expensive as her peasant father can provide; the Hakka bride arrives with both a dowry and a sizable amount of money that will remain under her control. Moreover, important parts of the Hakka wedding ritual include the presentation of money to the bride in exchange for tea and obeisances. The amount of money a bride receives is her own secret,

---

* Certainly the picture of Hakka women in the New Territories given later in this volume by Elizabeth Johnson is not far from the Hokkien stereotype.

TABLE 9. HAKKA AND HOKKIEN SUICIDE RATES
(*Crude rates per 100,000 of each sex*)

Year	Women		Men	
	Hokkien	Hakka	Hokkien	Hakka
1905	21.5	6.5	14.4	4.7
1915	20.8	12.0	20.7	11.0
1920	21.8	10.7	21.3	12.4
1925	18.9	12.9	18.3	10.8
1930	17.7	11.8	19.1	13.3

SOURCES: See Table 3.

and it would be in bad taste for her husband to even ask about the total. Although Hokkien women also have a private fund of money from similar sources, it is not likely among peasant women to survive the needs of the first year of marriage. Myron Cohen conceives of this money in Hakka society as *fang* money, the property of the new conjugal unit, but from his own description I think it might more accurately be described as money belonging to the woman's uterine family.[14] A widow who remarries takes the total amount with her, and Cohen describes the case of a young husband who is allowed to keep his deceased wife's private money *in trust* for her children. I would think that the sense of isolation and helplessness that dominates the first few years of many Hokkien women's married lives would be considerably alleviated by the presence of this secret money. It could serve both as the symbol of the uterine family she hopes to create as a bulwark against future insecurity and as a source of more immediate gratifications, from bus fare home when *she* wants it, to the ability to lend money to a friend at a crucial moment.

Another way of looking at the low suicide rates for Hakka, one that sheds some light on the equally low male rates, focuses on the equivocal status of the Hakka in Chinese society. Many students of suicide have observed that populations who feel themselves under attack, socially or physically, have lower suicide rates than their less threatened neighbors. Most examples are of religious groups—Orthodox Jewish communities in eastern Europe, Catholic counties in Protestant countries, and the predominantly Mormon states of Utah and Idaho. The suicide rates for these groups go up as they become more integrated with their neighbors. Religious teachings barring suicide naturally must affect the rates, but there are other beleaguered groups with low suicide rates who do not share any dogma addressing itself to suicide. Nations under attack in war have lower suicide rates; suicide was surprisingly rare among concentration camp internees (although many of those in World War II did share a religious orientation); and the Eta, a traditional outcast group in Japan, have slightly over half the suicide rate of their urban neighbors and one-third the rate of their rural neighbors. Perhaps the Hakka, too, as a large, self-conscious minority in Taiwan, benefit from the immunity to suicide of externally threatened groups.

Rural-Urban Differences in Suicide Rates

As one might expect from the way in which Chinese suicide rates differ from Western suicide patterns, the rural-urban differences in suicide also differ. In the West, suicide is more frequent in cities and rarer in the countryside, with a good deal of diversity among medium-sized towns. In Taiwan, the opposite is true. Rates are generally higher in the countryside and lower in the cities, although smaller and newly designated cities follow the Western pattern in their inconsistency. Omitting, for clarity, these smaller cities (Keelung, Changhua, and Chiayi), we see in Table 10 that in 1930, in four out of the five districts, rates for rural areas were higher than urban rates. In 1935 the balance shifts, with three out of five districts having higher urban rates, but in 1940 three out of five districts have higher rates in the rural areas.

Hsinchu is the one district in which in all three time periods the urban rates significantly exceed the rural rates. This apparent peculiarity is an intriguing example of the influence of ethnic differences on suicide. The city of Hsinchu is populated predominantly by Hokkien speakers, and it is surrounded by the largest concentration of Hakka speakers on Taiwan. The suicide rates for the three time periods suggest that the urban concentration of Hokkien speakers was not always as strong as it is now and was in 1940. Although there were marked rural-urban differences

TABLE 10. RURAL-URBAN SUICIDE RATES
(*Crude rates per 100,000*)

Area	1930	1935	1940
Taipei rural	21.0	19.7	17.0
Taipei city	10.8	21.2	17.8
Hsinchu rural	16.6	15.4	10.3
Hsinchu city	19.6	25.5	28.1
Taichung rural	15.6	17.2	15.1
Taichung city	13.2	16.4	13.7
Tainan rural	20.6	20.9	18.6
Tainan city	18.5	20.0	15.4
Kaohsiung rural	15.1	16.2	14.3
Kaohsiung city	11.1	19.7	8.4

SOURCES: See Table 3.

in the 1930 suicide rate in Hsinchu, the differences were less striking than they later became.

The only other area of China for which we can compare rural and urban suicide rates is Hong Kong. According to P. M. Yap, Hong Kong Island and Kowloon, both urban areas, had suicide rates of 14.8 and 16.3 per 100,000 population, respectively, and the New Territories, the rural area, had a rate of 8.7—the reverse of the Taiwan pattern.[15] Hong Kong, of course, is a very unusual population in a very unusual setting, but whether this accounts for its Western pattern of suicide is difficult to say. Aside from its somewhat cosmopolitan attitude, the population also has a strongly urban bias, with 1,950,000 people living in Hong Kong and Kowloon (at the time of Yap's study), and only 300,000 in the New Territories. Just how similar the large rural Hakka population of the New Territories is to the Hakka in Taiwan, at least with regard to its low propensity for suicide, is impossible to determine from Yap's material.

High urban suicide rates in Western countries are attributed to the isolation and anonymity of city life, the disintegration of family life, and a laxness of social controls. We could also use those terms to describe life in a Taiwanese city, but we would be speaking from an entirely different definition of what is normal. The laxness of social control in an urban environment that causes Westerners to become "disoriented" enables a Chinese to experience a sense of liberation, to know that if he commits one or two acts of poor judgment, he will not bear them for the rest of his life as part of his social identity—as he would have to in a village. The disintegration of family life that has such negative effects on Westerners means for a Chinese woman that she begins married life in a nuclear family without a domineering mother-in-law or suspicious sister-in-law, and in some form of partnership with her husband. The patterns of urban migration are different in China as well. Unless driven by a sudden disaster, most Chinese who migrate to cities go to neighborhoods in which they have at least one relative, and look for work in industries and businesses to which a relative or friend can recommend them. Starting, then, from different places on a scale measuring society's control over a person's behavior, it seems quite reasonable that the urban setting carries quite different meanings for Western and Chinese populations, and these meanings seem to be reflected in their suicide rates.

Attempted Suicide

The Japanese Colonial Administration either decided not to record statistics on attempted suicide or decided not to publish them. Attempt-

ed suicide is even more susceptible to concealment than suicide, and
the Japanese government may reasonably have concluded that such
statistics would not be worth the trouble. Were such records available,
I would expect to find low rates of attempted suicide among the Chinese
population, at least in the early periods, as compared with Western
populations. Students of Western suicide now seem agreed that suicide
and attempted suicide are acts with different meanings and, in general,
different motivations. Some would-be suicides approach the act with
near indifference to the outcome, presuming life could not get, or death
be, any worse. Others are making a desperate appeal for help. Still others
take the risk as a way of threatening persons who are important to them.
Young women in traditional China must have been keenly aware of the
unpleasant lot awaiting a girl who survived a suicide attempt. As an
appeal for help it was useless, and few would consider it a gamble having
as one possible outcome an improved domestic situation. As retaliation
against oppressors, an unsuccessful suicide attempt had limited value
and might make the survivor regret her halfway measures. If a young
woman wished to exact revenge, she had to forfeit her life. There was
little to be gained from suicide attempts in China, as catharses or as in-
strumental acts.

Another line of reasoning that makes me think rates of attempted
suicide would be lower among women in Taiwan than in the West is
fairly straightforward. All serious accidents and illnesses whether self-
induced or not were more likely to be fatal in rural areas, with their
minimal health standards. And for reasons both economic and moral,
Chinese families were loathe to seek medical attention for women, the
group in Western societies most prone to attempted suicide, thus further
depressing the attempted suicide rate and increasing the completed suicide rate. I was led to this grim thought while trying to reconcile the
flatness of the suicide profile P. M. Yap gives for women in Hong Kong.[16]
The Hong Kong women's profile for attempted suicide reveals a gradient
as sharp as that found in the completed suicide profiles in Taiwan. Compare the graph drawn from the Hong Kong data in Figure 5 with those
in Figure 3. Perhaps one factor that makes Hong Kong suicide statistics
so different from those in Taiwan is the presence of medical facilities and
the consequent greater likelihood that the young would-be suicide will
survive. The 1917 suicide statistics from Peking unfortunately do not
give age-specific rates for completed suicide, only for the combination
of completed and attempted suicide.[17] However, the resulting profile
(see Fig. 5) is very similar to the 1905 and 1910 profiles for Taiwan.
Thus it may well be that if health and medical facilities were held con-

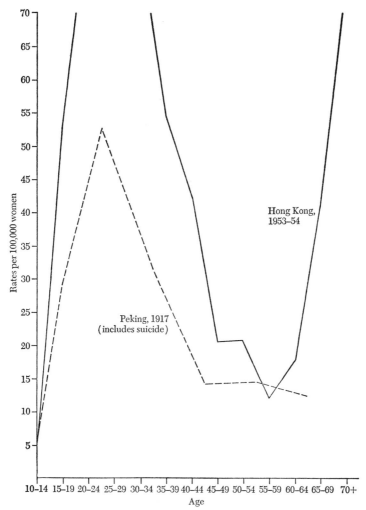

FIG. 5. ATTEMPTED SUICIDE IN HONG KONG (1953–54) AND PEKING (1917)
(Sources: P. M. Yap, *Suicide in Hong Kong*, Hong Kong, 1958;
Sidney D. Gamble, *Peking: A Social Survey*, Oxford, 1921.)

stant, the female suicide profiles for both Hong Kong in 1953 and Peking
in 1917 would resemble the Taiwan profiles.

Conclusions

This paper has not addressed itself particularly to sociologists or others
whose primary research interest is suicide. But as is so often the case

when Chinese, or for that matter Asian, data are introduced into an established Western field of inquiry, presumptions about the range of normal behavior have to be modified. The Chinese, equally convinced of the normality of their behavior, occasionally occupy parts of the scale never used in Western cultures and hence never considered by Western social scientists. In this very general sense, the more often Chinese or other Asian data can be introduced into social science, the more valid will be our understanding of what being human means. More specifically, in regard to suicide, the Chinese data refute Western research that says men are always more likely than women to commit suicide, and old people more likely than young; and the Chinese data suggest that urban life has very different meanings in different cultures. And then as further commentary on cultural variation, we find in the Chinese data two ethnic groups, Hokkien speakers and Hakka speakers, living cheek by jowl, engaged in the same occupations and with the same general range of social and economic classes, yet committing suicide at quite different rates.

The larger institutions of China, often so exotically different from those in Western societies, have occupied an inordinate amount of research energy to the neglect of the fundamental, if homely, domestic unit that is basic to them all. The number of pages devoted to the Chinese family as a political and ritual system is enormous when compared with the number devoted to the more mundane functions of the family, those functions dependent on women. Since it is within the fundamental unit that most if not all human beings learn to interact with their fellows, and this learning begins and in many cases is completed under the direction of the female half of the population, any source of insight into the operation of the family or the motives of its women is important. In the Chinese case, and, I suspect, in other cultures as well, the correlations between women's age-specific suicide rates, their life cycle, and the family cycle can tell us a great deal about the dynamics of the family as the primary unit of society.

In this paper I have presented a rather grim and at times unsympathetic view of the Chinese family. From the perspective of many young women and to a lesser extent their elders as well, the traditional Chinese family was indeed a grim setting for life and, as we have seen, for death. In many families women lived in harmony with their mothers-in-law, and husbands and wives established relations of mutual respect and honesty. Unfortunately, these families hold down one end of a scale firmly balanced on the opposite end by the families that furnish the statistics with which we have been dealing. Arthur Smith, that astute if often acid commentator on Chinese peasant society in the last century, sums up rather well when he says,

One of the weakest parts of the Chinese social fabric is the insecurity of the life and happiness of woman, but no structure is stronger than its weakest part, and Chinese society is no exception to this law. Every year thousands upon thousands of Chinese wives commit suicide, tens of thousands of other persons are thereby involved in serious trouble, hundreds of thousands of yet others are dragged in as co-partners in the difficulty, and millions of dollars are expended in extravagant funerals and ruinous lawsuits. And all this is the outcome of the Confucian theory that a wife has no rights which a husband is bound to respect. The law affords her no protection while she lives, and such justice as she is able with difficulty to exact is strictly a post mortem concession.[18]

Women as Writers in the 1920's and 1930's

YI-TSI FEUERWERKER

A New Generation of Women Writers

In the Preface to the collection of her short stories and essays published in 1954, Ping Hsin self-deprecatingly describes the new literature written after the May Fourth Movement in the following terms:

> I began writing at the time of the May Fourth Movement; . . . Chinese society was then plunged into darkness. My first stories, therefore, described and revealed the dark side of society, but I could see nothing but the darkness, without finding any source of light because I had not the courage to seek the light. . . . I was cut off from the people, my life was empty, and so the things I wrote kept getting poorer, emptier, and more forced, until I could write no longer.
>
> The reason for publishing a selection of these poor and empty things, however, is this: the current of the new literature after the May Fourth Movement followed a stage-by-stage course, which leads to the gate of socialist realism like a gradient staircase. If we are to see the whole of this development we must not dig up and throw away even the lowest and most crooked stone of this staircase. That is the reason why this collection is being published.[1]

Without agreeing on the reasons, many critics would concur that the literary achievement of the two decades following the May Fourth Movement is indeed something to be modest about. Yet even if the stage-by-stage course that led so inevitably and triumphantly to the gate of socialist realism is not to be applauded on purely literary grounds (supposing they were indeed possible to define), those "low and crooked stones" nevertheless represented momentous first steps toward a new direction for Chinese literature.

Perhaps we need to suspend temporarily the kind of criticism that would evaluate these literary products as autonomous, detached entities according to some transcendent esthetic standard: their interest lies precisely in their being so completely symptoms of a particular historical moment. It was a moment characterized above all by a state of continual upheaval, a moment when revolution was simultaneously political, social, and literary. Buffeted about on great tidal movements, writers had somehow to find their bearings, chart and record their experience—grappling all the while with formal and linguistic tools not yet fully mastered. It may well have been a period in which there was only the possibility of incomplete success, if not total failure. When the writer was also a woman, the literary enterprise was even more precarious. To write was to respond not only to a world in flux but also, in the wake of change, to a new and painfully evolving awareness of herself as a woman. Furthermore, to assume the role of writer she had the additional burden of finding an entering wedge that would allow her to make her way into an area of activity from which hitherto she had been largely excluded.

During the cultural self-questioning that marked the May Fourth Movement, the woman question (*fu nü wen-t'i*), together with literary reform or revolution, was recognized from the outset as one of the most urgent problems on the agenda. The subjugation of women had assumed such flagrant institutional forms—foot-binding, concubinage, female infanticide, the chastity cult—that women's liberation, initially understood as the elimination of these institutions, seemed an obvious, elementary matter. The experiences and writings of women authors, however, tell a more complex and difficult story, and show how pervasive and subtle were the effects of subjugation. With the bonds of literary tradition broken and women endeavoring to speak for themselves to their own condition, the true nature of some of the social and psychological pressures women had labored under began to emerge.

This paper examines the writings of the few women who, during the decade and a half after the May Fourth Movement, through a body of work established themselves as representatives of their generation. It was their fate, and perhaps also their opportunity, caught as they were in simultaneous literary, political, social, and feminist revolutions, to assume the task of transmuting unprecedented experiences and new self-awareness into untried art. Rather than considering them individually as writers who happened to be women, I shall be examining common characteristics and difficulties they shared as women who explored and articulated their identity through the act of writing. A 1931 book titled *Contemporary Women Writers in China*,[2] itself indicative of a degree of group self-consciousness, laments in its Preface that there are very few women writers and even fewer good ones. My samples, limited to writers of fiction, will not be very generous, but they will cover the preponderance of what there is.

The importance of the generation factor has been pointed out by students of modern Chinese intellectual history.[3] In analyzing writers confronted with new realities, the moment when their generation came of age is a key to the understanding of their literary preoccupations. All writers of the post–May Fourth period, regardless of sex, were from the beginning obsessed with their first, youthful responses to experience, but unlike some of their male counterparts, the women writers—with the major exception of Ting Ling—were unable to move on to a broader vision of reality. Most of our women writers began their careers early. The following list gives the years in which the women writers to be discussed reached the age of twenty-five, and the year their first *books* were published.* Individual stories by these authors had been appearing for some time in periodicals; thus the publication of a collection of stories in book form implied that by that early age, not a few of these women could already claim to be established writers. The pen names by which they were best known are used in the tabulation below and throughout this essay. In some cases the dates are approximate, because our sources conflict.

Name	Year reached 25	Year of 1st book	Name	Year reached 25	Year of 1st book
Ting Ling	1931	1928	Lu Yin	1923	1925
Su Hsüeh-lin	1922	1928	Ling Shu-hua	?	1928
Hsieh Ping-ying	1928	1928	Feng Yüan-chün	1927	1926
Ping Hsin	1927	1923			

When Western scholars, having been matured and aged by the expenditure of over one-third of their lives in learning the Chinese language and mastering their intellectual disciplines, feel finally prepared to assess modern China's cataclysmic history with some authority, they are in many cases taken aback by the relative youth of the Chinese who had such a serious impact on their time. The creation of a new literature was thrust upon a generation of writers who were in their early and impressionable twenties deep in a period of political and social upheaval. Their baptism by fire included experiences of hope, idealism, conflict,

---

* In his *Culture and Society, 1780–1950* (New York, 1958), Raymond Williams includes a table giving the date at which the writers he mentions were twenty-five (pp. vii–viii), and discusses the importance of the artist's age in relation to his experience of a "qualitative change in society" (p. 31). I have not been able to find any reference to Ling Shu-hua's birth date, even an "unreliable" one.

dislocation, and suffering. No thinking person escaped. Every public event was deeply felt as a personal, internal experience. How necessary, or from another point of view how debilitating, was the factor of their youth? In times of change, youth is a double-edged quality. The young were in the vanguard of the cultural generational shift that occurred during the May Fourth period, for both the belief that the past had to be overcome if not obliterated and an openness to experimentation in life and writing were prerogatives of youth. On the other hand, the confrontation with newly emerging realities combined with the young person's struggle for self-discovery may have been too engulfing an experience during that unique time to be easily outgrown. The situation of women seeking self-affirmation in a masculine world may be in some ways analogous to that of youth striving for adult identity; for those post–May Fourth writers who were both young and female, the effort to assimilate experience was so intense and problematic it seems to have absorbed almost all their creative energies. The only major literary themes for some women writers throughout their writing careers remained themselves when young, themselves as female, and the acute relationship to past and present entailed in this double predicament. In the following pages I shall first discuss briefly women in traditional Chinese literature as the past that had to be rebelled against, then describe the post–May Fourth inclination to explore contemporary reality through fiction, and, finally, examine women's writings both as acts of self-affirmation and as purveyors of new images of women's condition.

Women in Traditional Chinese Literature

While discussing in *A Room of One's Own* the obstacles confronting early-nineteenth-century English women novelists, Virginia Woolf singles out one difficulty as an even greater deterrent than "discouragement and criticism," namely that "when they came to set their thoughts on paper . . . they had no tradition behind them."[4] She was referring specifically to prose style and literary forms "unsuited for a woman's use" because they were "made by men out of their needs for their own uses." The aspiring woman writer in China suffered not only from the absence of a tradition for her, but from the presence of a tradition heavily loaded against her, a tradition that kept her in her place by perpetuating particular modes of thinking and feeling about women. Many of the positive images of women in traditional literature—beginning with the two Han works *Lieh-nü chuan* (Biographies of model women) and *Nü chieh* (Exhortations for women) and continued in their numerous imitators —were wise mothers, virtuous wives, or chaste widows extolled mainly for their support of men and their fidelity toward them. In forging new self-conceptions, the modern woman had to reject these models of self-effacing nobility. Other images of women developed in traditional poetry and fiction and particularly germane to our considerations relate directly to sexual relations and the life of the emotions, themes that dominated the writings of post–May Fourth women. The meanings of these images are enormously complicated and no doubt reach deep into the sources of creativity; for our present purposes, I shall mention only three particularly restrictive images: woman as *femme fatale*, as desirable object, and as sentimentalist.*

Warnings against the Chinese version of the *femme fatale* abound in historical and political writings. *Nü-huo* (disasters due to female influence), the fatal face that overturns kingdoms and destroys cities (*ch'ing-kuo ch'ing-ch'eng*), is a standard explanation for moral decline and hence dynastic ruin. On the personal, or perhaps one should say physiological, level, feminine allurements are a deadly threat to a man's vital powers. "A maiden fair, just sweet sixteen" is "more vicious than a hungry *yaksha*";[5] thus Taoist and Buddhist notions reinforce Confucian moralism.

A man done in by lust, for which the woman is to blame, was a common theme in popular fiction. One of the most powerful projections of male fantasy appears in the novel *Chin p'ing mei* (Golden Lotus), which has been hailed as the "first Chinese novel with convincing women characters."[6] Its heroine Golden Lotus combines in her person both the fascination and the horror felt toward female sexuality; her unmatched beauty, lovingly described, and insatiable sexual appetite bring destruction to others and her own life to a gruesome end. The novel's curious mix of exhortations to virtue and blatant pornography, as well as its lack of moral coherence, is attributable at least in part to the unresolved ambivalence toward the image of women that Golden

---

* Another image frequently found in popular literature is the Mu-lan type, i.e. the woman who assumes a male disguise and for a time enjoys a career in the world of men, either as a warrior in battle like Mu-lan herself, or as a degree candidate (*nü-hsiu-ts'ai* or *nü-chuang-yüan*). Roxane Witke's inquiry into the meaning of the "Mu-lan complex" emphasizes that the female warrior was admired precisely because she adopted what were considered to be the higher masculine traits. See Witke, "Transformation of Attitudes Towards Women During the May Fourth Era of Modern China" (Ph.D. dissertation, University of California, Berkeley, 1970), pp. 45–49. We might also note that at the end of the story these "defeminized" superfemales always literally shed their masculine guise and revert to traditional domesticity. Is there a parallel here with the life stories of many post–May Fourth women writers? Were their very brief literary careers likewise only partial and temporary departures from conventional roles?

Lotus represents. Fear and contempt of women are carried to extremes in *Shui-hu chuan* (Men of the marshes), in which one test of male virility and qualification for joining the bandit brotherhood is the ability to resist (and in several episodes to decapitate, stab, mutilate, etc.) members of the female sex.[7]

The other side of the coin is the image of women as objects of desire, longing, and ecstatic contemplation. This is the dominant mode of love poetry in the *tz'u* form (usually but somewhat inaccurately translated as poems in irregular meter), which originated in close association with the courtesan milieu, and therefore, unlike Western love poetry, is completely devoid of Platonic or chivalric posturing. Woman is never seen in Chinese literature as an unattainable ideal with the power to transform and ennoble her worshiper. She is firmly placed in the poem as a material object, although a certain reticence is maintained in that, apart from the face, the description always stops short of the physical body, hovering suggestively around clothing and toilet articles:

> On the bedscreen's folding panels, gold glimmers and fades.
> Clouds of hair verge upon the fragrant snow of cheeks.
> Languorous she rises, pencils the moth-eyebrows,
> Dawdles over her toilet, slowly washing, combing.
> Mirror front and back reflect her flowers;
> Face and blossoms illumine one the other.
> Upon her new-embroidered silken jacket
> Pairs and pairs of partridges in gold.[8]

Screens, panels, mirrors, silk jackets, gold flowers—love poetry has moved into the bedroom, which is richly decorated with objects that appeal to all the senses at once: in the middle of all this, almost too fragile to withstand the rigors of applying make-up, is the most expensive, ornamental, sense-gratifying object of all, the woman.

The notion of woman as sentimentalist is closely associated with a kind of lyricism central to the Chinese poetic tradition. One traditional view of poetry has always stressed the expression of personal feelings (*shih yen chih*),* and certain moods and sensibilities were associated specifically with women. The male poet expressing himself through the voice of a real or imaginary woman has been a common feature of Chi-

---

* James J. Y. Liu provides a clear exposition of the relationship between poetry and feelings according to this view in *The Art of Chinese Poetry* (London, 1962), pp. 70–73. For an account of the varied interpretations of the *shih yen chih* theory through history, see David E. Pollard, *A Chinese Look at Literature: The Literary Values of Chou Tso-jen in Relation to the Tradition* (Berkeley, Calif., 1973), pp. 4–13.

nese poetry from the time the courtship songs in the Book of Odes were interpreted as political allegories: the languishing mistress is in truth the loyal but unrecognized minister longing to serve his lord. The continued popularity of this poetic device can be explained by the usefulness to the lyric poet of the characteristics attributed to women: extraordinary sensitivity, capacity for suffering, melancholy. Like the Golden Lotus image, this one was given its most memorable personification in a work of fiction, *Dream of the Red Chamber*. It was an important part of the author's conception that Lin Tai-yü (Black Jade) also composed beautiful verses; in her person are merged physical fragility, emotional sensitivity, and poetic talent.

Ts'ao Hsüeh-ch'in's great novel, which was motivated by his desire to acknowledge the superiority of women he had known, is in many ways an exception that proves the rule:

Toiling in the world of dust, I have been an utter failure. Suddenly I thought of the women of that time; going over them one by one in my mind, I felt that their conduct and their insights were all superior to mine. . . . My sins are many . . . but I must not, in order to conceal my own inadequacies, let them [those women] be lost to oblivion.[9]

With a genuine sensitivity to the tragedy that is a woman's lot once she emerges from girlhood and the innocent delights of *ta-kuan-yüan* (Grand Prospect Garden), plus a deft rendering of psychological states through individualized speech, Ts'ao Hsüeh-ch'in, though he failed to complete his novel, fulfilled his goal of leaving a gallery of complex and unforgettable female characters, a unique achievement in traditional Chinese fiction.

Love, marriage, sexual relations, and the emotional states these engendered, all explored from the woman's point of view, form a substantial part of women's writings in the 1920's. In proclaiming their right to love freely, even their right to suffer for love, they were repudiating the traditional treatment of women as depersonalized objects, whether contemplated with desire or with a combination of fascination and horror. But the close alliance between feminine and "poetic" sensibility that marks the third image discussed continued to form part of their self-conception. To be "laden with sorrow and illness" (*tuo-ch'ou tuo-ping*) like Lin Tai-yü was a badge of artistic creativity. In a sense they were carrying on, albeit with a difference, the rather limited self-image of the few women who did make their mark as writers in traditional literature.

A 1957 study of Chinese women's writings through the ages,[10] based on extensive searches of dynastic bibliographies, local gazetteers, literary collections, notes (*pi-chi*), etc., lists over 4,000 names of women writers. Many of these are recorded only as wife of so-and-so, or Madam so-and-so, and many of the works themselves, having never received the attention of commentators, collectors, anthologists, or historians, have disappeared or exist only in fragments. With the exception of a few famous tz'u poets and a handful of frequently anthologized individual poems, women's writings have not been endorsed or authenticated as part of the great classical literary tradition. In the categories of literature that deal with the serious, profound aspects of culture and experience (philosophy, history, political and moral essays, which constitute by far the greatest portion of Chinese literature [*wen*], though most of it is now ignored by scholars and translators), if we leave aside the writings instructing women on proper behavior, there are hardly any women writers at all. With respect to colloquial literature, women have always been important as performers in the oral traditions, but seem to have written just a few plays, some *t'an-tz'u*,* and one or two short stories.[11]

Chu Shu-chen, ranked by hierarchy-conscious traditional critics as the second-greatest woman poet after Li Ch'ing-chao, wrote ruefully a Poem of Self-Incrimination (*tzu-tse shih*):

> A woman writing literature is truly culpable,
> How bear the praising of the moon and singing of the wind!
> Grinding down an iron inkslab is not my duty,
> Merit is achieved by wearing out the gold embroidery needle.[12]

When she did turn to grinding ink on the inkslab, she wrote sorrowful, melancholy verses about longing and parting, about being deserted by her lover, and similar variations on a few standard themes. Without denying that some of the lyrics by women poets are beautiful and moving, one cannot help seeing in their poems an analogy to women actors playing female roles in the Peking Opera. When women actors were first permitted on stage in the early twentieth century, they had arduously to master the moves, gestures, walk—those little mincing steps—stan-

---

* Twelfth- and thirteenth-century descriptions of the Northern and Southern Sung capitals include numerous women's names in their lists of performers and storytellers. These accounts have been collected in *Tung-ching meng hua lu* (*wai ssu chung*) (Reminiscences of the Eastern Capitol [and four others]; Peking, 1962); see pp. 29–30, 123–24, 312–13, 454–59. Later novels mention women storytellers in a variety of genres. *T'an-tz'u*—a long romantic or historical narrative, part of which is in rhyme and is sung—is the only popular genre that can claim several known women authors. See T'an Cheng-pi, *Chung-kuo nü-hsing te wen-hsüeh sheng-huo* (The literary life of Chinese women; Shanghai, 1930), pp. 383–466. Cheng Chen-t'o, in his *Chung-kuo su wen-hsüeh shih* (History of Chinese popular literature; Peking, 1954), discusses the relationship between women and t'an-tz'u, 2: 348–83.

dardized by previous generations of male actors impersonating females.[13] The majority of the small number of traditional women writers, some of whom have been accorded the highest praise, have tended to be poets with a rather limited range of subject matter and attitudes and confined themselves to the modes of thinking and feeling ascribed to women in the literary tradition.

Tradition, Fiction, and the New Realism

The search for new self-definitions by women through literature in the post–May Fourth period had to go beyond the rejection of conventionally appointed roles. One condition that made such a search possible was the questioning of old literary techniques, indeed the effort to redefine the nature of literature itself. It was in part what the literary revolution of May Fourth was all about. The jettisoning of the classical language as the medium of serious literature entailed a radical change in the approach to writing, and opened the way for the incorporation of vast new areas of experience, including the experience of women, as proper subjects for serious literature.

The close relationship between the classical literary tradition and the hierarchical power structure of the Confucian state, exemplified in the examination system, had ensured that the scholar-official who was also the man of letters would support a specific ideology and specific set of values in his writings. In turn he had the satisfaction of knowing that his literary output served an exalted, well-defined function in society. It was partly because women had no public role that they were largely cut off from the serious business of classical literature. But the authority of tradition extended well beyond political and moral direction and even more deeply and pervasively affected literary practice, the way literature was written. Reverence for the past along with the arduous discipline required to master the language and craft of classical writing encouraged imitation, allusion, reiteration with variation, and writing based on earlier writings. The conventions of a genre governed not only style and form, but also the kinds of social values, philosophical ideas, and even emotional experiences admissible within that genre.* A traditional poet did not simply sit down to fix on paper a particular experience or observation; he was also consciously adding to a long line

---

* There was, for example, a hierarchy of seriousness with respect to the various poetic forms. The Sung poet Su Tung-p'o is credited with liberating *tz'u* from its previously narrow erotic concerns and infusing it with new vitality and substance by "writing *tz'u* as if it were *shih*"; he was criticized by traditional critics for breaking generic conventions. See Hu Yün-i, ed., *Sung tz'u hsüan* (Selections of Sung tz'u; Shanghai, 1962), pp. 9–12.

of poetic examples, all existing contemporaneously for him because of the deathless classical language, his own exemplification of the genre.[*] He had at his disposal, and assumed in his reader, a knowledge of images, rhetorical devices, historical allusions, and emotional formulas, inherited from the past.

The formal requirements of poetry are partly responsible for this reliance on the "consensual reflex," the "resonance effect."[14] But by the T'ang dynasty even biography, whose subject was supposed to be a particular flesh-and-blood person, was being written to formula.[15]

Literary conventionalism extended to popular literary works, even those regarded as entertainment. Fiction, after evolving from the storyteller's tale in the marketplace into long, complex written narratives by individual authors, never attained the status of literature but nonetheless remained subservient to conventions that bespoke its oral origins. Since fiction addressed itself to domestic and social relations in everyday life, women (at least as they were seen by men) became increasingly important as characters. One novel, *Ching-hua yüan* (Flowers in the mirror), even adopts the woman's point of view in describing an imaginary Country of Women where sex roles are reversed, and portrays the sufferings of males who travel there.[16] This was followed by some late-nineteenth-century "courtesan novels," but the high point in the novelistic treatment of women remained the mid-eighteenth-century *Dream of the Red Chamber*. Even Ts'ao Hsüeh-ch'in's masterpiece was bound and at times marred by formal conservatism in such matters as chapter division, narrative pace, and structure. Not until Chinese fiction writers broke altogether with the constraints of traditional convention

---

[*] Burton Watson has counted and classified nature images in the standard anthology *T'ang-shih san-pai shou* (Three hundred T'ang poems) and demonstrates statistically that the T'ang poet was not so much describing what he actually saw as manipulating with individual variations a conventionalized stock of images. See Watson's *Chinese Lyricism: Shih Poetry from the Second to the Twelfth Century* (New York, 1971), pp. 122–37. See also Jaroslav Průšek, "The Importance of Tradition in Chinese Literature," *Archiv Orientalni*, 26 (1958): 212–23. Průšek observes that a given work by a writer like P'u Sung-ling has more in common with works by others in the same genre than with his own other works in different genres, and that it is difficult to reconstruct an individual artistic personality from his literary corpus. He discusses the problem of "literary regimentation" in traditional authors and contrasts it with the situation of the new writer "who alone must seek out his own path to reality and to its expression." See his *Three Sketches of Chinese Literature* (Prague, 1969), pp. 5–8. Every writer, of course, must take his departure from writing he knows, and works with conventions even when he is revolting against them. There was nonetheless a change in emphasis and even more in the writers' conscious attitude that distinctly separates modern from traditional Chinese literature.

could the novel become the vehicle of radically new ideas and perceptions.

The increasing presence of women in novels notwithstanding, there seems to have been in traditional China little of the special affinity between women, either as readers or as authors, and realistic fiction that is assumed in the West. George Henry Lewes was voicing a widespread sentiment when he wrote in 1852, "Of all departments of literature, fiction is the one to which by nature and circumstance, women are best adapted . . . ; novels are their forte."* From the time of the novel's appearance in the eighteenth century, its reading public was composed largely of women, and novel writing, in England at least, seems to have been one of the very few areas of cultural activity (if not the only one) in which women practitioners outnumbered men. We can assume that in China novels had some women readers, but their effect on the form is difficult to gauge; there were no recognized lady fiction writers.

After the May Fourth Movement fiction became in both quality and quantity the most important literary form among women writers. It was a fiction governed by the new principle of "realism." There is uncertainty enough over the proper application of the term "realism" even in Western literary history; should it be treated as a style, as a characteristic present in literature of all ages, or as a period concept designating a specific, self-conscious literary movement of the nineteenth century? Once Western labels are imposed on Chinese writings, and become part of the modish jargon, clarity of definition becomes even more difficult.† But in intercultural transmissions, what counts is not the concept itself, but the perception of it by the recipient. Whatever else realism

---

* This was some five years before George Eliot, whom he already knew, had begun to write and introduce a new dimension of moral and philosophical seriousness into the English novel. His statement is quoted by Vineta Colby in her *The Singular Anomaly: Women Novelists of the Nineteenth Century* (New York, 1970), p. 4. On the relationship between women and the novel in England, see Ian Watt, *The Rise of the Novel, Studies in Defoe, Richardson, and Fielding* (London, 1957), pp. 43–47, 151–73, 298–99.

† Bonnie S. McDougall gives examples of what she calls the "superficial syncreticism" among Chinese writers using Western literary concepts in *The Introduction of Western Literary Theories into Modern China, 1919–1925* (Tokyo, 1971), pp. 88–108, 260–63. In *The Romantic Generation of Modern Chinese Writers* (Cambridge, Mass., 1973), Leo Ou-fan Lee writes, "despite their theoretical espousal of realism or naturalism the Chinese writers were motivated by an emotional ethos more akin to romanticism" (p. 277), a statement he documents in a masterly fashion for the writers he has selected to deal with. My point here is that "realism" (*hsieh-shih chu-i*) as a consciously applied literary doctrine was used by Chinese writers as a conceptual tool to break the hold of past conventions and redefine the nature and task of literature.

might mean, during the early stages of the literary revolution, in Ch'en Tu-hsiu's articles in *New Youth*,[17] for example, or Mao Tun's many critical writings during the twenties,[18] it meant the overthrow of classical tradition, the discarding of age-old conventions, and a new orientation toward reality. Literature was to be a "reflection [Mao Tun's English word] of life," based on the direct observation and depiction of experience and firmly grounded in a contemporary social setting. It would deal with reality without the mediation of literary conventions, directly, at first hand.

Traditional novels and short stories had of course been "realistic" in their notations of speech and behavior, but even in *Golden Lotus* and *Dream of the Red Chamber*, the novels' action occurred within a transcendent framework of religious retribution or moral symbolism. It was above all the elevation of realism into a comprehensive, self-conscious literary doctrine that destroyed the habit of traditionalism in literature and marked a definitive break with the past. Though later qualified by "revolutionary" or "socialist," realism has remained the official literary doctrine in China today, the ultimate, indeed the only method appropriate to all literature.

The break with classical literary conventions, and concomitantly with the concepts, values, and images of life embodied and perpetuated in them, set off an explosive expansion of literary material. The lower social classes, the dark side of urban and rural life, excluded by convention from polite literature, now were proper and serious subjects. The experience of women, with a much greater awareness of its variety and complexities, assumed unprecedented prominence. In a literature eager to expose the hitherto neglected dark side of social reality, women—the prime victims of feudal oppression—took on special interest. Hsianglin's wife (Lu Hsün), the slave mother (Jou Shih), are only two of many memorable examples. In a time of political upheaval, women (e.g. Mao Tun's heroines) became the sensitive registers of emotional turmoil. In the new poetry of erotic mysticism, a Western import, women became idealized objects of love. Later, in proletarian writings, she is warrior and labor heroine, in the vanguard of revolution and production. Images of suffering but heroic women, e.g. in the ballets "White-Haired Girl" and "The Red Detachment of Women," have dominated the stage and screen in recent years. For young women writers brimming with the need to test and conquer experience, who came into literature for the first time in the 1920's, realistic fiction became almost the sole literary form. Ping Hsin launched her career with poetry, but soon turned to the short story. A few women wrote poetic dramas on the theme of love,

and dramatizations of traditional stories made a momentary splash.*
Otherwise, serious women writers stayed with the novel and the short
story, the genres best suited to their purposes of exploring the world
about them and their individual selves within it.

We tend in retrospect to think of writers in groups, pursuing common
goals and arriving at turning points in literary history together. But for
each writer, and in particular each woman writer, the rejection of authority and acquiring the freedom to confront reality head on was an
individual struggle. Every woman writer had to set out alone on an independent and in some cases heroic path.

Self-Affirmation: Struggles for Education and Career

In the case of Ping Hsin, an idyllic childhood (according to her own
account),[19] enriched by love, the ocean, and mother, gave her opportunities for reading and writing, and for listening in on the meetings
of the poetry club (*shih-she*) attended by her father and his friends.
Writing was mainly a matter of conquering diffidence, and the embarrassment of answering the editor's questions regarding her new poetry
("What is it?"). But most of the others had first to fight for something
more than the rudimentary education normally given to gentry daughters. Their education was usually restricted to instruction in the basic
characters and in the proper behavior for a young lady, which they received as hangers-on in the schoolroom of their brothers and male
cousins, or from half-educated aunts. Before they could attend one of
the newly established modern girls' schools away from home, some
women had to threaten suicide to break down family resistance. Hsieh
Ping-ying rejected six methods of suicide before hitting on the effective
one of fasting.[20] Su Hsüeh-lin reminisced in 1942 about her early days:

Next year [1913] we heard that the Provincial Girls' Normal School in An-
ch'ing . . . was admitting students . . . so I petitioned [*ch'ing-ch'iu*] my family
to let me take the entrance examination. It couldn't be considered petitioning,
it was really warfare, involving endless tears, crying, begging, arguing. Although mother softened, each time grandmother or the diehard elders in the
village clan casually stated their opposition, she would change her mind.
The more my desire to study was repressed, the more fervently it burned.
When it reached white heat, I could neither eat nor drink. As if in a mad
or drunken state, I would run to the woods called *shui-k'ou*, half a mile
[one *li*] from home, wander back and forth, and several times thought of
killing myself by jumping into the raging forest stream. Had my mother not

---

* Two better-known ones are Pai Wei's *Lin-li* (Linli; 1925) and Yüan Ch'ang-
ying's *Kung-ch'üeh tung-nan fei* (The peacock flies southeast).

overcome her submissiveness toward her elders out of love for her child and taken my cousin and me to the capital for the exam, then perhaps my little life would long ago have been ended in the water. Now I look back to analyze my state of mind [hsin-li] for wanting to attend school. Was it that education would bring me fame? The family considered young girls who left home to study to be violating precepts of female conduct [kuei-hsün]; what fame could I expect? Was it in hopes that I could thus secure a position in society, so that my future life would be freer and more comfortable? I had not at that time thought as far as that. My state of mind then was very simple; it can be described as a kind of blind impulse, like tree shoots struggling up from the ground, like hidden springs gushing outward, supported by a force that could not easily be suppressed. Again, it was like a moth flying toward the flame, either to extinguish it or be burned to death. I entertained just one simple idea: to move ahead, or in other words, to pursue the brightness of my future.[21]

This desperate struggle for advanced schooling, a theme repeated with variations in the lives of many women, may have been carried on without conscious practical goals. It was nevertheless a prerequisite for becoming a writer, because it meant access to ideas, to high literacy, and above all because it meant physical and psychological liberation from the confines of home. The elders resisted hard, because they understood, more clearly perhaps even than the rebellious young themselves, that women's struggle for education marked the end of the old order. Su Hsüeh-lin's scholarly ambitions eventually took her to France for three years, but after a protracted emotional struggle, described in her semi-autobiographical novel *The Bitter Heart* (*Chi-hsin*), she deferred to her mother's wishes and returned to marry the husband her family had selected. Many other women writers suffered imprisonment, expulsion, financial deprivation, and (most difficult) had to resist emotional blackmail by their mothers to avoid marriage to husbands not of their own choosing. To many young men and women, the conflict over marriage seemed the fundamental one. In Feng Yüan-chün's story "Separation" (Ke-chüeh), a young girl imprisoned by her mother writes to her lover: "Life can be sacrificed, but not freedom of will. If I cannot have freedom, I prefer death. If people do not fight for the freedom to love [lien-ai tzu-yu], then nothing is worthwhile. This is my declaration."[22] The letter includes a poem she had written earlier to celebrate their love. Three days later, as the date of her arranged marriage approaches and escape plans go awry, she takes a fatal dose of poison.

As a threat self-destruction was useful, but it was by no means the only possible outcome. Ting Ling got a head start in her path to liberation by having a mother who herself had left home for school to train as a teacher when she was a widow of thirty with two young children and whose personal heroine was Madame Roland. Ting Ling herself broke off her arranged marriage with a cousin and went to school in Shanghai, where she found herself in a heady atmosphere among vaguely anarchist intellectuals and writers. Called a truly "modern girl" (Lu Yin uses the English term),[23] Ting Ling was on her own, so to speak, but her relationship with Hu Yeh-p'in, then an aspiring poet and later one of the celebrated five martyrs kidnaped and executed by the Kuomintang in 1931, had a double-edged effect on her initiation as a writer. A sensitive account of this relationship and its effects is given in Shen Ts'ung-wen's reminiscences of Ting Ling,[24] written in 1933, when she had disappeared and was presumed to have been executed. Although Hu Yeh-p'in, referred to as the naval cadet, had "nurtured the seeds of her creative writing" and provided her with certain opportunities, without him, Shen believes, Ting Ling's output would have been of higher quality and double the quantity.[25]

After she had launched her career with *Miss Sophie's Diary*, Ting Ling became convinced she had achieved a certain notoriety because she was a *woman* writer, while editors unjustly continued to reject Hu's poetry. "In her success she had to say smilingly to old friends, 'It is all P'in's achievement'—without the naval cadet, there would have been no book." According to Shen, she would tear up her own almost finished manuscripts in her indignation over the rejection of Hu's works.[26] Earlier his lack of success and their impoverished life together had turned Ting Ling to jobs as a governess or private secretary. She also tested her fate as a movie actress in Shanghai. This attempt (the basis for her early story "Meng-k'o") failed, in part because she could not bear to be regarded as a commodity:

That day, whether it was in the lounge, office, dining room, shooting room, or dressing room ... she was sated by the vulgar, flippant talk between actresses and actors or the director, by the tiny shrieks emitted when a thigh was pinched, the kinds of looks that passed back and forth; everyone was so comfortably laughing, happily chatting, playing. She alone was astonished, suspicious, as if she, too, had become a prostitute and was there letting those utterly disrespectful eyes roam over her.[27]

Getting away to the city, to school, leaving home and an arranged marriage, were only the first steps; it was also necessary to reject the obvious, demeaning female occupations, and perhaps most difficult of all, to find relationships that would support rather than insidiously in-

hibit one's development as a writer. As Shen Ts'ung-wen writes, Ting
Ling had to achieve the pride that came from exaggerating, and thus
despising, the common behavior of men in general before it was possible for her to engage in political or literary work.[28]

I have dwelled on Shen Ts'ung-wen's account of Ting Ling's early
experiences as a writer because he got from her, personally "liberated"
as she was, a sense of the multiple restrictions from which a woman had
to free herself before she could write. It seems evident that a woman
had to be more of a rebel and iconoclast, to push her way past far
greater obstacles, than a man who wanted to write. The effort involved,
the resistance overcome, were in some cases so tremendous that writing
became an existential act of self-definition. Since at that juncture in
history there were no available precedents for either their lives or their
writings, women writers were, among other things, struggling to *be*,
through words, to make something of themselves, to discover what they
were through self-expression. But in most cases the struggle did not last
very long. Women's careers as creative writers were marked by extreme
brevity. Feng Yüan-chün and Su Hsüeh-lin soon became (and have remained) literary historians and teachers; Ling Shu-hua, a diplomat's
wife and painter; Lu Yin died in childbirth at thirty-six. Ping Hsin married a professor of sociology and, apart from some children's stories and
essays, has added very little to the slim output of her early years. Hsieh
Ping-ying continued to write mainly patriotic stories relating to the war
against Japan and later to the Civil War; she also did editorial work and
became a teacher. Ting Ling is the only woman writer who actively pursued a serious literary career for more than twenty years until she was
silenced, by the Communist Party, in 1957. In other words the creative
phase in the lives of most women writers was mainly coterminous with,
and often did not outlast, the period following emergence from adolescence. About the reasons for this, one can only speculate. Could it have
been that domesticity or the academic life either so satisfied or so stul-
tified the creative urge that fiction writing was no longer possible? Or
that once the youthful search for self-definition was over, the impetus
to write was lost? They wrote at the time in their personal lives when,
having made the brave effort to break away from traditional molds, they
were rebellious and defiant, but also lonely and anxious, and they wrote
to clarify and interpret to themselves the rush of impetuous, unsettling
experiences they were living through. In these works of their youth
they wrote to keep up with their own lives; they wrote, over and over
again, the story of their own lives. Perhaps herein lies the explanation
of the personal and limited nature of their art.

Subjectivism and the New Images of Women's Condition

With self-affirmation such a strong motivating force for women who made the great effort to become writers, their tendency to stay within the range of their own experiences is understandable. The overthrowing of tradition made available a whole new range of literary subjects, but it is their evolving consciousness as individual women and their perception of the female condition that form the substance of their fiction.

It would be a mistake to read every piece of writing as literal transcriptions of actual experience, even those works that take the favored forms of diaries or letters, or stories that use the personal names of the author and her friends. At the same time, it must be recognized that the new principle of realism produced literature that was not so much the direct reflection or mirror of reality that the theorists had prescribed, as reality refracted through a very subjective consciousness. The tendency toward subjectivism after the May Fourth Movement was not limited to women and arose, among other things, out of the writer's new alienation from society, the emphasis on sensibility, and the impact of Western romanticism. The male writer, too, in emulation of his great hero Byron, was deploying the "pageant of his bleeding heart" in his life and writings.* But whereas many male writers managed to move beyond self-indulgent, confessional writing, no women of the post–May Fourth period painted the broad social canvases of Mao Tun or achieved the ironic perspective of Lu Hsün or the satiric force of Chang T'ien-i. Even if we confine ourselves to "romantic" writing, the range of women writers is comparatively narrow; their work shows a greater preoccupation with the self, more particularly with the self as woman. In 1931, Lu Yin summarized the essential quality of contemporary women writers this way:

In the works of women writers in general, there seems to be an indelible, covert sign. All you have to do is open the book, and you can immediately tell the writer is a woman. The main reason is that they use their fervent emotions as the ink of their creative writing, their old-fashioned temperament becomes the heart of their characters' temperament. Most of their writing expresses emotions, and is autobiographical in form. All problems remain within the confines of their individual lives, and feelings predominate over reason.[29]

Lu Yin suggests that this narcissistic emotionalism is a "residual quality from old times" (*chiu-shih-tai te hsing-ke*), a vestige of the traditional

---

* The phenomenon of Byron as the most popular English poet among non-English-speaking nations continued long after Matthew Arnold's famous 1855 description in his "Stanzas from the Grande Chartreuse" of how "Byron bore, . . . Through Europe

image of woman as sentimentalist. The predominance of autobiographical or semi-autobiographical forms in women's writings up till the time of her book (1931) is significant and revealing. Many writers wrote autobiographies, published their love letters, and used personal experiences, thinly disguised in their fiction. Stories themselves often were presented in the form of diaries and letters, used as vehicles to bare the soul, to chart the course of inner feelings.

The confessional form was well-suited to the writers' favorite themes, such as the complications and tragedies, particularly generational conflicts and triangular situations, that follow in the wake of love. The individual young woman's rebellion against the authoritarian family most often took the form of true love versus an arranged marriage; throughout the 1920's this struggle was used to dramatize in concrete terms the emotional turmoil that accompanied China's transition from the old world to the new. In many cases the tragedies are not brought on solely by outside pressures: the human heart, on which one must rely in fighting the evil system, is itself discovered to be a great betrayer. A person will court self-destruction by willfully falling in love with the wrong person.[30] Most often a woman falls in love with a married man, whose wife and brood of children cannot in good conscience be sacrificed; a man may become enamored of his step-mother or sister-in-law, against reason and moral sanctions, with disaster the only possible outcome. Love between women is also subject to jealousies, inconstancy, or social scorn, and thus is also likely to occasion anguish.

In some stories, however, tragedy is attributed not so much to social institutions or the wayward heart as to a general victimization by men. This pathos of the female condition is expressed as follows by a fictional diarist, on her deathbed, who has just been visited by the woman for whom her fiancé had deserted her: "I have always cursed mankind; because of her utter sincerity, however, I immediately forgave all the women of the world, and moreover wept for them. Because up till now there has never been a woman who has not been trifled with and humiliated by men."[31] The two women are united in tears; two rivals for a man's affections who now see themselves as fellow-victims of his perfidy. At the center of this and all the other tragedies is the fragile individual psyche, poised for extreme suffering, liable to be crushed at any

---

to the Aetolian shore / The pageant of his bleeding heart / That thousands counted every groan, / And Europe made his woe her own." And the phenomenon extended beyond Europe. See Leo Ou-fan Lee's discussion of Byron and the Byronic Hero, in *The Romantic Generation of Modern Chinese Writers* (Cambridge, Mass.), pp. 289–92.

moment by self-imposed emotional burdens. In many cases the heroine is also physically frail; a heart condition or consumption (blood is coughed up at bad moments) accompanies mental sufferings, and adds an undercurrent of feverish hysteria to the constant tear-shedding.

There are diverse sources of this self-centered emotionalism, with its paraphernalia of tears, sighs, consumption, deathbed scenes (supported in some cases by the sympathetic vibrations of moon, sea, wind, or flowers). Passionate and suffering lovers had earlier been celebrated in poetic drama, and passion and suffering carried to their neurotic, self-destructive extreme to culminate in death is a major theme of *Dream of the Red Chamber*. Post–May Fourth writers quote *Hsi-hsiang-chi* (Western chamber) and characterize themselves as modern successors to Lin Tai-yü. There is thus a continuity with the sentimentalist conception of women in the classical tradition, but more often European literature is consciously evoked as the source of inspiration. Shen Ts'ung-wen says of Ting Ling, "The three heroines in these three books . . . *Heart* [Maupassant], *La Dame aux Camélia*, and *Madame Bovary* . . . had taken full possession of the emotions of this future woman writer."[32] Feng Yüan-chün compares herself and her lover to Charlotte and Werther.[33]

The treatment of love in its various aspects—ecstasy, longing, frustration, despair, especially when combined with daringly intimate physical and psychological detail—was shocking for those days and was greeted excitedly as an example of the new realism. Readers today may find the suffusion of pseudopoetic sentiments, the loosely metaphorical and rhapsodic style rather vacuous and remote, but at the time these self-exposures represented a genuine emotional liberation, and as such struck a responsive chord among an emerging young reading public. The unprecedented exploration of the individual woman's sexual longings and frustrations, and even of her suicidal and self-defeating impulses, as in the heroines Meng-k'o and Miss Sophie through whom Ting Ling achieved her early fame, made them appear to contemporary readers to be more complex, intense characters than any women in traditional literature.

It was in part out of their need to affirm their newly liberated selves that this generation of women writers became so preoccupied with personal and emotional responses to experience. Having broken so drastically with authority, both literary and social, and with the old order and values that would have regulated her life, the woman writer was suddenly on her own, with nothing to fall back on but her feelings or uncertain new relationships, which were also dependent on tenuous feelings. The right to self-affirmation when finally won proved to be but a precarious thing, and the reliance on love and sensitivity for the management of her life only made a woman all the more vulnerable to other kinds of suffering.

Not all women writers remained locked into self-pitying contemplation of their unfulfilled love life. Some also turned to a consideration of other aspects of women's experience, aspects that had rarely, if ever, been given serious attention in literature. Ling Shu-hua wrote sympathetically of the pathos of old-fashioned women caught in a period of sudden social change, and with wry detachment of the trivial existence of middle-class, "modern," urban housewives. Both she and Ping Hsin took up the subject of women past their prime, burdened with intractable family cares, victims of indifferent or callous husbands, whose lives, when the vivaciousness or literary promise of their youth is recalled, are a record of bright hopes laid waste. Yet as described in stories by Hsieh Ping-ying and Ch'en Ying, the decision to relinquish motherhood is always full of pain, and the pain is never really overcome.* The physical agonies of childbirth or abortion, described in excruciating detail, paradoxically strengthen maternal feelings, making the anguish of suppressing them unbearable. The "victory" of marrying over family opposition quickly turns hollow. A wife is callously sacrified when her husband discards her for a woman who will advance his career. On the other hand there is the loneliness of a spinster schoolteacher, mocked by girl students, gradually cut out of general family activities, flutteringly anxious to do the right thing, or the desolation of an aging career woman when she meets again the lover rejected ten years ago, now radiant with his domestic happiness.[34]

There are many variations on all these themes, and one could multiply examples indefinitely. The overwhelming majority of stories are confined to the experiences of urban, upper- and lower-middle-class housewives, teachers, students; in short, they describe people from the same background as the writers themselves. There is a marked contrast between these stories and those which introduce characters from other social strata. While vacationing in a village, a schoolgirl befriends an adopted child-bride (t'ung-yang-hsi), who is cruelly abused by her mother-in-law, and watches helplessly as the peasant girl dies.[35] The dehumanizing conditions under which a textile factory girl works show

---

* Ch'en Ying (1908–), omitted from the tabulation at the beginning of this essay, is a less well-known writer, of relatively small literary output. After publishing a few short stories, she turned to teaching and translating.

the author that her own well-intentioned charity is useless.[36] A lady loses the old servant woman who out of ignorance and stubborn love sets out to find a son lost to the army.[37] The attempts in these stories, as contrasted to the stories described earlier, to depict the feelings of the sufferers have little understanding or conviction. The characters are seen sympathetically but from the outside; they have no inner life.

An exception is Ting Ling's story about an innocent country girl who is corrupted by her vision of the "good things in life," hitherto unknown, now passionately longed for. When her hopes come to naught, she is destroyed.[38] Although her internal evolution may not be totally convincing, the description of her successive mental states contains what T. A. Hsia calls the "occasional psychological subtleties, the little tremors of a sensitive mind" characteristic of Ting Ling's work.[39] The girl's changing attitudes are conveyed through specific experiences; there is an effort to construct through selective detail a feeling of place, of concrete happenings firmly grounded in a real, substantive world—as for example, the eye-opening first walk into the city. In many of the stories about love by other women authors, in contrast, one has the impression of abstract creatures, floating about in the void with their intense feelings, unanchored in any material reality, though the world of nature is occasionally drawn upon for easy metaphors to convey these feelings.

In looking over these writings by women, one cannot help but ask once more, is there a distinctly feminine mode of writing, characterized by subjectivism and sentimentality?* The passage by Lu Yin quoted at the beginning of this section suggests that fervent emotions in women are a holdover from earlier (and, one infers, more backward) times. Ting Ling likewise links the emphasis on emotions to social conditioning. In "Wild Grass" ("Yeh-ts'ao"), a slight story about a woman writer determinedly disentangling herself from a love affair, Ting Ling writes:

Today, she was feeling terribly vexed because she had written onto a very cool and rational woman in her story some excessively fervent feelings, and moreover had introduced a light layer of melancholy. This was really out of character for the woman of her imagination, but it was precisely one of the shortcomings of women that she could understand best. She didn't know what

---

* Mary Ellmann discusses the establishment in nineteenth-century England of a dichotomy between the "dominant and masculine mode possessing the properties of reason and knowledge" and the "subsidiary and feminine mode possessing feelings and intuition"; *Thinking About Women* (New York, 1968), p. 158. George Henry Lewes's statement on women and the novel quoted above continues: "the very nature of fiction calls for that predominance of Sentiment which we have already attributed to the feminine mind. Love is the very staple of fiction, for it 'forms the story of a woman's life.' "

to do, to tear up the manuscript and rewrite it, or to continue but without expressing sympathy toward this woman. She could not stop thinking about this vexing matter; gradually her thoughts turned to the social environment that led women to overemphasize emotions; she thought how pitiable women were; and then, as she reflected, she began to loathe herself.[40]

Elsewhere, Ting Ling speaks with strong dislike of women's failings, which she admits she often portrays sympathetically in spite of herself. In their statements of 1930 and 1931, Ting Ling and Lu Yin were looking back at less than a decade of new women's writing with a degree of self-knowledge and criticism; they realized that a woman emancipated from traditional culture could nonetheless remain encumbered by the condition of being female. Three years later Lu Yin was dead and Ting Ling's recognized predicament of being a woman writer was about to be submerged in the more urgent predicament of all writers, as the onrush of political events forced them to seriously examine the relevance of literary work to the anticipated political revolution.

From Shanghai to Yenan

With the rapid pace of political developments in the second half of the 20's—May Thirtieth, the first United Front, oppression and terror after 1927—the politicization of intellectuals is markedly accelerated. Subjective emotionalism takes a leftward turn, and the role of the writer in relation to society undergoes agonizing reappraisal. Now young women are in suicidal despair because revolutionary experiences can be as disillusioning as love.[41] There appears a group of novels in which romance and revolution are blended in various proportions. Having had her own fling at the conflict between sex and revolutionary duty,[42] Ting Ling clearly signals the move toward a new direction. The following classic passage on the disenchantment of writers with their individualistic, sentimental writing occurs in her story "Shanghai, Spring 1930":

About literary composition, I sometimes feel that it would not be a serious loss if we gave it up entirely. We write, and the people read. Time passes, and no influence whatsoever. Then what is the meaning of all this, except that we get paid for it? It is of course possible that some readers are touched by a turn in the plot or by certain passages of writing—but who are these readers? Students of the petty-bourgeois class above the high school level who have just reached adolescence and are subject to melancholy. . . . But the consequences, I now understand, are harmful. We do them a great wrong by leading them to the paths that we ourselves have trodden: sentimentalism, individualism, grumblings or sorrows for finding no way out. . . . Where is the way out indeed? They will sink deeper and deeper in their moroseness, not seeing the relation between society and their sufferings. Even if they could improve their language and produce essays and poems that win praise from some old writers, what good, I ask you, is that to them? And what good to society? Therefore, personally, I am willing to give up writing.[43]

The recognition that both her life and her writings had reached a state of sterile emotionalism ultimately leads Mei-lin, the heroine of the story, to join the revolution, but her activities, beyond attendance at meetings and demonstrations and meeting with a female worker, remain rather vague. What is definite is her new feeling of elation, and a kind of self-assertion that inevitably leads to a break with her lover. As for Ting Ling herself, her writing becomes "proletarianized"; she experiments with depictions of collective life—for example, of peasants whose political consciousness is raised following a disastrous flood.[44] In her later attempts at socialist realism her literary technique will be much more secure, as in *The Sun Shines on the Sang-kan River*; but that novel of 1949, remote in concept and concern from early post–May Fourth writings, is beyond the scope of this paper.

In the transition from the works of the first generation of writers following the May Fourth Movement to the new revolutionary literature, Ting Ling is an important figure. If she seems to dominate the early 1930's and the closing pages of this paper, it is because almost alone among her female colleagues, she endured and developed as a serious writer. Her literary output of over twenty years, unrivaled in duration and range by that of any other woman writer, is not merely a chronological series of books, but the sensitive register of a historical process, reflecting in its successive stages the changing relationship between modern Chinese writers and their times. Her early feminist semi-autobiographical stories, with their overtones of bohemia and anarchism, expressed the evolving consciousness of a young woman reaching for a liberated life-style. Then revolution appears, as the vaguely romantic alternative to sexual love. Subsequently she extends her reach to a broader portrayal of social reality, which culminates in her last long novel, on land reform. But even while dedicating her writing to the cause of revolution, she did not put aside altogether either her perception of the plight of women or her serious commitment to the idea of literature. These two concerns were eventually to cost her the condemnation of the Chinese Communist Party, and her fate illustrates how difficult it is to reconcile the claims of either feminism or literature with the more immediate claims of socialist revolution. But in the 1930's, the tragic dénouement of her story lay far ahead.

In 1931, after Hu Yeh-p'in's martyrdom, Ting Ling plunged into political activity. She herself is betrayed; arrested in 1933, she escapes three years later under obscure circumstances, and sets out for the Border Region to join the party. The story has never been fully told,[45] but it calls to mind the forthright daring typical of her life and career. One can picture her in her Manchurian soldier disguise, spending nine days on foot and horseback from Lo-ch'uan to Pao-an, making her way through the treacherous northern landscape toward Yenan. This tableau will serve to bring down the curtain on the women writers of the May Fourth generation.

Conclusion

Yenan, situated in the hinterland where Chinese civilization once began, was to represent a new direction for literature: attempts to develop national forms, to accommodate folk traditions, and to use literature as a tool for mobilizing mass consciousness. Although literature continued to be produced in Shanghai, the "Shanghai phase" of the modern literary movement was over. To that Westernized coastal city a generation of writers had flocked, free from the authoritarian control of outworn institutions, from their traditional roles as son, daughter, or daughter-in-law, and from the restrictive influence of a classical education and literature. There the Western imports were glittering and fashionable, but they could not always be put to effective use. Thus this restless, rootless generation was left mainly to its own devices, and forced to fall back on its subjective self.

It was during this period that women writers were most concerned with exploring their identity through writing. The extreme iconoclasm that had encouraged them to break out of the fetters of the past and endeavor to speak for themselves was, however, also fraught with unforeseen consequences for the practice of literature. The writers' severance from the verbal and conceptual resources deep-rooted within their cultural tradition, although incomplete, left a vacuum that could not be adequately filled by hastily imported Western literary doctrines and models. Would-be creators of a new Chinese literature were thus caught (artistically, but not necessarily politically, speaking) "Wandering between two worlds, one dead, the other powerless to be born."*

It is easy now to forget how little time the post–May Fourth generation had for literary experiment. The national crisis brought on by war with Japan, the pressing need for radical social and political change, soon

---

* In these lines from his "Stanzas from the Grande Chartreuse," Arnold is lamenting the passing of the age of religious faith, now "But a dead time's exploded dream," while nothing has come to take its place.

curtailed the progress of modern literature and prevented it from reaching maturity. And with the coming to power of the Communist revolution, the premises and indeed the entire direction of literature were changed. Writing as a means of working out one's identity, of attaining an independent, privileged existence for the individual, was no longer possible. The urgencies of socialist construction have in fact led to a questioning of the validity of literature itself.

What is remarkable about the women writers of the late 1920's and early 1930's is not their modest literary achievement under the difficult circumstances of cultural transition, but what they managed to convey, through their unpracticed art, of their own condition. They showed that the cultural revolution of May Fourth, like other revolutions in which women have taken part—trying to find an opening as traditional structures start to tumble, hoping this time to attain their own emancipation —was for women yet another betrayal. It held out promises of easy solutions, illusions that women, in human and artistic terms, could quickly and finally come into their own. These illusions turned out to be false. The crumbling of the old structures made it possible for a few gifted women, the articulate, self-conscious vanguard, to break out into the open. There they discovered that whereas women had been repressed and confined under the traditional system, they now were in a precarious and exposed situation, and no less vulnerable. In a limited period of time, their writings touched on an unprecedentedly wide variety of female experiences. But the grievances that had appeared attributable to specific institutions or adventitious circumstances—a callous husband, a despotic father, an unwanted pregnancy, a fickle lover— and therefore had seemed remediable, proved to be inherent in the fundamental condition of being female. Freedom from an authoritarian tradition mainly enabled women to get closer to, become more aware of, the basic, inescapable contradictions of their existence. Hence the recurring situation of a woman's seeming to be at war with her own nature and the frequent note of suicidal despair.

The women writers of the post–May Fourth generation were not self-consciously engaged in a literary women's liberation movement. Together in the lifeboat with the young men of their generation, especially their lovers, they were attempting a joint escape from oppression and quest for salvation. They were just beginning to grope toward the idea that the liberation of all human beings through total social revolution might be the precondition of their personal liberation. The much more severe oppression of peasant women, factory girls, bondmaids, figured in their stories, but not prominently. As partially free, articulate, modernized, urban, intellectual writers, they were still largely absorbed in their private griefs.

The line between literature and their agitated lives was difficult to draw. Too much of their experience, overwhelming and inextricable from the historic upheavals around them, entered their writing in a half-processed state. They lacked the balance, the mature detachment, the finality, that make for great works of literature. Yet their efforts to record their own autobiographies in a shifting world heighten our consciousness of the tragedy of woman's condition. It is because these writers remain so much a part of their history that their voices speak to us with such immediacy.

Chiang Ch'ing's Coming of Age

ROXANE WITKE

> I have some memories, but fragmentary in the extreme. They
> remind me of the fish scales scraped off by a knife, some of
> which stick to the fish while others fall into the water. When
> the water is stirred, a few scales may swirl up, glimmering, but
> they are streaked with blood, and even to me they seem likely to
> spoil the enjoyment of connoisseurs.
> —Lu Hsün, "In Memory of Wei Su-yüan"

This first chapter in the life story of Mao Tse-tung's wife, Chiang Ch'ing,
is based on personal interviews conducted in Peking and Canton in August 1972—the first time, according to Chiang Ch'ing, that she had
disclosed her past to a foreigner. To appreciate the full significance of her
disclosures one must recognize that she was addressing herself not only
to the world beyond China, but also to the internal record, where, she
feels, her past has been inadequately and inaccurately set down. In the
absence of documentary information on her origins and early years, a
few writers and biographical services have yielded to the temptation
to supply a past for her, one compounded of the reminiscences of former
friends and enemies, hearsay, and sheer speculation.[1] Because of the
traditional and surviving Chinese proclivity for preserving the anonymity of informants (a proclivity Chiang Ch'ing shares), the differences
among such sources, as well as their relative authenticity, are almost
impossible to sort out. A cursory glance at previous accounts, all by men
and none by Communists, reveals a common distortion, which is to over-
spice the substance of her story with sexual motive and salacious adventure. However titillating such accounts may be to readers from
cultures unused to women in positions of power, they neither add to
history nor add up to biography.

On the assumption that any person is a singularly well-informed
source on his own past, I have chosen to represent Chiang Ch'ing largely
as she presented herself to me. In my view, what she chose to say about

The author wishes to thank the Joint Committee on Contemporary China of the
Social Science Research Council and the American Council of Learned Societies
and the Johnson Foundation, Racine, Wisconsin, for their generous support during
the time this paper was written.

herself, however selective that may have been, has a certain authenticity, for it shows the past in the process of being recovered and reappraised in the light of a present cast of mind. Regardless of political positions, moreover, what Chiang Ch'ing chose to say of her youthful self was not all favorable.

To cleave as closely as possible to her thought processes, I have presented her narrative in direct quotation or paraphrase. The difference between her account and my explanatory material is evident. Our interviews, which lasted some sixty hours, stretched over the better part of seven nights and a day. They covered far more of her life than the first nineteen years discussed here, and far more of her thoughts on China and human affairs. The voluminous notes I took during that extraordinary time in her company will appear in a book about Chiang Ch'ing's life in revolution.

From the rhetoric of her speeches during the Cultural Revolution, published speculations of male expatriates staggered by the thought of a woman married to the ruler of China and wielding national power, a few photos, and observations of her acting officially during a banquet at the Great Hall of the People, I expected Chiang Ch'ing to be a stern, severely single-minded revolutionary. That harsh image began to dissolve during my first evening as her guest, on August 12 at the Great Hall. There she was attired as usually photographed, in the unadorned gray tunic and trousers of the high-echelon leaders. Yet her official-looking exterior barely concealed an imagination and personal style that were as original and sometimes shocking as conscientiously "revolutionary." On that first encounter she spoke provocatively and emotionally of her childhood and a spectrum of other matters. Some two weeks later, during our "secret" rendezvous in Canton, a softer, far more gracious personality emerged in the tropical ambience of this southern city, remote from the political pressures and ungentle rivalries of the northern capital. On her own, with no other leaders of comparable rank in the area, she exercised greater freedom of performance and imagination.

In Canton she always dressed for our meetings in a pastel crêpe-de-Chine dress of simple Western cut, sheer nylon anklets, and white plastic sandals. Each evening began with an aesthetic ritual from which she took obvious pleasure: attendants brought her jasmine and tiny orchids threaded on silk tasselled cords, and deftly she tied them to the handles of delicately carved sandalwood fans, one for each of us. Only then did we begin sustained conversation, lazily moving with our perfumed fans the hot, humid air of a Cantonese summer night.

With the nocturnal work habits typical of the leadership, Chiang Ch'ing summoned her aides, my aides, and me to her villa each evening around dusk, and kept us, with pauses for dinner and occasional refreshing strolls or other recreation, until three or four in the morning, by which time her formidable energies still had not flagged. Although the setting of our conversations seemed informal, the social climate was in fact skillfully controlled by Chiang Ch'ing in the style to which she and the others were accustomed. Often she smiled and laughed, yet even in deep seriousness and severity her manner was winsome. Provoked by her glance, graceful arm gesture, or quick word, we found ourselves sitting, rising, moving to another room, going for dinner, or taking a stroll indoors or in a garden. If an aide hesitantly interrupted a sustained monologue to remind her of a waiting dinner, she might with equal aplomb either break off and lead us to the dining room, or, if unwilling to break the flow of her narrative, ignore the aide's presence. Her retinue during our meetings was not small: two bodyguards, two doctors, some nurses, two interpreters, one recorder of all conversation, a Deputy Minister of Information, a Vice-Chief of Protocol, my two assistants, and on occasion some others. But *her* presence was always the active factor in the environment. The others were as eager and at times appalled to learn about her past as I was.

Her power to dominate a room full of people is most readily attributable to her being the wife of the Chairman, and to authority inherent in leadership in her own right: she is the only woman on the Political Bureau of the Tenth Central Committee (1973) of the Chinese Communist Party. However, these objective statuses are bolstered by unique personal qualities, enhanced perhaps by training in the dramatic arts. Even so, after spending a week in her company, I found myself less conscious of her political position and skills as a performer than of the strength and complexity of a personality developed in adversity.

Chiang Ch'ing entered the world as Li Chin in March 1914. She would not reveal the exact date of her birth because, she said, she did not want to make it possible for the masses to celebrate her birthday. Her first home was in the town of Chu-ch'eng, a hsien capital of some 80,000 persons located on the south bank of the Wei River, some fifty miles from the port city of Tsingtao in Shantung province. Vulnerably situated between the Gulf of Chihli and the Yellow Sea, Shantung was one of the first provinces to fall prey to imperialism. In 1860 the coastal city of Chefoo (Yen-t'ai) was ceded to France. In 1898 the port of Weihaiwei was leased to the British and the Tsingtao Peninsula to Germany. In the year of Chiang Ch'ing's birth the Japanese appropriated the German-held areas of Shantung as a foothold from which China could ultimately be drawn into the swelling Japanese empire. In the years of her childhood the nagging military presence of Japan with its supportive colonial installations engendered throughout Shantung province a chronic instability punctuated by occasional crises.

Despite the lengthening shadow of imperialism, Shantung could boast an impressive revolutionary legacy. During the Taiping and Boxer rebellions of the middle and late nineteenth century, Shantung produced major forces and also a fair share of "martyrs" for the Revolution of 1911. Shantung was the diplomatic *cause célèbre* of the May Fourth Movement of 1919, and its capital, Tsinan, was the site of the May Third Incident of 1928, which opened a new era of Sino-Japanese military confrontation.

Living standards in Shantung, China's second largest province, were abysmal, a condition amply reflected in Chiang Ch'ing's childhood recollections. Even without famine the ordinary people often ate but one or two full meals a week; the incidence of intestinal disorders and slow death from malnutrition was high. Yet in a material sense Chu-ch'eng hsien was better off than most, and its cultural and educational standards were relatively high. During the great wave of student migrations abroad during the first two decades of the twentieth century, Chu-ch'eng exported more students than any other hsien in Shantung. Chiang Ch'ing was not among them, though eventually she fell under the influence of some who returned as teachers, writers, and political conspirators.

Chiang Ch'ing first spoke of her childhood the night of our first meeting in Peking. She began cautiously, cleaving to well-worn political guidelines, but later continued more freely with minimal ideological restructuring.

I

"Since you are eager to know about my past, I can tell you briefly," she began. "I grew up in the old society and had a miserable childhood. Not only did I hate the landlords of China, but I also felt a spontaneous sense of resistance against foreign countries, because foreign devils from both the East and the West used to bully us. We did not have enough food and clothing. Foreigners looked down on us and called us 'the sick man of the Orient.'"

Li Chin was the first of several names she would use before taking Chiang Ch'ing, her name in the community of Communism. She had numerous brothers and sisters—how many she would not say—all of them at least a dozen years older than she was.* Her father was an "old

* If there was a conscious motive for her vagueness about numbers and names of family members and subsequently of friends, it was probably the desire to protect those still living from public attention, investigation, or recrimination in the event of renewed political struggle.

man" of about sixty when she was born. Though her mother was over forty, she remembered her as being much younger than her father and with far greater tenderness. Her father started out in life as a carpenter's apprentice and eventually became the owner of a handicraft workshop that specialized in making wheels. "Because we were poor and had little to eat, my father was always beating or cursing my mother." Such behavior earned him the name *ma-jen i-shu-chia*, an artist in insulting others. He beat the children whenever he felt the urge, but when he savagely attacked the mother all the children rallied around her, trying their best to protect her.

Some of his rages were unforgettable. At the time of the Lantern Festival, which falls on the fifteenth day of the first lunar month, a vast number of lanterns had been put up by a host of landlords. Seemingly maddened by this display of wealth beyond his reach, Chiang Ch'ing's father seized a spade and tore after her mother, striking her first on the back, then on the hand, breaking her little finger. When Chiang Ch'ing threw herself in front of her mother to shield her, her own mouth was struck and a tooth broken. As Chiang Ch'ing described this violent scene, which left her mother's finger crippled, she lifted her upper lip with her index finger to show where the baby tooth had been broken. As an ideological afterthought she remarked, "At first I thought that all men were no good because of the way my father bullied mother and us children. Actually, it was grinding poverty that made him act as he did." Whatever his reasons, this incident seems to have been the last straw for her mother. She strapped Chiang Ch'ing to her back and the two fled, never to return. Though only a small child, Chiang Ch'ing added mysteriously, from that point on she began to learn first to grope her way in the dark, then to walk alone at night.

A landlord in Chu-ch'eng hsien who had a wife and several concubines but still no male offspring asked Chiang Ch'ing's mother to join his family as a servant. Chiang Ch'ing refused to go with her at first, but later agreed. She remembered her mother as being surrounded by lots of people from then on. Her mother's motive may have perplexed Chiang Ch'ing, for she justified it in the following terms: "My mother had gone out to work so that I might be able to go to school. Yet I was able to complete that stage of primary school only because tuition and books were free. But even then I often went hungry or ate cold meals, which gave rise to a chronic gastrointestinal condition." She remembers vomiting after forcing down coarse cold pancakes given her by relatives to relieve her hunger pangs, and being nauseated for long periods. Since childhood, she said, she has suffered from digestive problems.

As a child she was never given new clothes or real girls' clothes to wear, she continued with a discernible tone of resentment. All were hand-me-downs from a brother. Her hair was always dressed in two pigtails, which invited trouble. In the family her mother worked for, one of the landlord's little girls made it her business to mock Chiang Ch'ing's curious appearance. Once when the child was in a taunting mood, she yanked at Chiang Ch'ing's hair. Furious, Chiang Ch'ing pushed her away with all her might. There followed a terrible scene. Other members of the household rushed to the child's defense. The up-shot: Chiang Ch'ing's mother was fired.

Her mother soon found another position, this time in the home of a "bankrupt landlord" whose decline in fortune meant there was almost nothing to eat. One night when Chiang Ch'ing was left alone in the room she shared with her mother, driving rain poured through the di-lapidated window frame, which lacked a paper covering. With only a small oil lamp to provide illumination, Chiang Ch'ing, who had nothing to do, sat motionlessly for hours on the *k'ang* (the broad stone bed typ-ical of northern Chinese homes) awaiting her mother's return. When the rain stopped at dawn, her mother reappeared. Astounded to find her in the same upright position in which she had left her, she burst into tears and cradled her in her arms. From her pocket she withdrew a biscuit called *ho-tzu* in Shantung. Exhausted, Chiang Ch'ing could eat just one bite, and her mother none at all, so she quietly pocketed that precious bit of foodstuff for them to share later.

"When I was only five or six, I learned to walk in the dark in search of my mother." That opaque motif was repeated several times in the course of her childhood recollections, leaving her listeners wondering just what her mother's nocturnal employment was. Other people, Chiang Ch'ing went on to say, fear that when they walk in the dark they will encounter devils, ghosts, or gods; she had never had such fears. But there was one thing she feared: wolves.[2] For years she lived with the lingering terror that they would track her down and eat her. The un-settling thought of wolves reminded her of another time when she was staying at a certain Ch'en village where everyone, like her family, was surnamed Li. Having had but one meal that day, she was driven by hunger pangs to wander out into the alleys in search of her mother. The sparsely populated village was infested with dogs. Suddenly she was attacked by a pack of ravenous dogs and one bit her on the leg. Lifting the hem of her dress, she showed us the faintly discernible scars just above her ankle. Alerted by the dogs' barking, her mother arrived on the run, swept Chiang Ch'ing up into her arms, and carried her home on her back, tears streaming down her face.

As a result of her mother's change of position, Chiang Ch'ing was admitted to another primary school at Chu-ch'eng. She was sponsored by a man named Hsüeh Huan-teng, who was prominent in the May Fourth period and later professor at the Peking Girls' Normal School. When she enrolled in the school, Professor Hsüeh gave her a new name, Yün-ho, "Cloud Crane," as suitable for one of her height and slenderness. A county-run girls' school, it was established mainly for landlords' daughters, with a few girls like herself—daughters of laboring people—included "for show." Too poor to buy a uniform, Chiang Ch'ing wore any clothes she could get, most of them castoffs from boys. The other children found her appearance ludicrous. One of her dilapidated shoes revealed her big toe, which they scornfully called her "big brother"; her heels, mocked as "duck's eggs," protruded at the other end.

She was subjected to similar sarcasm by an aunt and a niece in the household of her mother's employer.* Once she flew into a rage at their mockery and struck the aunt on the breast. Both women howled in self-pity, but did not fight back. Why? Because she was too small, she explained. Horribly upset by the incident, she dashed to school and announced to the principal that she would quit school and run away. To her amazement, he received her sympathetically, dried her tears, and told her she should not allow such things to bother her. All that mattered was that she study hard and persist in school work. She relented. In time her teachers grew to respect her, and some even to be fond of her.

But school engendered other antagonisms. The course she most hated was *hsiu-shen*—self-cultivation in Confucian morality.† One day when she was daydreaming in the Confucian morality class, the teacher became enraged and dragged her to the toilet, where he hit her five times with a board. (That particular teacher, she remarked, was known to have also beaten the daughter of her mother's employer.) After class, he seemed apologetic and went over to make peace with her. She became involved in other conflicts, though, and was dismissed from school after one semester. She then vowed, as she remembered now, never

---

* Possibly other members of the household who were not actually blood relations.
† Literally "cultivation of the self," Hsiu-shen came to mean something like self-discipline or self-abnegation. In classrooms down to 1949 hsiu-shen was systematically invoked to make the young conscious of their lowly place and responsive to authority.

again let anyone bully her. Thus her experience of primary school ended abruptly in the fifth year.

People often marvel how the Chinese have long been a "civilized" people, Chiang Ch'ing commented skeptically. Yet she has known since childhood the depths of their barbarism. It was customary where she used to live for the "bullies" to decapitate their countrymen and display the freshly severed heads on the city wall to terrify the local populace. When she saw this as a child, she fell ill and realized that "people have no hearts." When her mother knew that such bloody events were scheduled for a time when she would be occupied with household chores, she asked neighbors to cover her child's eyes. Even with her eyes blinded, Chiang Ch'ing could still visualize the awful carnage.

Other childhood images of violence were indelibly impressed on her earliest memory. Chu-ch'eng hsien was a fertile area. Yet each year at harvest time local bandits and even some landlords plundered other people's crops. Those caught in the act were imprisoned, and some were executed by rifle, broadsword, or both. Two military officers in the Chu-ch'eng area regularly checked the prisons and decided who should die. As a child listening to the sounds of the city, Chiang Ch'ing learned to read the rifle reports resounding against the high brick city wall; from the number of shots she surmised how many had died. Her curiosity aroused, one day she made a walking tour of the long city wall. She learned that the officers, in the course of their daily inspection of the prisons, often killed a dozen or more people, including some who were obviously innocent. Why were the innocent destroyed? The policy of the military governors, whose first concern was their own security, was to open the city gates just a crack at dawn and to lock them tightly at dusk. Because they feared that aliens and other unidentified people might cause trouble, intruders were shot on sight. Through cautious observation she learned that the executions were carried out at the Little East Gate, which was situated near a suspension bridge. She remembered its sway and the sinking feeling one had walking over it. She was not frightened because the place she lived in was built on a cliff and she was used to heights.

Why should some people want to kill others, she wondered as a child. Still more perplexing was the public enthusiasm for such events. When the time came for scheduled executions at Chu-ch'eng, the "rich people" viewed the spectacle from high on the city wall. She knew the scene to be sharply impressive. Red tassels fluttered from the broadswords used to decapitate the victims. The prisoners filed in, each one wearing a placard on his back. Even when she did not watch the execution but only listened, she understood the sound of hands clapping. Each round of applause signaled a death. And she knew that those who clapped loudest were the rich.

"Once I saw heads hanging," she continued. In those days she and members of her family were living between the inner and outer walls of the town of Chu-ch'eng, while she attended a school inside the walls. As she was returning home from school one day, her attention was drawn to the sound of an odd gait. She looked up. Approaching her was an old man bearing a shoulder pole with two men's heads, one dangling from each end, still dripping blood. Stunned, she turned away blindly, ran home, threw her books on the floor, and collapsed in bed, where she sank into a high fever. "I think this is enough to show you something of my childhood," Chiang Ch'ing said calmly.

II

Chiang Ch'ing grew up in perilous times that left a permanent stamp of threat and uncertainty on her consciousness. From the early 1920's on, the rise of imperialism, warlordism, and urban industrialism in the treaty ports of Shanghai and Tsingtao pricked the political consciousness of the young May Fourth generation. Communist and Nationalist Party agents, seeking to promote revolution by stirring up urban insurrection, made clandestine contact with workers in foreign-owned factories, disseminated Marxist propaganda, and fomented strikes protesting the physical abuse of laborers, long hours, the employment of children, and deplorable dormitory conditions. When strikes broke out against Japanese-owned cotton mills in Tsingtao and Shanghai, the Japanese responded by arresting "radicals," many of them students. The most memorable confrontation of the twenties took place in Shanghai on May 30, 1925, when university students demonstrating on behalf of Chinese workers exploited by Japanese- and British-owned factories were fired on by British police. The news of that bloody event, which touched off an intense and widespread public response, quickly spread to Tsingtao and other Chinese cities.

The Japanese had long-term interests in Shantung, and in the late 1920's thousands of Japanese were stationed in Tsinan and Tsingtao. Although Chiang Ch'ing did not elaborate upon this phase of China's political history, it left its mark clearly. In the spring of 1928, when she was just fourteen, Nationalist forces led by Chiang Kai-shek and the warlords Feng Yü-hsiang and Yen Hsi-shan launched the second stage of the Northern Expedition to complete the unification of China. Japan immediately dispatched an expeditionary force to protect the interests

of two thousand Japanese residents of Tsinan, and to obstruct the northward march of the Nationalist forces. On May 2, Chiang Kai-shek moved
his headquarters to Tsinan to forestall the Japanese expedition. During
the first week of May, Japanese and Nationalist troops coexisted in
Tsinan in an uneasy truce, punctuated by disrupted communications
and numerous small incidents. Then on May 7 Chiang Kai-shek pulled
out his troops and resumed his northward march, leaving in his wake
a reign of terror that lasted almost a year. The Japanese took over the
city, administered it through Chinese underlings, suspended freedom of
the press and of public assembly, and slaughtered Chinese citizens suspected of sympathy with Chiang Kai-shek's cause.[3] Chiang Ch'ing mentioned these crises in passing as they impinged on her life.

After the last Ch'ing Emperor was overthrown, the military governor
Chu Yü-p'u controlled Chihli province (later Hopeh), she recalled. By
1927 she and her mother had moved to Tientsin, to live with an elder
sister who was married to a minor official serving under Chu Yü-p'u
and other northern warlords. She remembered 1927 as the year when
"Chiang Kai-shek betrayed the revolution. I was only thirteen or so. I
had to do all the household chores—mopping the floor, cleaning the
rooms, shopping, and going to the pawnshops. But this also tempered
us. I wanted very much to continue school. But tuition in all the schools
there was too high and I could not afford it. Moreover, my brother-in-
law lost his job." Later that year, at a point she remembered as close in
time to the arrival of the Northern Expedition,* she decided to leave
home, hoping to become a worker in a Chinese cigarette factory; cig-
arettes then were still being rolled by hand, and the work was done
mostly by children. But her brother-in-law forbade her to go despite
the straitened circumstances that had forced him to pawn almost all
the family's belongings. He told her that working in a place like that
would turn her into a "little bureaucrat" (an epithet she did not explain). Though vexed by his opposition, she deferred to his wishes. In
1929 he and her sister moved to Tsinan, the provincial capital, taking
Chiang Ch'ing and her mother with them.

Located in western Shantung just six miles from the Yellow River,
Tsinan had been a vital cultural center since the Ming dynasty, when
its inner city wall, replete with impressive gates and towers, was erected.
The city's outer wall dated from the Ch'ing, by which time Tsinan
served as the civil service examination center for Shantung province.
By the time Chiang Ch'ing moved there the city's population exceeded

* The Northern Expedition reached Tientsin on June 6, 1928.

400,000, and its internal transportation system and external rail connections were the best in the province. The level of public education was high: there were over two hundred elementary schools, plus several high schools and colleges, including Chi-lu University. The city's racial composition had been complex since the late nineteenth century, when the municipal government opened the city to foreign residents, primarily Europeans. But the city's most recent immigrants were the Japanese, some 5,000 strong by the time Chiang Ch'ing arrived.[4] Since the Ming the city had been renowned for its theaters, in which, contrary to the custom prevailing elsewhere in China, some of the performers were women. Tsinan was also famous for its drum singers, most of whom were women. It was here that Chiang Ch'ing found her vocation as an actress. Her studies began at the Shantung Provincial Experimental Art Theater, a boarding school where tuition, room, and board were provided by the government. In Republican China such an arrangement was quite common. In return for government support, graduates of the school were usually obliged to work for an unspecified period as apprentices with the experimental troupe.

"In 1929 I was admitted to the Shantung Provincial Experimental Art Theater at Tsinan. This was an art school, where I studied mainly modern drama but also some classical music and drama. I was only fifteen then. The school provided free tuition and meals and an allowance of two *yüan* a month. Because the school sought to enroll graduates of junior and senior high schools and even university students, I did not technically qualify for admission. I was accepted only because the school had too few girls. I studied there only one year, but I learned a lot. I studied everything that came my way. I got up before daylight and strove to learn as much as possible." Not only did she read extensively in dramatic literature and learn to sing traditional opera and perform modern drama, but she was introduced to a variety of musical instruments. Among these was the piano, then an exotic instrument in China, which she studied for three months. Although her teacher was fond of her, she recalled, when it came to music he was a tough disciplinarian. To regulate the tempo of her playing, he struck her wrist with sticks, a pedagogical technique she deplored. With so little training she never got beyond the scales and basic exercises. This was the first time she had mentioned her piano training to a foreigner, Chiang Ch'ing added parenthetically; when President Nixon visited China earlier in 1972 she had been tempted to tell him, but decided against it because she was sure that he played far better than she.

In Chiang Ch'ing's class there were only three girls, of whom she was the youngest. The other two, along with the rest of the school's students, looked down on her because of her threadbare clothes. The director's wife, Yü Shan, who had been a student at the First Girls' Normal School in Tientsin (where Teng Ying-ch'ao, the wife of Chou En-lai, had also studied), was the sister of one of these two girls.[5] The director's wife was a "reactionary" who bullied her endlessly. But Chiang Ch'ing held her own against her and managed to play pranks of her own on the other girl students. Now, over forty years later, she recalled one with a pleasure not unmixed with a spite to which she freely admitted.

The school was situated in an old Confucian temple, which was completely airless during the scorching summers. After classes students went to the temple's main hall to cool off. Chiang Ch'ing recalled with particular vividness the huge statue of Confucius that stood at the center of the hall. Confucius wore an enormous hat with bead screens in front and behind; he was flanked by 72 sages who were his disciples. One hot evening Chiang Ch'ing entered the main hall and sat down in an old rattan chair. The two other girl students sauntered in and demanded that she move chairs for them. Chiang Ch'ing decided to comply in her own fashion. First she offered to hold up the lamp to assist them, then she moved two chairs into the hall for their use. As they proudly sat down, she slipped out the door with the lamp, slammed the gate behind her, and fled. Unexpectedly isolated in that eerie hall, the girls screamed, calling for others to come to their rescue.

Soon several boy students came running to console them. The boys found some lanterns and set out into the night to track down Chiang Ch'ing and "teach her a lesson," as she put it. She had run as fast as she could into some tall bushes beside a stream, where they could not find her. But the girls knew that eventually she would have to return to the room they all shared, and they would get even. When she thought they were asleep, she slipped back into the room, tunneled into bed, and pulled the mosquito netting closely around her. They knew, however, that she was terribly ticklish. When she saw fingers poking menacingly through the netting, she screamed. The angry girls tried to force her to promise never to do such a wicked thing again. "That depends," she hedged.

There was also much good that they shared. To perform drama Chiang Ch'ing first had to master the Peking dialect, which was standard in China for all official and cultural purposes. Her own dialect was that of Shantung province, modified by the local dialect of her birthplace. The other students, already fluent in Peking pronunciation, roared with laughter at her clumsy efforts to master their tongue. Nevertheless she persisted, she recalled good-naturedly, and one of her schoolmates coached her and listened patiently to her practice recitations.

Once the school mounted an experimental production of *Tragedy on a Lake*, a "bourgeois drama" by the well-known playwright T'ien Han, who founded the Southern Society (Nan Kuo She), a famous drama group of that era. The student who was the sister of the director's wife was first assigned the lead in this production, but Chiang Ch'ing was given the role on a Monday, a day when the audience typically was scant. She threw herself entirely into the part. The audience was moved to tears, and their emotion caused tears to pour from her own eyes—the effect of following the "naturalist" school of acting. (As Chiang Ch'ing observed later, the "naturalist" school was to be thoroughly repudiated by the present regime.) When she was removing her makeup after the show, the school's director and her teacher strode into the dressing room to commend her performance and hail her promise as a tragic actress. Overwhelmed by their praise, she dissolved into tears and dashed from the dressing room. Despite this incident, recaptured as melodrama, she remembered the general aura of this period with vexation. "As a matter of fact, I was insulted everywhere in Tsinan," she added without further elaboration.

"The school was closed down when Han Fu-ch'ü, the warlord of the Northwestern Army, came to Tsinan.[6] I joined some of the school's teachers and students in organizing a touring theatrical group that went to Peking. I departed without telling my mother, only mailing her a letter at the railway station just before the train pulled out.

"That year [1930] I was only sixteen, and life in Peking was very hard indeed. I was so poorly equipped that I did not even have any underclothes. Although I had taken my family's best quilt with me, I still shivered with cold because its cotton wadding was worn thin from age. That season in Peking there were heavy sandstorms and the nights were dismal. I had not yet come to know politics. I had no notion of the significance of 'Kuomintang' and 'Communist Party.' All I knew was that I wanted to feed myself and that I adored drama."

"Then in spring 1931 I went to Tsingtao," she said. "My former teacher [Chao T'ai-mou], a fellow townsman who used to be Director of the Experimental Theater in Tsinan, now had become Dean of Tsingtao University, serving currently as Professor in the Literature Department. Through these connections, he arranged my admission to Tsingtao University."[*]

[*] In 1932 its name was changed to Shantung University.

When Chao T'ai-mou first presented her with this opportunity, she was tempted, but she felt uneasy about moving to the wholly unfamiliar environment of Tsingtao. To encourage her, he promised to set up an art department (presumably dramatic arts, though she did not specify) at Tsingtao University and offered to pay her travel expenses to Tsingtao. Her classmates from the Experimental Art Theater at Tsinan urged her to accept, and she finally agreed. "Actually, he [Chao] belonged to the Reformist Group of the Kuomintang. His views on literature and art were close to those of Hu Shih.[7] I was once appreciated by the bourgeoisie," she added with a smile. "There was a time when members of Hu Shih's group, which included people like Liang Shih-ch'iu and Wen I-to, tried to win me over to their side.[8] Wen I-to was one of my teachers at Tsingtao University, where I audited many of his lectures.*

"Our greatest teacher by negative example was Japanese imperialism. After the September 18, 1931, incident at Mukden, our three northeastern provinces [Manchuria] were seized by the Japanese imperialists. That we could not tolerate. We could not become slaves to a foreign nation. As for myself, I too felt compelled to resist Japanese aggression. By that time, the whole of China was surging up in a high tide of national democratic revolution. Many students went on strike or petitioned government authorities, and the workers supported them. The movement engaged a broad spectrum of the people.

"Aroused by the situation, I said to my teacher [Chao], 'I want to join the petitioning.' He shot back, 'You want to make trouble, too?' I was dumbfounded and could scarcely say anything. So I turned and left, knowing full well that he was greatly displeased with me. I walked alone to the hills and wandered in the woods, deeply perplexed by what he meant when he said that the students' patriotic movement was 'trouble-making.' When at last I realized that his views were wrong, I decided to join the League of Left-Wing Dramatists in Tsingtao.

"At Tsingtao University, there were mass student boycotts of classes and examinations. Under these circumstances, I refused to accept any more assistance from my teacher. So I joined the university staff as library clerk. My job was to write out cards. At the same time, I continued to audit classes. Each month I earned thirty yüan [about $9] and sent ten to my mother. Because the cost of living at Tsingtao was

---

* Yao Wen-yüan, who was present during the conversation, interjected matter-of-factly, "Wen I-to was assassinated by Chiang Kai-shek's thugs in the latter stage of the democratic revolution because of his participation in the progressive anti–Chiang Kai-shek movement. He was highly spoken of by Chairman Mao in an article he wrote in August 1949."

very high, the twenty yüan remaining was not enough for me. For you
see, I was not only supporting myself, I had to help out other comrades.
We had to pay out of our own pockets the costs of staging plays calling
for National Salvation—no one helped us with money.* When we took
our performances to factories or to the villages, the people welcomed
us and helped us, but they too were hard up. At that time, I did not
know that liberation must be won by the poor. Only later, after I joined
the Party, did I learn from other comrades that so naïve an understanding would not do, that one must serve the proletariat."

The university was but one dimension of Chiang Ch'ing's life at Tsingtao. Soon after she arrived there in January 1931, she and some fellow
dramatists (the "comrades" mentioned above) set up the Seaside Drama
Society (Hai-mo chü-she). She vividly recalled now the initial impact
of Tsingtao: chill fog and salty sea breeze at the harbor. How strange
it was, she remarked, that although her home town Chu-ch'eng was less
than fifty miles away, she had never laid eyes on the ocean before this
time. As for the Seaside Drama Society, its purpose was less artistic than
political: to make theatrical propaganda against the Japanese at schools
and factories and in the rural areas.† After performing in the city at
the height of the New Year's festivities, the troupe left for the countryside with the purpose of spreading news of the soviet districts being
developed by the Chinese Red Army in Kiangsi. In 1931 substantial
knowledge of the Red leaders and the emerging way of life in the soviets
was scant, and their forces did not yet seriously threaten the security
of the Nationalist regime. Even so, public mention of the soviets' existence was risky. To avoid arrest by Kuomintang agents who had infiltrated the countryside, the Seaside Drama Society decided to minimize
its conspicuousness by dividing into small units, which made their way
separately into the rural areas.

The plunge into the countryside caused unforeseen problems for
young idealists used to urban amenities. The rural areas were poor, food
was scarce, and public restaurants and inns were almost nonexistent.
Consequently, they were forced to go for long periods without eating, an experience that sapped their morale. Other naïvetés emerged as

---

* National Salvation (*chiu-kuo*) was a term popularly used from the 1920's
through the 1940's to refer to all organized patriotic efforts to "save the nation" from
the Japanese.

† Though Chiang Ch'ing was then a novice at impromptu political theater, it had
a tradition in China going back nearly three decades; at the turn of the century young
radicals performed songs and skits to show the evils of foreign imperialism. See Mary
C. Wright, ed., *China in Revolution: The First Phase, 1900–1913* (New Haven,
Conn., 1968), p. 9.

the troupe progressed through the countryside. The first village they reached was Lao-shan-wan, a few miles up the coast from Tsingtao. When the actors presented themselves, the villagers were shocked by the men's Western-style suits and the women's *ch'i-p'ao* (the Mandarin-collared, slit-skirted dresses worn by urban women of Republican China). Obviously disturbed by their presence, the villagers sent someone to present them with a silver dollar, apparently to speed them on their way. Villagers who were outraged by their strange appearance accused them of coming there just for fun rather than for a serious performance. Nor did the troupe's propaganda have any noticeable effect. In those years, Chiang Ch'ing added with the advantage of hindsight, they knew nothing of the "summing-up experience," by which political workers trained in Communist methods immediately follow up a performance or work session with a collective assessment of the performers' good and bad points.

As they prepared to leave Lao-shan-wan, the villagers recommended that they go to Wang-ke-chuang, a larger village with several inns situated just a few miles down the coast from Tsingtao. There Chiang Ch'ing was assigned to work with children. Since by then the Japanese had infiltrated the entire coastal area around Tsingtao, Chiang Ch'ing established rapport with the children by teaching them anti-Japanese songs. The children responded readily, having already been alerted by their parents to the viciousness of "Western and Eastern devils." The children took to her, and a few invited her to visit their homes. Though obviously gratified by this recollection, she noted that other members of the troupe enjoyed equal success.

During the troupe's few days in Wang-ke-chuang, Chiang Ch'ing gradually became attuned to local ways, and the peasants took a liking to her. They singled her out from the group, she recalled with pleasure, and begged her to sing favorite arias from Peking opera. Even then she did not adore Peking opera, yet to please them she obliged. After a while they would join in, singing in the local operatic style. Once the troupe gained the people's confidence, they introduced political messages into the songs and skits. Such innovations went over best with the younger peasants. Yet how astonished they were when the players began to tell them about life in the soviet areas (about which they had previously heard only second-hand reports), especially the communal ownership of food and clothing.

Most of the Seaside Drama Society's political work was still at the experimental stage. One of the trial performances given at Wang-ke-chuang was the original version of *Lay Down Your Whip* (Fang-hsia ni-te pien-tzu), a one-act play set to song and instrumentation, about Manchurian refugees living under Japanese occupation, an example of street theater (*chieh-t'ou chü*) that became a highly popular encapsulation of the national defense theme in the 1930's. Since that version still had flaws, Chiang Ch'ing did not want the draft score circulated. When some local musicians tried to get a copy from her, she quickly tucked it into her pocket, slipped away from the gathering, and ran straight to the graveyard, where she hid it under a tombstone. No one found it there.

The audience at Wang-ke-chuang included a good many soldiers, who obviously liked the troupe's performance. Warming to their praise, Chiang Ch'ing agreed to spend time with three of them. As they were chatting about political affairs, the soldiers kept stressing the virtues of cooperation between the Chinese Communist Party and the Kuomintang, a notion that seemed implausible to her even then. Despite their political differences, they parted amicably, the soldiers insisting that she accept some gifts for herself and her friends as a token of appreciation for their cultural work. That evening she returned to the inn laden with bounty: cotton quilts, the steamed cabbage famous in that area of Shantung, and the steamed bread (*mo*) popular in North China. Only later did she discover that among the soldiers she had spoken with that day were some who had taken part in the Shanghai Uprising of 1927—which resulted in the Kuomintang's bloody purge of the Communist Party from its ranks—and that a branch of the Communist Party had been established in Wang-ke-chuang prior to their arrival. She was never in touch with that branch; her first contact with the party was made later, in the city of Tsingtao.

After several days at Wang-ke-chuang, the players prepared to leave. Some villagers urged Chiang Ch'ing to stay, and she was touched by their hospitality, but the players had to move on. Whenever they took to the road in those out-of-the-way places, their cash ran out and their hungry stomachs growled. On one occasion, penniless as usual, they all piled onto a bus. Some hours later the driver halted at a bus stop on a narrow mountain road and demanded their fares. They tried to convince him they would pay when they reached their destination, but he objected loudly and would have left them stranded on the mountain road had some local people not rescued them by putting up the fare. That embarrassing meeting between "poor" mountain folk and "rich" urban intellectuals made a sharp impression on Chiang Ch'ing. Not long afterward she explored the social implications in a long article published in Tsingtao.

Mention of that article, written in 1931, reminded Chiang Ch'ing of a more recent incident. During the Cultural Revolution, the "Lin Piao clique" (Lin Piao was celebrated as her major political helpmate until the fall of 1971) authorized two groups of people to search for materials that could be used against her. One, which called itself the May Sixteenth Group,* amassed information about her past that it hoped to embarrass her with. The May Sixteenth Group demanded of Chou En-lai that he personally search for articles Chiang Ch'ing had written years earlier, including the one composed when she was a member of Tsing-tao's Seaside Drama Society. Under pressure Chou complied, but his search failed to uncover anything. Besides the article that had appeared in Tsingtao, another that eluded them was one called "My Open Letter," which had appeared some years later in Shanghai's *Ta-kung-pao*. Hesitating momentarily, she corrected her earlier statement: actually, Chou had managed to track down a piece she had written for a women's magazine. Having written it so long ago, Chiang Ch'ing had all but forgotten it. When she was questioned about this, her interrogators accused her of having written it just to make money. She confounded them by agreeing! Living a hand-to-mouth existence, she had written that article *only* to make money.

III

In the Republican era it was not unusual for a poor student to attend university classes as an auditor, doing the same work as a regular student but with no right to a degree. In this capacity Chiang Ch'ing came into contact with renowned professors not only at Tsingtao University, but later at Peking University and at universities in Shanghai. As an auditor at Tsingtao University, she gained her first exposure to intellectuals as personalities and as fresh sources of ideas. Although she would later repudiate open-ended academic inquiry, at the susceptible age of

* That curious twist in her narrative, a sign of the ongoing dialectic between past recollection and present politics, was later clarified by Chiang Ch'ing. She was a key member of the May 16 Group set up in May 1966 to discredit the authors of the February Outline, who were identified as supporters of Mao Tse-tung's chief opponent in the Cultural Revolution, Liu Shao-ch'i. One of the May 16 Group's initial goals was to rout out reactionary elements in the regional branches of the People's Liberation Army, which was then headed by Lin Piao, Chiang Ch'ing's major patron as of February. By summer that patronage backfired, as evidenced by "ultra-leftist" attacks on Chou En-lai (whom Chiang Ch'ing always credited as her supporter), herself, and other members of the Cultural Revolution Group identified with Mao. For an analysis of these Byzantine politics based on the published record, see Barry Burton, "The Cultural Revolution's Ultra-Left Conspiracy: The 'May 16 Group,'" *Asian Survey*, 11.11 (Nov. 1971).

seventeen she was exhilarated by the free play of thought in a university environment.

She had not thought back on her Tsingtao experience for years, Chiang Ch'ing confessed, and reconstructed events elliptically. With some experience in drama, she was intensely interested in literature, ancient and modern, and in trying her hand at writing. The first teacher she recalled was Wen I-to, who taught courses on T'ang poetry, on novels and drama, and on the history of Chinese literature. There was also Yang Chen-sheng, author of the novel *Jade Gentleman* (*Yü chün*, 1925) and then President of Tsingtao University. With him she studied creative writing, and got to know him better than Wen I-to. She attended the classes of Fang Ling-lu, a woman writer whom Chiang Ch'ing believed to have served in her own student days as Chairman of the Literary Association of Chekiang. Wen I-to, Yang Chen-sheng, and Fang Ling-lu had all studied in the United States, Chiang Ch'ing remarked, and Yang and Fang were still alive at the time of Liberation in 1949.

She could not at the moment recall the names of her other teachers. What she remembered best were impressions of her own first literary efforts. She wrote her first short story in a course taught by Yang Chen-sheng, who enthusiastically praised it as very much like the work of the celebrated woman writer Hsieh Ping-hsin.* A great admirer of Ping-hsin, Chiang Ch'ing was overwhelmed by the comparison. A subsequent story did not fare as well. Though Yang rated it the best in the class, he had one criticism to make. "Miss Li," he said, "your robber is too genteel. When he curses a person he uses the expression 'Drop dead' [*kai ssu*]. Now that's refined language—not rough enough for a robber." Humiliated by this criticism, she never returned to his class.

In the summer of 1931 Chiang Ch'ing wrote a play entitled *Whose Crime?* about a young revolutionary who lived with his sickly mother. He broke the law in some way, and when he eluded the police the mother was seized in his stead. Eventually the son was arrested and the mother died. Reference to the plot of her play reminded her of the name of her play-writing teacher, Chao Ping-o, with whom she also had a distressing exchange in the early fall. He commended her style, but expressed bewilderment at the political ambiguities in the text. He asked her bluntly whether her "revolutionaries" belonged to the Communist Party or the Kuomintang. Still desperately ignorant of the substantive differences between the two and frustrated with embarrassment, she

---

* For a discussion of Ping-hsin's career, see the preceding paper.

retorted, "*You* tell *me* what's the difference between the Chinese Communist Party and the Kuomintang!" His sharp laughter at her sophomoric response showed her he thought her a fool. Yet he liked the play well enough to urge her to expand it from one act to three. The play was not all that important, she said; what mattered was that his needling aroused her curiosity. Although during the Seaside Drama Society's tour she had made some simple propaganda for the soviets, she began to wonder now just what were the ideological differences between the Communist and Kuomintang parties. "From that point on, I began to observe."

That fall the usual calm of university life was shattered by the Mukden Incident of September 1931: Japanese troops marched on Manchuria. In the heat of that crisis she was still ignorant of the meaning of "reformism" and its relation to the Kuomintang. Although she and others like her had assumed that these "nationalists," so heavily concentrated in the university environment, were patriots who valued their country's integrity above everything else, they were wrong. She now perceived that these respected reformists were not really determined to resist Japanese aggression at all costs. When in the heat of the reaction to the Mukden Incident she declared herself openly for resistance, they criticized *her* for being a troublemaker. With Chao Ping-o's sarcasm still ringing in her ears, she wandered by herself into the woods outside Tsingtao to mull over his words. It dawned on her that Chao had to be a member of the Kuomintang, the "Nationalist" Party that was not following the hard line of resistance. When students at the university began to make trouble for her, she surmised that they too had to be working for the Kuomintang. After that she accepted no more help from Chao Ping-o, and set out on her own course.

The reception room in which Chiang Ch'ing and I were talking was hugely proportioned. Yet on a sultry August evening in Canton, its air began to close in on us. She proposed that we change to another room. Standing up, she stretched her limbs pleasurably, adjusted and smoothed her dress, and led the way. The room to which we moved was comparably grand. Seating arrangements, tables, writing and recording equipment, refreshments, and the full service of hot, cold, wet, and dry towels were set up exactly as they had been in the first room. We sat down, and she resumed her narrative.

She had also studied with the writer Shen Ts'ung-wen, who also taught fiction at Tsingtao University. As his student, she gradually got to know him. He had a sister named Shen Chou-chou who was often with him, and who often invited Chiang Ch'ing to visit their home. Apparently impressed with her literary talent, Shen wanted her to improve her style by writing a story a week. He was in earnest, she thought, but she never made the effort. From her perspective as a poor student, the Shen family seemed rich.[9] When Shen's sister, seeing that Chiang Ch'ing needed money, offered to pay her for knitting Shen a sweater, she refused. Later she learned that Shen Chou-chou had studied at the French Missionary School in Peking, an elitist institution where tuition was high —five or six hundred silver dollars a term.

Summing up the cultural significance of her Tsinan, Peking, and Tsingtao years, Chiang Ch'ing said that she had spent one year (1929–30) at an arts academy and two years (1931–33) in the "upper strata of culture," referring to the intellectual circle of Tsingtao University and the cultural circle of the Seaside Drama Society. In those years she developed a love of novels and poetry. She also enjoyed foreign poetry in translation, reading most extensively in "old foreign poetry," though she observed that most poetry is not translatable and so cannot be genuinely understood by foreigners. When she was young, she said, she composed verse that she considered publishing and also wrote essays, some of which were published. But in the 1930's she decided that writing poems and essays was far less important than actively making revolution. As for formal education, counting five years of primary school, in all she had but eight years. Her real learning, like Mao's, was "social education," education in the school of experience. And in 1933 that was just beginning.

In this early interview, Chiang Ch'ing revealed the first of what would unfold as some twenty chapters of her lifetime as of the summer of 1972. Her beginnings, as she was aware, were quite ordinary, and for that reason not worth dwelling upon in exhaustive detail. Yet in her earliest years one can perceive certain distinctive modes of reacting to experience and of handling situations. She displays a quick temper, swift defensive and aggressive energies, and a keen sense of opportunity. Still more important, she exhibits what we might call a spontaneous radicalism— a willingness to take risks so as to increase her control over her own life and her environment. All these are character traits she would use to cut through the social and cultural bondage of being born an impoverished female.

Her break with conventional constraints on women by repudiating her family, negotiating a position as university student, and gaining recognition as an actress, all before she was twenty, is important in itself, but this was merely the first stage in the development of wide-ranging cultural pursuits and the formation of a "revolutionary" character. Her relations to her parents were fairly typical of commoners of her generation: resistance to a harsh father, the original "bully" of her life, was balanced by tenderness and instinctual protectiveness toward her vulnerable mother. Her contemptuous assessment of her father set her against an unthinking patriarchalism from an early age. Her natal family and the landlord families into which her mother moved offered no positive model of family life, and her recollections reveal no significant awareness of positive domestic roles for women. She speaks unsentimentally and apolitically of poverty, hunger, and instability, an attitude that contrasts with the learned pride in poverty that is the hallmark of proletarian class character and a fundamental element in current Chinese ideology. Sadism was the norm in the social environment she first knew. With images of executions and decapitations surreally fresh in her memory, she has no illusion about man's capacity for violence.

From her youth, politics was but one side of the double-faced fabric of her life. Culture, especially the performing arts, was the other, and soon the two would be bonded together. Her involvement with the Seaside Drama Society marks both a turning point in the political history of modern Chinese culture and the first convergence of the political and cultural dimensions of her own career. The Society's naïvely conceived jaunts to the countryside were a backward reflection of the romantic revolutionary notion, inspired by the Russian Narodniks, of "going to the people" to rouse their torpid consciousness. Now as Chiang Ch'ing explained her youthful experience from the vantage point of a seasoned Communist, her group's initiation into countryside drama cast a forward reflection toward Mao Tse-tung's formula for the popular promotion of literary and art works: all art is political and must serve the people.

A brief look at her subsequent life may be of interest. In the early 1930's, she joined several leftist leagues of artists and professionals determined to make a collective statement of their objections to the policies of the Kuomintang government. In 1933 she joined the Communist Party in Tsingtao, though she lost that membership when she moved to Shanghai later that year. In Shanghai, then caught in the paradoxical spell of extraordinary cultural diversity subjected to totalitarian repression, she joined popular demonstrations against the Japanese and their Chinese collaborators, was kidnapped and imprisoned for suspected Communist associations, participated in the mass education movement as a teacher of women workers, and acted in amateur and professional theater and in films. By 1936 the forces of political and public persecution drove her, along with other women writers, artists, and actresses, to the brink of suicide.

With the renewal of the Japanese attack in 1937, Chiang Ch'ing joined the exodus of young radicals from Shanghai to Yenan, the barren north-west outpost where Mao and the other beleaguered survivors of the Long March had settled the year before. There she underwent a rigor-ous course in military arts and Marxist politics, taught drama at the Lu Hsün Academy of Literature and Art, and married Mao. In the late 1940's she participated in the liberation wars, an experience savored as much for its lessons in political strategy as for its military drama. Dur-ing much of the 1950's she was ill: brief periods of political activity alternated with long stretches of convalescent retreat. Soon after Lib-eration she participated anonymously in the arduous and often violent movements of land and marriage reform. As Mao's closest associate she was embroiled in the public debates over the films, plays, and novels that allegedly upheld a disfiguring mirror to leading personalities of their times. She also initiated the renewal of literary debate over the great eighteenth-century family saga *Dream of the Red Chamber*, of which she spoke with nearly inexhaustible enthusiasm and detail, devot-ing particular attention to an analysis of the leading female characters.

In the early 1960's Chiang Ch'ing began an independent investigation of the performing arts—opera, modern drama, music, and film. Paradox-ically, the flourishing of these increasingly popular genres indicated to her the extent to which the Chairman's *diktat* on the creation of a pro-letarian culture (spelled out in his 1942 "Talks to the Yenan Forum on Art and Literature") had been largely forgotten in the wake of material progress, and also convinced her of the ultimate insubstantiality of pre-vious rectification movements against intellectuals. Working alongside musicians, performers, directors, and cultural administrators, few of whom were eager instruments of change, she launched a new movement to proletarianize the cultural environment in accordance with Mao's political principles and her own aesthetic sensibilities. In that spirit she authorized the creation of the *yang-pan-hsi*, the small repertoire of model operas and ballets that stand as palpable cultural evidence of the Cultural Revolution she helped to engender in the mid-1960's. On this new stage the common people were neither absent nor fools, but stars, and proletarian women achieved a sexual parity unmatched by art or life in the revolution to that time.

Although she is the only woman among the leading comrades of the Politburo, Chiang Ch'ing does not restrict her political horizon to women's affairs. She has never been among the leaders of the national women's movement. Yet she is the first woman in Chinese history to assume an authoritative role in the nation's cultural policy, one focused on the performing arts but extending to literary criticism and education at all levels. However inimitable she is by virtue of being the Chairman's wife (though not every Chairman's wife would have acted as she has), she is China's most conspicuous model of woman in revolution. More important in the long run, the positive and egalitarian female roles she has established in art will serve as models in the people's lives for years to come.

The Power and Pollution of Chinese Women

EMILY M. AHERN

In many societies women are considered ritually polluting and unclean. This means in part that a woman's sexual parts and their emissions are regarded as potentially harmful to others. When women are in a state considered unclean, therefore, they must carefully abstain from certain activities, and other people must take precautions before coming into contact with them.

In Chinese society women are regarded as both ritually unclean and dangerously powerful, and they are barred from certain activities because of the harm they threaten to inflict on others.* In the following analysis I explore from three different approaches the question of why Chinese women should be considered unclean or polluting: the first looks to the nature of allegedly unclean substances and their connection with birth and death; the second views the ascription of pollution to women as a reflection of their social role; and the third sees women's putative pollution as part of a system of ideas relating pollution to breaking the boundaries of social groups. In the conclusion I assess the relative merits of the three approaches.

I. Unclean Substances

In *A Daughter of Han* Lao T'ai T'ai declares, "Women were not considered clean."[1] What has made Chinese women unclean, and what other

---

* The material used here was gathered from June to August 1972, during a field project made possible by the Department of Epidemiology and International Health, University of Washington. The study was done in Ch'i-nan, a village in northern Taiwan, the same village I lived in from 1969 to 1970. Although I refer to "Chinese" for convenience, most of my data come from this Hokkien-speaking Taiwanese community. For background information on Ch'i-nan, see Emily M. Ahern, *The Cult of the Dead in a Chinese Village* (Stanford, Calif., 1973).

persons or substances are similarly counted as unclean? Principally, bodily effluvia associated exclusively with women are unclean: menstrual blood and postpartum discharge, which are believed to be the same substance. When a woman becomes pregnant, menstrual fluids accumulate in her body. These fluids emerge during childbirth and continue to flow, less and less heavily, for about a month afterward. Both menstrual and postpartum discharges are unclean, though the quantities of effluvia associated with birth make that event much dirtier. As one of my informants put it, "Menstruation is like one-hundredth of a birth."

In describing these substances, people used the word *la-sam*, a word also used to describe ordinary sorts of dirty things—a child's dirty face, for instance, or a dirty shirt. Alternatively, they described unclean substances as not clean, *bou chieng-khi*. Menstrual fluids are considered unclean in part because they are bad for the body. A woman is well rid of them. Numerous informants said something like this: "You want to get all the dirty stuff out. It's good to get rid of it; that blood is dirty. It is blood the body doesn't need." Such remarks make an implicit distinction between beneficent blood, i.e. the blood that flows through the veins, which is essential to health, and the blood that flows out during menstruation, which is harmful. Both kinds of blood escape during childbirth. A woman hopes to replace the good, ordinary blood by eating tonic foods after childbirth; the dirty blood, she feels, is a kind "no one would want."

Anyone who comes into contact with menstrual blood—male or female—is barred from worshiping the gods. Given the serious consequence of contact with menstrual blood, one would expect great care to be taken in its disposition. In fact, however, women treat the problem quite casually. They put the soiled papers or pads in the latrine, where they disintegrate. The fact that a latrine's contents ordinarily end up on rice fields in the form of nightsoil might be taken as indicating scant concern with unclean substances. Actually, however, concern with dirt reappears in another form: anything that has come into contact with the dirt on the ground is potentially offensive to the gods because unclean menstrual substances may be mixed in with ordinary dirt. A god's image, I was told, cannot be carried under a clothes-drying pole because pants (men's and women's) have probably been hung on it. "Pants are dirty because people's feet have passed through them when they put them on. People's feet are dirty because they often touch the ground and can come into contact with dirt even though we ourselves may not know it. The ground is full of dirty stuff—both real dirt [earth] and

women's dirt. Our feet can't help coming into contact with this dirt."
Even though in theory everyone comes into contact with menstrual
blood in walking on the ground, in practice not everyone is prevented
from worshiping the gods on that account. Only things touched by the
feet must be kept away from the gods.

As the statement about dirt on the ground indicates, there are other
kinds of dirt besides menstrual fluids. At this point, I will briefly introduce the other unclean substances as they were explained to me. Later
in the paper, I will relate the unclean substances women produce to the
entire class of unclean things. People talked about dirty substances in
two basic ways. One approach was to consider any discharge from the
body dirty; menstrual blood, semen, urine, feces, pus, and mucus are all
dirty. One woman told me, "Menstrual blood, semen, urine, feces—all
that stuff—is dirty." When I asked why, she replied, "How could something coming out from inside the skin be clean?" (*Baq-lai chut-lai na u
chieng-khi?*)* The other approach to unclean substances was to divide them into two major types, the dirt associated with happy events
(births) and the dirt associated with unhappy events (deaths). As one
informant explained it, "The dirt from birth—menstrual fluids—is the
dirtiest of all. Then there is the dirt from death—the corpse. Both of
them are dirty in the same way, but the dirt of birth is the dirt of happy
events (*hi-su*), and the dirt of a corpse is the dirt of unhappy events
(*song-su*)." Ghosts, too, are said to be unclean by virtue of their association with death. Ghosts are spirits of dead persons, who for one reason or another cannot follow the normal route to the underworld. Rites
to propitiate these ghosts are said to make the places they frequent
cleaner. Most things people referred to as dirty were covered by the
happy-unhappy typology. The major omission is sexual intercourse,
which is not explicitly classified with the dirt of happy events despite
its recognized connection with pregnancy and birth. I will discuss the
dirt of sexual intercourse in more detail later.

The effect of contact with most dirty substances is the same as the
effect of contact with menstrual blood: women who are menstruating
or within a month of childbirth, anyone who enters a room in which a
woman has given birth within the previous month, anyone who is in
mourning, and anyone who has recently had sexual intercourse cannot

* Recent anthropological analyses of ritual pollution have shown the frequency
with which bodily excretions are invested with special properties. Often they are considered both polluting and dangerously powerful. See, for example, Mary Douglas,
Purity and Danger: An Analysis of Concepts of Pollution and Taboo (New York,
1966), pp. 114–28.

worship the gods. Here the term polluting will be applied only to dirty substances that break communication between man and gods upon contact. Unclean things that do not affect the relationship between man and gods are peripheral to my analysis. Some people made this distinction themselves, saying that bodily substances like urine, feces, and pus (which do not affect worship of the gods) are "really" dirty, whereas menstrual blood and corpses are dirty in a different sense. Someone who has been in contact with a "really" dirty substance can be cleaned with soap and water, whereas the dirtiness of someone who has been in contact with menstrual blood or with a corpse cannot be alleviated by soap and water.

The polluting substances associated exclusively with women—menstrual and birth fluids—are closely associated with dangerous power. Menstrual blood is most directly powerful in that, in the villagers' understanding, it creates babies. Some of the menstrual blood a woman produces during pregnancy flows out during childbirth. The remaining accumulated menstrual blood *becomes* the body of the child; "it creates flesh and bones" (*si:-kut si:-baq*), informants said. The blood discharged when a baby is born is residue of the creation process. To be sure, menstrual blood alone cannot produce a child. For that, "you need both the mother's blood and the father's semen. The semen has '*thang*' in it, which make the child start to grow. The thang are like seeds in the ground from which a plant grows." The role of semen and the role of plant seed are not identical. Whereas a seed itself turns into a grown plant, semen merely starts the growth of a child; what turns into the body of a child, into its flesh and bones, is menstrual blood. The woman's role in procreation is thus seen as very substantial.*

The blood that surrounds the fetus and emerges during childbirth also has great power. Beliefs about the potentially dangerous power of this superfluous blood are related to beliefs about the behavior of a spiritual entity called the Thai Sin. Although the name means Placenta God, Thai Sin is also, and more importantly, regarded as the child's soul. One informant said, "You could say that just as adults have a *lieng-hun* [a soul], so infants have a Thai Sin." The Thai Sin comes into existence the moment the child is conceived and stays until four months after birth. During its first nine months the spirit is not confined to the fetus, but moves about inside the pregnant woman's bedroom. This movement causes

---

* Ancient ideas about women also depict them as the fount of life-giving forces. Whereas men must copulate with women to absorb women's yin essence, women themselves have an endless supply, which is not depleted by intercourse. R. H. Van Gulick, *Sexual Life in Ancient China* (Leiden, 1961), pp. 46, 48.

difficulties: if one should happen to strike, break, or cut something in the woman's room when the Thai Sin is in the way, the child's body may be injured. If one cuts cloth at the wrong time, the child may be born with a cleft palate; if one breaks a stick, one of the child's limbs may be damaged; if one drives a nail in the wall or digs a hole in the floor, the child may be aborted or born prematurely. After birth the Thai Sin becomes attached to the child's body with increasing firmness, until, at about four months, there is no need to fear striking it inadvertently.[2]

Because the newborn child's soul is not firmly settled within his body, anything close to the child can affect his body through the medium of the Thai Sin. Because the Thai Sin may be present in the birth fluids, their disposal is most problematic. If they are disturbed while being removed, the infant may fall seriously ill. One informant said,

The birth fluids are caught on paper so they won't spill on the floor or bed. Afterward, the midwife takes the paper away and drops it gently into a large, free-running stream. She must be sure to drop it softly, because if she drops it with a jolt, the child will vomit continuously. The blood is very strong and powerful [*li-hai*]. If there is no stream, it can be buried but not burned. If fire were to touch the blood, the child itself would burn up, or else be marked with red spots. All the blood must be disposed of; if some soaks into an earthen floor you should dig up the earth in that place and dispose of it, too.

The power of this blood derives from its relation to the child; because the baby's soul is likely to be present in the blood, the treatment it receives can directly affect the baby's well-being.

In the case of birth fluids, every effort is made to avoid harming the child. In other cases, the potentially harmful power of menstrual blood may be deliberately exploited. About twenty years ago, I was told, two Ch'i-nan men named Li and Peq quarreled because chickens that belonged to one man ate some grain that belonged to the other. The quarrel finally escalated into a fight with long knives, in which Peq killed Li. Afterward, fearing the revenge the Li man's soul might exact, the Peqs hired a Taoist priest. The Taoist performed esoteric rituals using two key substances to ward off the vengeful soul: the blood of a black dog (a euphemism for menstrual blood) and a brass needle. The Taoist not only kept the soul away but also destroyed its power; as a result, it was said, the Li family has been declining ever since.

Other substances, similar to menstrual blood, are invested with similar powers. To be specific, blood flowing from bodies is in many cases regarded as powerful. In Ch'i-nan when a pig or chicken is slaughtered for the gods, the butcher captures a cupful of the blood that spurts from the jugular vein. A wad of ritual paper money may also be thrust into the stream of blood. These two items are presented to the gods as embodiments of the strength and life force of the slaughtered animal.

The power released at the moment when blood is spilled in slaughter, like menstrual blood, has potential for both good and evil. The man hired to slaughter a pig pastes a charm written on red paper (a prophylactic color) on the handle of the slaughtering knife. One such charm was used in Ch'i-nan when a man fell sick at the exact moment of the kill. The butcher soaked the charm in water and administered the resulting drink to the sick man. He soon recovered.

The double-edged power of blood is evident also from its use in exorcising evil spirits. The blood protects those who use it on the one hand and destroys those against whom it is used on the other. David Graham tells us that the blood of humans, chickens, or ducks can be used to exorcise demons.[3] According to J. J. M. de Groot, the blood of dogs is used for the same purpose.[4] Finally, *tang-ki*, spirit mediums who become possessed with the spirit of a god, commonly mutilate themselves and daub the resulting blood on charms that are then used to ward off evil spirits.[5]

Slaughter and exorcism seem a long way from menstruation and childbirth. Yet one element links them all, the escape and flow of blood. Moreover, in at least one instance menstrual blood is explicitly linked to the blood shed by tang-ki. A. J. A. Elliott notes that menstruating women are expected to stay away when a tang-ki is possessed: "If a menstruating woman is present while the *dang-ki* [sic] is possessed by the *shen* [god], she places both herself and him in great danger. If the *dang-ki* has cut himself as part of the performance, he may have great difficulty in stopping the flow of blood if such a woman is near him."[6] The escape of blood, any blood, from a living body seems to be associated with power. The life force in this power can be harnessed to produce a child, to please the gods with a potent offering, or to protect a person threatened by an evil spirit. At the same time, the destructive force in the power of blood portends death and danger—to the newborn child, the bystander at a slaughter, vulnerable spirits, and bleeding tang-ki.

The association of blood with both beneficial and destructive power may derive in part from the involvement of blood in both life and death. Blood is necessary for the development of a new life, but the menstrual blood that flows when a woman is not pregnant is, in a sense, a dead fetus. In earlier times, too, childbirth itself and the accompanying blood flow were all too often associated with the death of the mother, the child, or both. Moreover, the powerful blood that flows at a slaughter

is necessarily accompanied by the death of an animal. The close association of both life and death with flowing blood is epitomized by a custom De Groot reported for Amoy: the blood that spurted from decapi-
tated criminals was collected and used for life-strengthening medicines.[7]
It may be partly the fundamental emotional response of people confronted with the momentous events of birth and death that invests flowing blood—which partakes of both—with its ambivalent power.

II. *Power and Danger in Women's Social Roles*

The comparison with other kinds of flowing blood gives us some understanding of the dangerous power of menstrual blood. For another
kind of explanation we ask the question, what kinds of social powers
do women have that might parallel the powers and dangers of menstrual blood?[8] If there are parallels between the characteristics of menstrual blood and the characteristics of women's social activities, one
might hypothesize that the power of menstrual blood is an expression
or a reflection of women's social role.

In searching for social parallels to the dangerous powers of menstrual
blood, let us begin with the woman who has married but has not yet
reached menopause. From the viewpoint of her husband's family, the
woman's most important desirable power is her ability to produce offspring (chiefly sons) who will form the next generation in her husband's
line of descent and ensure that offerings will be made to her husband's
parents when they die. Although this capacity means great potential
advantages for her husband's family, it is also potentially threatening.
Like the menstrual blood that produces children, a woman's reproductive power is double-edged. A woman not only bears children, she also
strives to form close, affectionate bonds with them so that she will be
assured of a secure place for herself in the alien environment of her husband's family and security in her old age. Her ultimate goal is the separation of her uterine family (the term is Margery Wolf's) from the
families of her sisters-in-law. This enables her to escape much of her
mother-in-law's domination and to strengthen her influence within her
own uterine family.[9]

A married woman's loyalties, at least initially, do not lie firmly with
her new husband's family. As an outsider, an intruder, she is expected
to make her own way, if need be by undermining her husband's authority. The few people I could persuade to talk about sorcery mentioned
one form of sorcery almost to the exclusion of any other: attempts by
a new bride to dominate her husband. In one incident recounted to me,
a man and his wife quarreled. The wife packed up her things and set

out for her natal family as if for good. To everyone's surprise she returned a few days later with her own mother. Not long afterward, the husband's behavior changed: he stopped cooperating with his brothers and sisters-in-law in paying their joint land tax, and he became very subservient to his wife. In my informant's opinion, the mother and daughter had procured a charm that would produce this effect and had devised a way to have the husband ingest it. The woman was assumed to be bent on manipulating her husband so that he would defer to her and weaken his own family ties.

The power young women wield as they build their uterine families and attempt to manipulate their husbands is of a peculiar kind. It consists in subverting and disrupting the family form that most Chinese men hold dear—the family that grows from generation to generation without interruption and without division. Sons, their wives, and their children should live in harmony under the guidance of the eldest male. The goals and desires of young married women conflict with this ideal, and it is largely their machinations that prevent its attainment. The *power* women have is their capacity to alter a family's form by adding members to it, dividing it, and disturbing male authority; the *danger* they pose is their capacity to break up what men consider the ideal family.

The kind of power married women exercise before menopause is, then, analogous to the kind of power inherent in menstrual blood in its two-sided potential for both great harm and great good. Does the parallel between women's social roles and the qualities of menstrual blood apply as well to other stages in the woman's life cycle? The pattern holds to some extent for a nubile but unmarried girl. At this stage, the girl's menstrual fluids are not likely to create a fetus; nor is she able to contribute in any crucial way to her natal family, as a young wife does to her conjugal family by bearing sons. The potential benefits both of the young woman's menstrual flow and of her social role are absent. What about the potential for harm? It is hard to see any parallel here. For the most part unmarried girls identify closely with the wishes of their elders and have little capacity or inclination for disruption. The most that can be said is that when they marry out they disrupt the family's finances and the emotional ties between themselves and others, but these are temporary problems that seem not to have a lasting, deep-felt effect.

Is there a clearer parallel in the stage of a woman's life that follows the menopause? We would expect women's potential for either good or evil to diminish along with the flow of menstrual blood. Their power to add to the family directly does indeed fall away. But activities that threaten male ideals continue, even though many of a woman's interests at this stage of her life seem to coincide with her husband's. Like him, she desires filial and obedient sons and daughters-in-law who will work to sustain the family and extend it to the next generation. In other ways, however, a woman's interests diverge from her husband's. Through what Margery Wolf has called the women's community, women—especially older women, established in the community—indirectly influence men's behavior in ways that men find threatening. The women's community, composed of loose, overlapping groups of women in a village, is most visible when women gather to wash clothes or do chores together. Much information is exchanged in this setting, some of it about the affairs of men.[10] Because, according to tenets accepted by everyone, to be talked about is to lose face, women affect men's behavior merely by talking about them:

We once asked a male friend in Peihotien just what "having face" amounted to. He replied, "When no one is talking about a family, you can say it has face." This is precisely where women wield their power. When a man behaves in a way that they consider wrong, they talk about him—not only among themselves, but to their sons and husbands. No one "tells him how to mind his own business," but it becomes abundantly clear that he is losing face and by continuing in this manner may bring shame to the family of his ancestors and descendants. Few men will risk that.[11]

According to the male ideal, power should be exercised by male heads of households, managers of lineages, and community leaders. No wonder the ability of women to exercise power of a very different kind, power wielded behind the scenes, unsupported by recognized social position, is seen as a threat to the male order. No matter how well-ensconced men are in the established positions of power, the surreptitious influence of women remains beyond their capacity to control.

Of course, this mode of influencing men is to some extent open to younger women as well. But it is the older women, themselves mothers-in-law, who set the tone of the women's community.[12] Outside the women's community, older women have ways of wielding power and influence that are not open to younger women. If they have gained the loyalty of their sons, they can exert considerable control over them, even after they are grown men with wives and children of their own. In many cases, too, older women take a strong hand in decisions about household management, investment, or social affairs. The gradual accretion of influence and power by older women by no means coincides with the end of menstruation. But the two processes work in opposite directions: as a woman's menstrual flow ends in her 40's or 50's, she gains increasing power over the people around her.

In sum, although the parallels between a woman's social power and the power of menstrual blood are at best tenuous before marriage or after menopause, they are quite convincing for the stage of life just after marriage. During this stage of women's lives their capacities are complex: the production of children for male lines of descent is regarded as essential and desirable, but in other respects their power is from a male point of view threatening and even dangerous. There is a clear parallel between these attributes and those of menstrual blood: both are able to cause substantial, desirable change, and both are potentially dangerous. Young women produce sons who form the next links in their husbands' lines of descent; menstrual blood creates the body and bones of the fetus. Young women can threaten male ideals of the family; menstrual blood can threaten the life of the fetus (at birth) and the wellbeing of anyone against whom it is directed by a sorcerer. The power of menstrual blood, then, can be seen as a symbolic representation of the actual social power of young married women. The power attributed to menstrual blood may also be the culture's way of recognizing that social power, which otherwise goes virtually unacknowledged in Chinese society.

The parallel between menstrual blood and young women's social role has one other noteworthy aspect. Young married women clearly use their powers intentionally, in order to achieve certain goals. The disruption caused by the men's perception of their activities as threatening is more than compensated by the increased security they gain. Is there a parallel with respect to pollution? Do women wield their supposed capacity to pollute as a weapon, intentionally directing it at others to gain their own ends? For an answer we must try to place beliefs about women's polluting capacities within the wider system of beliefs about pollution, including pollution from death. There we will uncover yet another way of interpreting the relation between women and pollution.

III. *The System of Ritual Pollution*

The defining characteristic of a polluting substance in Chinese society is that it prevents those who come in contact with it from associating with the gods. The prohibition is most rigorous for those who come into closest contact with birth fluids—the new mother and her baby. Both are confined to the house for one month to spare T'ien Kung, the highest god, the sight of them. While the mother is "within the month," she must not bathe or wash her hair; she must ingest only certain strengthening tonics. Only when the month is up may she resume normal activities.[13] As for the baby, during the first two or three days of life, efforts are made to cleanse him of the birth fluids he has been in contact with. The herbal tea he is given to drink is sweetened with brown sugar, a "clean" substance that will rid his stomach of any "dirty" blood swallowed during birth.* In Ch'i-nan this appears to be the sole act needed to cleanse the child of the mother's blood. An additional cleansing takes place one month after birth—the child's hair is shaved and he is given a bath in water mixed with several kinds of "clean" herbs—but this cleansing is said to rid the child of the dirt associated with death. "It is in case someone in mourning came into the child's room or touched him."

In some Chinese communities the dirt associated with birth requires more extensive cleaning. In Peihotien (also in northern Taiwan) Margery Wolf reports that one month after birth, a child is "ritually cleansed of the dirt she got from passing through 'the dirty part of a woman' by having her head and eyebrows shaved."[14] Marjorie Topley's Hong Kong informants believed the contamination from the womb to last well past infancy. The pustules that erupt during measles are caused by poison in the body that "came from the womb and was passed to the child. It was 'unclean' because of its origin."† In Ch'i-nan the sores accompanying measles are also considered a release of poison from the body, but my informants made no link between that poison and contact with the womb or birth fluids.‡

Even outside the immediate context of childbirth, women must take care to avoid offending the gods. The gods take offense if they are ex-

---

* In accord with a four-part classification of foodstuffs and herbs as cool, clean, hot, or poison, certain substances are considered clean and able to rid the body of unwanted poisons or dirt.

† Marjorie Topley, "Chinese Traditional Ideas and the Treatment of Disease: Two Examples from Hong Kong," *Man*, 5 (1970): 426. Topley also reports a serious disease called *so-lo*, contracted by men who have intercourse with a woman within 100 days of childbirth (*ibid.*, p. 424). I found no notion of any such disease in Ch'i-nan.

‡ This difference may reflect a more general difference in ideas about pollution prevalent in Hong Kong and in Ch'i-nan. In Ch'i-nan substances that exude from the body, e.g. pus, are often referred to as both poisonous and "really unclean." Ritually polluting substances or persons, however, such as menstrual blood and mourners, are called unclean (as opposed to "really unclean") but never poisonous. Hence it would make little sense for unclean substances associated with birth to appear later as bodily poisons. In Hong Kong, by contrast, the term poisonous can be applied both to things outside the body, like sex or pregnant women, and to ritually polluting things emanating from the body, like menstrual blood. (Marjorie Topley, "Cosmic Antagonisms: A Mother-Child Syndrome," in Arthur P. Wolf, ed., *Religion and Ritual in Chinese Society* [Stanford, Calif., 1974], p. 234.) Thus, the term poisonous provides a clear link between what my Ch'i-nan informants carefully distinguished as "unclean" and "really unclean." Such differences between Chinese communities make it premature to even attempt a description of beliefs about pollution for Chinese society as a whole.

posed to menstrual blood in any way; they may become angry and cause harm to the offender. The Stove God, whose abode is closest to women's work areas, will be angered if any article of women's clothing, any cloth used by a woman to wash, or any basket that has contained women's clothes should touch the stove. Outside the house, gods may take offense if a menstruating woman enters a temple, especially if she approaches the god's image too closely. Nor can she offer incense to the gods, a necessary part of the act of worship. This latter prohibition reportedly is not based on fear of the god's anger; people said that when you know you are dirty, you would not want to draw the gods' attention to your dirty state by worshiping them because it would be embarrassing. Besides, a communication from a menstruating worshiper would not "get through" to the gods anyway.

The presence of a polluted woman can prevent the gods from making close contact with other people as well. Sometimes gods are beseeched to diagnose an illness. To communicate his opinion, the god's spirit will possess the body of a spirit medium (a tang-ki), using the medium's voice to speak or hand to write. If a polluted woman is present at these proceedings, the god's spirit will not possess anyone. Periodically it is necessary to cleanse a god's image of polluting substances that have accidentally sullied it by carrying the image over a bed of hot coals. The men who carry the image cross the coals in bare feet. They are not burned because the god's spirit possesses them. The presence of a polluted woman prevents the god's spirit from entering the men; if the men are unaware of this interference and proceed with the firewalk, their feet may be severely burned.

To this point I have simplified the discussion in two ways. First, polluted women are not the only ones who are offensive to the gods and can prevent communication with them. Any person, male or female, child or adult, who sets foot inside the room in which a woman has given birth within the previous month is equally offensive to the gods. No such person can offer incense to the gods or attend a firewalk. The contamination lasts as long as the mother is within a month of childbirth. A man whose wife is within the month is automatically considered polluted; it is assumed that he cannot avoid polluting contact with his wife and child.

Second, other forms of pollution can produce the same effect. Gods are offended by exposure to the pollution of death as well as to the pollution of birth. Therefore the doors of any temple along the route of a funeral procession are closed until it passes; in the room where a corpse is laid out and encoffining takes place, ancestral tablets and gods' images are covered by baskets or mats; anyone who is within the prescribed 49-day mourning period refrains from offering incense to the gods. Further, although it is not absolutely essential because the gods will not necessarily be offended, people try to avoid sexual intercourse before worshiping, especially before a major festival. This is not just an extension of the pollution from women's bodies. Informants were quite clear that it is the act of sexual intercourse which is polluting, not just the male's contact with the female's genitals. At a firewalk, when a god is cleansed of all forms of pollution, those who are to carry the god's image must themselves be free of any form of pollution: they abstain from sex for six to twelve days prior to the event; they take care not to wear any clothes made of the cotton used in funeral dress (it goes without saying that they cannot be in mourning), and as a final ablution they pass each foot over an incense pot burning on the ground before beginning the walk.

Given the gods' extreme sensitivity to pollution, we are prompted to ask whether women are allowed less contact with the gods than men because they are more likely to generate pollution. When the higher gods are worshiped on special festival occasions, it is usually men who perform the act of worship. Unless they are menstruating, women are not barred from worshiping on such occasions, and they sometimes participate if the men of the household are absent. But men almost always make it their business to be home at those times. Special festivals are occasions on which a social group—a lineage or a village—is responsible for the celebration of a god's birthday. The group in charge provides sumptuous offerings and opera performances to please and honor the god. Two kinds of benefits may result. First, local leaders and the festival's organizers gain visibility in the community, and, if the festival goes well, political support. Second, it is hoped that the honored god will bestow on the festival's participants the universally sought-after blessings of wealth, many descendants, and family harmony. The same analysis applies when a lineage's early ancestors are worshiped: men worship when political and economic benefits are likely to ensue.

As far as I could determine, there are no festivals for high, powerful gods in Ch'i-nan in which women play a major role. Even cults that relate directly to women's interests and are given considerable prominence elsewhere are of minor importance there. The Weaving Maiden, for example, is worshiped in some areas by groups of women who ask for happy marriages.[15] The goddess is worshiped by some families in Ch'i-nan, but men perform the worship whenever they are home for the occasion.

Where low-ranking supernatural spirits are concerned, by contrast, women are quite free to play a predominant role. "Little low goddesses" like the Bed Mother or Cu-si: Niu-niu are often beseeched to bring sons or to cure a sickly child; their close association with childbirth makes them less clean than the other gods. These goddesses are worshiped regularly by most women in their own homes or at special altars in the back corners of temples, but there are no public festivals in their honor.*

Besides low-ranking supernaturals who reside in the world of the living, women are also permitted to traffic with residents of the world of the dead. When sessions are held in which villagers enter a trance, travel to the underworld, and visit deceased friends and kinsmen, women can participate fully either as observers or as mediums. Spirits of the dead and their world are unclean; hence women, also periodically unclean, may appropriately enter into contact with them. Indeed, in some parts of China practitioners who specialize in raising the souls of the dead are invariably women.[16]

Potentially malevolent spirits of the dead who are abroad among the living are often worshiped by women, not in hopes of their assistance, but in hopes of averting harm. For example, a *kho-kun* ceremony is held by every household on the first and fifteenth of each month. The spirits worshiped are *kui*, ghosts, who prey on the living, causing sickness and other misfortunes unless they are propitiated. Either men or women can worship these beings, but the responsibility seems to fall by default to women. Of the twenty households I observed performing kho-kun in one section of Ch'i-nan, in eighteen the worship was performed by women. In ten cases the woman's husband was not home, but in eight he was home yet made no move to take over the worship.†

It seems clear that there is a hierarchy of spiritual beings depicted here: at the top are clean, high gods worshiped at important times by men; at the bottom, dirty, low spirits and ghosts worshiped and tended by women. The common relegation of women to the worship of the low, unclean end of the hierarchy is appropriate because women are so frequently unclean themselves. Conversely, the near-monopoly by

* For lack of space I will not discuss here the other ritual roles in which women guard the welfare of children. There are principally two: in one the mother performs a certain ritual to call back the lost soul of her ailing child; in the other a child can be taken to a female ritual expert called a Sian-si:-ma, who can also call back the soul.

† These offerings are made privately by each household. Once a year, on the fifteenth day of the seventh month, a community propitiation for the ghosts is held. My notes from 1970 are unclear on whether men or women predominate in this rite, but my impression is that women do. If so, this may be the only public festival on which women more often worship than men. Still, its character is utterly different from that of festivals for the gods. One's only hope in worshiping is to be left alone.

men of the clean, high end of the hierarchy is appropriate because they are much less often unclean.

For a more accurate, albeit more complex, analysis of pollution, I turn now to consider the system of pollution, thus far presented piecemeal, as a whole. The idea of dirty or polluting substances as "matter out of place" is a familiar one.[17] The Chinese material lends itself to a similar notion: things the Chinese consider unclean threaten the order of or are a result of disorder in the family or in the human body. Disorder here has two specific meanings: anything that pierces the boundaries of these two entities is unclean, whether it is something that enters or something that leaves; anything that tends to undermine the tenets of order, any external threat to orderly entities, is unclean. This abstract formulation can be illustrated by drawing together the material already presented, supplemented occasionally by additional information.

In the family, for example, the entrance or exit of members is problematic and requires ritual action. The act of entering or exiting seems to make people dirty (productive of disorder) and in need of cleansing. For this purpose a special plant called *bua-a-chau* is cultivated and protected so its purity is ensured. It is grown in a fenced enclosure so that animals cannot defecate nearby. It is sheltered from birth and death: a woman who is menstruating or within the month cannot touch it; anyone in mourning cannot approach it. If the family cultivating it is in mourning, the plant, too, wears a mourning bracelet, which protects it from the pollution of death. This plant is then used to cleanse those who enter or leave the family. An infant is washed in water infused with it one month after birth, both to rid it of the dirt associated with leaving its mother's body and to mark its entrance into the mother's family.* A woman is washed with it on the day she marries out of her natal family.

When a person leaves a family through death, he or she becomes one of the most polluting objects—a corpse. Everyone who comes into association with the corpse takes measures to protect his family. When a mourner returns home from a funeral, he sets off firecrackers, burns incense, and prepares a tea infused with a charm to ward off the dead person's influence. This is drunk by the most vulnerable family members, the children. Even the deceased's immediate family takes mea-

---

* Adopted children seem to be an exception to this rule. If a child is adopted after the one-month washing, he need not be washed again. It may be that one cleansing of the dirt associated with entering a family is sufficient to cover a subsequent entrance into another family. Or the primary object of this cleansing may be to rid the baby of the pollution associated with birth, a cleansing that would not have to be repeated upon adoption.

sures to protect itself. Some of the ceremonies that follow a death are designed to separate the dead person from all his living relatives.[18]

After death, a spirit is normally reintegrated into his family as an ancestor, whereupon he ceases to be unclean. Those with no descendants to care for them, however, may become wandering, hungry ghosts and be termed unclean on that account. "Hungry ghosts without descendants are the dirtiest of all spirits. They come wandering around with missing heads or limbs, covered with filth and dressed in rags." These ghosts are the epitome of social disorder, contravening the most valued elements of orderly existence. They have no one to carry on their lines of descent, they are without resources, and they are excluded from any social group. Even worse, they destroy order where they can, causing illness and family quarrels.

If ghosts are the dirtiest supernatural beings, gods are the cleanest. They are so clean that besides taking the precautions discussed in the last section, people often wash in a bua-a-chau bath before worshiping them. In contrast to ghosts, gods are the epitome of social order. They are the source of all the things a ghost lacks: descendants, wealth, and peace. Moreover, in their capacity as supernatural magistrates, they can control and subdue disorderly ghosts.* In this same capacity, gods of various ranks literally define the boundaries of social groups, both large and small. In Ch'i-nan, each family worships the Kitchen God; each of the four lineage communities within the village worships the particular Earth God that governs its precincts; the village as a whole worships another Earth God in a central location; and the three villages that share the local market share responsibility for the worship of two more powerful gods called the Ang Kong. In short, most important social groups, from the family on up, are delineated by the worship of gods. The gods' cleanliness seems to derive from their association with right order and neatly bounded social groups.

Just as uncleanness in families is associated with the crossing of boundaries, so it is with the human body. We have already seen how substances that escape across body boundaries are considered unclean. Some of these, such as pus from sores, are indicative of disorder within the body, usually an imbalance of hot elements or an excess of poisonous ones.

Is the pollution attributed to sexual intercourse related to ideas of order and disorder in the body? It is hard to say, in part because vil-

---

* Villagers in Ch'i-nan said that some gods are unclean, i.e. corrupt gods who perform evil acts. Like corrupt government officials, corrupt gods encourage social disorder. Their association with disorder makes them unclean.

lagers are so reluctant to talk about sex that I am uncertain how it relates in their minds to pollution. Perhaps ideas about sexual intercourse
widespread in China since ancient times influence the attitudes of country people today. According to these ideas, during intercourse a man
absorbs the female yin essence, which strengthens his vital powers.
Ejaculation, however, results in the debilitating loss of vital yang essence. Too frequent intercourse so drains a man's vital essence that he
is vulnerable to several serious diseases. For this reason numerous techniques are recommended that enable men to avoid ejaculation; women
are in no danger, for their supply of yin essence is inexhaustible.[19]

If some such ideas as these are believed by the villagers of Ch'i-nan
(a possibility I can neither confirm nor reject), sexual intercourse may
be considered polluting in part because it threatens to disrupt the balance of yang and yin in a man's body. If he cannot avoid emitting semen,
his health may be impaired by the resulting imbalance. This would not
differ greatly from an imbalance of hot and cold elements or an excess
of poison in the body, which are sometimes associated with the emission
of pus and other unclean fluids across corporeal boundaries.

Even if these ideas have influenced the villagers of Ch'i-nan, they
take us only part way toward understanding why sexual intercourse
should be considered polluting, for imbalance in the man's body would
not pollute the woman. Future investigations may tell us whether the
pollution of sex is related to order and disorder in the body, or to the
crossing of body boundaries when the male enters the female or the
fetal soul (the Thai Sin) enters the woman's body at the moment of
conception.

The problematic case of sexual intercourse aside, if it is true that the
system of pollution is based on the crossing of bodily or social boundaries, we should now be able to account for facts that initially seem
puzzling. Why, for example, should birth be so extremely polluting that
anyone who enters the room where it occurs becomes polluted, i.e. is
barred from worshiping the gods? Even death pollutes only those in
mourning, not all those who venture near a corpse or place of death.
Our analysis shows us that unlike death, birth entails crossing both bodily and familial boundaries. Blood flows from the mother's body, and
the family must be redefined to include the new member.

Again, why should the birth of a boy be considered less polluting by
some Chinese than the birth of a girl? Doolittle writes that a woman is
unclean for one month after bearing a son, but for four months after
bearing a daughter.[20] And some of Margery Wolf's informants told her
that if a newborn baby is a boy, only the mother is unclean, "and the

visitors to her room would not suffer the same restrictions as they would had the child been a girl."[21] More graphically, Johannes Frick says that according to folk belief in Tsinghai:

At the time a boy is born, the pure sun sees the birth room submerged in blood and the mother sunk up to her neck in blood. At the birth of a girl the woman in childbed is so immersed in blood that her hair drips with it. The blood overflows out of the birth room onto the whole courtyard. After the birth of a boy the lying-in period lasts by custom thirty days, but the birth of a girl requires forty days because she is more unclean than a boy.[22]

If integration into a family is part of what makes birth polluting, then it is reasonable that a boy should be less polluting than a girl. A male occupies a firm, permanent position in his family as a future heir to the family estate and as one of those who will perpetuate descent lines. His integration is therefore in a sense less problematic than a girl's, for she belongs to her natal family only temporarily, until she marries out and becomes part of her husband's family.

Beliefs in polluting and unclean things—because of their close association with birth and death, and with the entrance and departure of people from social groups—involve problems or dilemmas of serious concern to both men and women.* The central dilemma might be expressed this way: how can we keep families pure and homogeneous and their members united and loyal when, in order to grow, they need outsiders (women with competing loyalties and children whose loyalties are unformed) and when, in addition, all family members must eventually die? The answer is that by ritual means, outsiders can be cleansed before entering the family, and mourners cleansed of the defiling contact with death. Temporary pollution remains a problem, and it is the cause of temporary ruptures between men and the gods. As long as a person's body or family harbors polluting disorder, he or she cannot establish communication with the gods, the most certain representatives of order.

In the foregoing section I have shown that women are not the sole source of pollution. The impression may still remain, however, that when a woman is involved in pollution, the invariable source is the woman's body. It is more accurate to say that problematic events—birth and death—are the sources of pollution, and both men and women are implicated in them. My informants pointed to this interpretation when

---

* See Sherry B. Ortner, "Sherpa Purity," *American Anthropologist* 75 (1973): 49–63, for an analysis that stresses the importance of concepts of pollution as a guide to action for people faced with fundamental problems of the human condition.

they referred to the dirt of happy and of sad events. Sometimes women are more closely associated with these events than men, as in childbirth. At other times men come to be polluted independently of women, as when a relative dies. Even for an event closely associated with women, men seem to be polluted not by the woman in question, but by the event itself. Pollution emanates from the place where childbirth occurs, not from the new mother. Now that more women have their children outside the home, in hospitals and clinics, within-the-month pollution is disappearing. When a baby is born in a hospital, only the delivery room is polluting; when the mother returns home, she leaves the contagion behind. Beyond this, some would say that a husband is automatically polluted when his wife gives birth and that he must wait as long as she to be clean again; it is as if he were affected by the birth in the same way as she.

Moreover, when women are in certain states they are considered dangerous and vulnerable, but not, in the sense used here, polluting. Pregnant women, for example, are often considered a menace to others: they can make children fall sick and cause difficulties for brides.[23] Because of the danger pregnant women pose for brides, in Ch'i-nan a ceremony called Sifting Four Eyes is performed before the bride's dowry is sent to the groom's house. All items in the dowry are passed over a large sieve so that pernicious influences, including those of pregnant women, can be sifted out. "Four Eyes" refers to the two beings in one that a pregnant woman represents—two eyes for her and two for the fetus. As Doolittle explains:

After the articles have been sifted, contact with them is carefully avoided by the female members of [the bride's] family. It is supposed that it would be especially unlucky for her and her affianced husband should any pregnant woman, or any person wearing mourning, handle, or in any manner come in contact with, any of the articles already sifted before they are carried over to the future home of the girl. Such a contact would be expected to produce death in her husband's family, or a future miscarriage on her part, or quarrels and misunderstandings between him and her, or some undesirable result.[24]

In I-ch'ang, Hupeh, during an initiation ceremony for young men on the eve of marriage, comparable protective measures are taken against pregnant women and widows. On the groom's breast "hangs a small bronze mirror about three inches in diameter. This custom rests on the belief that the mirror can counteract the evil influence of widows and 'four-eyed persons,' (i.e., pregnant women). In spite of the power of the mirror, widows and pregnant women are usually excluded from the marriage ceremonies."[25]

At the same time, pregnant women are vulnerable: according to Topley, if a pregnant woman encounters a child with measles, the woman will fail to give birth.[26] Similarly, at a funeral attended by Margery and Arthur Wolf in northern Taiwan, a cry went out to warn pregnant women to stay away when nails were about to be hammered into the coffin "or else something will happen." The Wolfs were told that if "one of the dead person's daughters or granddaughters is pregnant, she must stand astride the threshold of the house, holding a piece of white cloth over her stomach. Other pregnant women should be far enough away so as not to be able to hear the noise of the nails being pounded into the coffin."

We plainly have here a class of anomalous, marginal, or transitional people—pregnant women, widows, brides, grooms, mourners, children —who are both vulnerable and dangerous to others.* A full analysis of the beliefs underlying this classification would go beyond the limits of this essay precisely because pollution is not at issue; people in this category are not called "dirty" for that reason, and, though danger lurks, it does not threaten the relationship between human beings and the gods. I have brought up these beliefs simply to illustrate the difference between women who are dangerous and vulnerable because of their condition (pregnancy or widowhood), and women as potential polluters. Pollution, with its consequent rupturing between people and gods, derives from association with the events of birth and death, which can affect both men and women; pregnancy and widowhood are states known only by women. In this sense the danger associated with pregnancy, pregnant women, and widows is sex-linked in a way that pollution itself is not. Only women can be pregnant or widows, but men as well as women can come into contact with polluting events, though men are less likely to do so.

Conclusion

We are left, then, with three different interpretations of the dangerous power of women. The first looks to the emotional significance of death and birth, the second to women's social role, and the third to the system of ideas about pollution. Are these mutually exclusive or mutually compatible interpretations? Must we choose one or can we keep them all? I would argue that we can reject the second in favor of the third on the grounds that the second leads to an inconsistency, which can be seen by reopening a question raised earlier: does it make sense

* Topley discusses the beliefs of her Hong Kong informants about this class of people in "Cosmic Antagonisms: A Mother-Child Syndrome."

to say that women intentionally hurt men by polluting them in the same way they may hurt men by interfering with their ideal of the family? Women stand to gain security and control over their lives from deliberate interference with male ideals of the family; no such gain accrues to women from deliberate exploitation of their capacity to pollute. Preventing communication between men and the gods is no more in the interest of women than it is of men. If a polluted woman intentionally entered an area where a god was being implored to possess men, her presence might cause either an abortive firewalk and injury to the participants, or the failure of the gods to diagnose an illness. In either event the benefits the gods can bring—health, plenty, and peace—would be denied to kinsmen and neighbors as dear to women as to men, an outcome unlikely to further any woman's interests. Aside from the possibility of interfering with worship, women seem to have no special ability to unleash the destructive power of their menstrual discharge. Menstrual blood is a powerful component of sorcerers' potions, but the knowledge to use it belongs to ritual experts, available for hire by men and women alike.

If the dangerous power of menstrual blood reflects the social role of young women, the two should be parallel in all important respects. But in one important respect they are not parallel: the element of intention in young women's manipulation of the family is not present in their capacity to pollute. This discrepancy leads me to reject the second interpretation in favor of the third, which sees certain events as sources of pollution because of their impact on the stability and integrity of the body and the family. The first interpretation need not be rejected, however. The hypothesis that the emotional significance of blood derives from its association with birth and death is not incompatible with the third interpretation, but rather helps us understand why certain events and not others are seen as disturbing.

But lest we too quickly rule out the relevance of women's social role, let me note that the system of ideas about polluting events does not exist in isolation from the Chinese kinship system. It is no accident that women rather than men are considered outsiders, and that the children women bear must be anchored to their families by elaborate ritual means. It is because the kinship system is focused on male lines of descent that women are depicted on the boundaries, breaking in as strangers. It may be events that are polluting rather than women *per se*, but polluting events are events that intrude new people or remove old ones in a male-oriented kinship system.

This brings us to a final question. If, as I believe to be the case, women do not deliberately use their capacity to pollute against men, what happens when the shoe is on the other foot? Do men deliberately use beliefs in pollution as a weapon against women? Many of the most polluting substances emanate from a woman's reproductive organs, the source of her greatest power over her husband's family—her ability to produce descendants. Once the polluting nature of the sex act (which begins the child's development), menstrual blood (which becomes the child's flesh and bones), and childbirth (which brings the child into the husband's family) is established, the source of a woman's power is obscured, if not rendered invisible by a layer of negative sentiment. While this line of thought is suggestive, I know of no evidence that men intentionally and self-servingly perpetuate these beliefs.

Nonetheless, one cannot ignore the numerous messages that deal with women's reproductive capacity in a negative way. Perhaps the most striking of these is the belief that women who have borne children (or, some say, who die in childbirth) are punished in the underworld for having produced polluting substances. According to Frick, people in Tsinghai say that women who die in childbed are sent to a special section of the underworld called *hsieh-k'eng*, blood pit. There the woman's soul is pinned down by a heavy stone:

The soul groans, yes, cries out in agony. As its eyes anxiously dart all around it sees only blood. It eats only blood clots; it drinks only bloody fluid. It is not the fresh blood of animals—which in its raw state is already an abomination for the people of Tsinghai—but inevitably foul vaginal blood and fluid. The soul cannot rest in the dreadful torment that it endures. Incessantly it groans and cries, but no friendly spirit approaches to help it. All good spirits shun the soul of a woman who has died in childbed.[27]

Sometimes, however, a woman's sons will show their love and pity for her and attempt to lessen or eliminate this punishment by ritual means. As Doolittle explains it:

The object of the *Bloody-Pond ceremony* is to save the spirit of a deceased mother from the punishment of the *Bloody Pond*. Sometimes it is performed several times on the death of the mother of a family of children. This is one way by which they manifest their *filial love* for the deceased.[28]

It is remarkable that in the same ceremony, the fate that women suffer for engendering pollution in the exercise of their procreative powers and the gratitude and pity that at least some men feel for them should be so dramatically juxtaposed.

Women and Childbearing in Kwan Mun Hau Village: A Study of Social Change

ELIZABETH JOHNSON

In traditional Chinese society, children, particularly male children, were highly valued. Male descendants were needed to continue the worship of the ancestors, to inherit family property, and to support the parents in their old age. Without sons, a woman's existence was without meaning, and she and her husband had little security in this life or the next.

When a woman married—and marriage was nearly universal—her physical and spiritual home was transferred to that of her husband and his family. The pressures on her to produce sons were intense. Should she fail, the family might try to secure male descendants through adoption, uxorilocal marriage, or, if the husband had the means, the acquisition of a second wife. Any of these alternatives undermined the woman's status and security. The value placed on descendants does not mean that unlimited numbers of children were desired, except by the wealthy, but under conditions of high mortality, unlimited births may have been necessary to produce the desired number of descendants, and infanticide or adoption out of the household resorted to if too many children survived, especially if they were female.*

Chinese society has followed distinctive paths of development in China, Taiwan, and Hong Kong. As a result of modernization, fertility-related values and practices are also changing, though not everywhere in the same way.[1] Certain aspects of the situation in Kwan Mun Hau Village, on the southern coast of Hong Kong's New Territories, are

* I spent the years 1968 to 1970 in Tsuen Wan, living in Kwan Mun Hau Village for eighteen months. I interviewed fourteen native and eleven outsider (immigrant) women, and twelve native men. I obtained additional information from a one-third sample census, from key informants, and from participant observation. The information given here pertains only to natives of Kwan Mun Hau unless specified otherwise. The research was supported by the Population Council (New York).

unique; others are typical of Chinese communities in Hong Kong and elsewhere. The women of Kwan Mun Hau have seen profound changes in certain areas of their lives. This paper deals with the effects of those changes upon attitudes and behavior with regard to childbearing.

Kwan Mun Hau and the Development of Tsuen Wan

Kwan Mun Hau is one of the twenty-odd original villages of Tsuen Wan District (formerly Tsuen Wan hsiang). The area was until recently very poor, there being little flat land between the slopes of Tai Mou Shan, the highest mountain in Hong Kong, and the sea. Settled by Hakka people in the seventeenth and eighteenth centuries, these villages remained a Hakka enclave until after World War II. Kwan Mun Hau was among the earliest villages settled. According to legend, its founders were men of the Hung and Ma (pseudonyms) surnames whose descendants now constitute the two lineages of the village. These lineages, though small by South Chinese standards (31 and 55 households), are among the larger lineages in Tsuen Wan. There are at present also two households of another surname, whose families have lived in Tsuen Wan for many generations.

Until World War II, the people of Kwan Mun Hau and neighboring villages derived their livelihood primarily from farming, fishing, and the cutting of firewood. Poverty drove many of the men to emigrate all over the world in search of work in the middle and late nineteenth century. Many émigrés never returned; others returned penniless. Those who returned with money bought land or started small businesses in Tsuen Wan. By the turn of the century, a market area of some importance had developed not far from Kwan Mun Hau. In the years before the war, new Hakka immigrants arrived, renting land and houses from the older settlers. In the 1930's, several factories were opened. Emigration declined as opportunities increased for regular employment in Kowloon and on Hong Kong Island, and for occasional employment in Tsuen Wan itself.

The postwar period brought dramatic change to Tsuen Wan. Its location on a harbor near Kowloon, together with a good supply of fresh water, made the area an attractive site for industrial development. Several big textile mills were moved there from Shanghai in 1948–49.[2] By 1968, Tsuen Wan had 405 registered factories, employing 42,707 workers, predominantly in the textile industry.[3] With the increased opportunities for employment and heavy immigration from China, the population of Tsuen Wan grew rapidly. In 1946 there were approximately 8,000 people in the District, primarily indigenous Hakka.[4] By 1971, the population was 271,892, of whom native Hakka were less than 5 percent.[5] In 1958 the Hong Kong government declared Tsuen Wan a satellite city, and plans were drawn for facilities to serve an eventual population of about one million.[6]

Thus, the original inhabitants of Tsuen Wan have witnessed a remarkable transformation in the past thirty years. Because Kwan Mun Hau Village was located in what is now central Tsuen Wan, growing population densities after the war made rice-growing impractical, and farmers turned instead to growing vegetables and raising pigs and chickens. In 1964, when the government moved the village to a new site on the periphery of the urban area, the villagers finally gave up agriculture. The development of local industry has assured Kwan Mun Hau natives of ready employment so that they have not had to emigrate either to other urban areas of Hong Kong or abroad to seek work, as have so many New Territories natives.[7] Employment in industry and service occupations is readily obtainable. Many Kwan Mun Hau men, however, work either not at all or only in businesses that demand little time or energy. This is because the land and houses owned by the villagers now earn lucrative rental income. Virtually all the families own their own houses, which gives them a significant advantage over recent immigrants, and most of them own additional rooms, houses, or land that they rent out. Some families own whole buildings in the city center, which bring them substantial income. Half the village population of about 1,000 now consists of postwar immigrants (primarily Cantonese-speakers from Kwangtung province) who rent rooms or floors in the village, in many cases to operate small factories and workshops.

The people of Kwan Mun Hau now have access to many urban amenities. Western medical care, modern education (now entirely in Cantonese), and good transportation to other urban areas of Hong Kong are readily available. There are several movie theaters in Tsuen Wan, and virtually every home has a television. In short, villagers enjoy many of the advantages of life in a modern city.

At the same time, they are sheltered from many of the demands of life in an industrial city. Spared the disruptive effects of migration, they have been able to continue within the long-established patterns of village society. As the area's original landowners, they enjoy a privileged status in the eyes of the government, which has tried to preserve the village's integrity. Few Kwan Mun Hau men have had to take employment in industry. Property ownership and the supportive social ties of lineage and village give them a kind of security enjoyed by few people in Hong Kong today.

Changes in Women's Role

Before the war and for some time after it, women who married into Kwan Mun Hau had the social and economic status typical of Hakka women in South China. They were in certain respects less subjugated than other Chinese women (they never had bound feet, for example) and enjoyed some degree of independence and freedom of movement. They paid a high price for these slight advantages, however, because their labor was essential to the village economy. Since in many cases the men were either abroad or working away from home, the burden of farm work fell mainly on the women. All the women of Kwan Mun Hau, regardless of their households' economic status, worked in agriculture until their fields were sold. The younger women worked the fields, growing rice and vegetables. They also raised pigs and chickens and cut grass in the mountains as fuel for their cooking stoves, carrying it down to the village in enormous loads on carrying poles. They often cut fuel in large groups, organized, according to one elderly woman, by age and marital status. In the rare hours young women spent at home, they carried water, washed clothes, and cared for children. The work was commonly divided among the women of a household, with most households including more than one adult woman. All but two of the women I interviewed married into a household that had at least one mother-in-law (polygyny meant that some households had two older women), although collateral extension, i.e. including the families of two or more married brothers, was less common. Old women did not do heavy farm work, but they worked hard at home nonetheless, cleaning, preparing pig food, and cooking. They had also to look after young children while their mothers were out working. Since the old women were so busy, babies were often left alone much of the time, perhaps tied to a table leg. Older children went to the fields with their mothers or ran about unsupervised, barefoot, and neglected. "Previously," I was told, "children were not so precious—they just fed them and put them to sleep, and let them crawl on the floor so that they were very dirty, because the women had to work and didn't have time."

In addition to farm work, most women also had some outside employment. Seven of the nine women over forty in my sample had had some form of remunerative employment. They typically had worked as laborers, carrying heavy loads at construction sites or at a nearby oil depot. They also earned money cutting and selling grass and firewood.

Women were able to keep at least some of the money they earned; a few women bought fields, and one woman built a house, into which she moved when her husband took a second wife. Clearly women had a degree of economic autonomy, though it may not have been commensurate with their responsibilities. Because they were willing and able to take jobs as manual laborers, women in need could support themselves, albeit at a marginal level. Desperately unhappy wives or adopted child-brides could run away and earn a living without resorting to prostitution, unlike such women elsewhere.[8]

Virtually all my informants, both men and women, emphasized that until recent years women had had difficult lives. They worked long hours, at very heavy work, "like horses or oxen," regardless of the weather or their health. They apparently worked as usual during pregnancy. They tried to do lighter work for a month after childbirth, but those whose mothers-in-law were unwilling or unable to help them had to continue to carry water and pig food.

When Kwan Mun Hau moved to its present location, virtually all the village fields had been sold. Pig-raising is forbidden in the new village, although a few elderly women raise pigs elsewhere, and most families raise chickens. During the negotiations that preceded the removal of the village, one of the village elders expressed his concern to the District Officer at the villagers' lack of the modern skills that would enable them to find work in Tsuen Wan, and in particular asked what the women would be able to do, now that agriculture had become impossible.[9] A few women miss their farm work, not only because they enjoyed it, but also because owning their own fields gave them a sense of security. An elderly woman told me, "Previously we had to work very hard in order to live. Now we don't because we have houses to rent out. But if the world situation changed we would starve to death. During the Japanese Occupation we farmed our own fields and survived."

The economic role formerly performed by women—providing their households' basic subsistence—has now been replaced, for most families, by rental income. Women do much less in the way of productive labor than they did a generation ago, producing virtually none of their families' food. Their work is much more confined to the domestic sphere than it was in the past. Yet I detected no feeling of anomie among the women. From their point of view, the loss of apparently meaningful and productive work in agriculture has been more than compensated for by the relative ease of their lives, particularly the absence of hard physical labor. The men seem to feel this change less keenly, and some felt a nostalgia for the past that was not expressed by the women. Perhaps this is because the work of basic farm labor and the carrying of fuel and water fell primarily to women; compounded by frequent child-bearing, this represented a burden few would regret losing.

Only 25 percent of the wives of native household heads in my sample census are now employed outside their homes. Of the fourteen women in my interview sample, only two (ages thirty and thirty-six) have full-time jobs in factories. Three others (ages seventy-two, seventy, and forty-four) do putting-out work from local factories at home, and one of these and another woman care for other women's children. Employment is readily available, in the form of factory, laboring, and putting-out work, for those women who want it, but many women eschew outside work. Standards of housework and childcare are higher than they used to be, and housework is very time-consuming, especially in households with many children. Women must go to the market each day to buy food; they wash clothes by hand, clean, and cook; and they now go not to the mountains but to construction sites to collect scrap wood for their cooking stoves. In any spare time they play Mah-Jongg and Hakka cards, or watch television.

Young women who have finished school but are not yet married work outside the home, typically in factories, though a few of the better-educated ones have clerical or teaching jobs. In dress, language, and life style, they present a striking contrast to their mothers. While most of the married women wear traditional clothes, the older women sticking to dark colors or black, the young women now wear Western clothes, often in the latest styles. They speak Cantonese, and those who have attended middle school speak English. I never saw an unmarried woman use a carrying pole, until recently the women's basic skill. Most important, all the girls and young women now attend school. Only five of the women in my interview sample had had any education, and I knew of only one village woman over fifty who could read at all.

Fertility and Infant Mortality

With the economic development of Tsuen Wan, the childbearing experiences of Kwan Mun Hau women have changed markedly. The experiences of elderly and middle-aged women were very different from those of women who are now of childbearing age. My purpose is to try to define not only how their experiences differ, but why; to indicate which aspects of their changing environment have affected attitudes and behavior that ultimately determine fertility.* Needless to say, I

---

* The terms "fertility" and "fecundity" are used here in accordance with demo-graphic practice. "Fertility" refers to children actually born; "fecundity" refers to childbearing potential.

cannot even approach a complete explanation of past and present fertility patterns. I have to rely on my informants' memories for knowledge of the past, and I lack the behavioral and physiological data necessary to explain even present fertility. Instead, I shall use the cases I have studied to point to probable causal relationships and to suggest patterns of change.[10]

Although almost all the Kwan Mun Hau women interviewed, regardless of age, have borne at least four children (see table) the number of children surviving has changed dramatically over time. All the women over sixty in my sample, and most of the elderly women I knew, had lost at least half the children born to them. Their experience was said to be typical. Children died primarily of measles, smallpox, and diarrhea. Malaria was also prevalent. Newborn infants were particularly vulnerable, and various ritual means were used to try to protect them. Any medical care available for sick infants and children was very expensive, and so seldom sought. If a child was sick, old women tried to cure the illness with herbal medicines, or by touching the child with pieces of burning grass or incense. These cures were often ineffective. "People couldn't raise babies because they boiled herbal medicines themselves—for example, if they had measles or smallpox, they boiled grass. How could you know if it was right? If it was not right, it killed the baby instead of curing it." The hard lives of their mothers presumably had a direct effect on the children's survival rates. Children born

FERTILITY AND CHILD MORTALITY

Current age of respondent	Age			Number of children	
	At marriage	At first birth	At last birth	Born	Surviving to adulthood
72	24	26	30[a]	3	1 boy
70	18	—	—[a]	0	(adopted 1 girl)
62	15	20	29[a]	6	1 girl (adopted 1 boy)
60	18	22[b]	38[b]	12	1 boy, 1 girl (1 stepson)
51	19	26	45	8	3 boys, 5 girls
48[c]	24	—	—[a]	0	(1 stepson)
47	29	30	35	4[d]	1 boy, 3 girls
45	16	21	41[a]	9[e]	4 boys, 5 girls
44	24	25	40	8	3 boys, 5 girls
36	17	22	36	4	3 boys, 1 girl
33	23	—	—	0	(adopted 1 boy)
32	20	21	30	6[d]	4 boys, 2 girls
30	19	20	30	4[d]	3 boys, 1 girl
29	19	20	29	5[d]	4 boys, 1 girl

[a] Marriage ended while respondent still of childbearing age
[b] Approximate age
[c] This woman had two children in her first marriage; one died and she gave one in adoption
[d] Used birth control
[e] Had abortion

to overworked mothers were born at risk. They were then neglected by their mothers and grandmothers, who were too busy to care for them properly. "That kind of bearing babies is useless. Women bore lots of children but only raised a few. Some women had seven or eight, but only three or four survived. This is because the women had to work all day, with no one to care for the children, so many died."

The women under fifty, by contrast, whose children were for the most part born after the Japanese occupation, lost virtually no children. In my census sample, women over fifty have an average of 3.3 surviving children, whereas women under fifty, some of whom may not have completed childbearing, have 5.2. By the end of the Occupation, modern medical care was available in Tsuen Wan, and health conditions in general had improved. The effect of these improved conditions has not been lost on the people of Kwan Mun Hau. Asked, "When did children die more, in the past (before the Occupation) or at present?", all but one of the women and all the men said unhesitatingly that children died more in the past. A number of people estimated that in the past only about half the children born survived, but now, "If one is born, you will have one." Consequently, women who have borne the number of children they consider desirable can make the decision to bear no more, confident that those already born will survive. According to a fifty-one-year-old woman:

Previously women had more babies but they were not all brought up. Now when a baby is born it will be raised. Previously women bore babies until they were unable to bear any more. Now they are sophisticated—after four or five they don't have any more. Some use birth control, others are sterilized. . . . People my age in this row all had eight, nine, or ten—the smallest number is five or six.

Precise information on the actual intervals between births is difficult to obtain because several different methods of calculating ages exist, and because many women do not know the exact ages of their children. In all cases the interval between births, if not affected by birth control, is between one and three years. There does not seem to be any striking difference between the older and younger women in this respect, although the sample is too small to generalize with confidence. There seems to be a trend toward a decreasing interval between marriage and the birth of the first child. A number of women confirmed this observation, adding that now many women are pregnant when they marry, a situation said to be unheard-of in the past. Since many of the women are still of childbearing age, no conclusions can be reached regarding the mother's last birth. Given the availability of contraception and sterilization, one would expect the age at last birth to fall.

Fecundity

The fecundity of Kwan Mun Hau women probably has been affected by changes in the work they do, in nutrition, and in the availability of medical care. Some informants asserted that women are now able to bear children closer together, and that girls now mature physically several years earlier than they did twenty years or more ago (a development that may be attributable to improved nutrition). One would expect that the availability of modern medical care would increase fecundity in several ways. First, diagnosis and treatment of problems causing sterility is offered by the Family Planning Association and by doctors; one hospital is reputed to offer particularly good care in this area. My informants were aware that apparently sterile couples could seek such help, and I interviewed one woman, a childless "outsider" (i.e. an immigrant from outside Kwan Mun Hau) who had done this. Similarly, medical treatment may be sought to prevent threatened miscarriages. Furthermore, all births now take place in hospitals or clinics, under hygienic conditions, so there should be less risk of fecundity-impairing infections or injuries. Before about 1950, women delivered at home, with the help of neighbors or midwives or sometimes even alone. Some older women also complained of having had to do hard, potentially injurious physical work, such as carrying water, soon after childbirth. According to one woman of fifty,

My first baby was born at ten o'clock in the evening. The next day I had to go out and get vegetables for the pigs. Several times when I had babies, we had small pigs that had to be fed. Once just after [one daughter] was born I didn't have enough vegetables, so I had to go in water almost up to my waist to get algae for them. The day after the first baby was born I fell down carrying two tins. No one could help me.

Changes in Marriage Patterns

Virtually all normal Kwan Mun Hau natives marry. There was only one normal native over thirty in my census sample who was unmarried. Outsiders have more difficulty finding marriage partners, and there are a number of unmarried immigrant men in the village. According to both my census sample and my interviews, native women were and are married at about age twenty although the oldest women were more likely to have married while still in their teens. There is some slight evidence that marriages were postponed during the Occupation. Otherwise, there is no obvious up- or downtrend in the woman's age at marriage. The age difference between husband and wife in the census sample is about four years. I think we can safely assume little, if any, difference between age at first sexual union and age at marriage, since early or casual dating is rare, and generally young people go out together in groups. When a young man and woman go out alone together, they are expected to marry shortly. Such couple may have intercourse, however—a fact that reflects a significant change in the emotional content of marriages.

Three women (one an outsider) told me that women have children sooner after marriage now because the couple has a chance to get acquainted before their wedding. They were contrasting the experiences of women who are now over sixty with those now in their twenties and thirties. The younger women interviewed were all introduced to their husbands (except for one woman, now forty-five, who was an adopted child-bride), and had some opportunity to meet or go out together before they were married. Except for a 51-year-old woman, who had seen her future husband once before marrying him, all the women over fifty married total strangers. A seventy-five-year-old woman described her marriage as follows:

When I was four years old, matchmakers came to the house saying how a man had a lot of fields, and so forth. When the eight characters [from which a person's horoscope is read] had been written and checked, I was engaged, and at eighteen I was married. It was a blind marriage. When I was married I was very shy. On the wedding day I didn't look at my husband, and not for several months afterward. Before I was married when the Hung people had an opera, I didn't dare go because I was engaged to that man and might see him. I was very shy and felt very ashamed. Even after I was married I didn't address him and didn't recognize his face because I didn't dare look at him— not like people now who are so free and can go out and go in cars and go to teahouses. The present is better . . . since people can go out and look at each other. When they like each other, they marry.

The younger women did not freely choose their own husbands, although this is now possible, but they did have a voice in the arrangement of their marriages and some opportunity to become acquainted with their fiancés. My informants feel there is now some communication and mutual attraction between a couple by the time they marry, whereas the initial months of the old marriages were characterized by distance, embarrassment, and a complete absence of communication. This must often have affected the quality of a couple's sexual relationship, and thus their fertility. A woman in her sixties said,

Now women have more babies. In the past women didn't usually have a baby until after four or five, or even seven or eight years of marriage. . . . Even after women were married they didn't know enough about their husbands. They dared not sit with them, and only took care of the farm work. There was no love between husband and wife. That is why they didn't have so many children.

She went on to say that she had had no children until she had been married for five or six years because there was no affinity between herself and her husband. In addition, it was believed that sexual activity would adversely affect her husband's studies.

A much younger outsider woman confirmed that marriage is now quite a different experience. "People could have more children now than in the past but they don't, because of birth control. They could have more now because they enjoy sex more. When they are young they can fall in love and get married and have children soon. Men in Hong Kong now know and understand more about sex—if a girl marries young she could have twelve children."

One woman said that sexual intimacy may exist even before marriage:

Previously there was a matchmaker and the two people didn't know each other very well. The woman was shy and there was some distance between husband and wife. Therefore it would be at least three years before they had a baby. Now it is different because they understand each other before they are married, and very often the girl is two or three months pregnant when they are married.

In the past, on the third day after a wedding, the husband's family would send a roast pig to the bride's natal family, indicating (according to my English-speaking informant) that "she had been a good girl," i.e., was a virgin. It may be significant that now the roast pig is sent on the wedding day, and eaten as part of the wedding feast. An elderly woman said that in the past there were never any pregnant brides in Kwan Mun Hau, but according to my informants premarital pregnancies are now common. This was true in the case of one of my neighbors, and one older woman mentioned to us the first time we talked that her daughter-in-law was pregnant when she married. This seemed to be a fact worth remarking on, but not condemning, although she did say that because the bride was pregnant they invited only a few people to the wedding, and therefore were criticized by other villagers. When I questioned informants they said that pregnancy at marriage is not a serious matter, although it is not particularly good. One woman said that mothers warn their daughters not to get pregnant before marriage because then they will not be able to demand a bride price, but will have to be sent to their husbands' families for free. A pregnant bride can worship at the ancestral hall only if the pregnancy is not visible. One woman said that a bride's pregnancy is referred to as a "modern dowry," a term with positive connotations. It is another matter entirely, however, for a girl to become pregnant by a man whom she is not going to marry. Promiscuity is not condoned, and a girl in this situation would be disgraced.

The frequency of intercourse within marriage is a subject I never heard discussed between women, and I did not want to jeopardize my relationship with my informants by asking direct questions. It would have been even more inappropriate for my assistants, who were unmarried, to ask such questions. The frequency of intercourse must be limited by the pattern of sleeping arrangements. All the women respondents slept (or had slept) in the same bed with their small children, and in many households the woman sleeps with the younger children while her husband sleeps separately. Furthermore, parents and children commonly go to bed at the same time. Lack of space was frequently given as a reason for a mother's having to sleep with her children, though many of the women also thought that in general it is a good idea, because the children can be kept warm and secure, and are easily fed and cared for. None of the women mentioned privacy for husband and wife as a problem.

Intercourse is proscribed in certain situations, although villagers say these proscriptions were more strictly adhered to in the past. It was formerly believed that a couple should not have intercourse for one hundred days after the birth of a child, because it would be physically weakening, especially to the man, and therefore dangerous.* Alison Bell, a gynecologist in Kowloon, says this is still an important factor in spacing births, except among the most modern-thinking women. Peggy Lam, Executive Secretary of the Hong Kong Family Planning Association, told me that most women wait at least two months, and many the full one hundred days. A neighbor told me, however, that very few people ("only those who listen to old people") wait longer than fifty or sixty days. A forty-five-year-old woman said old people used to say that intercourse within the one-hundred-day period was dangerous and could cause tuberculosis. She said she herself knew of cases in which the man contracted tuberculosis, but that now people pay no attention to this idea. Intercourse is considered particularly dangerous for men doing certain activities or in certain states of health. For example, I was told

---

* For a more extensive discussion of these beliefs, see the essay in this volume by Emily Ahern, "The Power and Pollution of Chinese Women."

that the thirty-six-year-old woman in my sample had been forced to abstain from intercourse for years because her husband had suffered from a brain disease. My informant said that intercourse would have meant the man's certain death, so he and his wife slept on different floors of the house and sometimes the husband lived with a friend in another town. This explains the nine-year interval between the births of their last two children.

Separation, Divorce, and Widowhood

A young informant told me that most of the older women in the village probably do not know what love is between a man and a woman. The lack of love between partners in some of the marriages was expressed by one old woman: "I wouldn't like to live to be very old and be helpless and bedridden. But if I have to be with that old man in the underworld, I'd just as soon live a little longer." Husbands who had the means could satisfy their need for love (and for descendants, if their wives were sterile) by taking second wives. The husbands of three of the oldest women in my sample had two wives, and out of about sixty native households, I knew of nine in which there was at least one case of polygyny involving people still living. In all these cases, the husbands were over fifty. I have since heard of one case involving a younger man, but this appears to be very unusual. In a polygynous marriage, I am told, although the husband may continue to live with the first wife or with both wives in one house, he typically sleeps with the second and the first normally bears no more children. This constitutes a form of separation. The children born to the second wife, if she is living in the village, are considered as much his descendants as those of the first wife. I even knew of a case in which the second wife had not been allowed into the village by the first, but the husband had brought two of the second wife's children into the household to live, so they were recognized as his descendants by the village.

A woman's fertility is also affected if her marriage ends in an actual separation, divorce, or the death of her husband. Most Kwan Mun Hau marriages are stable, although it was common before the war for adopted child-brides to run away either before or after marriage. Since then, marriages between girls adopted as infants and sons of their adoptive parents have ceased to be arranged. In my sample, the forty-eight-year-old woman had run away from an earlier marriage before she married a Kwan Mun Hau man, and the sixty-two-year-old woman separated from her husband when she was about thirty. She moved into another house in the village, and her husband took a second and later a third wife. In the case of divorce, when the wife leaves her husband and his village, she may also have to leave her children, though there is no clear prescription on this matter.

De facto separation arising not from marital incompatibility but from the husband's prolonged absence must have been very common when many Kwan Mun Hau men had to find work elsewhere, and must have had a substantial effect on fertility. The husband of the seventy-two-year-old woman left for Panama and died there two years after marrying her, his second wife; and the husband of the sixty-two-year-old woman was away working for several years. Such separations are now common elsewhere in the New Territories but not in Tsuen Wan anymore.

Women's fertility must also have been affected by the higher mortality rates prevailing in the past. Two of the older women in the interview sample lost their husbands while they themselves were still of childbearing age, as did two women now in their forties. It is possible that only one of the four would actually have borne more children. Of the others, one was forty-one when widowed and the other two had borne no children to their husbands. None of these women remarried. If a widow does remarry the residence and affiliation of her children by her first marriage are not definitely prescribed, although five women of nine asked said that if a widow remarried, her children would be left behind with her husband's brothers.

The Need for Children

Before the Japanese occupation, Kwan Mun Hau women had little control over aspects of their lives related to childbearing. Their marriages were arranged without their consent, and their husbands could and did take additional wives. High infant mortality rates meant there was no guarantee that the children born to them would survive. Now women have much more control in these areas, and in addition have access to effective means of birth control, so that they can limit the number of children they bear. For them to use birth control, however, they must not only have access to acceptable means of controlling births; they must also accept the idea of a limited number of children.

In Kwan Mun Hau it is important that a couple have at least one child. I know of no childless native couples who had not remedied the situation either through the husband's taking a second wife or through adoption. I remember one pathetic old woman who said she was "useless" because she had been unable to have children. She had not been able to adopt a child because her mother-in-law had said she would not help her care for one; her husband had taken as a second wife a widow with a son. Of the interview sample, the thirty-three-year-old woman listed in my table was childless and had adopted a son from her sister; and the seventy-year-old woman had adopted a daughter, although her husband's first wife had two surviving children. The sixty-two-year-old woman adopted a boy from within the lineage after separating from her husband, because she had only a daughter surviving. Many adoptions within the Ma lineage are recorded in their genealogy. In the fifth, sixth, and seventh generations, seven percent of the boys born were given to other members of the lineage (no adoptions are recorded in the first four generations, and the eighth and ninth are not yet written down). No adoptions from outside the lineage are noted, but there is at least one such case at present.

In my interviews I posed the question, "Why do people want to have children?" Twelve of the women gave a variety of answers, most giving several. Six stated that one reason people have children is to have someone to depend on in sickness and old age: "Raise crops to avoid starvation; raise children for old age." Six said that people have children to avoid loneliness, to bring happiness to the house, to give the couple something to talk about, and "to give spice and color to daily life." Five women said children must be born to continue the generations. "A family should have some young people and some old people. Then it becomes a family. It is like the trees: if a hillside has only old trees and no young trees, when the old ones die it will become a desert." One woman mentioned an obligation to reciprocate: "People raised you; you must raise others." Four women said people have children because it is their fate, because all married people have children, or because everyone wants them. One woman said people have children to avoid criticism.

My informants agreed that the traditional value favoring sons still exists, but that it is much weaker than it had been and that many of the older people have changed their thinking on this question. It is still important to have sons, but daughters are now much more highly valued than they were.* Couples are still under pressure to have sons, but they are in a better position to resist it, because, first, the younger generation

---

* Robert Mitchell presents data from urban areas of Hong Kong suggesting that, in general, boys are relatively more important. He found that the interval between the first and second child is shorter when the first child is a girl, and that families with no sons are more likely to have additional children. Freedman, Peng, Takeshita, and Sun found a strong preference for sons in Taichung, Taiwan. They concluded that whether or not more children are wanted depends on the number of living sons as well as on the total number of children in a family. Robert E. Mitchell, *Family Life in Urban Hong Kong* (Taipei, 1972), 1: 255; Ronald Freedman, J. Y. Peng, Y. Takeshita, and T. H. Sun, "Fertility Trends in Taiwan: Tradition and Change," *Population Studies*, 16.3 (March 1963): 228.

now has more power in relation to the older,* and, second, because they can now demonstrate that daughters are useful and can make a real economic contribution to the family. My neighbor, an outsider married into a Hakka family long resident in Tsuen Wan, became more emotional than I had ever seen her, shaking and perspiring, when a woman jokingly urged her to have another baby and try for a son. She said:

People used to give girls away or even smother them or put them out in the straw barn. Many old-thinking people still prefer boys. Many people tell me to have several more, and to have some boys. I say: and what if they were all girls? I know people who have as many as nine girls. A person's fate determines if she will have boys or girls—she is born that way and it can't be changed. What good would it do to have some more?—we couldn't feed so many and I would worry that I couldn't teach them. Anyway, I have my four girls and I wouldn't change them. Previously my mother-in-law said it is better for people to have more children, but now she is more enlightened and says two or three are enough, and it doesn't matter if they are boys or girls. After all, girls can now do many things that boys do.

Her emotion indicated to me that people's critical or concerned comments have an impact on sonless couples, even though they themselves may be satisfied only to have daughters.

The traditional Chinese value favoring sons is reinforced for Kwan Mun Hau natives by the lineages, both of which are now prospering. Lineage membership is accorded only to sons, and for a family to continue in the lineage and receive its share of lineage property in the next generation, it must have at least one son. Both lineages formerly held a ceremony on the fourteenth day of the New Year to recognize the sons born into the lineage during the previous year. The Hungs, who are reputed to be generally less conservative, now have just a banquet for families of new sons. The Mas have continued the traditional ceremony, in which fathers of new sons, each carrying a big paper lantern representing the child, form a procession through the village, accompanied by young men beating gongs and cymbals to a rhythm that means "produce sons." They march to the ancestral hall, where the lanterns are suspended from a beam and a feast is held for all the men of the lineage. I was told that a full-month celebration is much more likely to be held if the child is a boy, especially if it is not the first child.

* I observed that relationships between the generations seemed quite egalitarian and informants asserted that daughters-in-law have more power than they used to. This may be in part because young people, including women, are now literate and able to earn a substantial cash income; and in part because there are no longer arranged marriages, so a young husband and wife should have a stronger relationship to rely on for support against the older generation.

Of the eleven men I asked whether it is important to have sons, four said they did not care, boys and girls are the same. One or two of these men probably meant that both are equally important, not that it doesn't matter whether or not one has a son, but I think the others were really indifferent. "I don't care," said a fifty-year-old man. "Even when I had only three daughters I didn't care. Only my wife worried." The other seven men said it is important to have sons. Four of these indicated that this was an old-fashioned value that has persisted, though with diminished intensity. Several men expressed ideas similar to these: "The world has changed, but the idea is still maintained to some extent: one must have at least one son, at a minimum. After that it doesn't matter if one has boys or girls. The meaning is to continue the family and keep the property. Boys are more important because girls marry into another family."

The women all seemed to interpret my question as asking whether sons are more important than daughters. With one exception, their answers were remarkably consistent. They all said that boys and girls are equally important, and all but one expressed awareness and disapproval of the value favoring sons. Six women attributed this value to "other people," to other villagers, or to Hakka people in general, and three to the older generation. One woman said that the villagers used to feel that way but now have changed. Seven women mentioned in this context that they themselves want both sons and daughters.

There are very practical reasons for having children in Hong Kong, where, in the absence of a general system of social security, most people must depend either on their savings or on their children for support in old age. The people of Kwan Mun Hau are more fortunate than many, in that most of them have income-earning property. I asked those of my women respondents who were not already living with married sons whether they wanted to live with their sons in old age. The answers diverged. Two women said they want to live with sons, three do not, three don't know, and two said they would like to but doubted that they would.* A forty-five-year-old woman told me:

For Hakka people it's natural to live that way, but I don't know about the future. The world has changed and the younger people would not like to live with the old family, since my family is so big. The daughter-in-law would have a lot of washing and cooking to do. People seldom like to work so much for the family. I don't know about my son's wife. I don't even know what my son will be like after marriage.

---

* To elicit the information I wanted, this question should have been phrased differently, as in the research of Freedman et al.: "These days, for a family like yours how important is it to have a male heir?" "Fertility Trends in Taiwan," p. 228.

Of the nine men asked whether they would like their sons to live with them after marriage (a tenth man is already living with his son), five said they would like them to live separately, in several cases because the younger and older generations have different ways of thinking. Several men said young people will be living in a different world, which their parents might not understand. The remaining four would like to live with their sons, although three were uncertain that their sons would welcome them.

The men were also asked whether they wanted their sons to support them in old age, or thought it best to save for old age as Western people do. Of eleven men, two wanted their sons to support them (one said he should also support his son if necessary). The others said either that saving is preferable (or that they do not have to save because they have property), or that they wanted to depend both on savings and on their sons. Of the women asked, more than half said they would like their sons to support them. I asked informants only about support in old age, but parents clearly assume they will receive financial help from their unmarried children as soon as they start working. When the village depended on agriculture, children contributed their labor from an early age. Less such help is expected now because of the demands of schooling, although children, especially girls, are expected to give some help with household tasks. Now, childhood dependence is prolonged and education continues at least until fourteen. Once children begin working, however, both sons and daughters can and do make a substantial economic contribution to the family. A common pattern is for older children to leave school early, so they can help pay for the education of the younger children. Daughters are now real economic assets because from about fourteen on they can get factory jobs paying good wages, which in most cases they turn over almost entirely to their family during the years before they marry. One man said, "Some people say my daughters are like buildings, with rents coming in."

One can conclude that Kwan Mun Hau natives do not universally want or expect to live with their married sons. Most would like to receive some financial help from their children in old age, but they do not want to be totally dependent on them. Because they have property, most parents have the means to ensure their independence in old age. However, they expect and receive considerable financial help from their children before the children marry.

Children may be expected to provide their parents with more than just financial help and a home in old age. The majority of men, and a few women, mentioned other obligations: children should respect their parents, obey and serve them, and care for them when they are sick. Several people mentioned that daughters are generally more respectful and helpful to their parents than are sons. "The villagers previously considered that to have more sons is good, to have more daughters bad. Now the idea has changed quite a lot. People realize that daughters can help to earn money and sons are usually lazy and disobedient, so they will say to one another that it's better to have more daughters than a bad son."

The "Costs" of Children

Women said that in the past children were "cheaper" in their parents' eyes than they are now. Most people had neither the time nor the money to give children the special, individual consideration they receive now. In economic terms, it is probably relatively more costly to raise a child now than it was before the war. The cost of the birth itself need not be high, though children are now born in hospitals. Children are well-dressed, however, and they are fed well and given powdered milk after weaning. When sick, they are taken for prompt medical attention. A major expense nowadays is education. Girls received no education until after World War II, and many boys received very little. Now all children study at least through primary school, and most parents have high aspirations for their children's education. The great majority of those interviewed hoped that their children would study through middle school or university, or as much as possible. However, five of eleven men and four of eleven women said that girls should study less than boys or would have to do so if the family could not afford to educate all the children. Primary education is quite cheap at the local government school, although other primary schools are more expensive. Secondary school is very expensive, however, and in addition to the cost of school fees, uniforms, and books, there are transportation expenses and the loss of the child's earning power.

Children are also costly if they prevent a woman from working, but only one woman mentioned this as a consideration. Thirteen of the fourteen women had worked after marriage, most leaving their children with their mothers-in-law. In only a few cases did their children eventually prevent them from working, and none of the women said they had limited the number of births in order to work. Outsider women who wish to work are at a disadvantage because they are unlikely to have older family members living with them. For most families, the cost of sending more than two children to babysitters or nurseries would be prohibitive.

Were the mother able to share childcare duties with others, she might be under less pressure to limit her fertility. Godparenthood does not serve this function in Kwan Mun Hau, as it does in some other cultures, although the institution exists.[11] None of the children of the women interviewed had stayed with relatives for extended periods, but only two women had had no help at all in caring for their children. All the others had received help from relatives outside the nuclear family but sharing their household, usually their mothers-in-law. These patterns have not changed, except that now young mothers are more likely to be at home during the day and so do most of the child-tending themselves. The situation of outsider women is strikingly different. Only two of the twelve immigrant women asked had received help from relatives outside their nuclear family, the rest having turned instead to their husbands, neighbors, or servants. This contrasting response reflects the difference in household composition: native households are almost twice as large as the outsider households, and more than twice as likely to include relatives beyond the nuclear family.

Only two women mentioned problems of pregnancy and childbirth among the "costs" of having children. Pregnancy is attended by few restrictions. For a month after the birth, the woman is expected to rest and observe certain precautions, which may be inconvenient, because her health is considered to be delicate at this time. Ideally she should follow a special diet. Because her condition is "cool," she should eat "hot" food.* She should have pork, liver, salted eggs, rice wine, and ginger cooked in sweet vinegar. From twelve days after the birth (when a special ceremony is held), she should have chicken cooked in wine and ginger.[12] It is believed, although less strongly than in the past, that a woman who does not take special foods and rest after childbirth will suffer health problems later on.[13] A number of women said they couldn't afford the prescribed foods in the past, and some now don't bother with them. Believed by traditional-minded people to be particularly vulnerable, a new mother should not wash her hair or go out in the wind, and she should wear long-sleeved clothes and carry an umbrella if she ventures outside. Many women now disregard these precautions, and in the past women who worked could not always observe them. Their ability to rest and remain indoors depended on the presence of a cooperative mother-in-law.

According to my older informants, when their own children were born the idea that a woman is unclean after childbirth was taken very seriously. They had to wear a hat if they went outdoors to avoid offend-

* The terms "cool" and "hot" refer not to temperature but to properties of foods and states of the body, in accordance with the beliefs of Chinese folk medicine.

ing the gods. Their mothers-in-law made them stay in a bedroom, did not let them sit on chairs or eat with other people, or even serve rice to themselves. These restrictions are no longer observed, but during the first month after childbirth women still do not worship the gods or ancestors, or enter anyone else's house without being specifically invited, because they are considered unclean.

Attitudes Toward Family Size

All the variables discussed may affect a couple's decision on the number of children most suitable for them. Although one should not assume that an explicit decision is made in every case, some degree of rational planning is now possible for all. Each family can weigh the costs of additional children under its own particular circumstances.

My informants, both men and women, all agreed that before the war people wanted more children than they do now.* They perceive a clear change in attitudes in recent years. Several people mentioned that more children were desired in the past for farm labor, while others said that fewer are wanted now because of the burden of educating them. "Now they don't want so many because it's not so simple just to have a baby. You have to think of education, clothing, and food, and to bring him up to be a good person."

To learn women's present attitudes toward family size, I asked, "In general, what is the best number of children for a family to have?" Six out of twelve native women said that four children, two boys and two girls, is the most desirable number because then two would marry out (daughters) and two would marry in (daughters-in-law), so nothing would be lost. Of the others, one gave an ideal of four boys and two girls, two gave more than one ideal number, and one elderly woman said "the more the better." Two others could give an ideal family size only for themselves, rather than a general ideal number.[14] The majority of outsider women asked this question also gave an ideal of two boys and two girls, none recommending more than four children.

Six of the twelve native women asked have more children than they consider ideal. Two women have the same number as their ideal, and four have fewer. The latter are all too old to have more children and had less than their ideal number because of infant mortality, sterility,

---

* With regard to a similar response in Taichung, Freedman et al. comment, "The large numbers presumably desired at an earlier period probably referred to *births* rather than children. Since almost all children in Taiwan now survive to be adults, the three or four children now preferred is about the number that might have survived a generation ago under much higher mortality if parents were lucky." "Fertility Trends in Taiwan," p. 228.

marriages ended by death or separation, or a combination of these. None of the women of childbearing age want any more children, except for one, age forty-four, who has no definite opinion.

I asked seven of the younger women whether they had ever discussed with their husbands the number of children they wanted. Three (ages forty-seven, thirty-two, and twenty-nine) said they had, while four (ages forty-five, forty-four, thirty-six, and thirty) had not. Of the women who had not discussed this topic, two said simply that their husbands like children, one that these things are not men's concern, and one that it is not a matter to be discussed but a natural phenomenon. The forty-seven-year-old woman who had discussed this with her husband prides herself on her "modern" attitudes. She is also one of the few women in her age group who is literate.

The Limitation of Births

Infanticide has apparently not been practiced in Kwan Mun Hau within living memory, with one exception: the first child of the sixty-two-year-old woman was killed by her mother-in-law at birth, allegedly because it was born facing the wrong way. This was reported to me as an extraordinary, shocking act, committed by a "black-hearted" woman. Abortion, however, was and is occasionally resorted to. One middle-aged woman had tried in vain to induce an abortion with drugs bought from a traditional medicine shop. Another (age forty-five) had tried to abort her fifth pregnancy, taking various drugs and even deliberately taking a violent fall, but had failed. She succeeded in aborting her sixth pregnancy, taking a Chinese medicine in the fourth month. An outsider woman told me that her fourth pregnancy had been terminated at two months by a "professional" abortionist, using mechanical means. All but one of my informants knew it is possible to induce abortions, though two asserted they had never heard Kwan Mun Hau women talk about them. A few mentioned the means that could be used—injections, drugs, and surgery, and several women cited specific Chinese herbal medicines considered capable of inducing abortion because of their "cool" properties.

Most women think abortion is not a good idea. I asked my informants, "Suppose a woman with little money and many children was pregnant again—would it be wise for her to have an abortion or not?" Only two of eight women favored abortion in such circumstances. No one raised moral objections; the taking of life at this stage appears not to be considered immoral. Abortion is inadvisable, almost all the women said, because it is dangerous to the mother's health. Only one woman mentioned that it is illegal in Hong Kong. The threat to the mother's health was the overwhelming concern. "The woman should not have an abortion. There is a saying: 'It is better to have three babies than one abortion.' It would mean she could have no babies afterward, and it might kill her, because of infection. Some dirty things might be left in her womb, which would make her weaker and weaker." Two women said that under the circumstances described in my question, it would be better to let the baby be born and then give it away than to risk the mother's health with an abortion. An outsider woman said: "An abortion is not good. It hurts the woman. It is like picking an unripe papaya, which hurts the tree. It is better to pick it when ripe." A woman who has had an abortion should eat healing foods, such as chicken, wine, and ginger, to restore her health.

There were apparently no effective ways of controlling conception before modern methods of birth control were introduced. My informants said either that women previously had no means of preventing conception or that they had not heard of any. One elderly woman asserted that she had successfully prevented conception after her twelfth pregnancy by drinking a cup of unboiled water mixed with salt every night at bedtime.

Apart from one older woman who had been sterilized, only one woman now past childbearing age had used any modern means of contraception. This is the literate forty-seven-year-old woman, who is unusually well-informed about Western methods of health care and hygiene. Her husband, too, seems more inclined toward rational planning than many men his age. He said that from the outset of his marriage, with means of contraception then becoming available, he had planned to limit the number of children they had. According to his wife,

I had three children in three years, so I went to the health clinic and asked them for information. I had discussed this with my husband and we decided to use birth control, since our financal situation was very bad. They gave me a diaphragm because the IUD [intrauterine device] and pills were not used then. Then after several years the family decided it would be nice to have a second son. I didn't put in the diaphragm just once, and I became pregnant with the fourth child, who was a daughter. I was thirty-five. The next year I stopped menstruating.

Three of the five women who are now at risk of pregnancy have used and continue to use some form of birth control. Contraception was not used by these women or the woman just quoted either to postpone the first birth after marriage or to prolong the interval between births, but rather to stop having children. One woman of twenty-nine used an IUD after her fourth birth, but found that it made her "thin and tired" and had it removed. She then had a fifth child (and has since had two more, although she told me she wanted no more). A woman of thirty used an IUD after her third birth, but had it removed after several years because of internal bleeding. She then turned to birth control pills, but after taking them for six years she had an unplanned pregnancy, after which she was sterilized. The thirty-two-year-old woman also had an unsatisfactory experience:

After the fifth baby was born I went to see Dr. Fung, but I was already pregnant with the sixth so I couldn't take pills. If my health had been better I wouldn't have had the last two. When I used the IUD [after her fourth child] my periods were irregular but I suffered for over a year with it. I asked the Family Planning Association for pills but they said I had to use the IUD. Now I have had an injection, which lasts for three months, but I don't have periods so it's not good. I don't know what methods are good. I still don't know what to do.

The fourth woman at risk of pregnancy is now forty-four, while the fifth (age thirty-six), as described earlier, did not sleep with her husband for a number of years because of his brain disease. None of the women mentioned abstinence as a means of birth control. This is considered unnatural. According to village gossip, one elderly woman attempted to prevent her son and his wife from having any more children by forcing them to sleep separately (the mother slept with the son). People were amused when they had another baby anyway, conceived one night when the mother was at a meeting, and said that she was silly to attempt to force them to abstain because there are better ways of preventing births.

Modern means of birth control are inexpensive and readily available in Tsuen Wan. A month's supply of pills cost only about H.K. $2.50 in 1968. The Family Planning Association inserts IUD's without charge, and bases fees for other contraceptive supplies on the patient's income. Some women simply purchase pills themselves, whereas others get advice from a doctor. The majority of women receive information and advice from the Family Planning Association. The Association had three clinics in Tsuen Wan at that time. In these clinics, older methods (diaphragm, condoms, foam) have been offered but now are not emphasized. The IUD, available since 1965 in all clinics, was strongly emphasized when first introduced. Pills have been available in Hong Kong on a small scale since 1959 (perhaps not that early in Tsuen Wan) and emphasized since 1967. Pills are now given about four times as frequently as the IUD, according to the Family Planning Association. The Association also refers and screens cases for sterilization.[15]

All the women knew of at least one modern method of contraception (IUD, pills, sterilization), and many of them mentioned several in the course of their interviews. Furthermore, most had some understanding of how the methods are used. I found this degree of awareness quite remarkable, given that over half of the women are illiterate and some are quite elderly. Birth control is a common topic of discussion in the village, and the various methods are talked about openly and without embarrassment. Even men mentioned the use of birth control to me in interviews or told me that their wives had been sterilized. Gossip and informal discussion are an important source of information for elderly women, but the most important source for women in general is the Family Planning Association. Since there is an Association clinic at Grantham Hospital, where most village babies are born, many women do not distinguish between the maternity and family planning clinics. The Association approaches women when they visit the maternity clinic for prenatal or postpartum checkups, or when their babies are born. This policy seems to be highly effective. The women interviewed have a good opinion of the Association workers, and seem to feel no reluctance about seeking information from them. Because most of the women are illiterate, only one mentioned newspapers as a source of information.

I found virtually no objection to the idea of contraception.* None of the women interviewed expressed any more reservations, although of the six men who mentioned birth control, two opposed it. A forty-year-old man said fatalistically that whether or not a child is conceived should be decided by the gods. The second man, a Christian, said that it is better to have more children and unnatural to limit births, and that it is wrong to kill them because God sends them. Both men expanded on the dire effects of contraception on women's health, maintaining it makes them thin, irritable, and even insane. Their attitudes may represent the opinion of a small proportion of older men. Four women also expressed rather fatalistic attitudes, i.e., that really nothing can be done to limit births.

In Kwan Mun Hau there do not seem to be the sorts of problems of communication and agreement about contraception which Stycos describes in Puerto Rican culture:

* Researchers in other Chinese communities have found a similar receptivity to contraception. Robert E. Mitchell, *Family Life in Urban Hong Kong* (Taipei, 1972), 1: 246–47; Ronald Freedman et al., "Fertility Trends in Taiwan," *Population Studies*, 16.3 (March 1963): 229–30.

Differential sex statuses and roles are such as to encourage family limitation on the part of the wife and discourage it on the part of the husband. These roles and statuses are often sufficiently disparate to limit adequate communication between husband and wife on matters of family limitation; and to frustrate the wife's desires where such communication may exist.[16]

Although women seem to have more definite opinions on the subject than men, few people in the village believe that an unlimited number of children is good. There is no value corresponding to the Latin American machismo—no belief that many children are proof of a man's virility. The rational calculation of the costs and benefits of additional children seems paramount in most cases. Most men and virtually all women believe it desirable to limit the number of children born. Although there is a considerable degree of role differentiation, especially in the marriages of older Kwan Mun Hau natives, when husband and wife discuss this topic they usually agree. In my sample the husbands either approved of their wives' use of birth control, or were indifferent to or ignorant of it.

Even elderly women, as mentioned earlier, are quite well-informed about birth control and apparently feel no strong objection to its use. I know of no case in which an older family member prevented a younger couple from using birth control. In one or two cases young couples may have voluntarily postponed the use of birth control because the old people wanted more grandchildren. One man said he and his wife simply concealed from his father that they were using birth control because they knew he would object.

The women interviewed did have serious doubts about the use of birth control in one area: its effect on a woman's health. The consensus seems to be that birth control should be used only by healthy women, who are strong enough to tolerate it. I was told of women who could not use birth control because they were in poor health. More pregnancies were considered better for them than contraception. Women brought up problems they believed to be caused by the various methods. Although only one woman had tried pills, several raised objections to them, saying that they are not always effective, or that they make women pale, fat, or thin. Sterilization seemed generally acceptable. Only two women mentioned objections to it, one saying that women cannot do heavy work afterward and the other that it is bad for women with a certain type of disposition. Only one woman mentioned problems with the IUD, but the three who had actually used it had had to discontinue its use. The advantages and risks of the different methods are a common topic of discussion in the village. In all, eleven of thirteen women expressed objections to one or more of the methods they knew. One can conclude that although in general the women interviewed are receptive to the idea of birth control, they have reservations about most of the methods currently available.

Conclusions

The childbearing experiences of Kwan Mun Hau women have changed in two principal ways since World War II. First, almost all the children born now survive. Second, within the last ten years modern means of birth control have become readily available in Tsuen Wan, so that women need no longer bear unlimited numbers of children. In general, women regardless of age are well-informed about the availability of birth control. In common with other young women in Hong Kong, the younger women in the village are attempting, with varying success, to limit the number of children they bear.

Although the people in Kwan Mun Hau are now living in an industrial city, in many ways their lives remain those of rural villagers. One would expect certain aspects of their situation to foster high-fertility attitudes. The villagers have steadily been becoming more prosperous in recent years, particularly in relation to other people in Hong Kong. Although few villagers are really wealthy, most families enjoy a basic economic security because of their property holdings. Because they own their own homes, they have space for larger families than many immigrants have. Because the men need not migrate to seek employment, families (about half of which are extended) remain intact. This means that most women can share the burden of childcare with grandparents and other relatives. One might also expect that the presence of old people in the households, and the persistence of traditional lineage and village organization, would work to maintain high-fertility values.

All these factors together must mean there is less pressure on Kwan Mun Hau natives than on most immigrants to limit fertility, and more resistance to the idea of smaller families. Nevertheless, most of the women interviewed accept the idea of birth control and feel that in general four children are enough. In this respect they perceive a clear change in values in recent years.

Women in the Countryside of China

DELIA DAVIN

One of the greatest social achievements of the Chinese Communist Party has been the change brought about in the lives of Chinese women since 1949. Indeed, women have always had a special place in party policy because they are considered to have been subjected to a special kind of oppression—both within the family and within society as a whole. This idea of the special oppression of women is to be found in classical Marxism. Engels observed that the husband's obligation to earn a living and support his family gives him a position of supremacy so that "within the family he is the bourgeois and the wife represents the proletariat."[1] And Mao Tse-tung, writing of China in 1927, put it like this: "A man in China is usually subject to the domination of three systems of authority (political authority, clan authority, and religious authority). . . . As for women, in addition to being dominated by these three systems of authority, they are also dominated by men (the authority of the husband)."[2]

By the time of Liberation the position of urban women in China, though still in many respects unsatisfactory, was certainly in flux. The countryside, by contrast, presents a more static picture. Such Kuomintang legislation as might have been expected to affect women, notably the marriage law and the law on equal inheritance, was not only unheeded, but in rural areas was even largely unknown. Women were still regarded and treated as inferior. In theory they still owed obedience to their fathers until marriage and to their husbands ever after, and in practice they had a very subservient position all their lives unless they achieved a prestigious old age by raising at least one son to adulthood. In the long years of war before Liberation, women in many areas stricken by famine had lost even the limited security that had been afforded them in normal times. The sale of girl children had always been a possible solution for impoverished families, but these grim times saw adult women change hands, sometimes sold by their starving husbands. Such cases, an exceptional but nonetheless real part of twentieth-century experience, have not been allowed to drop out of the public consciousness. These stories, kept alive by the media along with tales of women's sufferings under the old marriage system, have proved a great stimulus to women's struggles.

Practical policies to deal with the special situation of women were first applied in the early days of the Kiangsi Soviet. Over the next twenty years these policies underwent considerable development and refinement.[3] By 1949, when the Communists faced the task of administering the whole of mainland China, they had long experience of mobilizing people for social revolution and moderating their ideas of what should be to what the economic, social, and political situation made possible. Since problems and possibilities varied enormously from class to class, from city to countryside, and from one region to another, a complex range of policies, practices, and institutions had to be developed in the campaign to change the position of Chinese women. In this paper I examine the changes that occurred in the lives of rural women in the first decade of the People's Republic. Though I touch upon the effects of the marriage law, I will concentrate on land reform and collectivization, on women's role in traditional agriculture and the mixed success of the campaign to change it, and on the institutional barriers to sex equality in the countryside.

The idea that women are oppressed because they are cut off from productive work is central to Marxist thought. Engels wrote, "To emancipate woman and make her the equal of man is and remains an impossibility so long as the woman is shut out from social productive labor and restricted to private domestic labor."[4] Accordingly, much effort in China has been directed toward getting women to work outside the home. There has, however, been considerable fluctuation in this effort over time. The explanation is not hard to find. Women's labor has been desperately needed in some places, at some times, as for example in contested areas during the Liberation War, when so many men were away fighting. In other circumstances chronic unemployment and rapidly diminishing returns to labor have made it difficult to employ women productively outside the home. Moreover, the party has in practice acknowledged that mere participation in productive labor will not of itself automatically liberate women. Formal legislative protection is afforded by the marriage law, but more important, women are encouraged to struggle for equality through their special organization, the Women's Association, and through discussion and argument in every context their lives afford. Attacks on male chauvinism, whether made laughingly between teasing husbands and wives or joking colleagues, or in earnest at family meetings or enterprise assemblies, are commonplace in People's China.

The switch of attention to the cities, which was a general feature of Communist policy from 1947 onward, was echoed in the women's movement. The importance of organizing urban women was constantly stressed, and many of the best, most experienced organizers of village women were transferred to cities and urged to make their first priority the restoration and development of industrial and handicraft production in the urban areas. Publications of the women's movement in those years were full of stories about the situation in the cities and had much less to say about the villages.

Organizational efforts among rural women at first received little attention because they could continue on the basis of policies and techniques already developed in the Liberated Areas. Obviously conditions in many of the newly Liberated Areas differed from those in the old, and policies were adapted to meet them. It was a process of adaptation, however, rather than innovation, and cadres who worked with rural women were recommended, as late as the early 1950's, to take as their guideline a resolution passed by the Central Committee of the CCP in September 1948.[5] This resolution was itself largely a reiteration of one adopted by the Central Committee in February 1943. The main thesis of that resolution had been that women's path to liberation lay in participation in productive labor.[6] The resolution was actually part of an attack on the "feminism" of certain women intellectuals (notably Ting Ling), who favored an all-out and no doubt socially disruptive attack on the feudal marriage system, and who were accused of failing to understand the importance of developing women's economic role.[7] The resolution of 1948 continued the economic emphasis, though it stipulated that the remnants of feudalism still constraining women would not just disappear spontaneously once women took part in production, and anticipated a prolonged period of education and even struggle before traditional attitudes toward them were eradicated.

In the countryside, then, 1949 was not a great watershed for the women's movement. Land reform, with its momentous impact on women, would not take place for a considerable time in the south, yet it was already complete in some of the older Liberated Areas in the north, where indeed a few mutual-aid teams and cooperatives existed long before they became nationwide during the 1950's. Land reform and collectivization revolutionized what the party recognized as the key to the position of rural women: their relationship to production and to the ownership of the main means of production, the land. It is on this relationship that I will first focus.

Women and the Land

The role played by women in agriculture varied from one area to another and from one class to another. But, as a rule, in traditional China women did not own land. Inheritance went from father to sons or other male relations. Occasionally widows held land on behalf of their infant sons, though it was usual to entrust it to a male relative of the dead father so that it could be worked by a man. Neither as wives nor as daughters were women themselves able to inherit land. Only in the odd situation when the family had no male offspring and chose to continue their line of descent by keeping their daughter at home and arranging an uxorilocal marriage for her was the land passed through the female line.* This was still the case in most of China at Liberation, although in the older Liberated Areas it had long been different.[8] Land reform, which overthrew the landlord system, also upset the male monopoly of landownership. The agrarian law provided that men and women should receive equal shares of the land, and that separate property deeds should be issued where necessary.[9] In Long Bow village, Shansi province, women knew even before land reform had taken place that they were to receive land, and they were fully aware of the great significance this could have. One of the leaders of the Women's Association said: "Still, there are beating cases and most men despise women's words and think women are no use. We have to struggle for a long time to win equality. When we have land of our own it will help a lot. In the past, men always said, 'You depend on me for a living. You just stay home and eat the things I earn.' But after women get their share they can say, 'I got this grain from my own land and I can live without you by my own labor.' When it comes to labor on the land, women can work just as hard as men even if they are weaker. They can do everything except

---

* This is one of the many instances where custom triumphed over law in Nationalist China. Legislation of 1931 gave sons and daughters equal rights of inheritance and made the wife her husband's legal heir, but it remained ineffective and probably largely unknown outside the cities—a situation that in Taiwan has changed little even today. For a description of the law, see M. H. van der Valk, *Conservatism in Modern Chinese Family Law* (Leiden, 1956). For the situation in contemporary Taiwan, see Margery Wolf, *Women and the Family in Rural Taiwan* (Stanford, Calif., 1972), pp. 203–4.

plowing. They can even hoe if they can't hoe so fast. But they cannot drive carts. Well, even this they can do, but some of the animals are pretty hard to handle."[10] In fact the Women's Association in Long Bow would soon start plowing classes for women. But the campaign to get village women to involve themselves directly in production was closely linked to the transition from individual to collective farming. Before examining these stages in detail, I will briefly survey woman's traditional relation to production in the countryside.

It is often said that women did not work the land in traditional China. This statement requires considerable qualification. In some villages in the north it was exceptional for women to do farm work. But in certain areas of the south women played an important part in agriculture.

From his surveys in the early 1930's, J. L. Buck estimated that "in terms of work accomplished, men performed 80 percent of all the farm labor in China, women 13 percent, and children 7 percent."[11] His figures show a general difference between north and south, with 16 percent of farm work being performed by women in the rice-growing areas as a whole as opposed to only 9 percent in the wheat region. A breakdown of the figures within these areas shows more striking contrasts, particularly for the rice areas: in the double-cropping rice area for example (mainly Kwangtung province, southern Kiangsi, and southern Fukien), 29 percent of the labor was performed by women, whereas in the rice-tea area directly to the north (northern Fukien, Chekiang, Kiangsi, and southern Hunan), their share was only 5 percent. Between these two extremes, the women's share was 22 percent in the southwestern rice area, 19 percent in the Yangtze rice-wheat area, and 11 percent in the Szechwan rice area. North of the Yangtze the differences were less marked. Women performed 14 percent of the farm work in the spring wheat area, 8 percent in the winter wheat–kaoliang area, and 5 percent in the winter wheat–millet area.

Here it may be useful to apply the economist Ester Boserup's analysis of sex roles in farming, of which she has made this excellent summary: "In very sparsely populated regions where shifting cultivation is used, men do little farm work, the women doing most. In somewhat more densely populated regions, where the agricultural system is that of extensive plough cultivation, women do little farm work and men do much more. Finally, in regions of intensive cultivation of irrigated land, both men and women must put hard work into agriculture in order to earn enough to support a family on a small piece of land."[12]

If we apply this framework to China, we can see that all of North China and part of South China belong to the second category, of extensive plow cultivation. In such areas women's contribution to agriculture was small, and probably was made mostly in the busiest seasons of the farming year. In the far south and the southwest, where several crops were grown each year and much of the land was irrigated, the demand for labor was high throughout the year. Consequently many women performed farm work as part of their normal routine. During the busy periods of planting or transplanting and harvesting which occurred several times a year, even women who did not go daily to the fields might be drawn into the work. Since the cultivation of rice is especially labor-intensive, women's participation rate was highest in the double-cropping rice area. This serves as a general explanation for the most striking regional differences, but there remain contrasts that cannot be explained by relative intensity of cultivation.

The spring wheat area of the far north, which showed the comparatively high female participation rate of 14 percent, was a sparsely populated area with a short growing season, low productivity per acre, and a correspondingly extensive agriculture. Buck, who suggested an association between female labor participation rates and regional variations in the prevalence of foot-binding, was troubled by this high figure of 14 percent. He was aware that foot-binding was still widespread in the spring wheat area, and that the bindings were so tight that women, unable to stand for any length of time, were compelled to do field work on their knees.

Perhaps climate was the significant factor here. In this region the growing season was so short and the winter so bitter that only one crop could be produced each year. Labor-demand peaks were therefore concentrated in the spring sowing and autumn harvest periods. These must have been even more pressing than the four main peaks that occurred in the other northern regions, where winter wheat was grown with kaoliang or with millet. Adverse climatic and soil conditions and, according to Buck a high rate of opium addiction, combined to produce the lowest labor productivity in China. It would therefore have been impossible for a man to support as many dependents as he could elsewhere in China. Thus a harsh climate and low productivity together raised the rate of women's participation in farm work, although their role remained a minor one.

A comparatively low-intensity agriculture may have been a factor in the rice-tea region of the south, where women did only 5 percent of the farm work. Here the grain crop yield was only 86 percent of the average for China. With much of the region consisting of barren hills, there was less cultivated land per person than in the Yangtze rice region, where women were responsible for 19 percent of the work. Furthermore, though the same proportion of land was double-cropped as in the Yangtze region, very little land had to be artificially drained, and mountain streams were utilized for irrigation so that water control was less labor-intensive than in the Yangtze plain. Nevertheless, the 5 percent figure, so extraordinarily low for the south, is difficult to explain. Rice, tea, and rapeseed, the three main crops of the region, all have heavy labor requirements, and tea cultivation in particular usually involves large numbers of women in the workforce. Here we encounter a basic difficulty in the comparative use of these percentages: they must contain distortions attributable to differences in perception that we cannot now determine. In this case tea-picking, which absorbed much of the women's time but was not heavy work, may have been assessed as a small part of the total work done on the land.

Subsidiary work, such as tea-processing, hog and poultry raising, spinning, weaving, basket making and other handicrafts, was separately listed in Buck's survey. Such pursuits brought the peasants considerable supplementary income, and occupied time when other work was slack. But Buck's figures do not show a consistent relationship between the proportion of subsidiary work done by women and the amount they did on the farm. For example, though in the wheat-millet area, where women rarely went to the fields, they were responsible for 25 percent of the subsidiary work, in the rice-tea area, where they did equally little farm work, they performed only 13 percent of the subsidiary work. Secondary occupations provided 15 percent of the farm incomes in the former area and 13 percent in the latter, so their economic importance to the two areas was similar.

In some prosperous areas women may have had to spend more time working at home because food and clothing requirements were more elaborate, while in others the extra production that accrued from additional labor power in the fields may have been enough to tempt them out to work. While it is hard to know to what extent decreasing marginal returns to labor discouraged women from working, it seems likely to have sometimes been a factor in so labor-intensive an agriculture. Certainly in the 1950's steeply declining marginal returns to labor impeded the campaign to get women to work in the fields.

Women's participation in agriculture was thus part of a complex pattern. Some local variations cannot be explained by any of the factors mentioned, and might be better understood in terms of local history or ethnic and subethnic differences. Any village with a significant proportion of Hakka residents, for example, would produce quite different figures from villages without them, because Hakka women did not have bound feet and normally worked in the fields. In villages whose cultivated land was at some distance from home, women may have been discouraged from working by problems with children. This was especially serious if work areas were deep in the hills, as were the tea-growing districts.

For China as a whole only a very broad generalization can be made: although women did more farm work in the south than in the north, their agricultural role in all but a few localities was relatively minor and highly seasonal. They helped with the harvest, especially in those areas where it coincided with the planting of another crop, and did secondary, low-prestige chores such as weeding. Except in a few places in the south, it remained the ideal that women should not do agricultural work. An adage from I-liang, Yunnan province, quoted by Buck, expresses the reluctant acceptance of women in the fields at rush periods that was general in China:[13]

> In the two busy seasons
> Maidens may leave their chambers.
>
> Erh chi nung mang
> Kui-nü tou yao ch'u hsiu fang.

Ramon Myers, in his detailed study of North China in the 1930's, clearly indicates the seasonal and auxiliary basis on which women worked. Of the early summer in a Hopei village, where cotton and millet had to be thinned at the same time the wheat was harvested, he says, "the demand for labor was so great, even women came to the fields to help the men." Again, in a Shantung village Myers studied, a seasonal labor shortage was met by women, but only from the poorer households: "During the wheat harvest when the spring crop was also being planted, women and children in poor households of only 10–30 mow even worked in the fields because so much labor was needed."[14] In the richer households this need was met by temporary hired labor.

In China as a whole, Buck found that subsidiary occupations provided 14 percent of farm families' income.[15] It was thus a significant though minor source of income. But the contribution of women was quite a small one here, too: they provided only 16 percent of the labor. This aggregate figure masks wide regional variations (from 25 percent in the winter wheat–millet region, to as little as 7 percent in the spring wheat region), but it confirms the implication of our data on agricultural production: women played an unquestionably minor part in rural production. This had a bearing on their status, since within the family productive labor might contribute to power and prestige, as landowner-ship did within the village.

Organizing Women to Work Outside the Home

Although women's participation in directly remunerative work was minor, their share of work was not. The household work for which they were responsible was demanding and often arduous, and was indis-pensable to the family's well-being. Providing meals, for example, did not simply mean cooking; it could include the gathering of fuel, the drawing and fetching of water, the husking and grinding or polishing of grain, and the preserving of surplus vegetables and fruits. Many women mentioned the processing of grain as their heaviest task. Rudolf Hommel, writing of China in 1937, said: "In almost every village in the rice-growing districts of Chekiang province there is a rice-hulling mill, the property of the community.... Every farmer owning a draught an-imal can use it, the others have to be content to use their hand mill."[16] Descriptions of northern villages also mention both large, animal-powered equipment for husking and grinding grain and household querns. So, presumably, north or south, it was the poorer women (whose incentive to work outside the house was greatest), who would be com-pelled to give the most time to one of the basic household tasks. In some households the women made beancurd, fermented alcoholic drinks, and prepared tobacco leaves for pipe-smoking. Clothes were usually made at home, and so sometimes were the cloth and the thread that went into them. Cloth shoes stitched by women took two or three days to make but lasted only five or six months. In impoverished and backward rural areas, where even water and soap cost much effort to procure, housework and childcare were more burdensome than in advanced societies. In the slack seasons men might sometimes help by carrying firewood or fetch-ing water, but in general domestic tasks were the exclusive responsibility of women.* To increase their share in productive work was therefore clearly impossible, or at least would make their lives still harder, unless household work and childcare could be reorganized. Otherwise they would suffer from the double burden of which the early Bolshevik Alexandra Kollontai had warned.[17]

There were other obstacles to women's working in the fields. Arduous

---

* There is an interesting exception in northern Shensi, where men do the family knitting in the slack season. This was a very practical arrangement since the long northern winter brings more leisure to men than it does to women, whose busy household routine continues. Jan Myrdal, *Report from a Chinese Village* (London, 1965), p. 13.

though housework was, much agricultural work could be heavier still. This had been a factor in the traditional division of labor and had to be considered if this division were to be changed. Many women were permanently handicapped by bound feet, which precluded them from carrying heavy loads or even walking any distance. Until recently, moreover, a woman might expect that for much of what would otherwise have been her prime, she would be continuously pregnant, her health and strength progressively undermined by childbearing in primitive conditions. The surveys make by J. L. Buck in the 1930's indicated that Chinese women who lived to complete their fertile period bore an average of between five and six children.[18] This figure is likely to be too low; high infant mortality and the tendency to omit female births probably led to underreporting. Moreover, since many pregnancies no doubt ended in miscarriages brought on by hardship, poor nutrition, and heavy work, women must have undergone many months of pregnancy that did not result in births.

Where it was not customary for women to work on the land, they lacked the many skills and techniques needed in order to do so. They were therefore thought incapable, so that a lack of trust on the part of men, and of self-confidence on the part of women, were serious obstacles. A further prejudice in such areas was the one against women leaving their homes at all, especially if it meant being in the company of men. When women began to break this convention, they were often thought to have disgraced both themselves and their families. They were sometimes criticized by other peasants for "immorality," beaten by their husbands, or refused food by their mothers-in-law, who attacked them just as fiercely as did the men. Nor, prejudice apart, was it possible to involve women in productive labor everywhere at the same rate; although labor shortages made extra workers welcome in some areas, surpluses made them unusable in others.

When these problems could be solved at all following Liberation, it was only in a gradual and piecemeal way. At each stage of the collectivization of agriculture, one finds the same claims made about the great numbers of women being mobilized for agricultural work. The repetitive nature of these claims tends to make the reader feel much effort is being expended for little progress, and this effect is aggravated when, by claiming "unprecedented" successes at every stage, the CCP's publicity machine devalues all earlier, equally vaunted achievements. For a historical perspective I think it better to stress the continuous and gradual nature of the mobilization. Since throughout the campaign the essential problems did not change, one can discuss the general approach to them before going into detail on the particular way each stage in the transformation of agriculture affected women.

The conflict between domestic and outside work was dealt with in part by the exchange of labor, improved amenities, labor-saving consumer products, and communal childcare and eating facilities. The bulk of housework and childcare in traditional society had fallen on the younger women. As mothers grew older, their elder children helped by caring for the younger ones; on the marriage of sons, the new daughters-in-law took over the worst of the burden; and though the older women remained in charge of the house, their role was less active. But once the younger women began to work outside the house, this balance was changed, and a greater share of the chores fell to the mother-in-law. While the girl was out at work, the older woman would look after her grandchildren and do menial tasks that would once have been reserved for the younger woman. The older woman cooked for the family, including the daughter-in-law, who would formerly have had to serve her. This reversal of roles was certainly felt in a society that was highly role-conscious. The older women, not surprisingly, were often resentful. In the 1950's, publications for women carried many articles clearly directed at this unlucky generation of middle-aged women, reminding them that in enabling their daughters-in-law to work, they were themselves making a contribution to the welfare of society and of their family. Judging from this material, the care of children was a far more popular task than housework, and there are even reports of grandfathers taking it on.

When no member of the family was available to take care of the children, an arrangement might be made with a neighbor. In such cases the household was effectively purchasing services from outside. Indeed, the payment for minding a child was sometimes even settled as a proportion of the mother's earnings, an indication that childcare was still firmly regarded as the mother's responsibility, although it was permissible for her to find a substitute when it was economically feasible.

Crèches and nurseries were a natural extension of such arrangements, especially when the formation of mutual-aid teams and cooperatives provided organizations on which they could be based. At their simplest they were informal and temporary, formed so that mothers could help with a rush harvest. Such ad hoc groups were usually housed in a borrowed building such as a temple, and were entrusted to old ladies or bound-footed women who could not do heavier work. Later, after the formation of co-ops, the best nurseries were sometimes quite well-equipped establishments managed by women who had trained for a few weeks in the hsien capital. Communal childcare facilities were usually subsidized at least to some degree.[19] This was an important principle, for as long as the mother is considered responsible for the cost of looking after her children, the value of her earnings is reduced, in her family's eyes, by the amount that must be paid for the children's care. A report from Anhwei province, in 1955, presented below in abridged form, gave much interesting detail on the care of the children of working mothers:

In the 581 households of Langk'ang hsiang, Ch'u hsien, Anhwei, there are 455 children under six who require day care. Arrangements were made within the family or with neighbors for the care of 360 of these children, so that 216 mothers could go to work with easy minds. The mothers of the other children either did not work, or worked and worried that their children would have accidents. The Women's Association organized a nursery for them in the rush seasons but it was not a great success. Investigation showed that some mothers still worried about leaving their children with others, especially if an only son were involved. Some did not like parting with their wages to pay nursery fees.

A meeting was held for the mothers, the child-minders, and the cadres (both men and women) of the hsiang. It was pointed out that women constituted 42 percent of the local labor force, and that if they worked it would be possible to increase yields, thus enriching both their families and the child-minders. The following rules were drawn up for the nursery:

Keep children away from matches and streams.
Have things ready to give the children to eat and stop them from quarreling.
Don't let things fall on the children.
Change diapers often, and don't let chickens or older children scratch babies' faces.

Vegetable leaves, clay, and empty matchboxes were recommended as economical and versatile play materials.

The nursery was to be in the charge of old ladies and children over ten if possible, otherwise a rota of mothers was to be drawn up. Charges for the nursery were decided according to the age of the child and the difficulty involved in looking after it. Thus the care of a baby was valued at ½ workpoint per day, against a whole workpoint for a toddler. Children who needed continuous attention were charged for at the rate of 1½ points, but there was no charge at all for children over seven.[20]

Such measures were thought to have solved the problems of working mothers in the hsiang.

In the countryside, communal eating facilities are less popular than nurseries. In 1953, at the Second National Congress of the Women's Federation, Teng Ying-ch'ao even spoke against sewing groups and canteens as misguided attempts to relieve country women of all housework.[21] This line was of course reversed during the Great Leap Forward (1958–59), but the new policy was not very successful, and today in most of rural China, canteens function on a large scale only at the busiest periods of the agricultural year.

Canteens had been expected to bring other advantages besides the obvious one of freeing more women for productive labor. Collective farming required a more exact sense of time than existed generally among peasants accustomed to planning their individual workday. If everyone ate together in a canteen, it was hoped, they would find it easier to report for work promptly. It was also argued that canteens would yield great economies of scale.

A complaint mentioned in almost every report on communal canteens was "You can't eat when you like."[22] Dissatisfaction with the quality and quantity of the food was aggravated by the food shortages of 1959–62. Even under ideal conditions it is of course difficult to cater to individual tastes, and conditions were far from ideal. Nor were the expected economies of scale always achieved. In the years before the canteens were established, the job of cooking at home had increasingly been undertaken by women who were too old or weak for outside work. Work in the canteens was heavy and the hours were long, so that the canteens had to employ able-bodied workers who might otherwise have been in the fields, while the older women were left idle. If public trust was to be preserved the canteens had to keep accurate accounts, but collectivization had already caused more demand than could be met for people who could keep books. The big stoves used in canteens did not warm the peasants' homes as private cooking stoves had done, and in the colder areas where some sort of domestic heating is indispensable, this separation of cooking and heating functions tended to increase fuel consumption. In the end most communes closed their big canteens, reopening them temporarily at the busiest times of year, when all available labor was needed.

Improved amenities and consumer goods, though still inconsiderable by Western standards, have helped lighten household work. Running water in the home remains rare in the countryside, but new taps and pumps have made it easier to draw, and in many cases have brought the water supply closer to the peasants' homes. Thermos bottles, which are proudly displayed in most peasant houses, have made it possible for people to take the ordinary country drink of hot water without always having to kindle a fire to heat the water. Soap, and more recently detergents, have become cheaper and more widely available, making all cleaning jobs easier. Husking and grinding by hand is less usual since many brigades have set up small mills to which their members take their grain. Jan Myrdal describes how the installation of an electric mill in Liu Ling, northern Shensi, in 1969 had affected one woman's life:

Li Yang-ching's household consisted of seven persons. They consumed about 1,500 kilos of grain a year. Formerly she used to grind all this herself, by hand. Now it was being ground for her in the brigade mill.

The brigade charges at cost for this service. The prices vary slightly for different sorts of grain. On an average it is 0.66 yuan per 100 kilos of grain. Last year Li Yang-ching paid about 10 yuan. This is deducted from the money she gets for her work. But since the mill has freed her—as it has the other women—from the hardest and most time-consuming part of her household work, and this has given her more time for agriculture, so her working income has risen.[23]

Products of the machine textile industry have gradually replaced the old handicraft industry, and peasants have even begun to buy some ready-made clothes. Factory-made cotton shoes with hard-wearing plastic soles have spared millions of housewives the old time-consuming job of stitching cloth shoes. "Sewing stations" have been set up in some communes. Equipped with sewing machines, these stations employ people who have become highly skilled at tailoring. They saved women an enormous amount of time, which could then be given to remunerative labor. To take another example from Liu Ling village, Shensi, women paid 2.5 workpoints to have a child's jacket and trousers made at the sewing stations. Formerly, working by hand, this job had taken them three days, the equivalent of 18 workpoints.[24] The sewing stations are also important because they put work previously done by women on an individual, private basis through a public measuring process and get it priced. Sewing thus enters the workpoint system.

Finally, mention should perhaps be made of a solution that was hardly adopted. Although men were occasionally urged in the mass media to assist their wives with household tasks, it was not suggested that they should divide them equally. Such persuasion as there was seems most often to have been directed at urban men whose wives worked. All the young women of Liu Ling village expressed pride or gratitude when they mentioned that their husbands helped with the house or children. They clearly recognized it as a difference between their generation and that of their parents, but they did not yet take it for granted. Women take more time off from the fields than men because they need it for housework. In the words of one peasant housewife, Li Yang-ching: "It isn't easy being a woman. My husband brings up four buckets of water a day from the well. I myself go down to the river to wash clothes once or twice a week. We often go down, a lot of us together. We do that when we have our day off. Or we do it during the midday rest, when our husbands are asleep. When we have our rest out in the field, we take out clothes to make or shoes to sew. The men either sleep then or walk about collecting fuel."[25]

By 1969, women in Liu Ling were in a more militant mood, demanding that men care for the children sometimes so their wives could attend meetings. Nevertheless, pay rate norms for an adult woman stood at six to seven workpoints a day, compared with seven to nine workpoints for a man. The women's workday was shorter to allow them time for household duties, which did not carry workpoints.[26] The official line was that eventually the drudgery of housework would be eliminated, but that in the meantime it was primarily the women's responsibility. No effort was made to explain or justify this assumption, presumably because in the traditionalist countryside, none was required. In unmechanized agriculture, productivity still is often closely related to strength and stamina, and the continuation in muted form of the old division of labor seems really to be a tacit acknowledgment that a man's time in the fields may be more productive than a woman's.

Women's capacity for farm labor, even for the lighter tasks like hoeing, picking, and transplanting, is of course affected by their state of health. The abolition of foot-binding, which in the most backward rural areas had continued into the 1940's, meant that in the future women would cease altogether to suffer from what had once been their worst physical handicap, though it continued until the end of their days to hamper those unfortunates too old to be helped by unbinding.

The damage previously inflicted by childbearing has been mitigated by improved knowledge of and facilities for pre- and postnatal care. Immediately after Liberation a huge program was initiated to train rural midwives.[27] Many of the "students" were village midwives who, though they had infected countless women with their unwashed hands and long fingernails, had years of practical experience, which when combined with a little theoretical knowledge, turned them into useful medical workers. Basic precautions against septicemia, such as scrubbed hands and sterilized instruments, reduced maternal and infant mortality. Later, "maternity stations" were built in some villages, so that many women, especially those for whom complications were feared, could have their babies in better conditions with trained medical assistance. But this effort has developed much more haltingly than the midwife-training program, and even by the late 1950's, medical care in remote country areas was still far from adequate.

The problem was not simply a shortage of personnel. Childbirth in

China, as in many societies, was associated with feelings of shame and fear, and tended to be shrouded in myth and superstition. The retrained midwives of the early 1950's were taught that the old Chinese customs of making a newly delivered mother sit up in bed for three days and of sealing her room to protect her from draughts were not only unnecessary, but could be harmful.* Twenty years later the barefoot doctors were still having to preach the same message.[28]

Even when maternal mortality rates began to fall, many women still suffered from ill health. A year-long survey taken in one Kiangsu hsien showed that 20 percent of the 151,000 women investigated were unable to take part in physical labor for reasons of health, and 50 percent suffered from some ailments.[29] Though the results were not wholly satisfactory, a great deal of effort was put into the maternal health campaigns from the earliest years. Both women's magazines and papers intended for the general public carried articles on feminine hygiene, pregnancy, childbirth, postnatal care, and related subjects, which were reproduced in primers for adult literacy classes.[30] These topics also became the subject of propaganda posters and radio talks. The real problem, both with propaganda and with facilities, was that of reaching the remote countryside.

Early efforts to popularize birth control were less sustained and effective. Its advocates were periodically charged with Malthusian heresy, and it was not until the early 1960's that there were really successful large-scale birth-control campaigns, urging later marriages and smaller, spaced families. When these did come, moreover, they met with much opposition in the countryside, where the longing to have many sons was still strong. In the Shensi village of Liu Ling, much of the resistance apparently came from men; women were more easily persuaded of the advantages of planned pregnancies.[31] Of course throughout the period contraceptives were legal and, in the cities at least, readily available without prescriptions. But without strong propaganda for smaller, spaced families and the instruction in techniques which was to be so widely promoted in the 1960's, modern birth control had little impact outside urban areas and the immediately adjacent countryside.

Although the model women workers held up for emulation were often praised for strength and hardiness (and indeed one occasionally meets rather worrying stories whose heroines insist on working almost up to the time of their delivery),[32] women were usually assigned the lighter

---

* As Emily Ahern's paper in this volume shows (pp. 202ff above), such practices might also reflect a desire to protect others from the polluting influences attributed to childbirth.

jobs, and there are frequent references to the importance of giving special consideration to older women or pregnant and nursing mothers in job allocation. This rational division of labor was facilitated by the formation of mutual-aid teams and cooperatives.

But perhaps through overenthusiasm, serious mistakes were sometimes made in job allocation. Occasional references to them can be found in the press throughout the 1950's. For example, in 1953 the *Fukien Daily* reported three miscarriages among women who had participated in the spring plowing and irrigation work, and complained that even after the first accident, cadres had continued to press other women to overwork.[33] The same article told of a four-year-old boy who was drowned when playing alone because his whole family was at work. Cadres were urged to take more notice of women's special situation when mobilizing them for field work. In 1956 and early 1957 there was a spate of similar reports, in the aftermath of the "High Tide of Socialism," when cooperatives were established all over China. This gave rise to many articles in which work-team leaders were urged to pay more attention to women's state of health when allocating work. Co-ops that arranged for women to have days off, or to be given very light work during menstrual periods and pregnancies, were praised. To facilitate such accommodation, mixed work teams were asked to appoint women deputy leaders if their leaders were men because women found it difficult to discuss intimate matters with men.[34]

Although the commune movement of the late 1950's was characterized by the sort of sweeping enthusiasm that pressured everybody to work harder, and some peasant women may have hurt their health by overwork, articles urging care continued to appear in the press and probably had some moderating influence. This was also a time when medical services were greatly extended in the countryside, and many new nurseries set up. But a negative feature of the period was that the family-planning campaign, which had gained some impetus in 1957, temporarily lapsed again. The use of contraception to safeguard the health of mothers and children was advocated, but at the same time large families were encouraged and the theory that population control was necessary to the economy was fiercely attacked.[35]

The health of country women certainly benefited in general, and during pregnancy and childbirth in particular, from the improved medical care available to them in the first decade after Liberation, but improvements were nevertheless limited by scarce resources and personnel. The same difficulties existed with regard to birth control, compounded by popular conservatism and, in the 1950's at least, ambivalence and vacillation in official attitudes. Access to reliable birth-control methods, essential though they are to women's health and to their liberation from heavy domestic burdens, was not widespread in the villages until the 1960's.

The prejudice against women doing farm work was variously attacked. It was most easily eliminated where there was a serious shortage of manpower. In other areas husbands and families were won over by the realization that women's earnings brought the family greater prosperity. Everywhere women activists, often officeholders in the local Women's Association, put enormous effort into learning how to do the work and, being young and highly motivated, they often succeeded. Their achievements were then widely praised and publicized, and other women were urged to follow suit. At district, hsien, provincial, and national levels, the campaign was buttressed by the election of a hierarchy of women "labor models" selected for their enthusiasm and accomplishments. They were also given great publicity in the mass media, and were rewarded with prizes of money, cloth, and farm implements.

Many of the heroines of this campaign were from the northeast, where the problems of organizing and assimilating large areas of the countryside within a short time were first tackled. Fairly typical of them was Teng Yü-lan of Fu-an village, Jehol.[36] The first time she was sent to the district seat as a model worker, she was given two yards of cloth and a towel. The next time she came back with a towel, a garden fork, a spade, and a laudatory banner. Her parents-in-law exclaimed, "What good fortune we have been granted in getting such a daughter-in-law!" She continued to win one honor after another until finally, as a national labor heroine, she saw Chairman Mao in Peking. Her fellow villagers were said to have been most impressed when, unspoiled by this great experience, she returned to work alongside them in the fields. A report called *Agricultural Production Heroines of the Northeast* tells us something of Yü-lan's background. She got on well with everyone, we are told, was a willing worker and often sought advice from the cadres. Though she was presented as a sort of pioneer, part of a new vanguard, the key to her success seems to have lain in her childhood, when she had started to work on the land with her two sisters, her parents being poor peasants with no sons to help them. A detailed description is given of all the different sorts of farm work Teng could do, and, the article adds, perhaps to reassure traditionalists, she was also an excellent needlewoman. Yü-lan was an active member of the Women's Association, and organized the women of her village for production so successfully that women in neighboring villages began to follow their example.

When one mother-in-law objected to her daughter-in-law's working, Yü-lan persuaded other old women to tell her how glad they were that their own girls worked, and to point out how much their families prospered as a result. When some women in her group had difficulty working because of their children, she involved them in such subsidiary occupations as hog and poultry raising, which allowed them to stay close to home.

One interesting aspect of this report and others like it is that it was preeminently poor peasants who emerged as leaders in the campaign to mobilize women for work in the fields. Their hard lives had forced them to acquire the skills necessary for agricultural work.* Most labor heroines originated from this class.

To overcome the dearth of agricultural skills among women, the Women's Association organized classes for them. The teachers, like the labor heroines, usually came from the poorest families. The classes encouraged them to take pride in abilities they had once been ashamed to possess and then to overcome the obstacles still in their way. For example, when Kao Shu-ch'in, a labor model from Heilungkiang, organized women in her village into a team to do hoeing, the men feared they would damage the young wheat shoots and would not let them try.[37] She persuaded her father-in-law to let the team give a demonstration on his land, and having been carefully instructed, the women hoed so well that the men were won over.

Even in those families where land reform brought women the ownership of land in their own right, women sometimes had little incentive to work in districts where even men were underemployed. Buck found that the proportion of able-bodied men over 15 and under 60 who were employed full-time was 35 percent; 58 percent worked only part-time.[38] The seasonal unemployment characteristic of agriculture in temperate zones is aggravated in China by the lack of a sizable livestock industry. Yet even in the areas where men were underemployed most of the year, there could be labor shortages resulting in lost production at rush periods like harvest time.[39] As the Chinese economist Ma Yin-ch'u put it: "The present key problem in rural areas is that of uneven busy and slack periods, as in South China, where the double rice-crop is being extended. In the 15 days which witness the cutting of early rice and the planting of the late rice, peasants have more work than can be accomplished. The

---

* Among the men, the situation was quite different. Their agricultural skills were not confined to one class. Indeed, the more prosperous farmers were often also more skillful and enterprising. Thus the party had at times to struggle against a tendency for a village's old leadership to regain all its former power under the new regime.

future key to rich increases in rural production is in mechanical assistance during the excessively busy period."[40] In such areas, when women did not work on the land, the men's labor had to produce enough surplus over their own needs to feed the women and the other nonproductive members of the community throughout the year.

But it still remains that in the areas where the land is untillable for much of the year, and in other areas where the marginal return on labor input fell very rapidly, the mobilization of women could not be carried out in the same way as in the lush south, where the growing season is longer and the double-cropping of rice was extended in the 1950's to all areas where it was feasible.[41] Subsidiary occupations and handicrafts were promoted or introduced in areas with short growing seasons to provide women with an alternative productive role. The Women's Association or marketing cooperatives were usually responsible for organizing such ventures, most of which produced traditional objects like mats, sacks, baskets, and brooms, for which there was a steady local demand.[42] Less commonly, their wares were sold much farther afield; some groups, for example, picked medicinal herbs to be sold all over China. As these small ventures became better capitalized, some of them acquired machinery and made buckets, cheap plastic goods, and other products for local consumption.

The great irrigation and flood-prevention works were also a rich source of extra employment for both men and women during the traditionally idle months. These projects sometimes required workers to live away from home for weeks on end, making them in traditional eyes completely unsuitable for young women. But to women activists the work, however arduous, had a touch of glamor: in the dramatic change it brought to the countryside it symbolized revolution in its most romantic form. Of course women had to fight for the right to participate, but it was a battle that many won. For example, of the 220 volunteers working on the Min River dam in Yangyi commune in Hopei during 1959, 80 were women.[43] And in other cases all the students of a middle school, boys and girls alike, would join great irrigation projects. No doubt, such experience gave young women all over rural China more independence from their families, wider horizons, and greater self-confidence.

Land Reform

Except in the older Liberated Areas, where great advances toward equality had already been made, the real revolution in the position of women in rural China began with another great revolutionary process— land reform. The relationship between the two movements was made very clear. In 1947 Teng Ying-ch'ao wrote that mobilizing the masses of laboring women was an urgent and indispensable part of land reform.[44] She criticized the inadequate attention given women by the party in most areas, and recalled the declaration of the National Land Reform Conference earlier in the year, that to carry out land reform properly and to abolish feudalism, all levels of the party should revitalize its work among women. She quoted the declaration:

With Land Reform as the focus, coordinate work among women with the Peasants' Association, for when the two are thoroughly integrated, they will stimulate each other and interact favorably together. Village women of the laboring classes have suffered the exploitation and oppression of the landlord class just like other peasants, and have the same demands, the same fierceness. Therefore, whenever land reform is moving ahead, when the peasants are being mobilized, the laboring women must be mobilized at the same time. There must be no division with "men first, then women," or worse still, patchy and irregular work. Nor must the work of going deeper among and mobilizing the hired hand and poor peasant woman be abandoned or allowed to lag with such excuses as they are backward, gossipers, bothersome, or irritating, with the work among them being left to take care of itself.

It was also resolved at the Land Reform Conference that women from poor peasant or farm laborers' families should be treated as the core and should be united with middle-peasant women. Cadres were told that they should unite with peasant women, teach them to "speak bitterness," make distinctions between social classes, and look for the causes of their poverty, so that they would become class-conscious. Typically, it was the poor peasant women who came to the fore in land reform, because it was they who stood to gain most from the movement. And among these women, it was widows and other women who were the economic mainstays of their families who were especially prominent.

The start of land reform in a village was marked by the arrival of the land-reform team. The team's first task was to find out as much as possible about the villagers by observing how they lived, by eating and working with the peasants, and by talking with everyone. Frequently the team included a woman whose independence served as an example to the village women. Even if the team consisted only of men, their willingness to listen to the opinions of village women and the respect they showed them began the long task of undermining the general contempt with which women had been regarded.

During land reform women were most active in those villages where many of the men were away fighting in either the Civil War, or later, the Korean War, yet they played their part in other villages, too. The Peasant Associations, through which the movement was run, were expected to have a minimum of 30–40 percent women members.[45] They had also to found either a Women's Department or a village branch of the Women's Federation. Women who spoke out at the fierce meetings that accompanied land reform could not but be affected by the experience. Having taken part in public life, learned to express opinions and to argue in front of crowds, and been stirred by the heady feeling of controlling their own destinies, they were not likely to settle back docilely into their former lives. Now when they saw a way of improving their lot, they might muster the courage to try to carry it out, even if it meant facing bitter opposition. Once they received land they could use it as a bargaining counter, and could threaten to leave with their title deeds when their treatment in the family was unbearable. A woman in Lucheng hsien, Shansi, said, "Always before when we quarrelled my husband said, 'Get out of my house.' Now I can give it right back to him. I can say 'Get out of my house yourself.'" Others simply said, "After we get our share, we will be masters of our own fate."[46] The old fatalism of peasant women had begun to crack. Moreover, people were receptive to new ideas introduced by the party. In the new vocabulary spread by the land-reform teams, "feudal" was an adjective applied to landlords and the old system of landownership. Thus for peasant men it acquired pejorative connotations, and they were uneasy at being accused of "feudalism" in their attitude toward their wives or toward women in general.

Collectivization

In China as elsewhere, peasants customarily exchanged help at harvest time. In the Liberated Areas such help was often formalized by a system of first temporary and eventually permanent mutual-aid or work-exchange teams. These made possible a more economical use of labor and eased the usual labor shortage during busy seasons, which in the Liberated Areas was often aggravated by the absence of men who were away fighting at the front. Since such teams were most often first organized in areas where women replaced their soldier-husbands in the fields, they included a high proportion of women members from the beginning. A report of late 1947, from Nanho village in the eighth district of Wuan hsien, Hopei province, where land reform was "fairly complete," indicated that with a population of 400 of whom 100 were away, the village relied on a labor force of 26 able-bodied men and 57 able-bodied women who were able to do a full day's work. Women able to do part-time or light work also far outnumbered men.[47] In this report, as in later discussions of the difficulties of collective work, the problem of payment receives much attention. Work was valued in terms of workpoints, since the variety of jobs to be done and the different levels of skill and effort required made simple exchange unsuitable. Because people work at different tempos and to different standards, it was difficult to allocate workpoints on a simple hourly or piecework basis. In Nanho village rates of payment were arrived at by discussion. Women were first given five points to a man's ten for the same number of hours, but when it was found that they were working as fast as the men, their points were doubled.

In an article of 1948, Lo Ch'iung, a leading member of the Women's Federation, reported that not only were women demanding the same number of workpoints as men when they did the same amount of work, they were raising the slogan, "Points of men and women in the same family should be recorded separately." She supported this demand as a justified attack on the old monopolistic authority of men, who should be prevented from grabbing their wives' workpoints and thus controlling their earnings.[48] Lo described the methods of recording workpoints then in use. The first was to consider all women as "half-labor powers," and thus to give them five points when men got ten. The second was to grade workers, male and female, once and for all, allowing good workers to be awarded more points than poor workers for a day's work. The third was separately to assess points for each job performed on the day it was done, giving points according to the quality of the work and the speed with which it had been done. She recommended the third method, which she claimed was the one most commonly used, because it gave women the greatest incentive to go to the fields and work hard there. However, the struggle for equal pay for equal work was still being waged twenty-five years later, and general arguments over the merits of different systems of work evaluation continue.

Producer cooperatives existed on a small scale even in the pre–1949 Liberated Areas, but their main development came in two stages in the 1950's. In the first stage several mutual-aid teams pooled their land, tools, animals, and labor, and the unit so formed came under unified management. The income of these cooperatives was divided partly on the basis of the work performed by members, but partly on the ownership of the means of production, which continued to be vested in individual peasants. These cooperatives were therefore considered "semi-socialist." Full socialization came in 1955–56, the period dubbed the "High Tide of Socialism," when all over the country low-level cooperatives and mutual-aid teams merged into larger units known as advanced cooperatives. In these, the dividend based on individual title to the means of production was abolished, and income was henceforth awarded purely on the basis of work performed. The lower-level cooperatives enlarged the unit under one management, thereby further rationalizing the division of labor. Of course this affected women. Small nurseries could be set up within the cooperatives, and women's work teams became quite commonplace since most cooperatives included enough able-bodied women to make them practicable.

The changes brought about by the formation of advanced cooperatives were more profound. Now that the division of the collective's income depended solely on labor, everybody had the maximum incentive to work. Ownership of the means of production ceased to be a factor in women's economic strength. All now depended on their part in productive labor.

The question of equal pay for equal work, which from the time of the first mutual-aid teams had periodically been raised in the press, began to receive a great deal of attention. During the High Tide this was accompanied by an enormous surge of directives, reports, and propaganda stories, many of which concerned the way individual co-ops functioned. Accounts of the role played by women nearly always raised the subject of equal pay. The policy of the party had consistently been one of equal pay for equal work. Peasant men put up a tenacious opposition to the principle, and it seems probable that male cadres, most of whom were themselves peasants, were not always very persistent about getting it applied.

Where equal pay was achieved, it was only after women had proved that they merited it. Sometimes this was actually done by means of an organized competition between men and women. In the Unity Cooperative of Tali hsien, Shensi province, a man objected when his wife's two mornings of cotton-picking were given the same value as his own two mornings of plowing.[49] He demanded to be put on to cotton-picking, which he considered a pleasanter job, if the remuneration was to remain the same. The management committee decided to make this a test case and allowed him to pick cotton. He exhausted himself but failed to keep pace with the women. He was thus convinced that equal pay for the two jobs was fair. Such conversions were probably rare, for the issue was usually difficult to settle. Yet where equal pay was not established women felt inadequately rewarded for their efforts and were unwilling to work. Their exasperation with the situation was reflected in the expression "those old five points," (lao wu fen), by which women's half-pay was familiarly known.[50]

In 1952 in a village of K'ouhsi district, Fuyang hsien, Anhwei province, the men of a mutual-aid team almost always got ten points a day, while women normally received only five or six and even the strongest never got more than eight.[51] Once when they were hoeing together, the women's team did as much as the men's. At the end of the day when points were being allocated, the men asked the women how many they thought they should get. The women replied, "It's up to you, but we did as much as you did." The men realized there was nothing for it but to give them equal points, though there was some grumbling that the women should try their hands at carrying loads or pulling carts. The women retorted that men should try making clothes and looking after children.

In other areas differentials continued. In June 1957, the *Shenyang Daily* published an article about discrimination against women in which it alleged that many cooperatives automatically gave women seven points to do jobs for which men would have been paid ten, and that piecework rates, by which men sometimes worked, were never applied to women for it was feared that their earnings might then rise too high.[52] In an article of September 1956 on pay, the *People's Daily* condemned both the idea that "equal work" should be defined as "the same work" so that men and women would be paid equally only where the jobs were identical, and the idea that if a man gets ten points for a day's work, a woman should too, irrespective of the nature of their jobs.[53] It urged instead that both quality and quantity be considered, so that women would earn more if they did more or better work than men, and less if they did less or worked to lower standards. But the article gave little guidance on the evaluation of jobs, which is the heart of the problem. All reports seem to indicate that evaluation was based on the skill or strength needed for the job. Of course this tended to favor men over women, though men's advantage in skills decreased as women learned more.

This problem, so complex, and so central to the practice of collective agriculture, continued to be a difficult one even under the communes. In 1958, the Central Committee added to its consistent line that men and women should receive equal pay a policy statement that was very relevant to job evaluation and workpoint allocation: "Existing differences in skill in rural areas are not such as to warrant wide pay differentials."[54] Nevertheless, in 1960 in Yangyi commune, Hopei, the tradition of assessing women's work at a low number of points still prevailed.[55] And reports by recent visitors to China indicate that the practice persists in some areas even today.

The formation of cooperatives helped certain groups of women who had benefited very little from mutual-aid teams. Article 7 of the Model Regulations for Cooperatives stated that all laboring peasants, men and women, who had reached the age of sixteen and were capable of performing labor in the cooperatives, might become members.[56] It went on to specify that dependents of revolutionary martyrs and servicemen, as well as the aged, the weak, widows, widowers, and the disabled, were also eligible for membership.

Mutual-aid teams were generally organized by friends and relatives coming together on a basis of choice. Often they were formed by peasants who had received a little land but no animal or only a share of one in land reform, and who had thus to pool their efforts in order to get their plowing done. Often they had to pull the plows themselves, and in such cases naturally tried to recruit strong members whom they expected to be of most use. The new, less personal cooperative organizations had to accept more people from groups like those mentioned above who were poor in labor power. Of these it was the women, whose handicap was more often a matter of social convention than of physical disability, who could most easily become more economically productive. A campaign to persuade them to do so became a major theme of the Women's Federation during the formation of the cooperatives.

In collective agriculture women sometimes worked in the same teams as men, but were more often organized into special women's teams. This helped to reduce the suspicion, which made difficulties for many young women when they first went into the fields, that women who left home to work were just looking for love affairs. All-women teams also made it easier to allocate suitable jobs to women. This continued to be important because, with a low level of mechanization, much of the farm work still consisted of jobs such as heavy portering.* A well-known rhyme expresses concern with the allocation of work to women:[57]

> When pregnant they must be given light work, not heavy.
> When nursing they must be given work close by, not far away.
> During monthly periods they must be given dry work, not wet.

Obviously in mixed teams such policies could be more difficult to implement.

Small manufacturing cooperatives also played an important part in

---

* As late as the mid-1960's, it was estimated that one-third of all agricultural labor was expended on carrying manure to the fields and bringing grain from them. Ts'ao Ting and Liang K'uang-pai, "The Role of Communications and Transport in Our National Economy," *Ching-chi yen-chiu* (Economic research), 2 (Feb. 20, 1965); quoted in Dwight H. Perkins, *Agricultural Development in China, 1368–1968* (Edinburgh, 1969), p. 58.

women's lives, often being run exclusively for women and occasionally even coming under the local women's organization. In the Liberated Areas these were often the first work groups organized because they were usually started to increase the income and self-sufficiency of an area or to supply the needs of the army. Thus, they were not only new as groups, their products were often new to the area. They were supplied with raw materials by a credit cooperative backed by the People's Bank, which also undertook the collection and marketing of the finished products. In the Liberated Areas the best-known examples of these were the textile cooperatives;[58] others made clothes, shoes, rope, straw hats, and so on. In the early 1950's such enterprises were set up in village after village, and they accounted for an important part of the income earned by women. Often the work was done on a "putting-out" basis in the homes of cooperative members, and so posed less problem to women with children.

Originally these cooperatives were designed to beat the economic blockade of the Liberated Areas. Then, after the Communists had won control of the great manufacturing centers and restored industrial production, the pattern of these small-scale handicraft industries changed. The handicraft textile industry, for example, contracted again, though in some cases new mills were set up in the same area to take advantage of the pool of skilled labor developed by the cooperatives. But in homes and workshops, rural women continued to make small consumer goods. In time the old handicraft cooperatives were absorbed into the higher-level agricultural co-ops and finally into the communes, under which they were developed still further in the campaign to increase the range of goods produced in each area.

If party policy toward women in rural China is to be judged on its own terms, one must first consider to what extent it succeeded in its aim of involving women in productive labor, and then analyze the effect of its success on the women concerned.

The data available on women working in the countryside are inadequate, and do not really admit of comparison over time. Definitions vary or are unstated, and figures are given for different localities each year so that it is not possible to trace the progress made in one area from year to year. In 1949, Teng Ying-ch'ao estimated that 50–70 percent of the women in the Liberated Areas (and 80 percent in the best-organized parts) were engaged in agriculture.[59] For areas liberated only in 1949, figures of the same order were being suggested ten years later.* We

* Neither Teng's reports nor the later ones quantify the work done, which makes it impossible to assess their real significance or to compare them with confidence.

know that local variations could be considerable: for example, in the Ten Mile Inn brigade, Yangyi commune, Hopei, two-thirds of the women between the ages of 16 and 45 turned out regularly for field work in 1960, whereas in Pailin brigade in the same commune, the figure was 97 percent.[60] But it seems that "regularly," in this context, could mean anything from a work record of 70 days a year to one of 200 or more. More significant is the 1956 figure of 25 percent, the percentage of total workpoints allocated to women by cooperatives all over China.[61]

Women undoubtedly still continued to work fewer days than men each year, and they often did lighter, less well-remunerated jobs. Where workpoints were allocated on a piecework basis, women probably earned less than men for heavy jobs such as shifting manure, and since pay discrimination persisted in some cooperatives, they would sometimes have had to do more than a man to earn the same number of workpoints. All these factors make it the more remarkable that women should have earned a quarter of the total workpoints in 1956, a figure that indicates a very high level of participation in production by peasant women. The communes, even as modified after 1962, seem to have provided more communal childcare, especially at the rush periods, and the percentage of workpoints earned by women must also have increased, though unfortunately we have no figures for this.

Although we cannot quantify the change, it is safe to say that until 1949 in most areas of China it was exceptional for women to work much in the fields. But by the late 1950's it was quite normal, and most able-bodied women did so, though to an extent that varied greatly with local conditions. Furthermore, a greater proportion of work performed by women now enters a formal accounting system, and thus has a value publicly set on it.

The change in women's economic status brought about by involvement in productive work has brought great changes in the peasant women's place in family and society. In 1957, 70–80 percent of the co-ops were said to have women as heads or deputy heads.[62] Thus even peasants who were not in an organization with a woman leader would at least know of one.* Even ordinary women became used to expressing their opinions in meetings at least at the work-team level, and to participating in the making of such important decisions as allocating workpoints. The involvement of women in rural leadership, though significant, is still far from equal to that of men. Obviously women are held back from cadre

---

* No doubt in the great majority of cases the woman was in fact the deputy head, but this does not invalidate the point that a woman was publicly seen to be in a leadership position.

posts just as they are held back from ordinary labor participation by household and childcare duties. Doubtless in China as elsewhere in the world, because women must give more of their energies to problems of home and family, they may tend to avoid the heavy commitment of both time and energy demanded by a responsible post.

Furthermore, even when the marriage law is properly implemented, marriage is still normally patrilocal, and the bride has often to move to another village. This is unfavorable to the unmarried woman because the probability of her joining another work team (that of her husband) upon marriage makes her own work team reluctant to send her to courses for cadre training or special agricultural skills. Once married, a girl is still less likely to be put forward as a candidate by her new team because she must first win the confidence of her teammates. By the time she has established a local reputation, she may be involved in child-bearing and -rearing.

In time these problems will possibly be moderated by changes that alleviate family responsibilities, or by an increase in the importance of the brigade at the expense of the work team. The most effective change in the first category would be a significant fall in the birth rate. The second kind of change would help women because where income is accrued at the brigade level, loyalty and identification are focused on the brigade rather than the smaller unit of the work team. Team members would be less reluctant to train someone who seemed likely to remain in the same brigade, and as young people choose their own partners, they will tend more to marry within their brigade, to which their social contacts are normally limited.

In the long term, however, a solution to the inequality of opportunity between men and women will probably require that women as a group campaign against it. This in turn will necessitate a strong group identification among women as women alongside their identification with a work team or brigade. At present, just as the older women of the traditional family once controlled the younger women on behalf of the male-dominated family power structure, their present strong commitment to the interests of the work team may lead experienced women to oppose the training of young women in special skills as actively as their menfolk.

Despite their limited prospects at work, within the family women's increased earning power has helped to change their position. Girl children are no longer regarded as liabilities to be partially redeemed by a profitable match. Young women find it far easier to delay marriage and to persuade parents at least to consider their views on a prospective partner. As married women they are treated with more respect. Not having been brought into the family at great expense, they are no longer viewed by their in-laws as a drain on the family's resources. Indeed, they contribute to the family income. Consultation between husband and wife is more natural in households where the woman, too, is gainfully employed. These changes were clearly recognized by a young peasant woman from Liu Ling village, Shensi, who said in an interview in 1962: "In the older families, it is the husband alone who decides [what to grow in the private plot], but my husband and I discuss everything together, because we are a young couple. Sometimes he gives in and sometimes I give in."[63] Another young woman from the same village said: "It [has] now become quite usual with our generation for husband and wife to discuss the family's problems and decide about them together. Women now no longer work just in the house; they also work in the fields and earn their own money. But the men of the older generation still say: 'What does a woman know? Women know nothing! What's a woman worth? Women are worth nothing!' In such families the men decide everything and their wives say: 'We are just women. We are not allowed to say anything.' "[64]

These achievements were slow to come. The young woman just quoted recalled that women had first taken part in open discussion at a meeting in 1956, when the higher cooperative was founded. Even at that late date, their right to put forward opinions was fiercely challenged, though Liu Ling village was part of an early Liberated Area.

Undeniably women pay a price for all they have gained. Even if there were a sufficient number of crèches and nurseries and the canteens had been a complete success, a certain amount of housework would remain. As it is, the surviving domestic burden is a heavy one, and it falls preponderantly on women. In 1953, an article on getting women to participate in field work listed the three main obstacles to their doing so: the need to care for children during the day, to find time to weave cloth for the family's clothes, and to cook at the end of a long day's work.[65] The solution urged by the article, which it claimed had been implemented in the area described, was that older women should help out whenever possible with the children, and that husbands should assist wives. When the older women take on an extra household burden, young women participate in production to some extent at the expense of their elders. In Yangyi commune in 1960, however, it was still the younger women who did most of the work in the house,[66] and in that commune at least, men gave only occasional help in the house. Women were certainly aware of their double burden. A young mother in Liu Ling stated: "Women work much more than men. We have two jobs: we work both in the fields and in our caves. I know my husband helps me, we're a young family, of course, but he isn't as particular about housework as a woman is. Life is a lot of hard work. I don't take part in any kind of women's activities, political or otherwise."[67]

Conclusion

Village life in China is still very tough. Survival requires hard work, and economic progress demands still more. Many women, playing a dual role, work even harder than men. Some are no doubt held back by this from playing an active part in politics and public affairs. Others, with great sacrifice of time and effort, become leaders in rural society. Women have not won equality of opportunity in the affairs of rural society. But inasmuch as they can rise in it, at least they have *more* opportunity, and can continue the struggle. Women now have a voice in decision-making in village, work-team, and family affairs. Girls grow up expecting to make an economic contribution to the family, and no longer wait for others to determine the whole course of their lives. Liberation is of course still far from complete, but women's place in rural China has undergone as tremendous a revolution as any other aspect of village society.

Reference Material

Notes

Lü K'un's New Audience: The Influence of
Women's Literacy on Sixteenth-Century Thought

The following abbreviations are used in the Notes:

CWCC   Lü K'un, Ch'u wei chai chi in Lü-tzu i-shu, edited by Wang Ch'ing-
            lin and Sung Yü-mei (K'ai-feng ed., 1827 Preface)
KF   Lü K'un, Kuei fan (Po-ju chai ts'ang pan ed., ca. 1613)
SCL   Lü K'un, Shih cheng lu in Lü-tzu i-shu
SPPY   Ssu-pu pei-yao
SYY   Lü K'un, Shen-yin yü, edited by Kōda Rentarō (Tokyo, 1956)

1. The best information on the legal status of women can be found in Chao
Feng-chiao, Chung-kuo fu-nü tsai fa-lü shang chih ti-wei (Peking, 1928);
and Ch'ü T'ung-tsu, Law and Society in Traditional China (Paris, 1961),
pp. 102–10.

2. Ch'en Tung-yüan, Chung-kuo fu-nü sheng-huo shih (Shanghai, 1937),
pp. 129–40.

3. Ibid., passim; Edwin O. Reischauer and John K. Fairbank, East Asia:
The Great Tradition (Boston, 1960), pp. 224–25.

4. Biographical material on Lü K'un can be found in Kuo-fang yen-chiu
yuan, ed., Ming shih (Taipei, 1962), ch. 226; Huang Tsung-hsi, Ming-ju
hsüeh-an (Taipei reprint of SPPY ed.), ch. 54; Wang T'u-ning, ed., Ning-
ling hsien-chih (1893 reprint of 1693 ed.), IX.10b–15b; and Hou Wai-lu,
Chung-kuo ssu-hsiang t'ung-shih (Peking, 1960), 4: 940–57. For information on the so-called eccentrics of the period, see William Theodore De Bary,
ed., Self and Society in Ming Thought (New York, 1970). Information on
Lü's admission to the Confucian Temple can be found in the prefaces to Lü-
tzu i-shu.

5. Ch'en Tung-yüan, Chung-kuo fu-nü sheng-huo shih, p. 188. Ch'en does
not indicate the grounds for this assertion. He also claims that the circulation
of didactic works for women abated for two hundred years after a period of
popularity at the beginning of the Ming.

6. See, for example, the preface of A.D. 1214 (Liu Hsiang, *Lieh nü chuan*, SPPY ed. *shih-pu*, vols. 1138–39).

7. KF, II.49a; Liu Hsiang, *Lieh nü chuan*, III.8b–9b.

8. KF, III.90b; Liu Hsiang, *Lieh nü chuan*, V.2b–3a.

9. KF, III.31b, III.63a.

10. In a postscript to a memorial in which Lü pleads innocent to charges that his *Kuei fan* had some nefarious intent in the heir-apparent controversy, Lü lists four editions of the work and remarks that the gentry were circulating it among themselves and merchants were selling it everywhere (CWCC, II.33b).

11. KF, Preface, 1a–b. In the postscript to the memorial of 1598 cited in n. 10, Lü claims he originally compiled the *Kuei fan* for his daughter (CWCC, II.33a–35b). Although his daughter might indeed have provided the first inspiration for the work, the preface clearly indicates that Lü had a much broader audience in mind.

12. For a description of the pornography of the period, see Robert Hans van Gulik, *Sexual Life in Ancient China* (Leiden, 1961), pp. 263–335; and van Gulik, *Erotic Colour Prints of the Ming Period* (Tokyo, 1951). For essays on such subjects as erotic paintings, "passing wine about in a courtesan's shoe," and men and women bathing together, see Shen Te-fu, *Pi-chou chai yü t'an*, in Kuo-hsüeh fu-lun she, ed., *Hsiang yen ts'ung-shu* (Shanghai, 1914), 3d *chi*, I. The same essays appear scattered throughout his *Yeh-hu-pien* (1619). Also illustrative of the decadence of the period are the novels *Chin P'ing Mei*, tr. as *The Golden Lotus* by Clement Egerton (New York, 1954), and Li Yü, *Jou p'u t'uan*, tr. by Richard Martin from the German version by Franz Kuhn (New York, 1966).

13. SCL, II.9a–b.

14. Lü K'un, *Tsung yüeh ko*, in *Lü-tzu i-shu*, 5a.

15. Pan Chao, *Nü chieh* in Tanahashi Ayako, ed., *Nü ssu-shu*, tr. into Japanese by Tsujihara Gempo (1656) (Tokyo, 1912), p. 155; Sung Jo-shao, *Nü lun-yü*, in *Nü ssu-shu*, p. 44; Jen Hsiao-wen Huang-hou, *Nei-hsun*, in *Nü ssu-shu*, pp. 91–92.

16. CWCC, III.34a.

17. John Meskill, *Ch'oe Pu's Diary: A Record of Drifting Across the Sea* (Tucson, Ariz., 1965), p. 155.

18. On academies, see John Meskill, "Academies and Politics in the Ming Dynasty," in Charles Hucker, ed., *Chinese Government in Ming Times* (New York, 1969), pp. 151–74. On popular educational works, see Tadao Sakai, "Confucianism and Popular Educational Works," in De Bary, *Self and Society*, pp. 331–62; and Tadao Sakai, *Chūgoku zensho no kenkyū* (Kyoto, 1960). For an ingenious estimate of literacy rates that might apply to the sixteenth century, see F. W. Mote, "China's Past in the Study of China Today: Some Comments on The Recent Work of Richard A. Solomon," *Journal of Asian Studies*, Nov. 1972, pp. 109–10.

19. During the Chia-ch'ing period the magistrate Hsiung Ping-yüan introduced many welfare and educational activities to Lü's native district (*Ning-ling hsien-chih*, III *passim*, V.6b). That Lü K'un must have been influenced by the magistrate's activities can be surmised from Hsiung's entrusting Lü

(then going by the name Li K'un) with the responsibility for compiling a gazetteer for Ning-ling (*ibid.*, Preface 5b, 16a–17b, Colophon 18a–b).

20. *Tsung yüeh ko*, Preface, 1a. In his preface to *Kuei chieh* (in *Lü-tzu i-shu*), Lü explains that he wrote the songs for women after nights of worrying about the neglect of education for rural women.

21. KF, Preface, 2a.

22. KF, III.87b.

23. KF, II.1a, IV.8b–9a. The tension between spoiling (and loving) children and the need to discipline them is vividly apparent in Lü's writings and in sixteenth-century fiction.

24. Lü, *Tsung yüeh ko*, 2a. A similar statement, "don't listen to women's talk," appears in the same work, 4a.

25. *Ibid.*, 1a. Similar tensions are evident in Wen Huang's *Wen-shih mu hsün* (photo reprint of *Hsüeh hai lei pien* ed., n.d.) and are worth further exploration.

26. KF, I.3a.

27. KF, II.1a–b.

28. KF, II.64a–b.

29. KF, III.49b; 54a–b; 56a; 57a–b.

30. KF, II.64a.

31. SYY, 92.

32. KF, III.63a. Also note Lü's criticism of "the excesses of the worthies" (*hsien che chih kuo*), KF, III.49b, IV.64a.

33. KF, III.81a–82a.

34. KF, III.83b.

35. KF, II.33b.

36. KF, III.90a–b.

37. KF, II.28b.

38. KF, III.45a–b.

39. KF, II.28b.

40. KF, III.102a–b.

41. E.g., Lü criticizes a mother who failed to persuade her son to relinquish three beauties to his prince (to avoid provoking the prince's jealousy). Ultimately the son was ruined. Writes Lü, "One could say that Lady Wei clearly understood her son's evil and was deeply worried about it. But she could not force her recalcitrant son and went to her ruin with him—was that not imbecilic? If, as his mother, she had reported it to the prince and presented [the beauties], then Duke K'ang [her son] would not dare but comply; and would not the disaster of having his state conquered have been avoided?" (KF, IV.40b–41a.) Of another wife, who sacrificed her life on her husband's behalf, Lü comments, "If there had been another plan—would one have preferred that it come to this?" (KF, III.37b–38a.)

42. KF, II.18b–19a.

43. KF, III.36b; *Lieh nü chuan*, V.11b.

44. KF, IV.92a.

45. KF, III.52a–b, 57a–b.

46. KF, III.59b.

47. KF, IV.34b.

48. KF, II.31a–32b.

49. KF, IV.92a.

50. KF, II.13a.

51. KF, II.17a.

52. KF, III.74b.

53. KF, II.31a–32b.

54. KF, III.100a–b.

55. KF, *fan-lieh*, 1b.

56. T'ien I-heng, *Liu-ch'ing jih-cha* (abridged ed., Taipei, 1969), pp. 98–100.

57. Jeannette Louise Faurot, "*Four Cries of a Gibbon: A Tsa-chü* Cycle by the Ming Dramatist Hsü Wei (1521–1593)" (Ph.D. dissertation, University of California, Berkeley, June 1972), pp. 136–37.

58. For a synopsis of "The Girl Graduate," see *ibid.*, pp. 97–100.

59. T'ien I-heng, *Liu-ch'ing jih-cha*, pp. 234–35. T'ien also tells of a monk who disguised himself as a woman to gain entrance to homes and seduce women (*ibid.*, p. 141); and of Lin Yu-yü, who took the examinations and received the *chin-shih* degree in the Sung period. Cited in Hsieh Wu-liang, *Chung-kuo fu-nü wen-hsüeh shih* (Shanghai, 1916), p. 38.

60. KF, II.16a. There are reports that some scholars of the sixteenth century were wearing such effeminate clothing that it was indeed difficult to distinguish men from women. Fu I-ling, *Ming-tai Chiang-nan shih-min ching-chi shih-t'an* (Shanghai, 1957), pp. 106–7.

61. KF, III.48a–b; cf. KF, IV.92a.

62. KF, III.17a.

63. See, for example, De Bary, "Individualism," pp. 157–60.

64. KF, II.66a. Also "Poverty cannot harm virtue. . . . Good birth cannot cover up evil" (KF, III.1b).

65. KF, IV.5b–6a.

66. Lü K'un, *Wu-ju*, in *Lü-tzu i-shu*, 3a–b.

67. Sung Ju-lin, *Sun-chiang fu-chih*, V. Cited in Yen Chung-p'ing, *Chung-kuo mien-fang-chih shih-kao* (Peking, 1955), pp. 39–40.

68. See, for example, De Bary, "Individualism," p. 168; and Tadao Sakai, "Confucianism and Popular Educational Works," p. 346.

69. Fu I-ling, *Ming-Ch'ing shih-tai shang-jen chi shang-yen tz'u-pen* (Peking, 1956), p. 11.

70. *Ibid.*, p. 12. Evelyn S. Rawski suggests that with the expansion of the cotton industry in sixteenth-century Fukien, it became more profitable for women to work at the looms rather than in the fields (Rawski, *Agricultural Change and the Peasant Economy of South China*, Cambridge, Mass., 1972, pp. 46–47; on the Soochow region, pp. 54–55).

71. Hai Jui, *Hai Jui chi*, Ch'en I-chung, ed. (Peking, 1962), pp. 445–46.

72. SCL, II.9b–10a.

73. *Ming shih*, ch. 175. Cited in T'ao Hsi-sheng, "Ming-tai mi-lo pai-lien chiao chi ch'i-t'a 'yao ts'ei,'" in T'ao Hsi-sheng, ed., *Ming-tai tsung-chiao* (Taipei, 1968), p. 7.

74. "Over one hundred men and women were caught" (*ibid.*). According to T'ao (*ibid.*), *Ming shih*, ch. 158, also notes that numerous women and nuns were arrested and questioned about their role in a rebellion. The *Ming ta cheng ch'uan yao*, ch. 60, also mentions men and women followers of the White Lotus. Cited in Li Shou-k'ung, "Ming-tai pai-lien chiao k'ao lüeh," in *Ming-tai tsung-chiao*, p. 44.

75. SCL, V.28a.

76. Ho Shih-chin, *Tsung-kuei*, in Ch'en Hung-mou, ed., *Hsün su i-kuei*, under the name Wang Shih-chin in *Wu chung i-kuei* (SPPY ed., *tzu-pu*, vols. 1540–47). Since Wang Shih-chin does not seem to be listed in any of the indexes, I am assuming that this is the work by Ho mentioned in Tadao Sakai, *Chūgoku zensho no kenkyū*, p. 55.

77. Shen Te-fu, *Pi-chou chai yü-t'an*, I.3a–4a.

78. See, for example, "Mai-fen-erh" ("The powder girl") in Li Fang, ed., *T'ai-p'ing kuang-chi* (typeset ed., Peking, 1961), ch. 274, p. 2,157.

79. Liu Ta-chieh, *Chung-kuo wen-hsüeh fa-ta shih* (Taipei, 1962), pp. 300–301.

80. T'ang Shun-chih, *Ching-ch'uan hsien-sheng wen-chi* (SPPY ed.), V.27a. I would like to thank Cheng Ch'ing-mao for directing me to T'ang's statements on women.

81. *Ibid.*, V.25b–26a.

82. Ho Shih-chin, *Tsung-kuei*, II.24b.

83. "Hua-teng ch'iao Lien-nü ch'eng fo chi" (Lien-nü attains Buddhahood on the way to her wedding), in Hung Pien, ed., *Ch'ing-p'ing shan-t'ang hua-pen* (Shanghai, 1959). The same story also appears in *P'ing yao chuan*, which, according to Patrick Hanan, was probably written earlier than the mid-sixteenth century (Hanan, "The Composition of the *P'ing yao chuan*," *Harvard Journal of Asian Studies*, 31 (1971): 201–19.

84. KF, III.4a–b.

85. KF, II.3b.

86. Feng Meng-lung, *Hsin tseng chih nang pu* (Ta-hsing t'ang ts'ang pan, n.d., Preface 1626), XXV.1a.

87. *Ibid.*, XXV.1b. 88. *Ibid.*, XXVI.23a.

89. Chao Ju-yüan, *Ku-chin nü-shih*. Cited in Ch'en Tung-yüan, *Chung-kuo fu-nü sheng-huo shih*, p. 191.

90. KF, II.49a. 91. KF, IV.90b.

92. KF, II.2b–3a.

93. KF, II.64b. Note also the contrast between Lü's criticism of a mother who condoned her son, who was imprisoned for expressing his political views, and Lü's praise of a mother who beat her son so he would not speak out rashly (KF, IV.16a, IV.32b–34m–34a). Even here, he mentions the need to preserve life in a disordered world.

94. KF, II.64b. 95. KF, III.31b.

96. KF, III.31a–b. 97. KF, Preface, 2a.

98. KF, IV.48b. Same phrase again, KF, II.12a.

99. KF, IV.28b.

100. KF, IV.50a.

101. For earlier statements about the need for restraints, see Tung Chung-shu, Wang Ch'ung, and Li Ao, cited in Feng Yu-lan, *A History of Chinese Philosophy*, tr. Derk Bodde (Princeton, N.J., 1953), 2: 35, 165, 414; and Wang Yang-ming ("One's mind is like a restless monkey and his feelings are like a galloping horse"), in Wang Yang-ming, *Instructions for Practical Living and Other Neo-Confucian Writings*, tr. and ed. Chan Wing-tsit (New York, 1963), p. 35. For Lü K'un, see SYY, p. 71.

102. Cited in Ch'ien Mu, *Chu-tzu hsin-hsüeh an* (Taipei, 1971), 2: 26.

103. Wang Yang-ming, *Instructions for Practical Living*, p. 34.

104. Ch'ien Mu, *Chu-tzu*, 2: 25–26; Wang Yang-ming, *Instructions for Practical Living*, p. 34.

105. Ch'ien Mu, *Chu-tzu*, 2: 26.

106. "The cultivation of the personal life is the part after the feelings are aroused, whereas the rectification of the mind is the part before the feelings are aroused. If the mind is rectified, there will be equilibrium" (cited in Wang Yang-ming, *Instructions for Practical Living*, p. 55).

107. "That is what is meant by saying that the feelings of the sage are in accord with all things and yet of himself he has no feelings" (_ibid._, p. 148).

108. SYY, p. 71.
109. SYY, p. 806.
110. SYY, p. 89.
111. SYY, p. 93.
112. SYY, p. 803. See also, Lü K'un, _Ssu-li i_, in a composite ed. of _Lü-tzu i-shu_ [1573–162?], Preface, 2a, on the need for li to be in accord with feelings.
113. SYY, p. 805.
114. _Ibid._
115. SYY, p. 806.
116. SYY, p. 81.
117. SYY, p. 80.
118. De Bary, "Individualism," p. 197.
119. Li Chih, _Fen shu_ (Peking, 1961), pp. 89–90.
120. KF, I.1b.
121. SYY, p. 71. The preface to this work is dated 1593.
122. KF, II.40a.
123. T'ang Shun-chih, _Ching-ch'uan hsien-sheng wen-chi_, V, _passim_.
124. Wen Huang, _Wen-shih mu hsün_.
125. Kuei Yu-kuang, _Chen-ch'uan wen-chi_ (photo reprint of SPPY ed., Taipei, 1971), III.3a–b.
126. KF, III.31a. For contrast, see the biography of "Wang lieh fu," _Ming shih, ch._ 301.3380. Worth further exploration are the efforts of the early Ming government to commemorate women who committed suicide to follow their husbands (see Ch'en Tung-yüan, _Chung-kuo fu-nü sheng-huo shih_, p. 179) in order, I suspect, to co-opt dissident parties (note the role of "demonic women" in early Ming rebellions).
127. SCL, III.29b.
128. KF, II.10a.
129. SYY, p. 90.
130. SCL, III.29a–b; Lü K'un, _Tsung yüeh ko_, 4a.
131. Lü, _Tsung yüeh ko_, 15a. According to the _Ming hui-tien_, women could inherit property when there were no male heirs. Cited in Chao Feng-chieh, _Chung-kuo fu-nü tsai fa-lü shang te ti-wei_, pp. 13–14. Also see SCL, III.26a, for regulations on inheritance for widows.
132. SCL, II.51b.
133. Lu Ch'i, "On respecting husbands," in _Hsin fu p'u_, in _Hsiang-yen ts'ung-shu_, 3d _chi_, III.12a.
134. Feng Meng-lung, _Hsin-tseng chih nang pu_, XXVI.28a–b.
135. Ch'en Tung-yüan, _Chung-kuo fu-nü sheng-huo shih_, p. 288. On what grounds he makes this statement is unclear.
136. Shen Te-fu, _Pi-chou chai yü-t'an_, I.3a–4a.
137. For a biography of Ch'en Hung-mou, see Arthur W. Hummel, _Eminent Chinese of the Ch'ing Period_ (Taipei, 1964), pp. 86–87.
138. On the grounds that his _Kuei fan_ was found in the women's quarters of the palace, Lü was accused of having a role in the heir-apparent intrigue.
139. Ch'en Hung-mou, _Chiao nü i-kuei_, in _Wu chung i-kuei_, II.4b–5a.
140. _Ibid._, Preface, 1a.
141. Lü K'un, _Kuei chieh_, Preface, 1a.
142. Ch'en Hung-mou, _Chiao nü i-kuei_, Preface, 1b.
143. _Ibid._, 1a.
144. _Ibid._, 1b–2a.

145. Arthur Waley, *Yuan Mei* (New York, n.d.), pp. 77, 179; Hummel, *Eminent Chinese*, p. 956.

146. David S. Nivison, *The Life and Thought of Chang Hsüeh-ch'eng* (Stanford, Calif., 1966), pp. 265–66, 274–75. Nivison also points out that Chang criticized Wang Chung for his view "that a wife's obligation of life-long loyalty to her husband does not begin until actual marriage" (*ibid.,* p. 262). There were precedents for this debate as well in the Ming (Chang Hsüeh-ch'eng, *Fu-hsüeh* in *Hsiang-yen ts'ung-shu*, 2d *chi*, IV.14b).

The Emergence of Women at the End of the Ch'ing: The Case of Ch'iu Chin

The abbreviation *CCC* is used in the Notes for *Ch'iu Chin chi* (The collected works of Ch'iu Chin; Shanghai, 1960).

1. For other discussion of Ch'iu Chin in the context of the revolutionary movement, see Mary Backus Rankin, *Early Chinese Revolutionaries: Radical Intellectuals in Shanghai and Chekiang, 1902–1911* (Cambridge, Mass., 1971), pp. 38–47, ch. 8 *passim*.

2. Roxane Witke, "Transformation of Attitudes Towards Women During the May Fourth Era of Modern China" (Ph.D. dissertation, University of California, Berkeley, 1970), pp. 260, 288, and *passim*.

3. The best source is Ch'en Tung-yüan, *Chung-kuo fu-nü sheng-huo shih* (A history of Chinese women; Shanghai, 1928), ch. 8.

4. Arthur W. Hummel, ed., *Eminent Chinese of the Ch'ing Period* (2 vols.; Washington, D.C., 1943–44), p. 683.

5. Ch'en Tung-yüan, pp. 275–78; Hummel, p. 441.

6. Chang Hsüeh-ch'eng, "Fu-hsüeh" (Women's education), in Kuo-hsüeh fu-lun she, ed., *Hsiang-yen ts'ung-shu* (Shanghai, 1914), 8: 14a. David S. Nivison, *The Life and Thought of Chang Hsüeh-ch'eng (1738–1801)* (Stanford, Calif., 1966), pp. 87, 262–66, is a guide to Chang's views on women.

7. Liang Ch'i-ch'ao, *Intellectual Trends in the Ch'ing Period*, tr. Immanuel C. Y. Hsü (Cambridge, Mass., 1959), p. 84.

8. Lin Yü-t'ang, "Feminist Thought in Ancient China," *T'ien-hsia Monthly*, 1.2: 134–45, surveys Yüan's writings on women.

9. Chang Hsüeh-ch'eng, 8: 13b, 15a.

10. Hummel, p. 433.

11. Lin Yü-t'ang, pp. 131–33; Witke, "Transformation of Attitudes," pp. 10–11; Hummel, pp. 936–37; Ch'en Tung-yüan, *Chung-kuo fu-nu sheng-huo shih*, p. 247; Yü Cheng-hsieh, *Kuei-ssu lei-kao* (Draft essays of 1833; reprint, Shanghai, 1957), pp. 493–504. On traditional anti-foot-binding, see Vincent Y. C. Shih, *The Taiping Ideology: Its Sources, Interpretations, and Influences* (Seattle, 1967), pp. 227–28; and Howard Levy, *Chinese Footbinding: The History of a Curious Erotic Custom* (New York, 1966), pp. 65–71.

12. Witke, pp. 12–13; Li Ju-chen, *Flowers in the Mirror*, tr. Lin Tai-yi (London, 1965).

13. Liang Ch'i-ch'ao, *Intellectual Trends*, pp. 88–89; Chang Hao, *Liang Ch'i-ch'ao and Intellectual Transition in China, 1890–1907* (Cambridge, Mass., 1971), pp. 22–25.

14. Winston Hsieh, "Triads, Salt-Smugglers, and Local Uprisings," in Jean

Chesneaux, ed., *Popular Movements and Secret Societies in China, 1840–1950* (Stanford, Calif., 1972), p. 154.

15. Excerpts from Wang Man, *Tu-shih* (Studying history), and Li Wan-fang, *Nü-hsüeh yen-hsing lu* (A record of words and deeds for the education of women), in Ch'en Tung-yüan, pp. 273, 278.

16. On nationalism, see Charlotte Beahan, "The Women's Press in China Prior to the Revolution of 1911" (unpublished ms., 1973), p. 8 and *passim*.

17. Liang Ch'i-ch'ao, "Pien-fa t'ung-i" (A thorough discussion of reform), in *Yin-ping-shih ho-chi, wen-chi* (Collected essays from the ice-drinker's studio, literary collection; Shanghai, 1936), 1.1: 37–43.

18. Excerpts in Ch'en Tung-yüan, pp. 330–41.

19. On problems of her birth date, see Shan Shih, "Ch'iu Chin nien-p'u" (A chronological biography of Ch'iu Chin), *Shih-hsüeh yüeh-k'an* (Historical studies monthly), 6: 21 (1957).

20. On Ch'iu Chin's family background, see *ibid.*; Hsü Shuang-yün, "Chi Ch'iu Chin" (Recollections of Ch'iu Chin), in Committee on Written Historical Materials of the National Committee of the Chinese People's Political Consultative Conference, ed., *Hsin-hai ko-ming hui-i lu* (Recorded recollections of the 1911 Revolution; 6 vols.; Peking, 1961–63), 4: 207; *Shang-hai hsien-chih*, Yü Yüeh and Fang Tsung-ch'eng, comps., 1871, 13: 16 a-b; Kuomintang, Committee for the Compilation of Materials on the Party History of the Central Executive Committee, ed., *Ko-ming hsien-lieh chuan-chi* (Biographies of revolutionary martyrs; Taipei, 1953), p. 209; and Ch'iu Ts'an-chih, *Ch'iu Chin ko-ming chuan* (A revolutionary biography of Ch'iu Chin; Taipei, 1953), p. 2.

21. Little is said of Ch'iu Chin's feet in the voluminous literature about her. The most reasonable assumption is that she unbound her feet when she left her husband to study in Japan. This is suggested in her poem "Yu-huai" (Longings), in *CCC*, p. 85. However, a former student at the Ta-t'ung School in 1907 remembers her as having bound feet. Chu Tsan-ching, "Ta-t'ung shih-fan hsüeh-t'ang" (The Ta-t'ung Normal School), in *Hsin-hai ko-ming hui-i lu*, 4: 147. A picture of her in Western male dress shows her wearing large leather shoes, but does not indicate the shape of the foot inside. *Ch'iu Chin shih-chi* (Manuscripts of Ch'iu Chin; Shanghai, 1958), p. 1. Takeda Haijun suggests that Ch'iu unbound her feet herself. Takeda Taijun, *Shūfū shūuhito o shūsamatsu* (The sad death of the woman of autumn rain and wind; Tokyo, 1968), p. 252.

22. "Ch'iu Chin nien-p'u," p. 21.

23. Hsü Shuang-yün, pp. 66–67; Ch'iu Ts'an-chih, pp. 3–4; P'eng Tzu-i, *Ch'iu Chin* (Shanghai, 1941), p. 5; T'ao Ch'eng-chang, "Che-an chi-lüeh" (A brief account of the revolts in Chekiang), in Chung-kuo shih-hsüeh hui (Chinese Historical Association), ed., *Hsin-hai ko-ming* (The 1911 Revolution; Ch'ai Te-kang et al., comps., 8 vols.; Shanghai, 1957), 3: 60.

24. "Ch'iu-jih kan-pieh" (Feelings at parting on an autumn day), *CCC*, p. 58.

25. E.g., "Chü" (Chrysanthemums), in *CCC*, p. 80; "Ch'iu-yen" (Autumn geese), in *CCC*, p. 65; "Wu-yeh" (Leaves of the Wu tree), in *CCC*, p. 63.

26. A scholarly and generally available collection of Ch'iu Chin's writing is *Ch'iu Chin chi* (The collected works of Ch'iu Chin; Shanghai, 1960), which

I have cited for this paper as *CCC*. Hsiao P'ing, *Hsin-hai ko-ming lieh-shih shih-wen hsüan* (A selection of writings by martyrs of the 1911 Revolution; Peking, 1962), usefully annotates a few of her most important poems and articles. Wang Ts'an-chih, *Ch'iu Chin nü-hsia i-chi* (A posthumous collection of Ch'iu Chin's writings; Shanghai, 1929), is an earlier major source. *Ch'iu Chin shih-chi* (Manuscripts of Ch'iu Chin; Shanghai, 1958) has good pictures and reproductions of handwritten originals.

27. Huang Hua, "Chi T'ung-ch'eng Wu Chih-ying nü-shih" (Recollections of Wu Chih-ying of T'ung-ch'eng), *Kuo-wen chou-pao*, 14.11: 33, 37 (Mar. 22, 1937); Ch'en Mi, "Wu Chih-ying chuan" (Biography of Wu Chih-ying), *Kuo-shih-kuan kuan-k'an* (Journal of the Institute of National History), 1.1: 86 (1947); *Ko-ming hsien-lieh chuan-chi*, p. 210; *CCC*, p. 31.

28. Ch'iu Ts'an-chih, *Ch'iu Chin ko-ming chuan*, p. 9; *CCC*, pp. 61, 74; "Ch'iu Chin nien-p'u," p. 21.

29. "Introduction" to *CCC*, p. 2; "Ch'i-jen yu" (Fears of the man of Ch'i), *CCC*, p. 8.

30. "Kan-shih" (Moving events), in *CCC*, p. 75; Hummel, p. 169; Ch'iu Ts'an-chih, pp. 13–14; *Ko-ming hsien-lieh chuan-chi*, p. 210.

31. E.g., "Chien-ko" (Sword song), in *CCC*, p. 81; "Ch'iu-feng ch'ü" (Song of the autumn wind), in *CCC*, p. 79.

32. For examples of nationalism, see *Ching-wei shih* (Stones of the ching-wei bird), in *CCC*, pp. 127–28; "Kan-huai" (Emotions), in *CCC*, pp. 79–80; "Ju-tzu chiang-shan" (Thus our rivers and mountains), in *CCC*, p. 107; and "Poem to Hsü Shuang-yün," in Hsü Shuang-yün, "Chi Ch'iu Chin," p. 211.

33. *Stones of the Ching-wei Bird*, in *CCC*, p. 152; "Introduction to the Chinese Women's Journal," in *CCC*, pp. 12–13; "Mien nü-ch'üan ko" (Urging women's rights), in *CCC*, p. 113.

34. *Ko-ming hsien-lieh chuan-chi*, pp. 216–17; "Man-chiang-hung tz'u," in *CCC*, p. 97.

35. A standard story; see, for example, T'ao Ch'eng-chang, "Che-an chi-lüeh," pp. 60–61. On the Wang Chao case, see *North China Herald*, 72: 861 (Apr. 29, 1904), and 72: 987, 1,007 (May 13, 1904).

36. On contrasting May Fourth approaches, see Witke, "Transformation of Attitudes," pp. 83–86.

37. "A warning to my sisters," in *CCC*, p. 15; "Introduction to the Chinese Women's Journal," in *CCC*, p. 12.

38. "Ching-kao wo chieh-mei" (A warning to my sisters), in *CCC*, p. 15; "Urging women's rights," in *CCC*, p. 113.

39. "Ching-kao Chung-kuo erh-wan-wan nü-t'ung-pao" (A warning to two million Chinese sisters), in *CCC*, p. 5; *Stones of the Ching-wei Bird*," in *CCC*, p. 122.

40. Yao Shun-sheng, *Chung-kuo fu-nü ta-shih nien-piao* (A yearly chronicle of major events concerning Chinese women; Shanghai, 1933), p. 137; Witke, p. 226; Wang Shih-tse, "Hui-i Ch'iu Chin" (Recollections of Ch'iu Chin), in *Hsin-hai ko-ming hui-i lu*, 4: 227. On numbers of Chinese students in Tokyo, see Roger F. Hackett, "Chinese Students in Japan, 1900–1910," *Papers on China*, 3: 142 (Harvard University, East Asian Research Center, 1949).

41. Committee on the Compilation of Documents on the Fiftieth Anniversary of the Founding of the Republic of China, *Chung-hua min-kuo k'ai-kuo*

wu-shih nien wen-hsien (Documents on the fiftieth anniversary of the found-ing of the Republic of China), vol. 1, pts. 9–10, *Hsing-Chung Hui* (The So-ciety to Restore China's Prosperity; 2 vols.; Taipei, 1963), 2: 95–98.

42. For evidence of Ho Chen's strong interest in Ch'iu Chin, see Lionel Giles, "The Life of Ch'iu Chin," *T'oung-pao*, series 2, 14.1: 225.

43. Wang Shih-tse, pp. 227–28; *Chung-hua min-kuo k'ai-kuo wu-shih nien wen-hsien*, vol. 1, pts. 11–15, *Chung-kuo T'ung-meng Hui* (The Chinese Revolutionary Alliance), 5: 199; *CCC*, pp. 9, 12, 32; Feng Tzu-yu, *Ko-ming i-shih* (Fragments of revolutionary history; 5 vols., Shanghai, 1945–47), 2: 178.

44. Sung Chiao-jen, *Wo chih li-shih* (My history; Taipei, 1962), p. 17. Ch'iu Chin's contributions appear in *CCC*, pp. 3–9.

45. Yü Chao-i, *Ch'iu Chin* (Hong Kong, 1956), p. 51.

46. Wang Shih-tse, pp. 225–26; Feng Tzu-yu, *Chung-hua min-kuo k'ai-kuo ch'ien ko-ming shih* (A history of the Revolution prior to the founding of the Republic of China; 3 vols.; Shanghai, 1928, 1930, Chungking, 1944), 2: 60.

47. T'ao Ch'eng-chang, "Che-an chi-lüeh," pp. 30, 61; Hsü Shuang-yün, "Chi Ch'iu Chin," p. 209; Feng, *I-shih*, 2: 178; Feng, *Chung-hua*, 2: 60.

48. "Testimony of Chiang Chi-yün," in *Hsin-hai ko-ming*, 3: 198.

49. Wang Shih-tse, pp. 226–27.

50. "Sword song," in *CCC*, pp. 74–75; "Tseng Chiang Lu-shan hsien-sheng yen chih chieh wei ta-jih ch'eng-kung chih hung-chao yeh" (Presenting Chiang Lu-shan with words of resolution and also with mementos of success in other days), in *CCC*, p. 78; "Chih Hsü Hsiao-shu chüeh-ming tzu" (Poem to Hsü Hsiao-shu in contemplation of death), in *CCC*, p. 26.

51. Robert Ruhlmann, "Traditional Heroes in Chinese Popular Fiction," in Arthur F. Wright, ed., *The Confucian Persuasion* (Stanford, Calif., 1960), pp. 151–52.

52. James J. Y. Liu, *The Chinese Knight-Errant* (Chicago, 1967), pp. 85–98 *passim*; Pearl S. Buck, tr., *All Men Are Brothers* (New York, 1937), ch. 47 (ch. 48 in several Chinese editions of *Shui-hu chuan*).

53. *Stones of the Ching-wei Bird*, in *CCC*, pp. 125–26; also see various poems in *CCC*, pp. 53, 71, 72, 82, 86, 91.

54. "T'i *Chih-k'an chi*" (Dedicated to *Chih-k'an chi*), in *CCC*, p. 82 (on the play *Chih-k'an chi*, see Hummel, p. 169).

55. "Dedicated to *Chih-k'an chi*," in *CCC*, p. 82.

56. "Urging women's rights," in *CCC*, p. 113.

57. "Fears of the man of Ch'i," in *CCC*, p. 8; "Tu-tui tz'u Ching-ming yün," in *CCC*, p. 64.

58. "Man-chiang-hung," in *CCC*, p. 97.

59. Chiang Wei-ch'iao, "Chung-kuo Chiao-yü hui chih hui-i" (Recollections of the Chinese Educational Association), in *Hsin-hai ko-ming*, 1: 487; *Ching-chung jih-pao* (The alarm bell; photolithograph, Taipei, 1968), p. 4 (July 26, 1904); Yang Chi-sun, *Chung-kuo fu-nü huo-tung chi* (A record of activities of Chinese women; Taipei, 1964), p. 334; Liang Chan-mei, *Chung-kuo fu-nü fen tou shih hua* (Words about the history of the struggles of Chinese women; Shanghai, 1928), pp. 77–78.

60. Li Hsüeh-li, *Chung-kuo fu-nü shih hua* (Words about the history of

Chinese women, 1947), p. 87; Tung Te-han, *Ai-kuo nü-ch'ing-nien shih-hua* (Words about the history of patriotic young women; Taipei, 1954), pp. 74–78.

61. Regulations of the school appear in *Shih-wu pao* (Reprint, Taipei, 1967), 6: 3186–91 (Dec. 4, 1897).

62. *Shang-hai hsien hsü-chih*, Yao Wen-nan and Wu Hsing, comps., 1918, 11: 9b–14b.

63. Sun Te-chung, ed., *Ts'ai Yüan-p'ei hsien-sheng i-wen lei-ch'ao* (Posthumous collection of the works of Ts'ai Yüan-p'ei; Taipei, 1961), pp. 153–54. On Ch'en Hsieh-fen and *Nü-pao*, see Feng, *I-shih*, 3: 86; and Feng Tzu-yu, *Chung-kuo ko-ming yün-tung erh-shih-liu nien tsu-chih shih* (Twenty-six years organizational history of the Chinese revolutionary movement; Shanghai, 1948), pp. 70–71. On all women's journals before 1911, see Beahan, "Women's Press," *passim*.

64. Chiang Wei-ch'iao, pp. 492–93; *Ching-chung jih-pao*, Mar. 29, 1904, p. 1; May 30, 1904, p. 3; June 16, 1904, p. 4; July 26, 1904, p. 4.

65. *Chen-hai hsien-chih*, Wang Yung-shang and Yang Ming-ts'eng, comps., 1924, 11: 16b–19b; *Nan-hsün chih*, Chou Ch'ing-yün, comp., 1922, 3: 5a. *Chü-hsien chih*, Chia Chen-lin and Ho Ch'ing-en, comps., 1929, 3: 26b–27a; Rankin, pp. 283–84.

66. Hsü Shuang-yün, "Chi Ch'iu Chin," pp. 210–12; T'ao Ch'eng-chang, "Che-an chi-lüeh," p. 61; *Nan-hsün chih*, 3: 5a.

67. Hsü Shuang-yün, p. 212; T'ao Ch'eng-chang, pp. 61, 87; Ch'iu Ts'an-chih, "Ch'iu Chin ko-ming chuan," p. 79; Feng, *I-shih*, 2: 179.

68. T'ao Ch'eng-chang, p. 32; *Ko-ming hsien-lieh chuan-chi*, p. 225; Chou Ya-wei, "Kuang-fu hui chien-wen tsa-i" (Miscellaneous experiences with the Restoration Society), in *Hsin-hai ko-ming hui-i lu*, 1: 624–36.

69. Hsü Shuang-yün, p. 212; "Draft regulations of the *Chinese Women's Journal*, in *CCC*, pp. 10–11.

70. "A warning to two million Chinese sisters," in *CCC*, p. 5; "A warning to my sisters," in *CCC*, p. 15.

71. E.g., letters in *CCC*, p. 9, 39.

72. "Introduction to the *Chinese Women's Journal*," in *CCC*, p. 12; "A warning to my sisters," in *CCC*, p. 15.

73. "Introduction to the *Chinese Women's Journal*," in *CCC*, p. 12.

74. *Stones of the Ching-wei Bird*, chs. 1–6, in *CCC*, pp. 117–60.

75. Chūzō Ichiko, "The Role of the Gentry: An Hypothesis," in Mary C. Wright, ed., *China in Revolution: The First Phase, 1900–1913* (New Haven, Conn., 1968), p. 302. On Shao-hsing, see Rankin, *Early Chinese Revolutionaries*, pp. 164, 174.

76. T'ao Ch'eng-chang, "Che-an chi-lüeh," pp. 62, 78–79; *CCC*, pp. 21–26.

77. T'ao Ch'eng-chang, pp. 31, 62; Chu Tsan-ch'ing, "Ta-t'ung shih-fan hsüeh-t'ang" (The Ta-t'ung Normal School), in *Hsin-hai ko-ming hui-i lu*, 4: 144, 147.

78. "T'ung-pao ku" (Our brothers' sorrows), in *CCC*, pp. 111–12; *Stones of the Ching-wei Bird*, in *CCC*, pp. 121–22; "Draft revolutionary proclamation of the Restoration Army," in *CCC*, p. 21.

79. "Our brothers' sorrows," in *CCC*, p. 111.

80. *Stones of the Ching-wei Bird*, in *CCC*, pp. 126–27.

81. "Letter to Wang Shih-tse," in *CCC*, p. 45.
82. See the collection from the Grand Council archives in *Hsin-hai ko-ming*, 3: 205–9.
83. Various sword songs in *CCC*, pp. 73–74, 74–75, 81; "To Chiang Lu-shan . . . ," in *CCC*, pp. 77–78; untitled poem, in *CCC*, pp. 82–83.
84. See nine letters to elder brother, June–Dec. 1905, especially nos. 3 and 7, in *CCC*, pp. 33–42; and "To Hsü Chi-ch'en," in *CCC*, p. 89.
85. E.g., "Thus our rivers and mountains" and "Che-ku t'ien," in *CCC*, p. 107; "Sword song," in *CCC*, p. 80; "To Chiang Lu-shan . . . ," in *CCC*, p. 78.
86. "Poem to Hsü Hsiao-shu in contemplation of death," in *CCC*, p. 26.
87. *Stones of the Ching-wei Bird*, in *CCC*, pp. 150–60 *passim*; Ch'iu used the phrase *nü-t'ung-pao*, e.g. in title of "A warning to two million Chinese sisters," in *CCC*, p. 4.
88. On vocation, see Dorothy Emmet, *Function, Purpose, and Powers* (London, 1958), ch. 9.
89. "Letter to Wang Shih-tse," in *CCC*, p. 44; "Che-ku t'ien," in *CCC*, p. 108; "Tui-chiu" (To wine), in *CCC*, p. 84.
90. See Witke, "Transformation of Attitudes," p. 323 and ch. 10 *passim*.
91. E.g., short untitled poem, in *CCC*, p. 91.
92. "Sword song," in *CCC*, p. 80. On Ching K'o, see James J. Y. Liu, *The Chinese Knight-Errant*, pp. 25–34.
93. "Mou kung-jen chuan" (Biography of a certain palace woman), in *CCC*, pp. 16–19.
94. Giles, "Life of Ch'iu Chin," pp. 225–26; Hsü Shuang-yün, "Chi Ch'iu Chin," pp. 218–22; T'ao Ch'eng-chang, "Che-an chi-lüeh," p. 42; Huang Hua, "Chi T'ung-ch'eng Wu Chih-ying nü-shih," pp. 34–35. Examples of fictitious treatments of Ch'iu Chin are Chang Shu-han, *Fen-nü te Chien-hu* (Furious Chien Lake; Taipei, 1965), and Ching-kuan-tzu, *Liu-yüeh shuang* (July frost; reprint, Shanghai, 1958).
95. Ch'en Tung-yüan, *Chung-kuo fu-nü sheng-huo shih*, pp. 357–58; Liang Chan-mei, *Chung-kuo fu-nü fen-tou shih hua*, p. 72.
96. Witke, pp. 166–67. She cites Kuo Mo-jo, " 'Na-la' te ta-an" (Nora's reply), *Mo-jo wen-chi* (Collected writings of Kuo Mo-jo; Peking, 1959), 12: 198–203.
97. Francis L. K. Hsü, "Chinese Kinship and Chinese Behavior," in Ping-ti Ho and Tang Tsou, eds., *China in Crisis* (2 vols.; Chicago, 1968), 1.2: 592–93.
98. Witke, pp. 333–34.

Marriage Resistance in Rural Kwangtung

1. Wu Shang-shih and Tseng Chao-hsüan, "*Chu chiang san chiao chou*" (The Pearl River delta), *Ling-nan hsüeh pao*, 8.1 (Dec. 1947): 105–22. Translated into English by Winston Hsieh and P. Buell in "Metaphysics Involved in Defining a Region: The Case of the Canton Delta Region" (background paper for the Canton Delta Conference, held at the University of Washington, Seattle, June 13–15, 1971).
2. Glenn T. Trewartha, "Field Observations on the Canton Delta of South China," *Economic Geography*, 15.1 (Jan. 1939): 9–10.
3. *Ibid.*, p. 8.

4. *Ibid.*, p. 6.

5. Benjamin Henry, *Ling-Nam: or, Interior Views of Southern China* (London, 1886), p. 66.

6. Trewartha, pp. 9–10.

7. Henry, p. 67.

8. John Kerr, *A Guide to the City and Suburbs of Canton* (rev. ed.; Hong Kong, 1904), p. 66.

9. Henry, p. 67.

10. Agnes Smedley, *Chinese Destinies* (New York, 1933), p. 178.

11. Robert F. Spencer and S. A. Barnett, "Notes on a Bachelor House in the South China Area," *American Anthropologist*, n.s., 50.3 (July–Sept. 1948): 463–78.

12. *Ibid.*, p. 474.

13. Henry, *Ling-Nam*, p. 68.

14. *Shun-te hsien-chih* (Shun-te county gazetteer), 1853, vol. 3: *Feng-ssu* (Customs), p. 39.

15. Marjorie Topley, "The Great Way of Former Heaven: A Group of Chinese Secret Religious Sects," *Bulletin of the School of Oriental and African Studies*, 26.2 (June 1963): 386–87.

16. Marjorie Topley, "Chinese Religion and Rural Cohesion in the Nineteenth Century," *Journal of the Royal Asiatic Society, Hong Kong Branch*, 8 (1968): 27.

17. *Ibid.*, p. 29.

18. Topley, "The Great Way," pp. 369–71.

19. Mrs. Edward Thomas Williams, "Some Popular Religious Literature of the Chinese," *Journal of the Royal Asiatic Society, China Branch*, n.s., 33 (1899–1900): 11–29.

20. Justus Doolittle, *Social Life of the Chinese* (2 vols.; New York, 1865), 1: 196–97.

21. I am grateful to Emily Ahern for this reference.

22. Ho It Chong, "The Cantonese Domestic Amah; a Study of a Small Occupahome Group of Chinese Women" (Research paper, University of Malaya [Singapore], 1958), p. 135.

23. James Dyer Ball, *The Shun-Tak Dialect* (Hong Kong, 1901), p. 6.

24. Cf. Ho It Chong, p. 47.

25. Marjorie Topley, "The Organisation and Social Function of Chinese Women's *Chai T'ang* in Singapore" (Ph.D. dissertation, University of London, 1958).

26. *Shun-te hsien-chih*, 1853, 3: 35.

27. W. P. Morgan, *Triad Societies in Hong Kong* (Hong Kong, 1960), p. 284.

28. James Dyer Ball, *Things Chinese* (5th ed.; Shanghai, 1925), p. 6.

29. Ch'en Tung-yuan, *Chung-kuo fu-nü sheng-huo shih* (History of women's life in China; Shanghai, 1928), chap. 8; *Chung-hua ch'üan-kuo feng-ssu chih* (Gazetteer of Chinese customs; n.p., n.d.), vol. 7: *Kuang-tung* (Kwangtung), Book 4, *hsia chieh*, pp. 30–33; S. H. Peplow and M. Barker, *Hong Kong Round and About* (Hong Kong, 1931), p. 118; Agnes Smedley, *Battle Hymn of China* (New York, 1943), p. 87.

30. Cf. *Chung-hua ch'üan-kuo feng-ssu chih,* loc. cit.
31. Ho It Chong, "Cantonese Domestic Amahs," p. 36.
32. Dyer Ball, *Things Chinese,* p. 372.
33. Arthur H. Smith, *Village Life in China* (New York, 1899), p. 287.
34. *Ibid.,* pp. 258–311; Margery Wolf, *Women and the Family in Rural Taiwan* (Stanford, Calif., 1972).
35. Cf. Olga Lang, *Chinese Family and Society* (reissue; New Haven, Conn., 1968), p. 43.
36. Smith, p. 262.
37. Ho It Chong, pp. 24, 135.
38. Smith, p. 287.
39. Ho It Chong, "Cantonese Domestic Amah," p. 28.
40. Lang, p. 42.
41. Cf. Doolittle, *Social Life of the Chinese,* 1: 61.
42. Smith, *Village Life,* p. 289.
43. Ho It Chong, p. 29.
44. *Chung-hua ch'üan-kuo feng-ssu chih,* loc. cit.
45. Ho It Chong, p. 25.
46. Smith, p. 287; Dyer Ball, *Things Chinese,* p. 375; and Peplow and Barker, *Hong Kong Round and About,* p. 117.
47. Dyer Ball, *Shun-Tak Dialect,* p. 7; cf. his *Things Chinese,* p. 375.
48. Cf. Ho It Chong, "Cantonese Domestic Amah," p. 30.
49. Cf. *Hsin-chiu hun-yin tui-pi t'u* (Chart comparing old and new marriage; Canton, 1952).
50. Ho It Chong, p. 36.
51. Maurice Freedman, "Ritual Aspects of Chinese Kinship and Marriage," in Freedman, ed., *Family and Kinship in Chinese Society* (Stanford, Calif., 1970), pp. 181, 183.
52. Cf. Ho It Chong, p. 115.
53. Lang, *Chinese Family,* p. 109.
54. Smedley, *Chinese Destinies,* p. 177.
55. W. L. Blythe, "Historical Sketch of Chinese Labour in Malaya," *Journal of the Royal Asiatic Society, Malaya Branch,* 20 (1947): 103.
56. *Hsin-chiu hun-yin tui-pi t'u.*
57. Cf. Ho It Chong, p. 120.
58. *Ibid.,* p. 21.
59. *Ibid.,* p. 27.
60. Topley, "Organisation and Social Function of Chinese Women's *Chai T'ang.*"
61. Janet Salaff, "Social and Demographic Determinants of Marital Age in Hong Kong," in Henry E. White, ed., *The Changing Family, East and West* (Hong Kong, 1973), pp. 72 *et seq.*
62. Fei Hsiao-t'ung, *Peasant Life in China* (London, 1943), p. 235.
63. Topley, "Organisation and Social Function of Chinese Women's *Chai T'ang.*"
64. Graham Johnson, "Rural Chinese Social Organization: Tradition and Change," *Pacific Affairs,* 46.4 (Winter 1973–74): 562.
65. *Ibid.,* pp. 563–64.

The Women of Hai-shan: A Demographic Portrait

1. Sidney D. Gamble, *Ting Hsien: A North China Rural Community* (New York, 1954), p. 29.

2. I am assuming that Barclay is thinking of sons and daughters when he refers to "the well-known [fact] that male offspring are especially cherished in Chinese families." His book does not mention female adoption. George W. Barclay, *Colonial Development and Population in Taiwan* (Princeton, N.J., 1954), p. 157.

3. Fei Hsiao-tung, *Peasant Life in China: A Field Study of Country Life in the Yangtze Valley* (New York, 1939), p. 54.

4. Arthur P. Wolf, "Childhood Association, Sexual Attraction, and the Incest Taboo: A Chinese Case," *American Anthropologist*, 68 (1966): 883–98. Also "Childhood Association and Sexual Attraction: A Further Test of the Westermarck Hypothesis," *American Anthropologist*, 72 (1970): 503–15.

5. L. A. Fallers, "Some Determinants of Marriage Stability in Busoga: A Reformulation of Gluckman's Hypothesis," *Africa*, 27–28 (1957–58): 121.

6. Margery Wolf, *Women and the Family in Rural Taiwan* (Stanford, Calif., 1972), pp. 32–41.

Women and Suicide in China

1. Ernest Alabaster, *Notes and Commentaries on Chinese Criminal Law and Cognate Topics* (London, 1899; reissued Taipei, 1968), pp. 316–17.

2. Adele M. Fielde, *Pagoda Shadows: Studies from Life in China* (London, 1887), p. 140.

3. Fei Hsiao-t'ung, *Peasant Life in China: A Field Study of Country Life in the Yangtze Valley* (New York, 1939), p. 49.

4. M.F.C., "The Chinese Daughter-in-Law," *Chinese Recorder*, 5 (1874): 212.

5. Alex Inkeles, "Sociology and Psychology," in Sigmund Koch, ed., *Psychology: A Study of Science*, 6 (New York, 1963): 325.

6. The sources are: (1) Sotoku-fu (Formosa Government-General), *Taiwan jinko dotai tokei* (Vital statistics of the population), 37 annual vols., 1906–42; (2) Sotoku-fu, *Rinji Taiwan kokō chōsa*, censuses of 1905 and 1915; (3) Sotoku-fu, *Taiwan kokusei chōsa*, censuses of 1920, 1925, 1930, and 1935; (4) Taiwan Provincial Government, Bureau of Accounting and Statistics, *Results of the Seventh Population Census of Taiwan, 1940* (Taiwan, 1953); and (5) Taiwan Provincial Government, Bureau of Accounting and Statistics, *Statistical Summary of the Past Fifty-one Years* (Taipei, 1946).

I am very grateful to Chieh-shan Huang and Stephen M. Olsen for their assistance in locating and translating statistical materials. I am also indebted to Arthur Wolf and William L. Parish for their comments and suggestions.

7. Sidney D. Gamble, *Peking: A Social Survey* (Oxford, 1921); Lin-po, pseud., "Chung-kuo ssu ta tu shih tzu sha hsing pi wen t'i" (The sex ratio of suicides in four major Chinese cities), *Ch'ing hua chou k'an*, 38.1 (Oct. 1, 1932).

8. P. M. Yap, *Suicide in Hong Kong* (Hong Kong, 1958). If the Hong Kong data were to be excluded from a study of Chinese suicide on any

grounds, the strong international influences on the population would be more appropriate.

9. World Health Organization, *Rapport épidémiologique et démographique*, 9.4 (1956).

10. Jack D. Douglas, *The Social Meanings of Suicide* (Princeton, N.J., 1967), p. 185.

11. Lin-po, p. 31.

12. *Ibid.*, pp. 39–40.

13. Margery Wolf, *Women and the Family in Rural Taiwan* (Stanford, Calif., 1972).

14. Myron L. Cohen, "A Case Study of Chinese Family Economy and Development," *Journal of Asian and African Studies*, 3.3–4 (1968): 169–70.

15. P. M. Yap, p. 12.

16. *Ibid.*, p. 13.

17. Gamble, p. 416.

18. Arthur H. Smith, *Village Life in China* (New York, 1899; reissued, Boston, 1970), p. 218.

Women as Writers in the 1920's and 1930's

1. *Ping Hsin hsiao-shuo san-wen hsüan-chi* (A collection of short stories and prose by Ping Hsin; Peking, 1954), Author's Preface, p. 3. This translation is adapted from Marcela Boušková, "The Stories of Ping Hsin," in J. Průšek, ed., *Studies in Modern Chinese Literature* (Berlin, 1964), p. 114.

2. Ho Yü-po, *Chung-kuo hsien-tai nü-tso-chia* (Contemporary women writers of China; Shanghai, 1931, reprint, 1936), p. 1.

3. Benjamin Schwartz, "The Intelligentsia in Communist China, A Tentative Comparison," *Daedalus*, Summer 1960, pp. 604–22.

4. Virginia Woolf, *A Room of One's Own* (New York, 1929, reprint, 1957), pp. 79–80.

5. An excerpt from *Hsi yu chi* (Journey to the West), tr. as "The Temptation of Saint Pigsy" by C. T. Hsia and Cyril Birch, contains the poetic warning against women from which these lines are taken. Cyril Birch, ed., *Anthology of Chinese Literature*, (New York, 1972) 2: 84. *Yaksha*, translated into Chinese as *yeh-ch'a*, is an ugly demon in Buddhist mythology. It is often feminized in such "human" epithets as *yeh-ch'a p'o* or *mu yeh-ch'a*.

6. James Robert Hightower, *Topics in Chinese Literature*, rev. ed. (Cambridge, Mass., 1953), p. 105.

7. For a perceptive, well-illustrated discussion of misogyny in *Shui-hu chuan*, see C. T. Hsia's chapter on this novel in his *The Classic Chinese Novel: A Critical Introduction* (New York, 1968), particularly pp. 105–6. See also his article "Comparative Approaches to *Water Margin*," *Yearbook of Comparative and General Literature*, 11 (1962): 121–28.

8. A *tz'u* to the tune of *P'u sa man* by Wen T'ing-yün, as translated by Glen W. Baxter in Cyril Birch, ed., *Anthology of Chinese Literature* (New York, 1965) 1: 336.

9. Ts'ao Hsüeh-ch'in, *Hung lou meng* (Dream of the red chamber; Peking, 1953), p. 1. This statement is actually part of the commentary that prefaces the first chapter of the novel, but has been printed as part of the main text

since its first publication. The commentator is quoting the author's own words; thus he speaks in the first person. (Unless otherwise indicated, all translations are my own.)

10. Hu Wen-k'ai, *Li-tai fu-nü chu-tso k'ao* (Writings of women through the ages; Shanghai, 1957).

11. T'an Cheng-pi, *Chung-kuo nü-hsing te wen-hsüeh sheng-huo* (The literary life of Chinese women; Shanghai, 1930), p. 389.

12. *Ibid.*, p. 287.

13. A. C. Scott, *The Classical Theatre of China* (London, 1957), pp. 68–70.

14. Two arresting phrases from George Steiner, "The Future of the Book," Part 1, *Times Literary Supplement*, Oct. 2, 1970: 1121.

15. D. C. Twitchett, "Chinese Biographical Writing," in W. G. Beasley and E. G. Pulleyblank, eds., *Historians of China and Japan* (London, 1961), pp. 95–114.

16. Li Ju-chen, *Flowers in the Mirror*, tr. and ed. Lin Tai-yi (Berkeley, Calif., 1965), pp. 107–25.

17. Collected in *Chung-kuo hsien-tai wen-hsüeh shih ts'an-k'ao tzu-liao* (Research materials on the history of modern Chinese literary history), ed. Peking Shih-fan Ta-hsüeh Chung-wen Hsi Hsien-tai Wen-hsüeh Chiao-hsüeh Kai-ke Hsiao-tsu (Committee to Revise the Teaching of Modern Literature, Dept. of Chinese Literature, Peking Normal University), 2 vols. (Peking, 1959), 1: 20–23.

18. *Ibid.*, pp. 132–49.

19. *Ping Hsin hsiao-shuo chi* (The short stories of Ping Hsin; 2d ed., Shanghai, 1947), Author's Preface, dated 1932, pp. 1–16.

20. Hsieh Ping-ying, *Shih-yeh yü lien-ai* (Career and love; Hong Kong, n.d.), pp. 25–27.

21. Su Hsüeh-lin, *Wo-te sheng-huo* (My life; Taipei, 1967), pp. 87–88.

22. Feng Yüan-chün, *Yüan-chün sa ch'ien hsüan-chi* (Selected writings of Yüan-chün before thirty; Shanghai, 1933), p. 15.

23. Huang Ying [Lu Yin], *Hsien-tai chung-kuo nü-tso-chia* (Women writers of contemporary China; 2d ed., Shanghai, 1934), p. 185.

24. Shen Ts'ung-wen, *Chi Ting Ling* (About Ting Ling). He also wrote *Chi Ting Ling hsü-chi* (More about Ting Ling). The two books were reprinted together, Shanghai, 1940.

25. See Shen Ts'ung-wen, *Chi Ting Ling*, pp. 67–68, 82–83, 84–85. Some twenty years after Hu Yeh-p'in's death, Ting Ling paid tribute to his "nurturing" and "cherishing" of her creative writing. See her "I-ke chen-shih jen te i-sheng—chi Hu Yeh-p'in" (The life of an upright man—on Hu Yeh-p'in), dated 1950, in *Hu Yeh-p'in hsiao-shuo hsüan-chi* (Selected stories of Hu Yeh-p'in; Peking, 1955), p. 14.

26. Shen Ts'ung-wen, *Chi Ting Ling*, p. 84.

27. Ting Ling, *Tsai hei-an chung* (In the darkness; 5th ed., Shanghai, 1933), p. 68.

28. Shen Ts'ung-wen, *Chi Ting Ling*, pp. 101–2.

29. Huang Ying [Lu Yin], *Hsien-tai chung-kuo nü-tso-chia*, p. 96.

30. Stories dealing with themes mentioned in this paragraph include Feng Yüan-chün, "Ke-chüeh" (Separation), "Ke-chüeh i-hou" (After separation),

and "Ch'ien-tao" (Secret mourning), in *Tang-tai shih ta nü-tso-chia chia-tso chi* (Best selected works of ten contemporary women writers; n.p., Preface dated 1937), pp. 703–23, 748–69; Lu Yin, "Li-shih te jih-chi" (Lise's diary), "Huo-jen te pei-ai" (The sorrow of a certain person), and "Hai-pin ku-jen" (Friends by the sea), in *Hai-pin ku-jen* (Shanghai, 1933), pp. 67–98; "Shih-tai te hsi-sheng-che" (Victim of the times) and "Fu-ch'in" (Father), in Hsü Ch'en-ssu and Yeh Wang-yu, eds., *Lu Yin hsüan-chi* (Selected writings of Lu Yin; Shanghai, 1936), pp. 43–55, 87–116; *Hsiang-ya chieh-chih* (Ivory ring; 2d ed., Shanghai, 1934); Lü I [Su Hsüeh-lin], *Chi-hsin* (Bitter heart; 4th ed., Peiping, 1931); Hsieh Ping-ying, "Kei S-mei te hsin" (Letter to Sister S), in *Hsieh Ping-ying ch'uang-tso hsüan* (Selected writings of Hsieh Ping-ying; Shanghai, 1936), pp. 75–98; Ting Ling, "Sha-fei nü-shih jih-chi" (The diary of Miss Sophie) and "Shu-chia chung" (During summer vacation), in her *Tsai hei-an chung*, pp. 73–202; and "Tzu-sha jih-chi" (A suicide's diary), in Hsü Ch'en-ssu and Yeh Wang-yu, eds., *Ting Ling hsüan-chi* (Selected writings of Ting Ling; Shanghai, 1935), pp. 119–28.

31. Lu Yin, "Lan-t'ien te ch'an-hui lu" (The confessions of Lan-t'ien), in *Ling-hai ch'ao-hsi* (Mental tides; 7th ed., Shanghai, 1949), p. 154.

32. Shen Ts'ung-wen, *Chi Ting Ling*, pp. 86–87.

33. Feng Yüan-chün, *Yüan-chün sa ch'ien hsüan-chi*, p. 26.

34. Stories referred to in this paragraph: Ling Shu-hua, "Hsiu-chen" (Embroidered pillows), in Su Hsüeh-lin, Chang Hsiu-ya, and Lin Hai-yin, eds., *Chin-tai chung-kuo tso-chia yü tso-p'in* (Modern Chinese writers and their works; Taipei, 1967), 1: 95–100, "Chiu-hou" (After wine-drinking), in *Tang-tai shih ta nü-tso-chia chia-tso chi*, pp. 409–17, and "Hsiao Liu" (Little Liu) and "Li hsien-sheng" (Schoolmistress Li), in her *Nü-jen* (Women; 3d ed., Shanghai, 1935), pp. 1–44; Ping Hsin, "Wo te lin-chü" (My neighbor), in her *Kuan-yü nü-jen* (Concerning women; Hong Kong, 1970), pp. 93–101; this collection of sketches about women was published under the humorous pen-name *Nan-shih* (Gentleman) in 1942, some years after the other stories mentioned in this paper. "Hsi-feng" (West wind), in *Ping Hsin hsiao-shuo chi*, pp. 287–303; Hsieh Ping-ying, "P'ao-ch'i" (Relinquishing), in *Hsieh Ping-ying ch'uang-tso hsüan*, pp. 123–94; Ch'en Ying, "Nü-shing" (Women), in *Tang-tai shih ta nü-tso-chia chia-tso chi*, pp. 556–89; Lu Yin, "Sheng-li i-hou" (After victory), in *Ling-hai ch'ao hsi*, pp. 52–70.

35. Ping Hsin, "Tsui-hou te an-hsi" (The last rest), in *Ping Hsin hsiao-shuo chi*, pp. 44–55.

36. Lu Yin, "Ling-hun k'e-i mai ma" (Can the soul be sold?), in *Hai-pin ku-jen*, pp. 32–43.

37. Ling Shu-hua, "Yang-ma" (Servant-woman Yang), in *Nü-jen*, pp. 47–69.

38. Ting Ling, "A-mao ku-niang" (Miss Ah-mao), in *Tsai hei-an chung*, pp. 203–70.

39. Tsi-an Hsia, *The Gate of Darkness: Studies on the Leftist Literary Movement in China* (Seattle, 1968), p. 182.

40. Ting Ling, *Ting Ling wen-chi* (Works of Ting Ling), *Ch'ing-nien wen-hsüeh tu-pen* (Literary readings for youth; n.p., n.d.), p. 312. See also her statement "Wo-te ch'uang-tso ching-yen" (My experience in creative writing), in Hsü and Yeh, eds., *Ting Ling hsüan-chi*, p. 142.

41. An example is Lu Yin's story "Man-li" (Mary) in Hsü and Yeh, eds., *Lu Yin hsüan-chi*, pp. 17–28.

42. Ting Ling, *Wei-hu* (Weihu; Shanghai, 1930).

43. *Ting Ling hsüan-chi*, pp. 84–85. This is the translation by Tsi-an Hsia in his *Gate of Darkness*, p. 188.

44. "Shui" (Flood), in *Ting Ling hsüan-chi*, pp. 36–79.

45. Ting Ling's autobiography as told to Helen Snow contains a brief account. Helen Snow, *Women in Modern China* (The Hague, 1967), pp. 194–221. L. Insun's "Ting Ling tsai Shan-pei" (Ting Ling in Northern Shensi) refers mainly to her adventures in crossing single-log bridges and falling into the water. See *Nü chan-shih Ting Ling* (Ting Ling, A female warrior; Shanghai, 1938), pp. 34–35.

Chiang Ch'ing's Coming of Age

1. See, for example, Chung Hua-min (pseud.), *Chiang Ch'ing cheng chuan* (Biography of Chiang Ch'ing; Hong Kong, 1967), translated as Chung Hua-min and Arthur C. Miller, *Madame Mao: A Profile of Chiang Ch'ing* (Hong Kong, 1968); "Chiang Ch'ing," *Biographical Service* 1405 (June 3, 1969); "Chiang Ch'ing," in *Who's Who in Communist China* (Hong Kong, 1969), 1: 132–34; "Chiang Ch'ing," in *Chinese Communist Who's Who* (Taipei, 1970), 1: 138–39.

2. Dogs and wolves are recurring themes not only in Chiang Ch'ing's life, but also in the art with which she has been associated. Literature of the 1930's commonly alludes to the Japanese invaders as "wolves." Chiang Ch'ing played a starring role in the film *Blood on Wolf Mountain* (1936), which was based on Shen Fu's story "Cold Moon and Wolf's Breath." Set in the 1930's, the film is a parable about wolves that threaten to kill members of an entire community one by one until they stand together against the predatory beasts. See Cheng Chi-hua, *Chung-kuo tien-ying fa-chin shih* (History of the development of the Chinese film; Peking, 1962), 1: 471–73. In the revolutionary opera *Taking Tiger Mountain by Strategy*, a product of the Cultural Revolution, the male lead slays a wolf to prove his valor. And in the revolutionary ballet *White-Haired Girl*, the female lead is threatened by wolves in her mountain exile.

3. See Akira Iriye, *After Imperialism: The Search for a New Order in the Far East, 1921–1931* (New York, 1969), pp. 193–205.

4. *Fen-sheng te-chih: Shantung* (Provincial directory of Shantung; Shanghai, 1935), pp. 81–86.

5. Yü Shan was a well-known opera singer and actress when she married Chao T'ai-mou. (Edgar Snow, *Red Star Over China*, rev. ed. [New York, 1961], p. 459.) By the time Chao became Director of the Experimental Art Theater in Tsinan, he had studied at Columbia and Johns Hopkins and taught at Peking University. See *Shan-tung sheng chiao-yü t'ing ti i tzu kung-tso pao-kao* (The first work report from the Education Department, Shantung Province; Shantung, 1929). See also *Chugoku bunkakai jimbutsu sokan* (Peking, 1940), pp. 643, 644, 651, and *Chung-hua min-kuo ta-hsueh chih* (Record of higher education in the Republic of China; Taipei, 1954), 1: 219–20.

6. Formerly the subordinate of warlord Feng Yü-hsiang, in 1930 Han became Governor of Shantung, at the same time switching his allegiance to

Chiang Kai-shek. For ineffective resistance to the Japanese, he was tried by a Kuomintang military tribunal and executed in January 1938. See Chalmers A. Johnson, *Peasant Nationalism and Communist Power* (Stanford, Calif., 1962), pp. 109–10.

7. Hu Shih led the American-oriented intellectuals at Peking University in the 1920's in the movement for a vernacular modern literature. To the Communist regime his career long was epitomized the worst in "bourgeois liberalism."

8. Liang Shih-ch'iu, who once studied at Harvard and Columbia, was a literary critic, professor, and translator of western literature. As a leader of the Crescent Moon Society in the 1920's, he professed aestheticism, individualism, and other theories of Western derivation. In his later years he wrote extensively on Shakespeare. In 1949 he moved to Taiwan.

Wen I-to, primarily a writer, was also a member of the middle-of-the-road China Democratic League, founded during World War II. The League drifted to the left after the war, and the Kuomintang engineered Wen's assassination at Kunming in July 1946.

9. Shen Ts'ung-wen was born to an old military family, which lost its fortune during the Boxer Rebellion. When Chiang Ch'ing knew him as a professor and short-story writer, his earnings would have been moderate but still markedly superior to her own. See Howard L. Boorman and Richard C. Howard, *Biographical Dictionary of Republican China*, 3 (New York, 1970): 107.

The Power and Pollution of Chinese Women

1. Ida Pruitt, *A Daughter of Han: The Autobiography of a Chinese Working Woman* (1945; reissue, Stanford, Calif., 1973), p. 179.

2. See Ho Lien-k'uei and Wei Hui-lin, *Tai-wan feng-t'u chih* (Customs of Taiwan; Taipei, 1970), pp. 65–66.

3. David C. Graham, *Folk Religion in Southwest China* (Washington, D.C., 1961), p. 140.

4. J. J. M. de Groot, *The Religious System of China*, 6 vols. (1892–1910; reissue, Taipei, 1967), 6: 1006–9.

5. A. J. A. Elliott, *Chinese Spirit Medium Cults in Singapore* (London, 1955), pp. 56–57, 88; Norma Diamond, *K'un Shen: A Taiwan Village* (New York, 1969), p. 103.

6. Elliott, p. 48.

7. De Groot, *Religious System of China*, 4: 377.

8. See Mary Douglas, *Purity and Danger: An Analysis of Concepts of Pollution and Taboo* (New York, 1966); Ian Hogbin, *The Island of Menstruating Men* (Scranton, Pa., 1970); and Marilyn Strathern, *Women in Between: Female Roles in a Male World: Mount Hagen, New Guinea* (New York, 1972) for other efforts to analyze the relationship between pollution and social roles.

9. Margery Wolf, *Women and the Family in Rural Taiwan* (Stanford, Calif., 1972), pp. 32–37, 164–67.

10. *Ibid.*, pp. 37–52.

11. *Ibid.*, p. 40.

12. *Ibid.*, pp. 39–40.

13. See Wu Ying-t'ao, *Tai-wan min-su* (Taiwanese customs; Taipei, 1970), p. 22.

14. Wolf, p. 57.

15. V. R. Burkhardt, *Chinese Creeds and Customs*, 1 (Hong Kong, 1955): 33.

16. Elliott, *Chinese Spirit Medium Cults*, p. 70; De Groot, *Religious System*, 6: 1323.

17. Douglas, *Purity and Danger*, pp. 1–4.

18. See Emily M. Ahern, *The Cult of the Dead in a Chinese Village* (Stanford, Calif., 1973), pp. 171–72.

19. R. H. Van Gulick, *Sexual Life in Ancient China* (Leiden, 1961), pp. 34, 46, 48, 144–47, 193–200, 279–84 *passim*.

20. The Rev. Justus Doolittle, *Social Life of the Chinese* (1865; reissue, Taipei, 1966), p. 196.

21. Wolf, *Women and the Family*, p. 57.

22. Johannes Frick, "Mutter und Kind bei den Chinesen in Tsinghai, I: Die Sozialreligiöse Unreinheit der Frau," *Anthropos* 50 (1955): 341–42.

23. Marjorie Topley, "Chinese Traditional Ideas and the Treatment of Disease: Two Examples from Hong Kong," *Man*, 5 (1970): 427.

24. Doolittle, p. 74.

25. Feng Han-yi and J. K. Shryock, "Marriage Customs in the Vicinity of I-Ch'ang," *Harvard Journal of Asiatic Studies*, 13 (1950): 393.

26. Topley, "Chinese Traditional Ideas," p. 427.

27. Frick, p. 358.

28. Doolittle, pp. 196–97.

Women and Childbearing in Kwan Mun Hau Village

1. See, for example, Ronald Freedman and John Y. Takeshita, *Family Planning in Taiwan* (Princeton, N.J., 1969); Leo A. Orleans, *Every Fifth Child: The Population of China* (Stanford, Calif., 1972); and *Studies in Family Planning*, 4 (Aug. 1973), an issue devoted entirely to family planning in China.

2. Graham E. Johnson, "From Rural Committee to Spirit Medium Cult: Voluntary Associations in the Development of a Chinese Town," *Contributions to Asian Studies*, 1 (The Hague, Jan. 1971): 128.

3. Unpublished records, District Office, Tsuen Wan.

4. Hong Kong Population and Housing Census, 1971 Main Report, p. 22. Graham E. Johnson, "Natives, Migrants, and Voluntary Associations in a Colonial Chinese Setting" (Ph.D. dissertation, Cornell University, 1970), pp. 42–43.

5. K. M. A. Barnett, *Hong Kong: Report on the 1966 By-census* (Hong Kong, n.d.), 2: 35.

6. David Podmore, "The Population of Hong Kong," in Keith Hopkins, ed., *Hong Kong: The Industrial Colony* (Hong Kong, 1971), p. 31.

7. L. G. Aijmer, "Expansion and Extension in Hakka Society," *Journal of the Royal Asiatic Society, Hong Kong Branch*, 7 (1967): 42–79; Hugh D. R. Baker, *A Chinese Lineage Village* (Stanford, Calif., 1968), pp. 207–8; Jack M. Potter, *Capitalism and the Chinese Peasant* (Berkeley, Calif., 1968), pp.

52–53; Jean Pratt, "Emigration and Unilineal Descent Groups: A Study of Marriage in a Hakka Village in the New Territories," *The Eastern Anthropologist* 13.4 (June-Aug. 1960): 147–58; James L. Watson, "A Chinese Emigrant Community: The Man Lineage in Hong Kong and London" (Ph.D. dissertation, University of California, Berkeley, 1972).

8. Margery Wolf, *Women and the Family in Rural Taiwan* (Stanford, Calif., 1972), pp. 205–17.

9. Unpublished records, District Office, Tsuen Wan.

10. In the conceptualization and ordering of these materials, I have drawn on Ronald Freedman, "The Sociology of Human Fertility," *Current Sociology*, 10-11.2 (1961–62): 35–68; Kingsley Davis and Judith Blake, "Social Structure and Fertility: An Analytic Framework," *Economic Development and Cultural Change*, 4.3 (April 1956): 211–35; and J. M. Stycos, "Experiments in Social Change: The Caribbean Fertility Studies," in Clyde V. Kiser, ed., *Research in Family Planning* (Princeton, N.J., 1962), pp. 305–16.

11. J. M. Stycos, "Family and Fertility in Puerto Rico," *American Sociological Review*, 17.5 (Oct. 1952): 576-80; G. W. Skinner, "Cultural Values, Social Structure, and Population Growth," *Population Bulletin of the United Nations*, 5 (July 1956): 5–12.

12. For the basis of these restrictions, see Marjorie Topley, "Cosmic Antagonisms: A Mother-Child Syndrome," in Arthur P. Wolf, ed., *Religion and Ritual in Chinese Society* (Stanford, Calif., 1974), pp. 234–37.

13. See also M. Wolf, *Women and the Family*, p. 56.

14. Robert Mitchell found that the women in his sample desired an average of 3.0–4.4 children for themselves, the number given increasing with the age of the respondent. Freedman et al. report that the great majority of their sample want three or four children for themselves, and say that about four children is ideal for Taiwanese couples in general. Robert E. Mitchell, *Family Life in Urban Hong Kong*, (Taipei, 1972), 1: 248; Ronald Freedman, J. Y. Peng, Y. Takeshita, and T. H. Sun, "Fertility Trends in Taiwan: Tradition and Change," *Population Studies*, 16.3 (March 1963): 227–28.

15. Peggy Lam, personal communication. Freedman et al. adjudge the work of the Family Planning Association very important in contributing to the declining birthrate in Hong Kong. Ronald Freedman, D. N. Namboothiri, A. Adlahka, and K. C. Chan, "Hong Kong: The Continuing Fertility Decline, 1967," *Studies in Family Planning*, 44 (Aug. 1969): 9, 12, 15.

16. J. M. Stycos, "Family and Fertility in Puerto Rico," *American Sociological Review*, 17.5 (Oct. 1952): 573.

Women in the Countryside of China

1. Frederick Engels, *The Origin of the Family, Private Property, and the State* (New York, 1972), p. 137.

2. Mao Tse-tung, "Report on an Investigation of the Peasant Movement in Hunan" (March 1927), as quoted in *Quotations from Chairman Mao Tsetung* (Peking, 1972).

3. Delia Davin, "Women in the Liberated Areas," in Marilyn B. Young, ed., *Women in China: Studies in Social Change and Feminism* (Ann Arbor, Mich., 1973).

4. Engels, p. 221.

5. "Chung-kuo kung-ch'an-tang chung-yang wei-yüan-hui kuan-yü mu-ch'ien chieh-fang-ch'ü nung-ts'un fu-nü kung-tso ti chüeh-ting" (Resolution of the Central Committee of the Chinese Communist Party on the present direction of work among women in the liberated areas), in *Chung-kuo chieh-fang-ch'ü fu-nü yün-tung wen-hsien* (Documents of the women's movement of the liberated areas of China, hereafter *Women's Movement Documents*; n.p., 1949).

6. "Chung-kuo kung-ch'an-tang chung-yang wei-yüan-hui kuan-yü ke k'ang-jih ken-chü-ti mu-ch'ien fu-nü kung-tso fang-chen ti chüeh-ting" (Resolutions of the Central Committee of the Chinese Communist Party on the present direction of work among women in the anti-Japanese base areas), in *Women's Movement Documents.*

7. See Gunther Stein, *The Challenge of Red China* (London, 1945), p. 206; and Ting Ling, "San-pa-chieh yu kan," (Thoughts on March 8th), *Chieh-fang jih-pao* (Liberation daily; Yenan), March 12, 1942.

8. "Nü-tsu ts'ai-ch'an chi-ch'eng ch'üan t'iao-li" (Regulations on women's property and rights of inheritance), in *Shan-Kan-Ning pien-ch'ü cheng-ts'e t'iao-li hui-chi* (Collection of political measures and regulations of the Shen-Kan-Ning Border Region; n.p., 1944).

9. *Chung-kuo t'u-ti-fa ta-kang* (Basic program of the Chinese agrarian law, Harbin, 1948), Article 6.

10. William Hinton, *Fanshen* (New York, 1966), pp. 159–60.

11. J. L. Buck, *Land Utilization in China* (Nanking, 1937), p. 292. All the data in the following discussion are taken from this work and its accompanying *Statistical Volume*. Buck's work is not altogether satisfactory for my purpose, not least because when percentages of farm work done by women are given, there is no indication of how the figure was obtained—whether, for example, the work is being measured only in terms of time taken on the job or instead an attempt has been made to "discount" lighter work against heavy work. Unfortunately, however, no better data exist.

12. Ester Boserup, *Women's Role in Economic Development* (London, 1970), p. 35.

13. Buck, p. 307; my translation.

14. Ramon H. Myers, *The Chinese Peasant Economy: Agricultural Development in Hopei and Shantung, 1890–1949* (Cambridge, Mass., 1970), pp. 75, 110.

15. Buck, p. 297.

16. Rudolf P. Hommel, *China at Work* (Cambridge, Mass., 1969), p. 96.

17. Alexandra Kollontai, *Communism and the Family* (London, 1972), p. 13.

18. Buck, p. 386.

19. See, for example, "Tung-yen nung-yeh sheng-ch'an ho-tso-she fa-tung fu-nü ts'an chia t'ien-chien lao-tung ti ching-yen" (The experience of Tung-yen Agricultural Producers' Cooperative in getting women to work in the

fields), in *Che-chiang nung-ts'un kung-tso ching-yen hui-pien* (Work experience in the countryside of Chekiang; Hangchow, 1955).

20. *Chung-kuo nung-ts'un ti she-hui chu-i kao-ch'ao* (High tide of socialism in the Chinese countryside; Peking, 1956), 2: 581.

21. Teng Ying-ch'ao, "Chung-kuo fu-nü yün-tung mu-ch'ien ti fang-chen jen-wu pao-kao" (Report on the present orientation and tasks of the Chinese women's movement), published among the documents of the Second National Congress of the Women's Federation, in *Hsin Chung-kuo fu-nü* (New Chinese women), 5 (Peking, 1953).

22. See, for example, Isabel and David Crook, *The First Years of Yangyi Commune* (London, 1966), p. 68.

23. Jan Myrdal and Gun Kessle, *China: The Revolution Continued* (New York, 1972), pp. 11–12.

24. *Ibid.*, p. 136.

25. Jan Myrdal, *Report from a Chinese Village* (London, 1965), p. 238.

26. Myrdal and Kessle, pp. 133–35.

27. "Ta-li kai-ke chiu chieh-ch'an-fa chi yu-erh-fa" (Vigorous reform of old delivery and child-rearing methods), published in Chung-hua ch'uan-kuo min-chu fu-nü lien-ho-hui (Democratic Women's Federation of China), *Fu-nü erh-t'ung fu-li kung-tso ching-yen* (Experience of welfare work among women and children; Peking, 1952).

28. Norman Webster, in *International Herald Tribune*, March 13–14, 1971, quoting information gathered in China.

29. *Ibid.*

30. See, for example, *Fu-nü tu-pen* (Women's reading primer; Shanghai, 1953).

31. Myrdal, *Report*, pp. 226–27.

32. *Chung-kuo nung-ts'un ti she-hui chu-i kao-ch'ao*, 1: 357.

33. "Pi-hsu chu-i chieh-chüeh fu-nü ts'an-chia lao-tung i-hsieh t'e-shu wen-t'i" (Some special problems of women at work that need attention), *Fu-chien jih-pao* (Fukien daily), March 30, 1953.

34. "Chao-ku fu-nü tsai lao-tung chung t'e-shu wen-t'i" (Attend to the special problems women have at work), *Nan-fang jih-pao* (Southern daily), July 20, 1957.

35. *Hsiang ta tzu-jan ch'uan-mien k'ai-chan* (Battling nature on many fronts; Peking, 1958), p. 134.

36. *Tung-pei nung-yeh sheng-ch'an ti nü-ying-hsiung* (Agricultural production heroines of the Northeast), ed. Tung-pei min-chu fu-nü lien-ho-hui (Northeastern Democratic Women's Federation; n.p., 1950), pp. 1–10.

37. *Ibid.*, pp. 10–20.

38. Buck, *Land Utilization*, p. 294.

39. For a detailed description of this problem see Dwight H. Perkins, *Agricultural Development in China, 1368–1968* (Edinburgh, 1969), chap. 4.

40. Ma Yin-ch'u, "My Philosophical Thoughts and Economic Theory," *Hsin chien-shih* (New construction), Nov. 1959, p. 30. Quoted by Kenneth

Walker in "Ma Yin-ch'u: A Chinese Discussion on Planning for Balanced Growth," in C. D. Cowan, ed., *Economic Growth of China and Japan* (London, 1964), p. 182.

41. Perkins, p. 189.

42. See, for example, Sun Yu's play about women's lives, *The Women's Representative* (Peking, 1956).

43. I. and D. Crook, *Yangyi Commune*, p. 80.

44. Teng Ying-ch'ao, "T'u-ti kai-ke yü fu-nü kung-tso ti hsin jen-wu" (New tasks of land reform and work among women; Dec. 1947), in *Women's Movement Documents*.

45. "Pei-yüeh ch'ü t'u-ti kai-ke yün-tung chung fa-tung fu-nü ching-yen" (Experience of mobilizing women during land reform in Pei-yüeh district; July 1947), in *Chung-kuo chieh-fang-ch'ü nung-ts'un fu-nü fan-shen yün-tung su-miao* (The rural women of the Liberated areas of China arise; n.p., 1949).

46. Hinton, *Fanshen*, p. 397.

47. Erh Tung, "Fu-nü erh-t'ung ting-liao ta-shih" (Women and children manage important affairs), in *Chung-kuo chieh-fang-ch'ü nung-ts'un fu-nü sheng-ch'an yün-tung* (The production movement of the rural women in the liberated areas of China; n.p., 1949), pp. 19–25.

48. Lo Ch'iung, "Chin-nien-lai chieh-fang-ch'ü nung-ts'un fu-nü sheng-ch'an shih-yeh" (Production work in the liberated countryside in the last year), in *ibid.*

49. Chung-kung Shan-hsi sheng-wei pan-kung-t'ing (Provincial Committee of the Communist Party in Shensi), *Shan-hsi nung-ts'un she-hui chu-i chien-shih* (Socialist construction in rural Shensi; Sian, 1956), pp. 61–70.

50. See the story of the women of Hsi-man village, P'ing-shun hsien, Shansi, who fought for and gained equal pay through production competitions against men after the woman deputy head of their cooperative had arranged training courses for them. Shen Chi-lan, "Nung-yeh sheng-ch'an chan-sheng ti nü mo-fan" (Women models on the agricultural production front), in *Nung-yeh ho-tso-hua tao-lu shang ti fu-nü* (Women in cooperativization; Shanghai, 1956).

51. All-China Democratic Women's Federation (Educational Bureau), *Fu-nü ts'an-chia sheng-ch'an chien-she ti hsien-chin pang-yang* (Outstanding examples of women taking part in production and construction; Peking, 1953), p. 43.

52. "Fan-tui ch'i-shih fu-nü, chia-wu lao tung yeh shih kuang-jung-ti" (Oppose contempt of women; housework is glorious too), *Shen-yang jih-pao* (Shenyang daily), June 5, 1957.

53. "Tsen-yang cheng-ch'üeh liao-chieh nan-nü t'ung-ch'ou" (How to deal correctly with equal pay for men and women), *Jen-min jih-pao*, Sept. 9, 1956.

54. Central Committee of the CCP, *Resolutions on Some Questions Concerning the People's Communes*, Sixth Plenary Session of the Eighth Central Committee of the CCP (pamphlet; Peking, 1958).

55. I. and D. Crook, *Yangyi Commune*, p. 127.

56. State Council, "Draft Model Regulations of the Agricultural Producer Cooperatives," Nov. 10, 1955.

57. I. and D. Crook, p. 126.

58. Lo Ch'iung, *Shan-Kan-Ning pien-ch'ü min-chien fang-chih-yeh* (The cottage textile industry in the Shen-Kan-Ning Border Region; n.p., 1946).

59. Teng Ying-ch'ao, "Chinese Women Help to Build a New China," *People's China,* 6 (1950).

60. I. and D. Crook, pp. 246, 247.

61. Chang Yün, "Ch'in-chien chien-kuo, ch'in-chien ch'i-chia, wei chien-she she-hui chu-i erh fen-tou" (Build the country and keep house thriftily; struggle for socialist construction), in *Chung-kuo fu-nü ti-san-ts'u ch'uan-kuo tai-piao ta-hui chung-yao wen-hsien* (Important documents of the Third National Representative Congress of Chinese Women; Peking, 1958), p. 13.

62. *Ibid.*

63. Myrdal, *Report,* p. 213.

64. *Ibid.,* p. 221.

65. All-China Democratic Women's Federation (Educational Bureau), *Fu-nü ts'an-chia sheng-ch'an chien-she ti hsien-chin pang-yang,* p. 43.

66. I. and D. Crook, *Yangyi Commune,* p. 245.

67. Myrdal, *Report,* p. 238.

Character List

Hokkien terms and expressions are identified with the letter H; all others are Mandarin. Common terms, place names, titles of literary works, and names that appear in Arthur W. Hummel, ed., *Eminent Chinese of the Ch'ing Period* (Washington, D.C., 1943), or Howard L. Boorman and Richard C. Howard, eds., *Biographical Dictionary of Republican China* (New York, 1970), are not included in this list.

Ang Kong (H) 尪公

bou chieng-khi (H) 無清潔
bua-a-chau (H) 麻仔草

ca-bo-kan (H) 婠媒嫺
chai-t'ang 齋堂
Chang Chu-chün 張竹君
chang-fu 丈夫
Ch'ang-fu Yen 長福岩
Chao T'ai-mou 趙太侔
Ch'en Chih-ch'ün 陳志群
Ch'en Fan 陳範
Ch'en Hsieh-fen 陳擷芬
Ch'en Ying 沉櫻
chieh-t'ou chü 街頭劇
Ch'ien-hu nü-hsia 鑑湖女俠
Chin I 金一
chin-lan hui 金蘭會
Ching K'o 荊軻
Ching-hsiung 競雄
ch'ing ko 情隔
Ch'iu Chin 秋瑾
Ch'iu-yü ch'iu-feng, chou-sha jen
　　秋雨秋風，愁煞人
Chu Shu-chen 朱淑真
Chu Yü-p'u 褚玉璞

ch'u pien chih li 處變之禮
ch'u pien chih ts'ai 處變之才
ch'u shih chih ch'üan 處事之
　　權
Cu-si: Niu-niu (H) 註生娘娘

Fang Ling-lu 方令孺
Feng Yüan-chün 馮沅君

hi-su (H) 喜事
Ho Chen 何震
ho-ch'ün 合群
ho-tzu 禾子
Hsiang-lin 祥林
Hsieh Tao-wei 謝道韞
Hsien-t'ien Ta-tao 先天大道
hsiu-shen 修身
Hsü Hsi-lin 徐錫麟
Hsü Tzu-hua 徐自華
Hsün-ch'i 潯溪
Hu Yün-i 胡雲翼
Hua Mu-lan 花木蘭

Jou Shih 柔石

ke-pang-kia: (H) 過房子
kho-kun (H) 犒軍

kuei-hsün 閨訓
kui (H) 鬼
Kung-ai hui 共愛會
K'ung Ssu-chen 孔四貞

la-sam (H) 污穢
lao wu fen 老五分
Li Chih-sheng 李直生
Li Chin 李進
Li Ch'ing-chao 李清照
Li Kuei 李閨
Li Tzu-p'ing 李自平
li-ch'ing 離情
li-hai (H) 厲害
liang-hsin 良心
lieng-hun (H) 靈魂
Lin Hsieh 林憐
Lin Tai-yü 林黛玉
Lin Tsung-su 林宗素
Ling Shu-hua 凌叔華
Lo Ch'iung 羅瓊
Lo Yen-pin 羅燕斌
Lu Yin 盧隱
Lü K'un 呂坤

Ma Feng-i 馬鳳義
Mei-lin 美琳
mei-tsai 妹仔
Meng-k'o 夢珂
Ming-tao 明道
mo 饝
mo tou-fu 磨豆腐
Mu-lan, see Hua Mu-lan

nü-ta pu chung-liu 女大不
中留

Pai Wei 白薇
pao-chüan 寶卷

pi-chi 筆記
pieng-lieng-kia: (H) 蜈蛉子
p'ing-i 平易
pu lo-chia 不落家

san-ts'ung 三從
shan-shu 善書
Shen Yün-ying 沈雲英
shih-p'o 師婆
shuang chieh-pai 雙結拜
si:-kut si:-baq (H) 生骨生肉
Sian-si:-ma (H) 先生媽
sim-pua (H) 媳婦仔
song-su (H) 喪事

Ta-t'ung 大通
t'ai-ko 臺閣
T'an Cheng-pi 譚正璧
t'an-tz'u 彈詞
tang-ki (H) 童乩
T'ao Ch'eng-chang 陶成章
Thai-sin (H) 胎神
thang (H) 蟲
T'ien Kung 天公
ts'ai-ch'ing 才情
Ts'ao Hsüeh-ch'in 曹雪芹
t'ung-yang-hsi 童養媳
tzu-sheng 資生
tzu-shu nü 自梳女

Wang (Ch'iu) Ts'an-chih 王秋
燦芝
Wang Fu-chen 王黻臣
Wang T'ing-chün 王廷鈞
Wang Yüan-te 王沅德
Wu Chih-ying 吳芝瑛

ya-t'ou 丫頭
yaksha [yeh-ch'a] 夜叉

Yang Chen-sheng 楊振聲
yang-pan-hsi 樣板戲
Yao Wen-yüan 姚文元
Yen-shuo lien-hsi hui 演說
　練習會

yin-chiao 陰教
Yü Cheng-hsieh 俞正燮
Yü Shan 俞珊
Yüan Ch'ang-ying 袁昌英

Index